The International Society of Business, Economics, and Ethics Book Series

Volume 3

Series Editors

Daryl Koehn
Laura Spence

The International Society for Business, Economics and Ethics is a global association for the study of social and moral aspects of business and the economy. This book series draws from the worldwide membership of ISBEE and its associates to present truly international research and scholarship. The primary objective of the series is to promote business ethics globally by giving a voice to top scholars from around the world and reaching a similarly global audience.

This series encompasses manuscripts that focus on ethics in the international arena of business, particularly enabling comparative studies. There is a focus on research on the responsibilities, values and behaviour of business people and organizations as they interact with stakeholders including shareholders, employees, suppliers, customers, competitors communities and governments. Incorporating a macro economic perspective, it is especially interested in considering new works dealing with globalization of business, **business in developing economies**, environmental questions, ethics and global communication, global economic growth, and sustainable development. The series embraces research and scholarship on all organisational forms relevant to business.

For further volumes:
http://www.springer.com/series/8074

The International Society of Business, Economics, and Ethics Book Series

Volume 3

Pauline J. Albert • Patricia Werhane • Tim Rolph
Editors

Global Poverty Alleviation: A Case Book

 Springer

Editors
Pauline J. Albert
St. Edward's University School
  of Management and Business
Chicago, IL, USA

Austin, TX, USA

Tim Rolph
School of Business
De Paul University
Chicago, IL, USA

Patricia Werhane
School of Business
De Paul University
Chicago, IL, USA

ISSN 1877-3176   ISSN 1877-3184 (electronic)
ISBN 978-94-007-7478-0   ISBN 978-94-007-7479-7 (eBook)
DOI 10.1007/978-94-007-7479-7
Springer Dordrecht Heidelberg New York London

Acknowledgements

Many people and organizations helped make this collection possible. We want to especially thank Darden Publishing at the University of Virginia and, in particular, Steve Momper, without whom the case book would not have been possible. Jenny Mead, Karen Musselman and Gerry Yemen at the Darden School of Business helped in case writing and editing. Tim Rolph at DePaul wrote the addenda updating older cases, and he was in charge of permissions, a thankless task.

We thank our institutions, DePaul University and St. Edwards University, for their support. The introductions and the particular selection of cases and their organization was the work of the editors, for which we take full responsibility.

Contents

1 Introduction.. 1
   References... 10

2 Technology and Capacity Building.. 13
   Introduction... 13
   Eskom and the South African Electrification Program (A) 14
     The Beginning of the Electrification Program 14
     How to Deliver Service 16
     Appendix 1: Eskom and the South African Electrification
     Program (A).. 17
     Appendix 2: Eskom and the South African Electrification
     Program (A).. 18
     Appendix 3: Eskom and the South African Electrification
     Program (A).. 20
     Appendix 4: Eskom and the South African Electrification
     Program (A).. 21
     Appendix 5: Eskom and the South African Electrification
     Program (A).. 23
   Eskom and the South African Electrification Program (B)....................... 25
     A Culture of Nonpayment.. 25
   Eskom and the South African Electrification Program (C)....................... 26
     Residential Tampering.. 26
   Eskom and the South African Electrification Program (D) 27
     Training to Tamper... 27
     Eskom 2013 Case Addendum 29
   The Volta River Project.. 30
     Introduction 30
     History of Ghana Before the Volta River Project........................... 31
     Negotiating a Dam 36
     When Power Fades... 44

Ghana Power Crisis: 1997–1998 46
What Lies Ahead for Ghana? 49
Some Other Options 51
Acknowledgments 52
Exhibit 1: Principal Agreements 53
Exhibit 2: Map of Ghana 54
Exhibit 3: Some Key Terms and Names 55
Volta River Project Addendum – 2013 56
Transforming Education in Rural Haiti: Intel and L'Ecole De Choix 56
Intel's Growth Strategy: Enabling the Next Generation 58
Intel's Programs to Transform Education 61
The Education Market Platforms Group (EMPG)
and the Intel Learning Series Products 62
Enter the Intel Education Service Corps (IESC) 64
Haiti: Land of Mountains 67
The State of Education in Haiti 70
L'Ecole de Choix in Mirebalais, Haiti 76
John Cartwright's Visits to Haiti's l'Ecole de Choix 78
The Postmortem and John Cartwright's Second Trip to Haiti 80
What Next for Intel's Partnership with l'Ecole de Choix? 83
Exhibit 1: Transforming Education in Rural Haiti:
Intel and L'Ecole De Choix 86
Exhibit 2: Transforming Education in Rural Haiti:
Intel and L'Ecole De Choix 86
Transformational Gaming: Zynga's Social Strategy (A) 88
Zynga and the Revolution in Social Gaming 89
Mark Pincus and Zynga's Development 90
The Closing Analysis 90
Transformational Gaming: Zynga's Social Strategy (B) 91
The Formalization of a New Social Strategy: Zynga.org 91
Moving Forward 93
Expectations 95
Implementation 96
FATEM and Fonkoze: The Partners and Their Context 96
Zynga.org's Inaugural Partners 97
FATEM 97
Fonkoze 98
The Original 50/50 Profitable Partnership Model 99
Monetization and Reputation Management 100
Exhibit 1: Transformational Gaming: Zynga's Social Strategy (B) 103
Exhibit 2: Transformational Gaming: Zynga's Social Strategy (B) 104
Exhibit 3: Transformational Gaming: Zynga's Social Strategy (B) 105
Exhibit 4: Transformational Gaming: Zynga's Social Strategy (B) 106
Exhibit 5: Transformational Gaming: Zynga's Social Strategy (B) 107

Our Vision 108

Our Values 108

Exhibit 6: Transformational Gaming: Zynga's Social Strategy (B) 110

Exhibit 7: Transformational Gaming: Zynga's Social Strategy (B) 111

3 Health 113

Introduction 113

The Novartis Foundation for Sustainable Development: Tackling
HIV/AIDS and Poverty in South Africa (A) 114

   The HIV/AIDS Crisis 115

   Novartis 116

   Origins of the Novartis Foundation for Sustainable Development 117

   Experimenting in Tanzania 119

   Exhibit 1: The Novartis Foundation for Sustainable Development:
   Tackling HIV/AIDS and Poverty in South Africa (A) 120

   Exhibit 2: The Novartis Foundation for Sustainable Development:
   Tackling HIV/AIDS and Poverty in South Africa (A) 120

The Novartis Foundation for Sustainable Development: Tackling
HIV/AIDS and Poverty in South Africa (B) 121

   Developing a Pilot Program 121

   Creation of REPSSI 123

   Exhibit 1: The Novartis Foundation for Sustainable Development:
   Tackling HIV/AIDS and Poverty in South Africa (B) 124

   Exhibit 2: The Novartis Foundation for Sustainable Development:
   Tackling HIV/AIDS and Poverty in South Africa (B) 125

   Exhibit 3: The Novartis Foundation for Sustainable Development:
   Tackling HIV/AIDS and Poverty in South Africa (A) 126

The Novartis Foundation for Sustainable Development: Tackling
HIV/AIDS and Poverty in South Africa (C) 126

   REPSSI: Growth and Evolution 126

   Novartis Foundation Philosophy 127

   Types of Cooperation 129

   REPSSI in 2006 131

   Motivation and Creative Partnerships 132

Procter & Gamble: Children's Safe Drinking Water (A) 133

   Procter & Gamble 133

   The Global Water Crisis 135

   The Search for a Solution 136

Procter & Gamble: Children's Safe Drinking Water (B) 136

   Development of PUR 137

   Strategic Partnerships 138

   Children's Safe Drinking Water 139

   Population Services International (PSI) 139

   Aquaya Institute and PURelief 140

   PUR Expands Globally 141

Procter & Gamble: The Search for Safe Drinking Water (C) 141
   Blogging from Borneo 141
The Female Health Company (A).. 143
   The Spread of HIV/AIDS in the United States 144
   From Concept to Market 144
   The Product and Its Launch 146
   What Now?.. 147
   Exhibit 1: The Female Health Company (A) 148
   Exhibit 2: The Female Health Company (A) 149
The Female Health Company (B) 149
   Perception Meets Reality 150
   The Public and Commercial Sectors 151
   Going International 152
   Zimbabwe's History, Economy, and Geography............................... 153
   HIV/AIDS in Zimbabwe 154
   Conclusion.. 155
   Exhibit 1: The Female Health Company (B) 156
   Exhibit 2: The Female Health Company (B) 158
   Exhibit 3: The Female Health Company (B) 162
The Female Health Company (C).. 162
   From Reality to FC2... 163
   Back Home in the United States 164
   Femy, Femidom, Reality, and FC2.. 165

4   Environmentally Sustainable Projects... 167
Husk Power Systems: Financing Expansion... 168
   Husk Power Systems 169
   GreenPoint Partners.. 170
   The Pitch 171
   A Unique Market... 171
   A Unique Technology 172
   Market Demographics... 174
   Alternative Revenue Streams 175
   Funding Expansion... 176
Solar Energy in Rural South Africa 177
   The Pilot Project.. 178
   Implementing the Project 179
   The Initial Assessment 180
   Exhibit 1: Solar Energy in Rural South Africa 181
   Exhibit 2: Solar Energy in Rural South Africa.................................. 182
   Exhibit 3: Solar Energy in Rural South Africa.................................. 184
BHP Billiton and Mozal (A)... 184
   BHP Billiton.. 185
BHP Billiton and Mozal (B) 186
   The Mozal Aluminum Smelter: Project Profile 186

Health and Safety Initiatives 187
Environmental Initiatives 188
Community Initiatives... 189
Socioeconomic Initiatives 190
Mozal: Focusing on Sustainability, for Business
and for the Community 195
Ecover and Green Marketing (A)... 195
Company History 196
Environmental Principles 197
Ecover at the Crossroads 199
Ecover and Green Marketing (B)... 201
The Ecological Factory 201
Green Marketing: Challenges and Opportunities.................................. 203
Ecover's Options 206
Ecover and Green Marketing (C)... 207
Recycling Advertisements.. 207
Marketing Principles 208
The Ecolabeling Conundrum 209
Compromising with Consumer Tastes 210
The Dilemma of Success.. 210
Ecover 2013 Case Addendum 211

5 **Environmentally Sustainable Processes** 213
Albina Ruiz and "Healthy City" 213
The Plan 214
Ciudad Saludable 215
A Case Study in the Evolution of Sustainability:
Baxter International Inc. 216
Introduction 216
External Forces.. 218
Model of Shareholder Value... 228
Sustainable Value Creation... 229
Application of Shareholder Value Model to Baxter.............................. 231
Where Does Baxter Go from Here?... 232
Sustainability Awards and Recognition for Baxter Inc. 239
Coca-Cola: Quenching More Than Thirst Around the World 240
125 Years of Selling Fizzy Water.. 242
Water: The Miracle Elixir 245
"Connected Capitalism" and the "Golden Triangle" 247
Coca-Cola's Water Stewardship Programs... 250
Working Through Partnerships 252
Addressing Water Shortages 254
The Coca-Cola 5 by 20 Project in Support of Women
Entrepreneurship 256
Lingering Problems... 257

Exhibit 1: 2011 Per Capita Consumption of Coke's
Beverage Products.. 258
Exhibit 2: Heads of Coca-Cola over Twentieth Century
to Present.. 258
Exhibit 3: Links Between the United Nations Millennium
Development Goals (MDGs) and Water..................................... 259
Exhibit 4: Coke's 2004 Manifesto and 2020 Vision Goals
(Established at the End of 2010)... 260
    Original Five Principles from the August 2004 Manifesto
    for Growth under Isdell's Direction 260
    2020 Vision (Established at the end of 2010)
    under Kent's Direction 260
Exhibit 5: Definitions Used in Water Footprinting 260

6 **Finance**... 263
    Introduction.. 263
    Enabling the Poor to Build Housing: Pursuing Profit
    and Social Development Together 264
        Pursuing Innovation and Global Expansion......................... 265
        Discovering Opportunity in Low-Income Markets 267
        Obstacles to Progress 268
        Replacing Resignation with Ambition................................. 269
        Banking on Social Capital... 270
        A New and Rewarding Experience 271
        High-Touch Outreach Builds Community and Trust 271
        Women Are the Key 272
        Safety in Numbers.. 273
        Partner #1 274
        Integrating Old and New Values 274
        Services Are Crucial to Low-Income Customers.................. 275
        Doing Well While Doing Good... 276
        Calle Digna: Financing City Infrastructure 276
        Patrimonio Hoy Services... 277
        Conclusion.. 282
    Bal Vikas Bank: Children as Bankers.. 282
        Rita Panicker 283
        Butterflies 283
        Street Children in India 284
        Bal Vikas Bank... 284
        Lessons Learned... 285
        Further Expansion 286

7 **Working at the Base of the Pyramid** 287
    Introduction.. 287
    Hindustan Lever Limited (HLL) and Project Sting (A)............... 288
        Hindustan Lever Limited.. 288

A New Business Model: The Nirma Way 290
Marketing, Packaging, and Other Innovative
Nirma Ploys... 292
Product Differences.. 292
Understanding the Rural Market 293
The Case of Rural India 293
HLL Slumbers While Nirma Overtakes Surf:
The War of the Bubbles.. 294
HLL Reacts 295
Exhibit 1: Hindustan Lever Limited (HLL)
and Project Sting (A)... 296
Hindustan Lever Limited (HLL) and Project Sting (B) 296
Hindustan Lever Limited's New Strategy 296
Analyzing the Market.. 298
Designing a Product to Fit the Needs of a Market 298
A New Definition of Product Design 300
Hindustan Lever 2013 Case Addendum.................................... 300
The Grameen Bank and Muhammad Yunus 302
A New Model 303
A Private Bank 304
The Sixteen Decisions... 305
Assessment... 306
Grameen II... 307
The e-Choupal Initiative 308
ITC Limited.. 309
International Business Division 310
Agriculture in India and the Plight of the Farmer 311
The e-Choupal Initiative... 313
The Sanchalak 314
The Samyojak... 314
The e-Choupal Process... 314
Leading Transformation in Rural India.................................... 315
The Road Ahead... 318
Exhibit 1: The e-Choupal Initiative.. 319

8 Global Corporations and Supply Chain Management....................... 321
Introduction... 321
Nike, Inc.: Corporate Social Responsibility and Workplace
Standard Initiatives in Vietnam.. 322
Corporate Overview 322
Evolution of Nike's Approach to Global Labor Issues 324
Nike, Inc.: Program Analyses 327
Nike Addendum 2013 337
Can Walmart Rise to a Transformational Challenge in China? 338
Introduction 338
How Did Lee Scott Arrive at His "Now Think" Moment?....... 340

Supplier Dependence Within Walmart's Ethical Supply
Chain Management System.. 342
Can Walmart Forge a More Collaborative Relationship with
Its Chinese Suppliers?... 344
Walmart's Authoritarian Management Model
of Cultural Solidarity.. 346
Conclusion... 347

About the Editors.. 349

Index.. 351

Chapter 1
Introduction

Social scientists are fond of theorizing about the world's biggest problems such as climate change, world hunger, and chronic illnesses. The people in this volume's case studies are not theorizing; they are all in the trenches making things happen for people who have been given very little opportunity in life. These are stories about people with significant moral imagination, willing to put aside old assumptions, engrained mental models, and not just envision a better world; but also make it happen. Moral imagination involves understanding the context of a situation, looking beyond one's preconceived biases and assumptions, imagining and carefully evaluating new possibilities, and then acting.[1] These cases demonstrate that adaptability, courage, and determination are also important ingredients for creating change.

While we have divided the book into seven chapters based on the organizations involved, there is amazing overlap in the underlying themes of the stories. All of these cases are about empowering people to create their own better worlds. The old Chinese proverb, "Give a man a fish, and you feed him for a day. Teach a man to fish and you feed him for a lifetime" seems overused and somewhat trite; but these cases illustrate that empowerment is an effective vehicle for changing people's lives and helping people become independent and self-supporting. This book is a collection of business case studies surrounding the premise from an earlier book about why profitable business partnerships could effectively alleviate the problem labeled as global poverty.[2] The thesis was that moral imagination, systems thinking, and deep dialogue were important ingredients for addressing poverty alleviation. These business cases effectively illustrate these concepts in action. This introduction provides a general context for the cases, and it summarizes how the narratives in these stories support the premise that businesses can grow and enhance their triple bottom line (people, profits, and planet) through partnerships with governments, non-government organizations (NGOs), and civil society.

---

[1] Werhane (1999).

[2] Werhane et al. (2010).

P.J. Albert et al. (eds.), *Global Poverty Alleviation: A Case Book*, The International Society of Business, Economics, and Ethics Book Series 3, DOI 10.1007/978-94-007-7479-7_1, © Springer Science+Business Media Dordrecht 2014

While corporate philanthropy is a nice feel-good activity, it is not necessarily sustainable, and corporate social responsibility (CSR), much like business ethics, has frequently been about adding yet again another new voluntary *program du jour*. There is increasing evidence that the twenty-first century calls for more systemic integration of the values associated with CSR. In other words, CSR has grown up and become refocused as a sustainability revolution. But, now the word sustainability cannot become another program or buzz word; it needs to become a new way of doing business. Some of the cases in this volume illustrate that for global corporations, strategically investing in emerging markets is increasingly critical to the long-term growth of these enterprises. These investments are self-serving and about the longer term survival and success of these global corporations. But these projects are also creating new markets and can offer new opportunities for those formerly living in abject poverty. McKinsey and Company refers to winning market share in developing countries as the "30 trillion dollar decathlon."[3] While going after new consumers for its global brands may be good business in general, an important question is whether this pursuit is exploitive or being executed using a moral compass. The cases in this book illustrate the latter. They also all illustrate that serving the poor is a complex endeavor with often surprising twists and turns. Moral courage is also involved in going after new business, as returns on investment may take longer. To be sustainable, success cannot be solely about this quarter's returns. Many visionary companies are tweaking their mission statements and evolving their values statements to incorporate people, profit, planet, for now and into the future. Thus, the cases that involve large companies have executive management involved, with all expressing a commitment to the importance of a sustainable future for a broader consumer base than ever before. Other cases feature social entrepreneurs who are both indigenous and ingenious, often having had the benefit of education, a key ingredient to changing the plight of those at the bottom of the pyramid.[4]

It is fascinating that technology is at the core of supporting many people in achieving a better life. The first chapter highlights how technology can be critical to the world's capacity-building efforts. Both the Eskom and Volta River cases illustrate the complexities associated with infrastructure development. Dams were once considered state-of-the-art for providing hydroelectric-based power. However, with increasing shortages of water around the world, both environmental tradeoffs, and exploiting new technological innovations must become part of the deep dialogue required for what is best for the future. Looking at the trade-offs between the natural environment and providing more people with electricity is an example of a situation where moral imagination is required. Rather than one thing or the other, the players in the Eskom and Volta River cases can possibly pave a third way, creating opportunities while trying to encourage buy-in by local people to the importance of water and electricity.

---

[3] Atsmon et al. (2012).

[4] Prahalad (2005), Werhane et al. (2010).

Intel has long had a commitment to education, but its newest programs in emerging markets incorporate both market building and making the company a great place to work. Employees are serving as ambassadors installing computer labs and supporting teachers to appropriately integrate completely new ways of learning reading, writing, and arithmetic. Many of the projects described in this book include skills-based training for workers, but the Intel case is one dedicated to giving children in Haiti a better start in life. Former chairman of Intel, Andy Grove, often commented that the Internet is a great equalizer, as screen-based learning technology is ordinarily unbiased. Intel's project in Haiti is an example of a partnership between several high-tech companies, government, and non-profits to help children in Haiti to build a better future for themselves and their country. Interestingly, there may be more children in emerging markets using small netbook computers to learn than there are in the United States. Zynga.org's efforts to share revenue generated from social media games is another innovative way for raising money to support the funding needed for rebuilding projects after natural disasters, such as the school in Haiti noted above.

The three cases in Chap. 3 address health care issues, and all are about for-profit companies partnering with others to support people in need. The United Nations deputy director recently noted that there are now more people worldwide who have access to a cell phone than to a toilet.[5] Every 20 s a child dies due to impure water, and this is an improvement from 2009 when a child died every 15 s.[6] The absence of proper sanitation is more complex than one might realize, and this issue is highlighted in the Proctor and Gamble (Chap. 3) and the Coca Cola (Chap. 5) cases. It is hard to believe that something as curable and devastating as leprosy still exists in the world. Novartis is a leader in addressing the needs of the poorest of the poor in accessing healthcare, and the case in this chapter is one of many examples in which the company is demonstrating its dedication to improving the well being of people from all walks of life. Procter & Gamble is one of the largest consumer products companies in the world, and its acquisition of the PUR water filter led to a product that could save people's lives, especially after natural disasters when clean water is in short supply. It developed small packets of powder that, when put in polluted and dirty water, clean that water within half an hour. It now distributes these packets through local salespersons in much of sub-Saharan Africa. The Female Health Company (FHC) case describes the company's early history and its development of a safe and effective female condom over the course of the late 1990s, when it began to explore going global. Having failed to market this product successfully in the United States, the company realized that there was a desperate need for female condoms in the developing world to protect women against HIV/AIDS infections when men do not protect themselves. FHC now distributes condoms in over 130 countries at very low prices, and since 2009 it has been profitable as well.[7]

---

[5] UN News Center (2013).

[6] Water.org (2013).

[7] The Female Health Company (2013).

Chapters 4 and 5 include cases relating to environmental sustainability. People in developed countries take electricity for granted, and we forget the challenges of building infrastructures that provide something as basic as electricity and clean water. Americans are up in arms when rolling blackouts occur during heat waves, but many people in Africa and India have no access whatsoever to the power grid. Chapter 4 begins with an innovative sustainability story. Entrepreneurial Indian MBA students at the University of Virginia are looking for financing to expand their business that provides electricity in small Indian villages using rice husks to power a simple mechanism to generate electricity in small villages. These M.B.A. students may be headed for Wall Street, but on the way, they are building a power company in their homeland that will help people who have never known the wonders of electricity, a technology that became widespread over a century ago.

The Solar Electric Power Fund (SELF) story in Chap. 4 is a classic example of helping people to help themselves, but it takes the narrative further by asking about the cultural implications of a more egalitarian community becoming one of *haves and have-nots*. This non-profit is committed to providing sustainable solutions and interestingly, it has trademarked its organization as supporting energy as a human right.[8] This issue of what is a *human right* and how should a right be accessed are also themes underlying many of these cases. If something is a human right does that imply that it must be free (not paid for) or does having a right mean that it is accessible? BHP Billiton and Escover are both examples of companies that are dedicated to environmentalism and global sustainability. BHP Billiton is a huge, global Australian/UK-based organization engaged in the business of identifying, developing, acquiring, and marketing natural resources, such as tin, aluminum, iron ore and coal. The Escover case study tells the story of a company so dedicated to environmental responsibility that it is hesitating to grow. This maker of safe detergents and cleaners exemplifies the importance of moral imagination, innovation, and consumer education in the collaborative plight to save the planet.

Chapter 5 starts with the story of an individual dedicated to making a difference in the world, and then moves to two huge companies whose scope makes them industry trend setters for environmental sustainability. The first case features Albina Ruiz, a social entrepreneur who has taken it upon herself to make her hometown of Lima, Peru cleaner, healthier, and more beautiful. She is an example of a person with a vision, courage, and the moral imagination to see that the world can be a better place when someone simply stands up and decides to change things. After graduating from college she could have gone elsewhere to pursue her dreams, but instead she is cleaning up her own backyard, and she has inspired a model that is now being used in Lima, Colombia, Mexico, Brazil, and India.

In 2010, Ceres, a nonprofit voluntary coalition of over 130 organizations dedicated to driving sustainable development that sits at the intersections of business, investment, and advocacy, issued a roadmap for what corporations should look like by 2020. In 2013, it issued its first report card on how 600 major global corporations

---

[8] Solar Electric Light Fund: Energy Is a Human Right (2013).

were doing based on its roadmap.[9] The assessment examines four major areas tied to sustainable business: Governance, stakeholder engagement, disclosure, and performance. Ceres is trying to put some teeth into companies' sustainability claims. Its aim is to help both investors and consumers to assess how deeply companies are engaged in efforts to incorporate the long-term implications of their decisions, which is at the heart of sustainability. Put slightly differently, this benchmark assesses how well companies are being morally imaginative in their strategic and day-to-day decision-making. Ceres' definition of sustainability is aligned with the examples outlined in this case book.

> For businesses in all sectors of the economy, sustainability is a strategy for building long-term shareholder value, managing environmental and social risks, and improving competitiveness. Environmental and social sustainability issues are material "balance sheet" issues. They pose risks and present opportunities that will drive the success of corporations.[10] (Ceres 2013a para. 1)

While there has been progress, the early 2013 results were disappointing. Based on its analysis of 600 companies, Ceres states that only 25 % are reporting on supply chain monitoring and performance (an issue highlighted in the Nike case in Chap. 8); 26 % have incorporated sustainability into their management and governance systems; and about 33 % have set targets for reducing greenhouse gas emissions.

Both The Coca-Cola Company and Baxter International are featured as exemplars of their industries in the Ceres report, and the final two cases in Chap. 5 should assist readers in seeing why they are considered leaders in their respective fields. The Coca-Cola Company, with its incredible distribution systems, is considering making use of all those people around the world with cell phones in helping them to locate both a Coca-Cola drink and a toilet. The Coca-Cola case tells a story about how the company bearing the most-valuable brand in the world is evolving from one that solely marketed soft drinks into a company with a huge product portfolio, and a major commitment to the 200 countries in which it does business. For example, Simon Berry is an innovative social entrepreneur and he discovered that the best way to get life-saving drugs to the most remote places in the world was to partner with Coca-Cola, which was driving to such locations to deliver its products. Berry now directs an independent non-profit based on this original idea.[11] Berry's story illustrates the ubiquitous nature of Coca-Cola and its power as a huge multinational to change the world. The case deals with the world's struggles with clean water availability and Coke's incredible commitment to work with its bottlers, governments, inventors, and numerous NGOs to replace and replenish the water it uses. Its plans are ambitious, but illustrative of how business is an integral vehicle for addressing poverty alleviation.

---

[9] Ceres (2013b).
[10] Ceres (2013a).
[11] ColaLife (2013).

Baxter International is a global, diversified healthcare company with almost 50,000 employees worldwide. The case in this chapter describes its sustainability journey dating back to the 1970s, and its evolution through five stages of development. The story illustrates that living out the sustainability promise is hard work, and it requires buy-in and innovation from all levels and parts of a large conglomerate, such as Baxter.

The lending model used by the Solar Electric Light Fund featured in Chap. 4 is carried forward into Chaps. 5 and 6 where issues of money and banking are explored in greater depth. While people can easily become overwhelmed and slide into poverty due to debt, many of the poor understand the importance of balancing borrowing with savings. In-depth studies of how those who live on $2 a day save money, borrow wisely, and even purchase insurance, reveal that the poorest of the poor are more resourceful than many people realize.[12] Microfinance goes back to the 1976 story told in Chap. 7 about Mohammad Yunus and the Grameen Bank, but Chap. 6 begins with a story about one of the world's largest building materials and cement producers who serves as banker for its customers. Cemex's Patrimonio Hoy program is an example of a for-profit company that has expanded its market reach by figuring out a way to sell its product to people who are very poor. The program helps people to build their own homes, and like Grameen Bank, Cemex found empowering women to be the key to its success.

Female empowerment is highlighted in a number of this book's cases, including the Female Health Company, the Coca-Cola Company and the Grameen Bank cases, as well as in the Hindustan Lever story in Chap. 7. Experts in global development have long seen the role that women can play in poverty alleviation,[13] and today that notion has evolved into the Half the Sky Movement. While it began as the title of a book,[14] the movement itself has evolved and today incorporates a 4-h documentary, online gaming, and a variety of both corporate for-profit and non-profit organizations working together to support women who are trying to change their lives.[15] For example, Coca-Cola has committed to supporting five million female entrepreneurs by 2020, and the company has identified its program as part of the Half the Sky Movement.[16]

Banking with women is good for business. But, who would have thought that homeless children could help themselves to create a better life by learning to run their own bank? The homeless boys of India were made famous by the Academy Award-winning film "Slumdog Millionaire,"[17] but that story was a fictionalized tale of redemption based on winning a game show. Not many of the millions of homeless children in India win the lottery and get chosen to be on a game show. Rita Panicker has long been engaged in creating a better life for these children, however

---

[12] Collins et al. (2009).

[13] Nussbaum (2000).

[14] Kristof and WuDunn (2009).

[15] Half the Sky Movement (2013).

[16] The Coca-Cola Company (2012).

[17] Boyle and Beaufoy (2008).

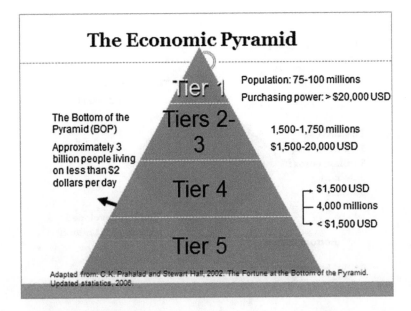

Fig. 1.1 The Economic Pyramid

her latest endeavor to help them to run their own banks is remarkable. Not only is the story inspiring, but it illustrates that with a little direction, and a strong belief in the power of the human spirit, even very young people can be empowered to change their own lives doing something as sophisticated as running a bank.

Chapter 7 is specifically dedicated to unique ways of supporting the poorest of the poor. All three cases feature innovators at local and global levels. Seeing the poor as a marketplace rich with possibilities for future profits that large multinationals from developed nations should pursue was the brainchild of C.K. Prahalad[18] in the early part of the twenty-first century. He elaborated further on his theory with case examples developed by his M.B.A. students at the University of Michigan[19] and his work has been carried forth by his colleagues after his untimely death in 2010.[20] Prahalad used a pyramid to describe and segment the world marketplace into a collection of tiers (See Fig. 1.1).

Because of the tremendous growth and the accompanying increases in prosperity of the BRIC countries (Brazil, Russia, India, and China), the shape of Prahalad's pyramid has changed, but there are still over 2 billion people who earn less than $1.25 a day (see Fig. 1.2).

There is controversy surrounding the ways to address the problems of the poor,[21] but the fact remains that there are still too many people unable to meet their needs

---

[18] Prahalad and Hart (2002).

[19] Prahalad (2005).

[20] Hart (2005), London and Hart (2011).

[21] Werhane et al. (2010).

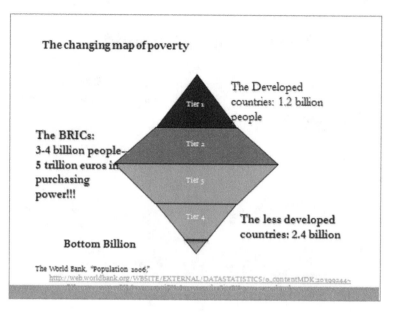

The changing map of poverty

The Developed countries: 1.2 billion people

The BRICs:
3-4 billion people—
5 trillion euros in
purchasing
power!!!

The less developed countries: 2.4 billion

Bottom Billion

The World Bank, "Population 2006,"
http://web.worldbank.org/WBSITE/EXTERNAL/DATASTATISTICS/0,,contentMDK:20399244~

Fig. 1.2 The Changing Map of Poverty

for basic nutrition and shelter. One can look at these people as victims or as opportunities. Both the for-profit and non-profit organizations featured in Chap. 7 have
learned that creativity and developing a deep understanding of the lives of the poor
is riddled with opportunities for positive change.

Unilever had not pursued selling products to the rural poor of India until it saw
how successful a local competitor was becoming, demonstrating how important
competition can be in motivating innovation in the bottom of the pyramid marketplace. Its local subsidiary, Hindustan Lever (today called Hindustan Unilever) made
the false assumption that these poor people had no money, when in fact many had
more disposable income than the typical poor urban dweller. What a perfect example
of an inaccurate mental model. Using innovative advertising, repackaging, and new
distribution systems, Hindustan Lever (HL) increased its sales and improved the
quality of the cleaning products and employment opportunities available to some of
the poorest people in the world. The case describes the company's long evolution
toward the development of a distribution system that employs women who sell HL's
products to serve the 630,000 small Indian villages inaccessible through standard
networks. Hindustan Unilever states that it plans to increase the number of Shakti
(meaning Strength) entrepreneurs from 45,000 in 2010 to 75,000 by 2015.[22]

Mohammed Yunus left his homeland to pursue a Ph.D. in Economics in the
United States, but later returned and began studying the plight of the poor of
Bangladesh. He saw how difficult it was to break the cycle of poverty and over

---

[22] Hindustan Unilever Limited (2013).

time realized that small loans, structured in a way that supported people in helping each other, could change people's destinies. His story is summarized in this chapter. Chapter 7 concludes with a case about helping farmers to work more cooperatively and become less dependent on oftentimes dishonest middlemen. The case of E-Choupal illustrates the power of the Internet as the great equalizer, as well as the power of education. The Indian Tobacco Company Limited (ITC) is one of the largest private diversified enterprises in India, and its e-Choupal project is another example of empowerment coupled with practical training in support of poverty alleviation. Started in 2000, the project began by helping rural soybean farmers while improving ITC's international competitiveness. The case tells the story of how India's *green revolution* of the 1960s helped some, but created huge negative consequences for many people, as well as for the farmland. The high-tech boom of the 1990s has in turn produced a series of lows for farmers, further creating poverty and vulnerability for those with less education and poor support systems. The case describes the unfortunate dilemmas faced by India's rural farmers, and the incredible impact that occurred after ITC facilitated farmers using Internet kiosks to provide them with information to help them to get fairer prices for their crops. It then added education to support farmers in how to better use ITC's products and increase their yields. Basically, through technology and education, the supply chain has been reorganized and optimized in support of farmers earning a better livelihood, all while making ITC more profitable, as well.

The last chapter, Chap. 8, is about two of the world's best-known and also most criticized corporate giants: Nike and Walmart. A few weeks before the 2012 Olympic Games in London, protesters were creating a rumble of complaints about the clothes that the Olympians would be wearing claiming that most were made in sweatshops in developing nations. If one ever wonders whether we as consumers have any power, the story of Nike is evidence that we all do. At the 2012 Olympics Nike was not among those being criticized. For the last 20 years Nike has been engaged in making its factories better places to work, but in the early 1990s people were boycotting its products, primarily because it initially denied that it had any responsibility for subcontracted factories.[23] A major turning point was the May 12, 1998, speech by Nike's founder and CEO, Phil Knight, in which he stated that the company was implementing a comprehensive program to raise wages, improve working conditions, and provide educational opportunities to workers. Nike's program and its monitoring tools are elaborated upon in great detail in the Chap. 8 case. In 2011, Greenpeace issued a Detox Challenge suggesting to major brands, such as Nike and Adidas, that it should stop dumping toxic chemicals into waterways near its factories. Within just a few weeks Nike had issued its game plan for being toxic-free by 2020, and then Adidas and Puma, its major competitors, issued similar plans within days.[24] Sound sustainable practices may not only change an individual company, but they can change an industry. Walmart's practices have changed the retail

[23] Birch (2012).
[24] Ibid.

industry, and while it is highly criticized, it also is evolving in terms of its environmental practices.

Walmart is the largest retailer in the world with over 2 million employees and 100,000 suppliers in 60 countries. As a huge employer possessing a gigantic footprint, it is under constant scrutiny on just about any front that one can imagine. The impact of Walmart on the supply-chain of the retailing industry has become known as the Walmart *effect*.[25] Making products inexpensive enough for millions of people who would otherwise not be able to afford them was the hallmark of the company's founder, Sam Walton. But the impact on suppliers changed the entire industry creating a power switch in which manufacturers lost power to the granddaddy of retailers, Walmart. Power is something that can be used or abused, and one can build an argument for either direction when it comes to an analysis of Walmart. Its most recent endeavor to create zero waste and sell products that sustain and renew our natural environment is huge and bold. It will require a great deal of moral imagination, and a change in mindset by all its suppliers and employees. The final case in this book asks some hard questions about how culture and bold visions can come together, or do Walmart's statements become no more than what have become known as greenwashing.[26]

In conclusion, while never wishing to minimize the extreme hardships suffered by the over three billion people (almost half the world) living on less than $2.50 per day,[27] poverty in and of itself can become a mindset. We should all feel ashamed of these statistics, because the world is an abundant place and with innovation, moral imagination, and human will no one needs to be without basic necessities. Alleviating poverty is complicated, but at its basic foundation, it is about people working together and seeing the potential of each and every human person. Alleviating poverty is about enhancing human dignity, and believing in what Muhtar Kent from Coca-Cola calls the Golden Triangle.[28] Kent's sentiments that business, governments, and society can and should work together to make the world a better place are echoed in the stories and by the executives, young entrepreneurs, and non-profit leaders featured in these cases. We offer them to help you to understand that with new mindsets, moral imagination, and partnerships we can alleviate poverty in our lifetimes.

References

Atsmon, Y., P. Child, R. Dobbs, L. Narasimhan, and A. Webb. 2012. *Winning the $30 trilliion decathlon (pp. 168)*. New York: McKinsey Quarterly.

---

[25] Fishman (2006), Johnson (2002).

[26] Karliner (2001).

[27] Shah (2013).

[28] Kent (2012).

Birch, S. 2012. How activism forced Nike to change its ethical game. Blog Retrieved from http://www.guardian.co.uk/environment/green-living-blog/2012/jul/06/activism-nike

Boyle, D. and S. Beaufoy (Writers). (2008). *Slumdog Millionaire*. In C. Colson (Producer): Foxlight.

Ceres. 2013a. The Road to 2020: Report Overview Executive Summary. http://www.ceres.org/roadmap-assessment/overview/executive-summary. Accessed 9 Apr 2013.

Ceres. 2013b. The Road to 2020: Corporate Progress on the Ceres Roadmap for Sustainability. http://www.ceres.org/roadmap-assessment. Accessed 31 Jan 2013.

ColaLife. 2013, August 8. About. http://www.colalife.org/about/colalife-about/. Accessed 2 Apr 2013

Collins, D., J. Morduch, S. Rutherford, and O. Ruthven. 2009. *Portfolios of the poor: How the world's poor live on $2 a day*. Princeton: Princeton University Press.

Fishman, C. 2006. *The Wal-Mart effect: How the world's most powerful company is transforming the rules of the American economy*. New York: Penguin.

Half the Sky Movement. 2013. Movement: Turning oppression into opportunity for women worldwide. http://www.halftheskymovement.org/pages/movement. Accessed 10 Apr 2013.

Hart, S.L. 2005. *Capitalism at the crossroads: The unlimited business opportunities in solving the world's most difficult problems*. Upper Saddle River: Wharton School.

Hindustan Unilever Limited. 2013. Project Shakti: Better livelihoods *Sustainable Living Case Studies*. http://www.hul.co.in/sustainable-living/casestudies/Casecategory/Project-Shakti.aspx. Accessed 11 Apr 2013.

Johnson, B. C. 2002. Retail: The Wal-Mart effect. *The McKinsey Quarterly* 1: 40–43.

Karliner, J. 2001. A brief history of greenwash. http://www.corpwatch.org/article.php?id=243.

Kent, M. 2012. The golden triangle: Spearheading change the smart way. http://www.coca-colacompany.com/opinions/muhtar-kent-on-the-golden-triangle. Accessed 12 Dec 2012.

Kristof, N.D., and S. WuDunn. 2009. *Half the sky*, Kindleth ed. New York: Alfred Knopf.

London, T., and S.L. Hart. 2011. *Next generation business strategies for the base of the pyramid: New approaches for building mutual value*, FT Pressth ed. Upper Saddle River: Pearson Education.

Nussbaum, M.C. 2000. *Women and human development: The capabilities approach*. New York: Cambridge University Press.

Prahalad, C.K. 2005. *The fortune at the bottom of the pyramid: Eradicating poverty through profits*. Upper Saddle River: Wharton School.

Prahalad, C. K. and S.L. Hart. 2002. The fortune at the bottom of the pyramid. *Strategy + Business* 26: 1–14.

Shah, A. 2013, January 7. Poverty facts and stats. *Global Issues*. http://www.globalissues.org/print/article/26. Accessed 10 Apr 2013.

Solar Electric Light Fund: Energy Is a Human Right. 2013. http://self.org/. Accessed 10Apr 2013.

The Coca-Cola Company. 2012. 5by20. http://www.coca-colacompany.com/stories/5by20. Accessed 15 Dec 2012.

The Female Health Company. 2013. Welcome. http://www.femalehealth.com/. Accessed 8 Apr 2013.

UN News Center. 2013. Deputy UN chief calls for urgent action to tackle global sanitation crisis March 21. http://www.un.org/apps/news/story.asp?NewsID=44452&Cr=sanitation&Cr1=#.UWMrqHBu_na. Accessed 8 Apr 2013.

Water.org. 2013. Water facts: Children. http://water.org/water-crisis/water-facts/children/. Accessed 8 Apr 2013.

Werhane, P.H. 1999. *Moral imagination and management decision making*. New York: Oxford University Press.

Werhane, P.H., S.P. Kelley, L.P. Hartman, and D.J. Moberg. 2010. *Alleviating global poverty through profitable business partnerships: Globalization, markets, and economic well-being*. New York: Routledge.

Chapter 2
Technology and Capacity Building

Introduction

Poverty is created and sustained by a system, not merely low income. A weak infrastructure precludes safe water, electricity, efficient food production and distribution. The absence of a rule of law and/or dangerous neighbors threatens security and confidence in safety and encourages corruption, thus depriving poor people of whatever resources might be available. Poor education weakens one's capabilities to compete for jobs and leadership. Scarcity of health care facilities exacerbates epidemics and curable diseases. Natural disasters create unpredictable havoc. Note that except for natural disasters, almost all of these phenomena are preventable. But almost all of them work together to create a system of poverty that becomes almost inescapable.

In this chapter we will take a more positive point of view. We include four cases of projects aimed at addressing the system of poverty. When apartheid came to an end, Eskom, the leading energy company in South Africa faced the daunting task of electrifying that country in areas that had either been neglected or where, in challenging the apartheid regime, the custom was to illegally tap into existing power lines. Its biggest challenge was to change mindsets of those previously excluded from the mainstream economy while ensuring that all communities would have power.

The second case, the Volta River Project, demonstrates the difficulties of providing adequate power and water to communities long deprived of those facilities. The third case, Transforming Education In Rural Haiti: Intel and L'Ecole De Choix, narrates a school project in earthquake-ravaged Haiti, and shows how an education initiative can work even in a very poor and allegedly corrupt country.

The chapter ends with Zynga, a large interactive social gaming company. Despite its commercial successes or maybe because of their impact on millions of players of its games, Zynga embarked on a series of efforts to raise funds for various antipoverty initiatives in the developing world. Its projects and challenges are narrated in this case.

P.J. Albert et al. (eds.), *Global Poverty Alleviation: A Case Book*, The International Society of Business, Economics, and Ethics Book Series 3, DOI 10.1007/978-94-007-7479-7_2, © Springer Science+Business Media Dordrecht 2014

All of these cases illustrate that a systemic approach to poverty alleviation, country by country, can make a difference, a big difference. And none of these are purely philanthropy. Each is trying to improve or eliminate the conditions under which poverty thrives, and each with success.

Eskom and the South African Electrification Program (A)[1]

The Beginning of the Electrification Program

The year was 1994, and Tienz[2] sat at his desk contemplating the enormous scope of the job that was in front of him. Eskom and the provision of electricity had always been an integral part of the economic and social evolution of the South African nation. Because of its important role in helping to shape the formation of South Africa, Eskom now saw itself as a necessary participant in the reconstruction process that the new African National Congress (ANC) government was outlining in an effort to rebuild the country in the postapartheid era.[3] The company even participated in the creation of upliftment programs under apartheid.[4] For example, in the late 1980s, the company had implemented an affirmative action policy to recruit black South Africans into management positions; they had also created programs to improve the school systems within black South African communities.

The present situation was somewhat more complicated than Eskom's past initiatives: in 1994, the new government had specifically stated that electrical access to all citizens was essential to the Reconstruction and Development Program (RDP), which laid out initiatives to help the country rebuild itself.[5] Management informed Tienz that the company had decided to aid the new government in its reconstruction process and implement a nation-wide electrification program – a far cry from simply extending the grid a few kilometers from urban centers.

---

[1] This case was prepared by Brian D. Cunningham under the supervision of Michael E. Gorman, and Patricia H. Werhane, Partial Support for this project was supplied by grants from the Ethics and Values in Science Program of the National Science Foundation and the Darden School. Copyright © 1999 by the University of Virginia Darden School Foundation, Charlottesville, VA. All rights reserved. The 2013 Case Addendum was prepared by Tim Rolph.

[2] Fictitious name.

[3] For a brief historical perspective of South Africa, see Appendix 1; a historical description of Eskom's background, Appendix 2; a description of the 1994 elections and the Reconstruction process that was outlined, Appendix 3; a description of Eskom's corporate initiatives and policies under Apartheid, Appendix 4; and for a description of Eskom's stated commitment to the South African reconstruction process, Appendix 5.

[4] Programs used to narrow the discriminatory gap between white and black South Africans.

[5] African National Congress, *The Reconstruction and Development Programme,* (Johannesburg, South Africa, 1994).

   The scope and scale of the proposed electrification program seemed overwhelming to Tienz. How was he going to develop a system to provide electrical connections to approximately 1.75 million homes (approximately nine million people) by the year 2000 in a cost-effective manner? Not only would new transmission lines have to be constructed, but safe and reliable distribution meters had to be designed to meet the unique conditions that existed in black South African townships, squatter camps, and villages.[6] The project would be demanding technologically – the possibility of recapturing the capital costs involved seemed impossible. The consumer market (i.e., the black South Africans) to whom Eskom was going to be providing electricity not only had grown accustomed to using coal, wood, and paraffin for all of their energy purposes, but they also had dramatically low and inconsistent monthly incomes. So how was Tienz supposed to develop a pricing structure for these new connections, given the depressed economic situation that existed in those areas?

   On his drive into work each morning, it was easy for Tienz to see the economic differences that apartheid had created between white and black South Africans. The highway was lined with hundreds of shacks that people had built out of spare wood, tin, and even cardboard in order to have a home closer to the city and the economic activity close to its borders, bizarre for a country that had a standard of living comparable to that of the highest-rated countries in the world. The average monthly income for a black South African was (South African Rand) ZAR294,[7] small when contrasted with the fact that average monthly expenditures for food and housing were ZAR28 and ZAR251 respectively. Half of all black South Africans lived below the poverty line; moreover, approximately 41 % of the black South African population was unemployed, and those who were employed had jobs either seasonal in nature or inequitable in salary structure.[8] For example, black South Africans made up 75 % of South Africa's population, but they earned only 28 % of the country's total income, whereas white South Africans were only 13 % of the population but earned 61 % of the country's income.

   The electrification program was seen as a "basic need" by the ANC government because only 20 % of black South Africans had access to electricity in 1994. Housing and water were identified as the two other basic needs: one-fourth of all blacks either had no housing or lived in shacks, and 40 % did not have access to clean water. These basic needs were identified because of the wide discrepancies between white and black South Africans, which were not only economic. For example, a typical black South African's life expectancy was 57 years compared to 73 years for a white South African, and infant mortality was 57 per 1,000 live births for blacks compared to 13 per 1,000 live births for whites.

---

[6] People could settle on municipal lands under new South African law, which meant that thousands of people were constructing make-shift structures for houses in areas that were not designed for residential development (e.g., areas beside freeways and even airport runways).

[7] The South African Rand fluctuated against the U.S. dollar in the range of 3:1 in 1994 to 6:1 in 1998.

[8] Reconstructed from *SA to Z: The Decision Maker's Encyclopedia of the South Africa Market* (Johannesburg: Eskom, 1996).

An electricity program was further seen as a viable option because the country already had an electrical grid in place to supply both residential areas and industry with electricity. In fact, there were approximately 240,000 km of lines currently employed in the country to transmit and distribute electricity. But extensions to the existing electrical grid would undoubtedly be capital-intensive; for example, a 1 km extension of low- medium-, and high-voltage lines would cost Eskom ZAR40,000, ZAR100,000, and ZAR1,000,000 respectively. Although the line extensions in the electrification process would use mostly low-voltage line extensions, some medium- and high-voltage extensions would be necessary to carry the needed electrical capacity to the areas being electrified. Although Eskom was operating at about 10 MW in excess capacity, the new customers would demand more electricity from the system, wiping out the excess capacity. The company could possibly find itself in the position of having to build more generation facilities and incur the associated capital expenditures in order to meet the new demand that they were in essence creating.[9]

The cost of the program had been estimated at ZAR1.2 billion annually. But Eskom's revenues were ZAR15,417 million, with operating expenditures at ZAR11,864 million, which left the company with a total operating income of ZAR3,553 million at its disposal.[10] The latter meant that Eskom needed to fund the program with approximately 35 % of its operating income annually, which would be an enormous expenditure for the company to make on a project that had an uncertain future. But three factors made the RDP's goals achievable by Eskom:

1. Eskom's policies were determined by the Electricity Council, which was linked closely to the government executive and the finance ministry;
2. Eskom had much experience with generating revenue by issuing bonds on financial markets;
3. Eskom had reserve generation capacity, which meant that capital expenditures for electrification excluded generation equipment, significantly reducing total expenditures.

Given the size of the capital expenditures that Eskom would undertake in the electrification program, the company needed to develop a program that would be affordable, add value to the lives of the people to whom they were providing electricity, and contribute to South Africa's reconstruction.

How to Deliver Service

Because of the possibility of not receiving a sufficient return on their investment, Eskom considered several options for the delivery of electricity. Of these options, two surfaced as being the most viable alternatives: (1) a prepayment metering

---

[9]One generation facility would cost approximately ZAR16 billion and take several years to build.
[10]Eskom annual report (Johannesburg), 1994.

system or (2) fixed-cost connections. In the former case, people pay for electricity before they actually use it, and, in the latter, people pay a monthly fixed fee for unlimited use at a fixed current level. Option (1) would allow Eskom the opportunity to offset the risk of people defaulting on their bills and the costs associated with recovering money owed, and option (2) would allow people to use as much electricity as they needed for growth at a low, fixed monthly fee.

The option of providing fixed-rate connections had already been used in other countries for similar electrification projects because of the lowered capital expenditures associated with being able to distribute electricity with low-voltage lines and not having to supply meters with each connection, which also offsets additional maintenance costs. But would it be possible for Eskom to set an affordable, fixed monthly fee that these consumers, who had variable monthly incomes at best, would be willing to pay each month? Again, the people being connected were struggling with high unemployment and sporadic monthly incomes. Since employment was variable at best, would the average person be able to afford the service that was being provided? If Eskom could develop an affordable monthly fee that people would agree to pay, would these people be willing to switch to a usage-based fee in the future if their electrical demands surpassed the amount of electricity available under a fixed-rate option? On the other hand, prepaid meters would cost more than fixed-rate connections and even more than traditional meters, thereby raising the capital costs associated with the electrification program. The advantage of the prepaid metering system was that consumers could stop using electricity and not pay whenever they did not have sufficient income or even a job.

Tienz now needed to decide which option would be better for the electrification program and why. He had to figure out how to finance a capital-intensive program that was projected to cost approximately ZAR20 billion to complete. So how was Eskom to raise the capital that was necessary for a program that would take ZAR1.2 billion annually? How was Eskom to develop sustainable communities to use the electricity that was being supplied to them?

Appendix 1: Eskom and the South African Electrification Program (A)

Early South African Beginnings

In 1652, an expedition by the Dutch East India Company landed at what is now South Africa to establish a garrison to supply East India ships with fresh water and food. Soon the garrison grew into a colony, and in 1657 the first settlers built their homes on the grazing land of the local indigenous people, which inevitably sparked conflict between these two groups of people in southern Africa.[11] In 1660, after

---

[11] The Khoikhoi (aka the Hottentots).

winning a number of conflicts with tribes, the Dutch settlers planted a thorn hedge across 6,000 acres of the Cape in order to separate the colony from the tribe.[12] This hedge, used to separate the races, serves as an early symbolic representation of the apartheid doctrine that would come later.

Although these periods of clashes between the white and black South Africans were frequent, there was a fair degree of trading and social interaction between the two groups.[13] Soon, however, further measures were placed into effect in order to regulate black and white interaction. For example, in 1829, a pass system was implemented to monitor and control the flow of black South Africans into white areas.

Then, as more Europeans settled in the country, stern competition arose between the two races for the limited amount of land and water in the country; this led to more frequent and serious conflicts. The fight for land started in the mid-1850s when 70 % of the white population was forced into black-controlled lands because of the limited land available in white-controlled areas.[14] The white population eventually learned to survive in these areas by dominating and controlling the black populations. The white population felt superior to the blacks, on both the battleground and in farming, and a master-servant relationship came into being with black indigenous people doing manual work for the white population in southern Africa.

The agricultural economy of southern Africa soon turned into one centered upon mining when, in 1867, diamonds were discovered. The master-servant relationship between the black and white populations deepened when the white-owned mines recruited cheap black labor, leading to a huge influx of blacks into white-controlled lands. The whites, to control race interaction, enacted the Native Land Act, granting blacks temporary status to live and work within South Africa. A portion of land was even set aside far from white areas for the incoming black population to inhabit. However, white control went even farther than controlling black populations in the white areas of South Africa. In the early 1900s, the white government went further in their control over the black populations in their midst by placing restrictions on black mobility, education, and housing.

Appendix 2: Eskom and the South African Electrification Program (A)

Beginning of Electricity Supply

It's hard to imagine that one of the far corners of the world was where electricity was first utilized, but given that "necessity is the mother of invention," South Africa's mining industry inevitably called for the use of electricity in the

---

[12]Louw, L., and F. Kendall. 1986. *South Africa: The solution* Ciskei, South Africa: Amagi Publications.

[13]Louw, L., and F. Kendall.

[14]Orpen. Productivity.

mid-1880s.[15] Mining companies installed their own electrical reticulation systems in order to supply electricity to the mines for illumination and power for equipment. These systems soon grew to the point of supplying the nearby cities with electricity, and it was soon recognized that large centralized power stations would supply more reliable and cheaper power than smaller dedicated mining power stations. This eventually led to the formation of the Rand Central Electric Works[16] and the Victoria Falls Power Company in 1906.

Eventually, the Electric Supply Commission (Escom) was established in 1923 in order to supply electricity more cheaply and efficiently to industry and local authorities.[17] In 1937, Eskom's headquarters was the tallest building in South Africa (21 stories tall), indicating the growth that Escom underwent to meet the growing needs of the mining industry. During the boom years after WWII, electrical demand was soaring, and Eskom had met these demands effectively. However, although South Africa was blessed with a wealth of natural resources,[18] the country did not have an adequate water supply, so Eskom recognized that they had to turn to the huge coal reserves to produce electricity. In fact, the coal seams in the country were abundant, thick, shallow, and unfaulted, which meant that extraction costs would be minimal and that these lowered costs could be passed on in the form of cheaper electricity prices.

During the 1960s more coal-fired generation facilities were constructed and Eskom successfully designed dry cooling towers for burning the lower-quality coal that was abundant in South Africa. In the 1970s, future electrical demand and load growth were expected to increase even more, so new facilities (one nuclear plant and several pumped storage plants) were built. However, load growth did not increase as planned, and Eskom was left with a surplus of generation capability at its disposal, which would ultimately lead to Eskom being able to supply even cheaper electricity in the 1990s.

At the end of 1997, Eskom was one of the five largest utilities in the world with total assets equaling ZAR96,894 million, total revenue equaling ZAR20,448, and approximately 40,000 employees.[19] The company supplied more than 98 % of the electricity used in South Africa, which constituted approximately 60 % of the electricity used on the entire continent of Africa. The electricity was generated by 20 power stations with a 39,154 total megawatt capacity. The power was distributed by way of more than 26,065 km of high-voltage power lines within South Africa. Because of the overanticipated electrical demand in the 1980s and the additional generation sites that were constructed as a result, Eskom was operating at a surplus

---

[15]The mining shafts were going deeper into the ground and needed to be ventilated.

[16]The first commercially supplied electricity in South Africa.

[17]Escom was renamed Eskom in 1987.

[18]South Africa has 91 % of the world's manganese reserves, 82 % of its platinum group metals, 58 % of its chrome, and 53 % of its gold. As a result, South African mines are deeper than any other country in the world, at depths of almost 4 km in places (e.g., Western Deep Levels Mine).

[19]Eskom annual report, 1997 (Johannesburg).

capacity of approximately 10,000 MW. Moreover, estimates showed that Eskom's surplus capacity would not be exceeded until the year 2007, even with the electrification project and growth in demand for industrial power.[20]

Appendix 3: Eskom and the South African Electrification Program (A)

The "New" South Africa

After winning the seat of government in the first open elections in South Africa[21] by receiving 62.5 % of the vote and obtaining 252 of 400 seats in the legislature, the African National Congress (ANC) then sought to implement a plan to make a better life for all.[22] Recognizing the need for infrastructure development, they created the Reconstruction and Development Program (RDP) to guide the post-Apartheid state in South Africa. RDP was a socio-economic policy that sought to mobilize all of South Africa's people and resources to eradicate the lingerings of apartheid and build a nonracially based, democratic government and nation. The program consisted of six basic principles and five key programs.

These were the six principles:

1. Maintain an integrated and sustainable program.
2. Center on a people-driven process.
3. Ensure peace and security for all.
4. Embark on nation-building.
5. Link reconstruction and development.
6. Democratize the nation.

The principles were set to be achieved by the five programs:

1. Meet basic needs.
2. Develop human resources.
3. Build the economy.
4. Democratize the state and society.
5. Implement the RDP.[23]

However, as the statistics in Tables 2.1 and 2.2 illustrate, the task would not be easy.

---

[20]Offei Ansah, Jon. 1995. South Africa: Large energy economy enjoyed by few. *African Economic Digest*, July 31. Although this fact is not emphasized in Eskom's literature, it is likely that this excess capacity may be one of the main reasons why Eskom began electrifying schools and homes as early as 1988 and the early electrification programs in 1990.

[21]April 26–April 28, 1994.

[22]"South Africa," *Hilfe Country Report* (July 1996).

[23]The Conference Board, 4.

Table 2.1 Income statistics for different ethnic groups [Constructed from data from *SA to Z: The decision maker's encyclopedia of the South African consumer market* (Johannesburg: Eskom, 1996)]

	Asians	Colored	Whites	Blacks
% of population (out of 42 million)	3	8	16	73
% unemployment	17.1	23.3	6.4	41.1
Avg. monthly personal income	ZAR1,304	ZAR711	ZAR2,875	ZAR294
Avg. spent monthly on food/housing	ZAR871/R640	ZAR521/R275	ZAR1,072/R827	ZAR251/R28

Table 2.2 South African statistical indicators (SA to Z: The decision maker's encyclopedia of the South African consumer market)

GDP	ZAR433 billion
GDP/capita	$3,004
Unemployment	32.6 %
Inflation	12.5 %
Interest rate	18.4 %

Appendix 4: Eskom and the South African Electrification Program (A)

Early Social Investment by Eskom

During the apartheid era, before the electrification program, an estimated 98 % of all white households had electricity; 80 % of black households lacked it.[24] In addition, the power that was sold to blacks was subjected to highly arbitrary rates. Eskom acted as a wholesaler of electricity to approximately 450 municipalities, which were typically white-controlled under the apartheid system. Because of the number of municipalities involved, over 2,000 different rate structures were constructed. In some areas, like Soweto, on the border of Johannesburg, black residents were paying double the rates of nearby whites within Johannesburg proper. Moreover, it could be argued that the electrical service for black areas was of much lower quality than for white customers: "If the power went out, you could wait a week, a month or even longer for a crew to show up."[25] Thus, Eskom's history of corporate social investment (CSI), not surprisingly, was racially directed.

[24]"South Africa: Large energy economy enjoyed by few, "*African Economic Digest* (July 31, 1995).
[25]Adams, Peter, and Eskom Spokesman, in Bob Drogin, "South Africa bringing power to the people," *Los Angeles Times*, January 31, 1996, A1.

In 1985, anticipating the likely changes in the apartheid regime,[26] Eskom committed to cultural change. It initiated an affirmative action program to create contact between the races and by the 1990s began to recruit talented black personnel into executive positions. In 1988 it launched its "New South African" program, a corporate social investment (CSI) program initially funded with ZAR4 million. About two-thirds of this budget was initially spent on electrifying 10 schools per year in Soweto. The rest of the budget was largely spent on funding education-oriented, nongovernment organizations, which sought to improve the educational conditions in poor, black regions.[27]

Moving to alleviate further some of the problems associated with the Apartheid system, Eskom accelerated its investments in electrification and expanded beyond schools to an "Electricity for All" program. At the end of 1990, it launched this program with the philosophy that economic development within South Africa's black communities would not occur until they had access to electricity. However, there were no accurate statistics on the proportion of the South African population that lacked electricity, and there was no accurate database of housing in South Africa. Accordingly, Eskom's first task was to compile housing statistics to determine the extent of electrification in South Africa's urban and rural areas. Results showed that out of 7.2 million homes in South Africa, only three million had access to electricity: i.e., approximately 23 million people – just over half of the population of South Africa at the time – were without electricity.[28,29] Almost all of these homes were in black impoverished urban, township, and rural regions.

Eskom piloted the first electrification program, and by the end of 1991, Eskom succeeded in connecting 31,000 residences to the electrical grid. Eskom worked with local government councils and offered incentives to regions if they could electrify homes in their areas. Viewed as a success, the program continued, connecting an additional 159,000 homes in 1992 at an average cost per connection of ZAR2,600. At the end of 1992, approximately 1 million black South Africans had been connected to the grid and over 260 electrification projects were underway. Eskom recognized that mere connections were not all that the poorer people in South Africa needed in order to have access to electricity. The company made it their goal to reduce the "real price"[30] of electricity in order to stimulate economic growth and provide an affordable service to their new customers. Eskom had achieved substantial momentum in electrification just at the time when political power was changing hands in South Africa.

---

[26] See Elling Njal Tjonneland. 1989. *Pax Pretoriana: The fall of apartheid and the politics of regional destabilization*. Uppsala, Sweden: Scandinavian Institute of African Studies.

[27] Alperson, Myra. 1995. *Foundations for a new democracy: Corporate social investment in South Africa*. Johannesburg: Ravan Press, 70.

[28] Eskom, "Bringing power to the people," video prepared for the Edison Electric Institute, 1996.

[29] Drogin, "South Africa bringing power to the people."

[30] Eskom's goal was to produce and distribute the cheapest electricity in the world.

Appendix 5: Eskom and the South African Electrification Program (A)

Eskom's Commitment to the RDP

John Maree[31] wrote in Eskom's 1992 annual report:

> As the new South Africa becomes a reality, large organizations will need to have relevance to our society and demonstrate that, through the conduct of their business, they bring value, not only to their own stakeholders, but also to the wider society. Their products and services will have to meet the emerging consumer needs and contribute to the well-being and progress of the community and particularly the disadvantaged.

Access to electricity was identified as one of the top two needs of the citizens of the country. Eskom's early electrification efforts had been embraced by the new government, and the electrification of homes was identified as one of the most important aspects of the "meeting basic needs" program. An accelerated and sustainable electrification program was planned to provide access to electricity for an additional 2.5 million households by the year 2000, thereby increasing the level of access to electricity to about 72 % of all South African households, double the 1992 number of households with access to electricity. Eskom would play a major role in meeting the goals set out by the RDP, and these goals became central to Eskom's electrification goals. Eskom's 1995 stated goals based on the RDP were:

1. Further reduce the real price of electricity by 15 %, to become the world's lowest-cost supplier of electricity.
2. Electrify an additional 1,750,000 homes, improving the lives of 11 million South Africans.
3. Change the staffing profile so that 50 % of management, professional, and supervisory staff are black South Africans.
4. Educate, train, and upgrade sufficient numbers of people to meet Eskom's future managerial, technical, and other professional staff needs, by employing 370 black trainees and bursars per year and enabling all Eskom employees to become literate.
5. Maintain transparency and worker consultation in decision-making.
6. Contribute ZAR50 million per year to electrification of schools and clinics, and other community development activities, particularly in rural areas.
7. Enable all Eskom employees to own a home.
8. Encourage small and medium enterprise development, through Eskom's buying policies and give managerial support.
9. Protect the environment.
10. Finance the above from Eskom's own resources and from overseas development funding.

---

[31]Chairman of the Electricity Council.

Because the company believed that electricity was a vital part of modern life and that it would encourage economic growth within the newly electrified areas, Eskom committed to the RDP goals of electrifying approximately 2.5 million of the 4.2 million homes (60 % of the people without electricity) through both grid and non-grid (solar) connections. The remaining number "would be difficult to electrify due to either structure of the dwelling, the distance from the existing grid, access to alternative energy sources, or simply as a matter of affordability." Other reasons why Eskom proclaimed commitment were: (1) the standard of living improved through access to hot water, stoves, and TV; (2) gender-specific roles could be revamped (e.g., time previously spent on collecting firewood could be used for other goals); (3) educational standards improved by access to lighting; and (4) health standards improved through access to refrigeration, since food and medicines could be kept handy and since smoke from cooking fires could be eliminated.[32] The company cited Japan, Taiwan, and Korea as "winning nations," and stated "economic growth could not reach impressive figures before the overwhelming number of homes in the country had electricity."[33] In addition to electrifying 300,000 homes per year until the year 2000, Eskom also made a pledge to reduce the price of electricity in real terms by 15 % by the year 2000 in order to provide the newly connected homes with an affordable service. The latter is in keeping with Eskom's overall vision of offering the lowest electricity rates in the world.[34] All such goals stem from Eskom's belief that little economic growth can occur without the widespread use of electricity.

In 1994, it was estimated that the electrification program would cost around ZAR12 billion (approx. USD3.5 billion), with annual investments peaking at around ZAR2 billion.[35] How would it be possible to implement such a large social investment project in a viable manner? Although Eskom was producing the lowest-priced electricity in the world at the time and was operating at an excess capacity, the capital expenditures that would be incurred would be astronomical. Moreover, given the history of apartheid, the people they were going to provide electricity to had become dependent on other sources of energy[36] for their daily needs. Was there a guarantee that these people would use the electricity when it was supplied to them? The unemployment rate in South Africa also lingered at approximately 45 %, and there was a history of "nonpayment" among the black population,[37] so how was Eskom going to implement a system that would lower the risk on return for their investment?

---

[32] Eskom, Eskom Corporate Profile, 1995.

[33] Eskom.

[34] Stephan, Rob. 1996. Challenges and innovations facing Eskom. *Transmission & Distribution World*. January 1996, 30.

[35] African National Congress. 1994. *The reconstruction and development programme: A policy framework*. Johannesburg: ANC, 31.

[36] Paraffin, coal, candles, dung, and wood.

[37] Used as a protest against the apartheid government. See Eskom B case.

Eskom and the South African Electrification Program (B)

A Culture of Nonpayment

During the apartheid years, there was a great deal of conflict between the black South Africans opposing the established government and the military and police of South Africa. The conflicts ranged from public demonstrations to covert ANC bombings. One of the most commonly used forms of protest against the apartheid state was the consumer boycott, when blacks used nonpayment as a form of protest against the government. The idea behind nonpayment was to withdraw support of the infrastructure that the apartheid government had forced upon black South Africans. Black South Africans boycotted rent, electricity, and consumables.

Boycotts started during apartheid as a method supported by the African National Congress (ANC) to undermine the South African government and spread widely through the poor population that was eager to avoid paying for anything out of their scarce incomes. Boycotting went further, when local authorities would typically respond by cutting off services to the areas boycotting payment. The residents of these areas naturally adapted by pirating the services (tampering with the electrical grid and water system) that were being denied them.[38] Many of the problems that the new South African government faced were a result of the past boycotts that they helped to support.

In fact, ANC members of government, who had anticipated the use of nonpayment to stop as soon as power was democratically held in the country, openly called for an end to the boycotts when the nonpayments were threatening the supply of services on a national scale. But a culture of nonpayment had permeated the country. It threatened the development of the new South African government and the RDP campaigns, and it also inhibited foreign investment when companies from abroad recognized the risk of negative returns on investments.[39] The government implemented extensive educational reforms in order to help the citizens recognize the need of payment for services.

In early 1999, Eskom executive Charles van Rooyen was assigned the task of determining what to do about Eskom being owed a total of (South African Rand) ZAR1.5 billion by black municipalities that had not paid for service during apartheid and that further nonpayment would hinder the electrification program.[40] Although van Rooyen remembered that the company had historically approached the problem of nonpayment with the threat of cutting off the power to municipalities, he soon decided that this policy was not viable for a number of reasons. First, there

---

[38] Johnson, R. W. 1997. Riots and bulldozers return to townships. *Overseas News-New York Times*, August 9, 1997.

[39] "Africa and Latin America," *BBC Weekly Economic Report*, Part 5, March 21, 1995.

[40] Kevin Morgan, legal adviser to the South African National Electricity Regulator, in an interview with *Africa News*, August 9, 1996.

was a question of equity and fair treatment of the people living within those communities who *were* paying their bills. Would it be fair to remove access to a service for which these people had in fact paid? Second, the effects of the apartheid regime were now more noticeable, and the company was committed to helping these people improve their living standards. Third, past action by municipal authorities against nonpayment had led to riots and violence. So van Rooyen had the difficult dual goals of both realizing a return on the company's investments *and* contributing to the quality of life of the citizens of South Africa.

Eskom and the South African Electrification Program (C)

Residential Tampering

Muenda,[41] one of Eskom's top managers, looked at the figures and couldn't believe what he was seeing. On average, as much as 40 % of Eskom's prepaid connections had been tampered with, and this led to a loss in revenue amounting to (South African Rand) ZAR300 million annually.[42] This wasn't surprising to him considering that even children in the sixth grade knew how to pull electricity illegally off the electrical grid. In fact, they could even demonstrate how the recoil would knock a person down if a mistake happened while tampering with the grid (many had been electrocuted while tampering).[43] During apartheid, the South African people living in these communities had learned that, in addition to not paying for services, they could further undermine the local white authority by tapping into the electrical grid and drawing service for free.[44]

Muenda looked again at the numbers and determined that it would be cheaper for the company to connect these people to electricity and not charge them for usage.[45] The cost per connection averaged ZAR3,000, and Eskom performed 1,000 connections on a daily basis, which amounted to approximately ZAR1.095 billion annually. Muenda decided to calculate the present value of this venture and determine the payback period, which would be a bit more complicated than simply looking at the overall costs and revenues associated with the program. In order to offset illegal draws from the grid, Eskom would have to go through the additional expenditures of monitoring the grid. Not only would Eskom have to pay for the man-hours and expenses associated with inspection, but many times these employees were attacked or had their

---

[41]Fictitious Zulu name.

[42]Robyn Chalmers. 1998. Meter tampering costs Eskom R300m. *Africa News,* May 21, 1998, http://www.africanews.com.

[43]Keller, Bill. 1993. Township gets electricity (and it's free, too). *New York Times,* September 1, 1993.

[44]Boycotting payment for service as a protest of the apartheid government.

[45]Interview with Paul Maree (Eskom manager for the Electrification Program).

cars hijacked in the areas they were inspecting, which was by itself a valid argument for supplying fixed-rate connections because of concern for employee safety.

After examining the figures again, Muenda discovered that, although the total annual sales per customer receiving electricity was ZAR96, the total annual operating cost per customer was ZAR104. Therefore, the excess costs of collection, maintenance, and inspection due to nonpayment and tampering reduced Eskom's return to a negative ZAR8 per customer. In other words, Eskom would not only absorb the initial capital expenditure of ZAR3, 000 per customer to connect people to electricity, it would also incur a ZAR8 fee annually for each customer connected to the electrical grid under the electrification program.

According to his figures, the program was providing the company with a return on its investment, even several years after the project began. In fact, Muenda determined that it would simply be more cost-effective for the company to give electricity away for free and thereby lower the costs associated with billing, maintenance, and metering equipment. But the company had not only committed to the RDP goal of electrifying 1.75 million households by the year 2000, but it was also attempting to foster a responsible culture of payment within the consumer base.[46]

Muenda wondered if he should recommend that the company stop the electrification program until his group could plan a way to generate adequate revenue from the consumer base. Although the costs of the program were increasing because some of the residents were tampering with their connections, there were people who were managing their connections responsibly within their communities and had been paying their bills. Would it be fair to these responsible consumers to stop the electrification program because of the people who were irresponsible? Should these responsible people be denied access because of what others in the community were doing?

From a theoretical perspective, it was easy to determine that it would not be fair to deny electrical connections to future responsible consumers because of the previous irresponsible behavior of some customers. But what was Muenda to do when he found hundreds of illegal connections coming off the grid in a community? The question of who was responsible, the individual or the community at large, became difficult to answer in this situation. Should Eskom disconnect the entire community?

Eskom and the South African Electrification Program (D)

Training to Tamper

Ralph Withers[47] was reading the newspaper, and he noticed the headline stating the unemployment rate for black South Africans currently hovered at 41.1 % of the total

---

[46] See "Eskom and the South African Electrification Program (A)" (E-0162).
[47] Fictitious name.

population in South Africa.[48] He remembered the issue of poverty recently being addressed by the African National Congress (ANC):

> Poverty is the single greatest burden of South Africa's people and is the direct result of the apartheid system and the grossly skewed nature of business and industrial development that accompanies it. Poverty affects millions of people, the majority of whom live in the rural areas and are women. It is estimated that there are at least 17 million people surviving below the minimum living level in South Africa, and of these at least 11 million live in the rural areas. For those intent on fomenting violence, these conditions provide fertile ground.[49]

In order to improve the quality of life for all South Africans, the poorer citizens needed help taking control of their lives. Part of the government's strategy to promote this empowerment was to improve living conditions, boost production, raise household income through job creation, and create opportunities for all citizens to sustain themselves. In fact, it was understood that job creation was specifically linked with public works projects and other projects aimed at meeting people's basic needs. Therefore, job creation was a primary focus of the ANC government, and Withers, a manager at Eskom, recognized the role that Eskom could play in the process.

With this in mind, Withers recommended that Eskom use local labor as part of the electrification process. By providing people with basic electrician skills, he was attempting to meet the problem of unemployment in South Africa. People trained in basic electrical wiring and repair would be paid for assisting in the electrification process of the surrounding areas. Although they would not be full-time employees with Eskom, because others would be trained to assist with the electrification process in their respective areas, these people would have marketable skills to help them procure jobs and start small businesses within their communities. As load growth and electrical demand increased in newly electrified areas, people would start to use more electrical appliances, creating a market for the repair and resale of these appliances, which would provide employment for the people trained by Eskom.

Withers was astonished to learn that, although illegal connections had been discouraged, electricity was being consumed by people had not purchased tokens for their prepaid meters. To find out what was going on, Withers chose pilot sites and placed meters on the connections going into these communities to determine how much electricity was going into the community in a given period of time. Then he looked at electricity sales for that community for the same time period and compared the amount of electricity going into the sales of electricity. He soon determined that tampering was prevalent in almost all of the communities that had been electrified – as high as 80 % in some areas.[50] And that was not all: Withers also noticed that the people who had been trained and paid to assist in the electrification

---

[48] *SA to Z: The decision maker's encyclopedia of the South African consumer market* (Johannesburg: Eskom, 1996).

[49] Section 2.1.1 of *The Reconstruction and Development Programme,* African National Congress, 1994.

[50] Soweto, South Africa.

process had actually been stealing electricity from Eskom. In other words, he had inadvertently trained people to steal from the company. These people would approach their neighbors and bypass prepaid meters for small fees, thereby providing free electricity to the people who would pay for illegal connections.

This situation only compounded the problem that Withers had encountered with residential tampering. If the company decided to continue with the electrification program, what type of message would the company be sending the residents when Eskom employees themselves were aiding in the illegal tampering? The purpose of training local laborers in the electrification process was to help curb the high unemployment rate for black South Africans. Withers wondered if Eskom should continue to train, pay, and use local labor in the electrification process. The company already had approximately 40,000 employees operating in a country that was little more than twice the size of Texas,[51] which meant that it had the existing infrastructure to perform the electrification process on its own without training and employing local labor. In fact, it even cost Eskom an additional amount on top of the electrification process to train these people at all. But now these same people were helping to steal from the company. Obviously, this type of employee behavior was driving the costs of operation even higher. But was providing people with marketable skills and curbing the unemployment rate more important than lowering the costs involved? How could Withers and his group achieve both?

Eskom 2013 Case Addendum

Since 1991, Eskom has connected over 4.2 million homes to the electricity grid, largely on a prepaid metering system, and it has provided non-grid access to 38,000 others. Many of these are extremely low-income homes– adding three million customers between 1994 and 2004 only increased Eskom's sales by 4 %, though industrial sales growth in the same period was 14 %.[52] In 2001, the South African Department of Energy began funding the Integrated National Electrification Programme (INEP), which Eskom implements on the department's behalf, and the company sponsors many of the new connections.[53]

In late 2007, Eskom received widespread criticism when demand for electricity exceeded supply forcing the company to introduce rolling blackouts, wherein certain sections of South Africa would be disconnected from power for 2 h at a time. The rationing seriously impacted several industrial sectors, such as mining.[54]

---

[51] Total area of 471,000 mi^2 as compared to 270,000 mi^2.

[52] Winkler, Harald, and Andrew Marquand. 2009. Changing development paths: From an energy-intensive to low-carbon economy in South Africa. *Climate and Development.*

[53] http://financialresults.co.za/2012/eskom_ar2012/fact-sheets/010.php. Accessed 10 June 2013.

[54] http://www.guardian.co.uk/world/2008/jan/26/southafrica.international. Accessed 10 June 2013.

Though Eskom has not resorted to such measures again since April 2008, some worry 2013 might see additional issues with the power grid, as the company continues to operate with a buffer of only 1 % of its capacity.[55]

The abundance and affordability of coal in South Africa has created few incentives for Eskom to move away from carbon-intensive energy generation, but it has recently partnered with the World Bank on the Eskom Renewables Support Project, a $1.2 billion initiative that will fund both a 100 MW wind plant and a 100 MW concentrated solar plant.[56]

Eskom is targeted to create an additional 724,000 connections over the next five years. At the current INEP funding rate, universal access to electricity is slated for 2033, though Eskom believes that, with addition resources, the goal could be reached by 2020.[57]

The Volta River Project[58]

In 1998, Ghana needed to consider new alternatives of electricity to counteract the recurring problem of power shortages due to droughts. With guidance by lessons from the past, the new alternatives would need to be practical, affordable, and sustainable choices for electricity in Ghana. The options included (1) thermal energy, (2) importing electricity, (3) construction of additional hydroelectric dams, and (4) other options such as nuclear energy, solar energy, and other fossil-fuel-powered plants and generators.

Introduction

March 6, 1997, marked the fortieth anniversary of Ghana's independence from British colonial rule. During the early years, Kwame Nkrumah, Ghana's first elected president, was keen on establishing Ghana's economic independence. In conjunction with multinational interests, his government oversaw the construction of Akosombo Dam on the Volta River. Akosombo would become the primary power source for the nation (Fig. 2.1). Nkrumah believed that industrialization was

---

[55] http://www.iol.co.za/business/companies/eskom-may-resort-to-blackouts-this-winter-1.1504409#.UbYE9HDo9xM. Accessed 10 June 2013.

[56] http://www.worldbank.org/projects/P122329/south-africa-eskom-renewables-support-project?lang=en. Accessed 10 June 2013.

[57] http://financialresults.co.za/2012/eskom_ar2012/fact-sheets/010.php. Accessed 10 June 2013.

[58] This case was prepared by John Riverton under the supervision of Patricia H. Werhane. Copyright © 1999; The Addendum was written by Tim Rolph, Copyright 2013 by the University of Virginia Darden School Foundation, Charlottesville, VA. All rights reserved.

Fig. 2.1 Akosombo Dam

dependent on ample and affordable electricity. Forty years later, the "miracle dam" was not able to supply enough power to meet energy needs in Ghana.

The Volta River Project was the name given to the association of the Volta River Authority (VRA), Ghana's statutory power provider, and the Volta Aluminum Corporation (Valco) whose power-intensive aluminum smelting operations justified the construction of the dam. Valco, which is 100 % owned by U.S. interests, lobbied heavily with the Ghanaian government and other contributors to see the speedy completion of the dam between 1963 and 1966. Although Akosombo Dam was a tremendous engineering feat which became a symbol of national pride, the effects of dam construction, the consequences of contractual negotiations and agreements with Valco, and Ghana's dependence on hydroelectric power continually resurfaced as Ghanaian policy-makers faced the challenges of meeting a growing power demand. During the worst droughts, water levels were not sufficient to generate enough power to meet Ghana's energy needs. Although other energy alternatives were considered, and some were implemented, Ghana's power infrastructure was dependent on the rise and fall of the water level in the Akosombo reservoir. Ghana's power infrastructure needed to change.

History of Ghana Before the Volta River Project

During the 1400s, the Portuguese were the first Europeans to arrive in what is known today as Ghana. Their primary objective was gold exploration. The Portuguese gave the name "Gold Coast" to the territory because of its wealth of gold and other natural resources. In 1482, they constructed Elmina Castle near Cape Coast; this castle would later become the last stopover for thousands of slaves before they were shipped to the new world. Between 1471 and 1957, several other European kingdoms explored the Gold Coast. Among these were Denmark, Holland, England, Prussia, and Sweden. They constructed elaborate castles and forts, to establish and protect their presence in the territory. When the British merchants arrived en masse during the 1700s, they sought to capitalize on natural and human resources: gold and slaves. The slave trade continued until the late 1800s when it was abolished in the western nations. The British finally colonized the territory in 1874; British colonial rule continued from 1874 until 1957, when the Gold Coast gained independence and became the Republic of Ghana.

In 1914, Sir Albert Kitson, director of the Gold Coast Geological Survey, discovered bauxite deposits near Mpraeso. Bauxite is a mineral ore containing aluminum oxide or hydroxides with several impurities. When refined, bauxite becomes alumina, the principal ingredient for aluminum production. The following year, while engaged in a rapid canoe voyage down the Volta, Kitson observed that the river flowed through a gorge surrounded by a large range of hills near Akosombo. He was the first person recorded to envision a dam at that location. Kitson's infrastructure proposals were not limited to Akosombo. He also identified Bui, on the Black Volta, as a second feasible site for a dam. He felt that a dam at that location, near the midwestern border of Ghana, would serve to electrify a future railway to the north.[59]

A Yorkshireman by the name of Duncan Rose would later carry Kitson's dream closer to reality. After graduating from Cambridge in 1930, Rose emigrated to South Africa to pursue his fascination with aluminum. He thought aluminum could be the metal of the century.[60] When he came across Kitson's bulletin in the public library at Johannesburg, Rose planned an exploratory trip to the Gold Coast. Working with his financing partner, T.W. Charles, Rose acquired the support of the Anglo-Transvaal Consolidated Investment Co., a leading South African mining finance house. Together, they formed the African Aluminum Syndicate, which would later be joined by a South African engineer by the name of Christopher St. John Bird. By 1939, St. John Bird was in the Gold Coast preparing preliminary reports while Rose was negotiating concessions for dam construction with the Gold Coast government.

World War II caused the Syndicate to suspend its physical operations in the Gold Coast. Rose left for duty in England to manage a munitions factory; however, while in England, he vigorously lobbied for support of the Gold Coast aluminum scheme in both government and business circles. Among his investor targets was British Unilever. After the war, momentum for the dam continued to build in the Gold Coast. Rose formed West African Aluminum Ltd. (Wafal), which replaced the prewar African Aluminum Syndicate. One indication of the growing success of the proposal was that in March 1946, Unilever, through its subsidiary, the United Africa Company, acquired financial interest in Wafal.

More on Colonial Interests

In 1949, Christopher St. John Bird and Duncan Rose were compiling proposals for the aluminum-hydroelectric dam. They reasoned that, since the land on the banks of the Volta River was of "low value," the dam, which was then estimated to cause about 5,180 km^2 (2,000 mile^2) of flooding, would not have a significant negative

---

[59]Moxon, James. 1984. *Volta, man's greatest lake*. London: Deutsch.
[60]Moxon, *Volta,* 52.

impact on the country. As retribution, St. John Bird suggested that a sum of £1 million be given to the Gold Coast government.[61]

St. John Bird had been a partner in an engineering consulting firm in South Africa before coming to the Gold Coast. His proposals were basically "apartheid" in nature.[62] In his plans for the Akosombo village, the European executives and senior workers would have their homes constructed on a ridge where they would enjoy a cool breeze. Their living area would include tennis courts, a swimming pool, and a dance hall, among other recreational amenities. The African workers would live in the valley within a mile of the humid riverbanks, where they would be closer to the work site. St. John Bird suggested constructing aluminum houses for the African laborers because those houses "would prove palatial in comparison with the local product."[63] The Europeans would be paid 14–25 times the salary of the African workers. The African laborers would be paid according to their skills and technical worth to the project. In his original proposals, no concessions were made for hiring Ghanaian managers or technical experts. St. John Bird anticipated that only a few Ghanaians would hold low-level management positions.

The White Paper Cmd 8702 of November 1952 illustrated the United Kingdom's mental model for the association between aluminum and hydroelectric power in Ghana. This document, bearing the title, "The Volta River Aluminum Scheme," strongly suggested that hydroelectric generation was more for the purpose of cheap electricity for aluminum production than for Ghanaian electrification. The preliminary plans presented in this document involved the production of 564 MegaWatts (MW) of power, of which 514 MW would go to the smelter and 50 MW to other users in Ghana.[64] As a part of the "scheme," the smelter would be obligated for 30 years to sell at least 75 % of the metal produced to buyers in the United Kingdom.

The White Paper concluded that:

Her Majesty's Government in the United Kingdom [is] favorable in principle to participation in the scheme, which would further their policy of encouraging the development of the resources of the [Gold Coast] as well as contributing to the raw material needs in the United Kingdom. They believe, on the basis of the information so far available, that it is soundly conceived [and] that its successful completion would bring substantial benefits to the two countries.[65]

Back in Ghana, the British Aluminum group (Wafal) and Aluminum Ltd. of Canada (Alcan) were actively compiling final reports from site investigations. During the preparation of these reports, African rights activist Kwame Nkrumah was released from prison. Nkrumah had been sentenced to two years for demonstrations surrounding his political action campaign, in which some demonstrators had died. Before the Gold Coast government could approve the Wafal-Alcan reports, the political climate changed.

[61] Hart, David. 1980. *The Volta river project*. Edinburgh, U.K.: Edinburgh University Press.

[62] *The Volta river project*, 35.

[63] Hart, *The Volta river project*.

[64] Hart, *The Volta river project*, 36.

[65] Hart, 37.

Nkrumah and the Volta River Project

In 1951, soon after his release from prison, Kwame Nkrumah's Convention People's Party (CPP) swept the polls at the February general election. He was appointed governor-general (a post that later became prime minister) of the Gold Coast under the Queen of England. The CPP became the first African-majority government to hold power in colonial Africa.

Nkrumah had started his career as a teacher before going abroad for 10 years to attend the London School of Economics and later Lincoln University and the University of Pennsylvania in the United States. Returning to Ghana, Dr. Nkrumah soon found his way among the intellectual elite. He believed that the key to securing African solidarity and independence from colonial rule was a unified Africa. One of the more revolutionary ideas Nkrumah held with other African leaders was forming a confederation of African nations and adopting Swahili as a continental language to unify all African peoples, and in 1963 they formed the Organization of African Unity (OAU). Some believe that Nkrumah wanted a more powerful, centralized structure where he could dominate continental politics. Much of his thinking was based on socialist theory and represented a unique blend of Christian and Marxist ideas.[66]

While president, Nkrumah emphasized the importance of diverse foreign investment in Ghana and national electrification as necessary precursors for development. He had embraced Kitson's vision of a dam at Akosombo in hopes of developing Ghana's bauxite reserves, among other interests. Nkrumah knew that involving an aluminum smelter was the only way to secure finances for the construction of Akosombo Dam.

Nkrumah maintained working relations with the Soviet Union and Red China as well as the West, while he solicited foreign investment to boost the economy of the newly independent Ghana. Nkrumah's government was overthrown in 1966 by a coup which occurred after the commissioning of Akosombo Dam. Suspicion of American involvement was verified when the *New York Times* published that "the CIA advised and supported the Ghanaian Army and police officers who took over the Government."[67] Before the coup, many Ghanaians had criticized Nkrumah for focusing too much on foreign policy and not enough on the needs of his own country, while others believed that these allegations were disseminated in CIA propaganda.[68] Nevertheless, African leaders were disappointed after his overthrow because Nkrumah's efforts for the cause of pan-African unity had brought about economic, social, and political benefits to the entire continent. Ever since Nkrumah had led Ghana to independence nearly 10 years before his overthrow, many other African colonies had taken steps toward achieving their own independence.

---

[66] Hart, *The Volta river project*, 6.

[67] Moxon, *Volta*, 270.

[68] Moxon, *Volta*, 270.

Aluminum and Hydroelectric Power

Refining aluminum from bauxite ore is an energy-intensive process. Bauxite is a mineral ore containing aluminum oxide or hydroxides with several impurities. Bauxite must be treated at a high enough temperature (around the melting point of aluminum: 660 °C/1,220 °F) to burn away all the impurities and leave behind the resulting alumina powder. When molten alumina is processed into marketable aluminum, it must be cooled at a slow rate to increase ductility and prevent a brittle product. Generating one six-pack of aluminum cans requires the same amount of electricity as running a 21-in. color TV for more than 11 h.[69] By 1998, the annual hydroelectric power used worldwide in aluminum production nearly equaled the annual power demand of Australia, or of about 35 million U.S. residents. On average, electricity accounted for about 20–30 % of the total cost of aluminum production.

Electrical energy, rather than direct heat (i.e., from burning fossil fuels), is the best form of energy for aluminum processing. Because aluminum is a poor current conductor, the electrical current is trapped and converted to heat energy. High electrical currents are required to perform the smelting operations.

Due to the high power costs associated with making aluminum, manufacturers usually seek the least expensive sources of power. During the 1960s and 1970s, world energy costs increased by 500 %, while serious doubts arose about the safety of nuclear power, which had once been a cheap and reliable power alternative for the aluminum industry worldwide.[70] Hydroelectric power was soon regarded as the next cheapest alternative for generating electricity. Throughout history, aluminum smelters have frequently been established in conjunction with new dams.[71]

Volta Aluminum Company (VALCO)

Valco was the name of the aluminum company associated with the Akosombo Dam. During preliminary negotiations in Ghana in the early 1960s, Valco representative Edgar Kaiser commented that Ghana's rich bauxite resources were part of the reason for the company's interest in Ghana.[72] President Nkrumah saw the link between aluminum and hydroelectric power as the best way to bolster Ghanaian economy. Furthermore, the presence of an aluminum smelter justified the construction of a hydroelectric dam to the foreign investors.

---

[69]Gitlitz, Jennifer. 1993. The relationship between primary aluminum production and the damming of the World's rivers. International Rivers Network (IRN) Working Paper #2 (August 1993).

[70]Graham, Ronald. 1986. Structural problems in the World economy: A case study of the Ghana-Valco renegotiations. In *Essays from Ghana-Valco renegotiations,* ed. Fui S. Tsikata. Accra: VRA, pp. 87–111.

[71]Gitlitz, "The Relationship."

[72]Tsikata, Fui. Dealing with a transnational corporation. *Essays from Ghana-Valco Renegotiations,* 1–14.

Kitson's vision for developing Ghana's aluminum industry was the framework around which Valco was established. A more wealthy country was invited to provide loans for the power infrastructure, establish a bauxite refinery and an aluminum smelter, and develop the local bauxite. It was a mutually benefiting design with very good intentions toward the host country. A host country that did not have the necessary infrastructure could cash in on an undeveloped natural resource, while a percentage of the production sales helped the foreign aluminum company liquidate their investments. It was envisioned that, after an agreed period of time, the contract would expire and the entire operation would be turned over to the host country.

In fact, ultimately Valco opted not to construct the bauxite refinery, because Kaiser's economists found that, for the time remaining on their contract, it was more profitable to continue importing alumina powder from Jamaica and Guinea than to invest high initial capital in a bauxite refinery in Ghana. Valco tests concluded that because of the impurities in Ghana bauxite, the same amount of energy would yield less alumina than bauxite refined elsewhere. The forgone bauxite factory left the Volta River Project vision incomplete, and Ghana's bauxite reserves untapped.

Valco would be 100 % owned by foreign interests, both of which were among the six most powerful corporations in the aluminum industry. One was Kaiser Aluminum Corporation (Kaiser, NYSE: KLU) of Houston, Texas. Kaiser, which would become one of the world's leading producers of alumina, primary aluminum, and fabricated aluminum products, owned 90 % of Valco. Kaiser would later be supported by MAXXAM Inc. (ASE: MXM), which directly and indirectly held about 78 % of the common stock. Kaiser's remaining 12 % belonged to other private interests. Reynolds Metal Company owned the other 10 % of Valco. The Valco smelting operation was designed as a service facility or a tolling station because it actually would not own any of the alumina or aluminum that it processed. Imported alumina was passed through the plant, processed at a fee, and exported for sale.

Valco would become the single largest consumer of electricity in Ghana. During the 1970s Valco consumed some 60 % of Ghana's electricity to produce 200,000 t of aluminum annually.[73] In July 1982, when a second smaller dam (Kpong Dam) was built downstream on the Volta River at Akuse, VRA's maximum electricity-generating capacity increased by 20 % to a total of about 1100 MW. By 1993, Valco consumed about 45 % of VRA's power production. Valco hired about 2% of the Ghanaian private sector labor force.[74]

Negotiating a Dam

Nkrumah needed President Kennedy's support in 1961 to bring international financial investors to the negotiating table. Beyond the financial needs for the Volta River

---

[73]Berry, LaVerle. ed. 1995. *Ghana: A country study*. Washington, D.C.: Federal Research Division, Library of Congress, 176.

[74]Sims, Rod, and Louis Casely-Hayford. Renegotiating the price and availability of energy. In *Essays from Ghana-Valco renegotiations,* ed. Fui Tsikata, 16.

Project, Nkrumah wanted to attract foreign investors to Ghana and establish a foundation for future development of other infrastructure, such as the Bui Dam. While the West was involved in building Akosombo Dam, the Soviet Union, after performing extensive investigations, was prepared to undertake construction of the Bui Dam. James Moxon, an Englishman who joined Ghana's Information Service in 1948 and worked closely with Volta River Project participants, suggests that Nkrumah used the Bui dam to maintain "some kind of political balance between the West and the East." In 1961, Nkrumah successfully completed a 2-month visit to Khrushchev and Mao Tse-tung, became the Kennedy family's first visiting head of state at the White House, and hosted Queen Elizabeth and Prince Philip in Accra.[75] With the support of President Kennedy, negotiations for the Volta River Project began.

In February 1962, over 20 agreements were signed concerning the financing, construction, and operation of Akosombo Dam. The parties represented in the negotiations included (1) the Ghana government and its agencies, (2) Valco and shareholders, (3) the International Bank of Reconstruction and Development (IBRD/World Bank), (4) the U.K. Government, and (5) some U.S. government institutions that insured U.S. corporations operating outside the United States.

Ghana's budget provided £35 million in cash ($98 million in 1962 dollars), which was half of the building costs for Akosombo Dam; the remaining finances consisted of loans from the World Bank, USAID, U.S. Export-Import Bank (EXIM), and the U.K. Board of Trade.[76] Valco shareholders gave $32 million for the building of the smelter, and another $20 million came as loans for other initial capital expenses required to establish aluminum operations in Ghana (see Exhibit 1: Principal Agreements).

The Ghana government and the Volta River Authority (VRA) agreed to a 30-year fixed rate of 2.625 mills (0.2625 cents) for every kilowatt-hr of energy supplied to Valco starting April 25, 1967.[77] This rate remained a controversial matter for various policy-makers over the decades. The Master Agreement is the document that resulted from the proceedings between VRA and Valco. As part of the agreement, Valco could demand power for an additional 20 years, on the same terms after the initial 30 years had passed, extending contractual agreements until the year 2017. This rate, however, was 40 % lower than that originally advised by the World Bank and other consultants to the Ghana government at the time. Under pressure from the World Bank and from Kaiser to commence the building project, the Ghana government agreed upon the lower rate. To Ghana, Kaiser would provide a long-term demand to generate revenue needed to amortize the dam. It was also reasoned that, since the hydroelectric plant would produce a surplus of electricity, the benefits of building the dam would jumpstart the economy and pay off in the long run. Akosombo began operations in January 1966 and the smelter in April 1967. After

---

[75] Moxon, *Volta*, 245, 249.

[76] Tsikata, "Dealing with a transnational corporation," 2.

[77] Tsikata, "Dealing with a transnational corporation," 2.

completion of the Volta River Project, Ghana would receive 99 % of its power from hydroelectric power for the next 30 years.

At the ground-breaking ceremony of the Valco Smelter in 1964, Kwame Nkrumah and Edgar Kaiser stood cordially side by side. In previous months, events associated with the Volta River Project operations had triggered mixed emotions from the Ghanaian citizens and the international participants. These had taken the form of anti-American demonstrations in the streets of Accra to months of heavy repairs near the foundation at Akosombo Dam caused by flooding. During the rainy season in 1963 (specifically in July), rains produced floods reaching 15,800 cubic meters per second (557,970 cubic feet per second), a level never recorded in the previous 25 years of records for the Volta River's natural cycles.[78] Furthermore, the assassination of President Kennedy and an assassination attempt on President Nkrumah less than 6 weeks later both cast a dark shadow on the fate of the Volta River Project. While Nkrumah was still balancing delicate political relations with the West and the Communist nations, the ongoing Volta River Project reassured him of at least one great victory for Ghana. At the ceremony, he quoted the words of the late President Kennedy when he said of "the new states whom we welcome to the land of the free. . . We shall not always expect to find them supporting our view. But we shall always hope to find them strongly supporting their own freedom."[79]

"Taming" the Volta

The catchment area of the Volta basin is about 390,000 km^2, of which 42 % (which contains the highest water volume) lies within Ghana. The Volta begins as a small stream in the Kong Mountains of Burkina Faso (Upper Volta). After flowing northeast, then due south for some 515 km (320 miles), it enters Ghana as the Black Volta. It then travels along the western border between Ghana and Ivory Coast before turning through a narrow gorge at Bui near the border. The river then meanders northeast until it joins the White Volta (which also finds its source in Burkina Faso). Together, they combine to flow the remaining 483 km (300 miles) to the sea. The Volta River basin is also fed by the Oti and the Afram Rivers (see Exhibit 2: Map of Ghana).

In 1963, construction of Akosombo Dam commenced under the management of Impregilo, an Italian contractor. As the world's fifth largest dam at the time, Akosombo stood 134 m high and approximately 700 m long (440 by 2,250 ft), with a power-rating capacity of 912 MW.[80] Because of the high surplus of electricity in Ghana at that time, many viewed Akosombo as a permanent solution to electricity provision in Ghana for many years to come. In due course, one of the first programs abandoned by the government, following Nkrumah's overthrow, was the Bui Dam.

---

[78] Impregilo. 1982. *1956/1981: Twenty-five years of worldwide activity*. Milan, Italy: Impregilo.
[79] Moxon, *Volta*, 270.
[80] Impregilo, *1956/1981*.

Lake Volta, which is the world's largest artificial lake (in terms of surface area), now lies behind Akosombo Dam. The damming of the Volta River resulted in 8,502 km^2 (3,275 mi^2) of flooded riverbanks. In comparison, the combined surface area of two U.S. states, Delaware and Rhode Island, is 8,466 km^2 (3,270 mi^2). About 80,000 people (more than 1 % of Ghana's population at the time) had to be resettled from the area. In addition to the resettlement of the river communities, damming affected local health, agriculture, fishing, and navigation. To this day, treetops can be seen above the waters of Lake Volta at various locations.

Effects on resettled communities

The spreading lake behind Akosombo Dam forced 739 villages along the banks to be moved. However, this was not the first time that Ghana had resettled citizens. In 1956, members of the Frafra people in the Northern Region first had their homes relocated because of overpopulation. They were settled in a less populated and more fertile land at Damongo. Despite the generous provisions, houses, bullocks, and plows, the people had a hard time departing from their traditional lands. For many years, they would send their dead to be buried back home in Frafra, which was over 200 miles away. The second resettlement was the Tema Manhean Project in 1959, which resulted from the construction of the Tema Harbor seaport. Some small fishing villages along the coast were moved about three miles from their original location to a modern village, where each house was replaced on a room-for-room basis.

The Volta Resettlement Scheme, Ghana's third of its kind, carried a budget of $9.8 million (£3.5 million). Before 80,000 people could be displaced, economic, social, physical, political, and psychological factors had to be addressed. Since resettlement would drastically affect the lifestyles of the people, it was essential to make the transition as smooth as possible, while preserving sacred traditions and rituals of life. Furthermore, there was a prevailing sentiment among the people that the government "owed them something." Many of the people needed to regain a sense of worth and to reestablish their contribution to society. Everyone was given the option of either monetary compensation or resettlement into one of the 52 specially constructed townships. Over 70,000 people chose resettlement over monetary compensation.

Before Akosombo, many of the people along the Volta lived in tiny scattered villages. The average village house was constructed with swish (soil-based) walls and thatch roofs. Subsistence farming, animal grazing, and river fishing were the most common practices in the area, and these traditions were passed down from generation to generation. According to 1956 preparatory studies, only about 6 % of the land to be covered by the lake was "used productively," while the rest was "unsuitable for agriculture or unoccupied."[81] The resettlement scheme offered a unique opportunity to consolidate the scattered villages into more organized communities and provide them with schools, improved sanitary facilities, and increased

---

[81] Hart, *The Volta river project,* 77.

revenue potential through mechanized farming techniques and organized livestock breeding. Furthermore, this consolidation would facilitate future electrification of the area.

A resettlement house was constructed with landcrete walls (landcrete is concrete made with local soil) and an aluminum roof. In terms of the *sturdiness* and *durability* of the building materials used, a resettlement house was superior to the average village house. The layouts of these houses were modeled after the traditional living quarters, which consisted of a central compound surrounded by several rooms. Because of time and cost constraints, VRA constructed the foundations, built the "core" one-bedroom house, and provided building materials (which would spread the cost to the tenant over a 5-year period) and training so that the resettled citizens themselves could finish the additional rooms. They aimed to cut down on labor costs, give the citizens a sense of ownership, and provide them with something to do during the first few months of transition, since many had lost their occupations with creation of the lake.

Although each family was given a "core" house, overcrowding was common because previously every household had built as many rooms as they needed. Also, many of the houses were never completed. In many of the resettlement villages, it was common to see the traditional swish houses constructed alongside the resettlement houses. During the cooler months of the year, many complained that their new houses were too cold. The landcrete walls and aluminum roofs could not insulate as well as the swish and thatch they had been using for hundreds of years.

The resettlement project also aimed to replace the common practice of subsistence farming with "cash-crop" farming. Each farmer would be taught new farming techniques to produce enough for his family and some extra crops to sell for income. In order to support crop rotation, virgin forests were cleared for farmlands, but this was not always done without resistance (the government often clashed with traditional chiefs over who owned the land). As a subsidy, the government also provided chicks, piglets, and other young livestock to the people to rear on the new livestock farms and later to sell for profit. After many of the animals began to die prematurely from disease and malnutrition (usually from improper care), the government stopped giving out the young livestock at no cost to the farmer.

Many agree that the Volta Resettlement project improved the physical environment for the average rural Volta citizen; however, the debate continues as to whether or not there were social and psychological improvements. VRA tried as much as possible to settle people of the same ethnic group into a village. But sometimes there were cultural conflicts because a Fanti would not want to be governed by an Ewe chief, for example. Other problems arose from lifestyle issues. Some who were seasoned fishermen did not want to become cash-crop farmers. Many left their resettlement homes and constructed wooden shacks along the lakeside so that they could be closer to their best-known source of income. As more people encroached on the lakeside and the communities diversified their activities, illegal clearing and farming along the banks led to increased sediment deposit into the lake. With the receding perimeter of the lake due to the drought in 1998, the government made efforts to replant trees along the lakeside to control erosion.

Effects on Health

The dam virtually halted the rate of water flow in the Volta River, increasing stagnant water conditions and consequently creating ideal breeding grounds for carriers of waterborne diseases. Before the Akosombo and Kpong Dams, malaria (from mosquitoes) was not much of a problem along the swift-flowing Volta River, but after it became a stagnant lake, malaria became a greater public health concern in lakeside villages. Likewise, only 1–5 % of the population had suffered from schistosomiasis (a disease transmitted by snails) before the dam was constructed. By 1979, urinary schistosomiasis had grown to become the most prevalent disease in the area, affecting some 75 % of lakeside residents.[82]

Humans are infected by urinary schistosomiasis through water that contains the larvae (cercariae) of the parasitic worm. When ingested, the larvae travel into the blood stream, where they may become lodged in the liver, lungs, or heart. Inside the human host, the cercariae mature into the parasitic worm. The worms may also travel through the blood stream, where they can sometimes clog arteries and veins, leading to cardiac failure. The worms lay eggs that leave the body through the urine. The eggs hatch on contact with water, releasing miracidia. The miracidia quickly find new hosts in certain species of stagnant water snails, whose numbers have increased in the lake environment. Inside the snails, the miracidia mature into cercariae, which return back to the water, completing the cycle. Symptoms include skin complaints, fever, inflammation, and coughing. In more advanced stages, one may notice blood in the urine. Schistosomiasis leads to death through cardiac failure, fibrosis of the lungs, an enlarged spleen, or secondary bacterial infection of the urinary tract.

During the construction of Kpong Dam in the early 1980s, flooding provided some health benefits. The dam was sited a few kilometers downstream from Kpong town, so that the backwaters would flood the Kpong Rapids, which was the largest breeding ground for the tsetse fly in Ghana. Sleeping sickness, carried by the tsetse fly, was a major problem for the British colonists, foreigners, and other people who did not have acquired biological defenses. Tsetse flies breed in the dense bush bordering bodies of water, and are most prevalent in the lower part of the Brong Ahafo Region, the Ashanti Region, and parts of the Eastern Region into the Volta Region. Sleeping sickness may linger quietly in a person for many years, causing a loss of energy and reduced immunity to other diseases. Full-blown sleeping sickness leads to quick death.

Effects on Agriculture

Long before Akosombo was constructed, the fertile banks along the Volta River were some of Ghana's richest agricultural land. Archeological finds show that the

---

[82]Gitlitz, "The Relationship."

Volta Basin was once well populated.[83] Much of the natural vegetation was burned down for agriculture over a period of more than a 1,000 years, which led to the eventual drying and erosion of the land. However, the floodplains along the raging Volta River provided a constant source of fertile agricultural land for local farmers.

Before Akosombo Dam, local farming along the Volta was structured around the rise and fall of the river. The damming put an end to the natural cycles that had deposited nutrient-laden silts along the flood plains. The river ecosystem was transformed into a lake ecosystem. Damming led to a drastic curtailment in subsistence agricultural production and animal grazing. Farming communities downstream continually petitioned VRA to coordinate its spillage with the traditional flooding cycles to simulate the natural flood cycles necessary for agricultural stability. Unfortunately, demands for electricity could not always be synchronized with the traditional flooding seasons. Furthermore, the reduced flow into the Gulf of Guinea resulted in saltwater intrusion at the Volta River delta and estuary. Salt water destroyed clam beds and lowered drinking water quality. Many of the stream and clam fishermen downstream moved north to the lake, where they hoped to restore their careers.

The Volta River Project also included plans for an irrigation network in the Afram Plains, which was considered Ghana's agricultural breadbasket. However, these plans were pushed down the agenda for various economic, social, and political reasons. The sudden change in government in 1966 led to budget restructuring during the first year of Akosombo's operation, which affected many of the original project initiatives, including the irrigation network and the resettlement scheme. Teaching new farming techniques was expensive, and there was no guarantee that the traditional farmers would embrace them. In 1998, only 2,000 ha of irrigated land existed in Ghana.

Effects on fishing industry

Although it was created primarily as a hydroelectric reservoir, Akosombo created a lake environment suitable for fish breeding. Lake Volta soon grew to become a highly productive fishing area yielding around 40,000 t annually.

Before dam construction began, St. John Bird wanted to remove the trees in the floodplains of the Volta River so that broken limbs would not damage the turbines. Only a few trees in the river section closest to the turbine intakes were removed. Those upstream were never removed. Further tree removal would have been good for fishermen. Submerged growth in the lake entangled and destroyed fishing nets. Mobile nets (winch nets) typically catch more fish than stationary nets. Not only would tree removal safeguard the turbines, but also local fishermen could use winch nets to increase their fish catch and consequently increase their earning potential.

Stationary fishing methods such as gill nets, traps, long lines, cast nets, and spears would remain the most widely used methods. Although fish were more

---

[83] Kaplan, Irving et al. 1971. *Area handbook for Ghana.* Washington, D.C.: Library of Congress, p. 17.

available, fishing was difficult for some fishermen because (1) finding an open area without too much submerged growth was difficult, (2) open areas, only accessible by boat, were typically located along the main channel, (3) open areas were often over-fished by winch fishermen, (4) fishing nets entangled in submerged trees required substantial time and energy to free, and (5) mending or replacing damaged nets was expensive in both time and money. Many fishermen in lakeside communities also engaged in complementary economic activities like farming and livestock-rearing.[84]

Life in lakeside communities is characterized by hardship. In 1998, policy makers of the Atebubu district in the Brong Ahafo Region were hesitant to build schools for the children of fishing communities located along the lake. Many of the fishermen and their families migrated with the fish, and those who were stationary chose not to send their children to school because they served as valuable labor hands. Many of these villages were also located within restricted lakeside areas reserved for farming. Most parents could not afford to send their children to better schools outside of the region; instead, their children were sent to earn money as menial labor hands for local fishermen. The wealthier fishermen, who would send their own children to better schools in the cities, overworked their neighbors' children. These children were usually between 8 and 11 years old. They could be found placing and retrieving bamboo traps and fishnets in the lake.[85] Not only were they subjected to deplorable working conditions, but these children were also deprived of education during critical years of social and mental development.

The growth of the fishing industry led to the migration of various people groups to the lakeside settlements. Survey data indicate that 80 % of the fishing villages near Yeji were inhabited by more than one tribe, and 50 % included two or three tribes.[86] Cultural differences were expressed in their intertribal relationships. Ewe fishermen, who principally used stationary nets clashed with Adangbe and Adas over their use of winch nets. Ewes and Adangbes, with established homes and livelihoods in the area, complained of Fantis and Adas, who came during prime fishing seasons to make money, and then returned home. Territorial clashes arose over who had the right to fish where.

Over time, the use of larger fishing boats and winch fishing nets in some parts of the lake proved quite profitable for those fishermen, some of whom had migrated from the coastal areas to Lake Volta. In 1998, the threat of overfishing in the lake became an issue of national concern, and the use of certain nets was prohibited. By request of the Ghana Fisheries Department, the Navy began monitoring fishing operations at Yeji. Fishery regulations restricted fishing to net with mesh sizes of less than two inches, as a means of preventing overfishing in the lake. To enforce these regulations, authorities confiscated the nets of fishermen suspected of using unauthorized nets.

---

[84] Agyenim-Boateng, conversations and interview; see Acknowledgements.

[85] "Rich Fishermen Exploiting Children," Ghana Focus, in *Africa News Online*, http://www.africanews.org/west/ghana/stories

[86] Agyenim-Boateng, conversations.

Effects on Aquatic Navigation

Between the time of Kitson's original vision (1915) and the actual construction of Akosombo Dam (1963), several proposals were drafted concerning the size and capacity of the dam. Each time, the conceptual size increased to generate more power capacity and a larger lake that would theoretically make navigation to the bauxite deposits easier (although Valco opted not to develop Ghana's bauxite resources). Before the dam, east-west routes were the most common mode of river navigation. Villagers could easily row across the river to trade goods and communicate with other villages. Most villages spoke the same language and exhibited similar lifestyles since they were separated by a relatively narrow Volta River that was hardly suitable for large-scale, north-south navigation.

With the construction of the dam, the immense lake consumed riparian land and increased east-west rowing distances an average of 24 km (15 miles). After dam construction, a shipyard was constructed at Akosombo, and ferries began navigation along Lake Volta between Akosombo and Yeji. The lake provided a 400-km (250-mile), north-south navigational corridor for an inland shipping route. Together, the Volta, Ankobra, and Tano Rivers provided 168 km of perennial navigation for launches and lighters; Lake Volta provided 1,125 km of arterial and feeder waterways.[87]

When Power Fades

During the 1970s, when oil prices reached record high prices worldwide, energy prices in Ghana increased by 900 % from their 1962 levels, making the Valco contractual agreements far less representative of the current state of affairs.[88] In 1972, 1973, and 1977, Valco agreed to some adjustments to the rate, but VRA and its lenders regarded the changes as unsatisfactory. By 1982, the power rate had been increased from the original 2.265 mills per kW/h to 5 mills per kW/h, an increase of 100 % over a time period during which energy prices had generally increased by 900 %.[89]

In 1982, Ghana called Valco into negotiations. The first question that arose was whether Ghana had the legal right to call for renegotiations of previously agreed contractual terms. If Valco was not willing to renegotiate, Ghana could take unilateral action under certain codes of international law. This right of a host country to pass sanctions against or regulate the activities of a foreign investor who

---

[87]U.S. Central Intelligence Agency, *The World Factbook*, 1, n.p. (September 7, 1995).

[88]Tsikata, "Dealing with a Transnational Corporation," 2.

[89]Sawyerr, Akilagpa. Some legal issues arising from the Valco agreement. In *Essays,* ed. Fui S. Tsikata, 60–86.

was viewed as exploiting natural resources within its jurisdiction was a controversial matter in international law.

Various resolutions of the United Nations General Assembly *Charter on the Economic Rights and Duties of States* state that a host country is free to "exercise full permanent sovereignty including possession, use, and disposal over all its wealth, natural resources, and economic activities." At the same time, Article 12 of the *Harvard Draft Convention on International Responsibility of States for Injuries to Aliens* also says that "the violation through arbitrary action of the state of a contract or concession to which the central government of that state and alien are parties is wrongful." Furthermore, under the Hickenlooper amendment to protect U.S. investors in foreign countries, the U.S. government is obligated to cut off all aid to any country that nationalizes the property or activities of any U.S. investor "without adequate compensation." Many considered it a bold move for Ghana to call Valco into renegotiations, but at the same time, Ghana's reasons were being heard internationally, and Valco needed to respond.

Between 1982 and 1985, Ghana and Valco engaged in renegotiations. Ghana's primary concern about the invalidity of the previous terms was that power production was calculated by *average* power. Valco was entitled to a percentage of VRA's average generating potential. In a country where there is a diversified, relatively stable power infrastructure, average power is an appropriate measure of available power. Ghana argued that due to the variable nature of hydroelectric power, the terms should have been assessed on a *firm* power basis, that is, by the actual generating potential at a given time. If the system faced a drought, with power generation being far less than average, Ghana argued that they would be unfairly obligated to provide power that would not be attainable for the system. Not only did the renegotiations result in rewriting the contracts in terms of firm power, but also Ghana's relations with the United States were preserved.

Under the Master Agreement, Valco was allowed to mine bauxite from about 40 $mile^2$ of land within Ghana without paying duties on mining or processing. However, the Agreement (under Article 20) also allowed Valco to import "all raw materials" from other countries duty-free as long as such materials were not locally available in quality, quantity, or at competitive prices. Since aluminum was Valco's primary resource, an exception was permitted to exclude it from Article 20. Valco was free to import aluminum *duty-free* from wherever it pleased, even if comparable aluminum was available in Ghana. Consequently, Ghana lost the import duty on aluminum as a levying weapon against increases in electricity production costs. As of 1998, VALCO imported 100 % of its alumina from Jamaica, which was processed in Ghana at a low electricity price rate. Only 10 % of the finished product remained in the country and 90 % was exported to Europe.[90]

In 1977 and 1978, rebellious struggles against the Ghana government resulted in "wildcat strike action." As a result of sabotage, power to Valco was interrupted without notice. Valco demanded compensation of $55 million from the government

---

[90] *The Independent* (Accra, Ghana), 11 June 1998.

for repair costs and lost profits, sighting the Master Agreement (Article 7(D)). The clause stated that the government must "make good to Valco all losses, damages, costs, and expenses incurred by Valco by reason of any default on the part of VRA in the fulfillment of its obligations." [91] It was determined that the government was not directly liable for the interruptions since the forces were beyond the control of VRA. To avoid litigation, the Ghana government paid Valco $10 million.

The "wildcat strike action" against the government may have been attributed to unrest between the military regime and labor unions. From the time of Nkrumah's overthrow well into the 1980s, the government's political climate was characterized by coups and passive military rule. Each successive government assumed power with both its supporters and rivals close at hand. Meanwhile, many believe that the rights of the people were often overlooked in the crossfire. At the time of the strike, labor unions made up of doctors, lawyers, and other professionals were in vocal disagreement with the government over unfair treatment and inadequate salary compensation. Some believe that the reason the government paid Valco $10 million was also to draw eyes away from the civil unrest within the country and put the government in favorable standing with investors.

In 1983, when a severe drought significantly reduced the water level in the dam, VRA began to question the sustainability of hydroelectric power as a sufficient source of electricity for Ghana's future. By August of 1994, the cumulative inflow into Lake Volta reached a 50-year record low, resulting in a water level of 73 m (239.5 ft), well below VRA's 75.5 m (248 ft) minimum level of generating power without risk of damaging the turbines. Some critics blamed the power shortages on VRA's poor management of the reservoir and accused them of "guesswork rather than science" in predicting water levels and spillage quantities.[92] The annual flooding cycles are between the months of July and November. The final level after this time often determines the power generating capacity for the following year. In 1992, the water level reached its highest level of 84 m (275 ft) since the 1982 drought. In June of 1997, VRA predicted satisfactory rainfall. But by the beginning of November 1997, the lake level still lingered around a meager 74 m (242 ft). After some rains in the northern region, the end of the flooding cycle saw water levels reach only 78 m (256 ft). As shown in Fig. 2.2, Akosombo Dam operated at or below 50 % capacity throughout the first half of 1998.

Ghana Power Crisis: 1997–1998

Meteorologists attributed the Volta River droughts and the subsequent 1997–1998 Ghana power crisis to El Nino, the worldwide weather phenomenon responsible for climate fluctuations, storms, natural disasters, floods, and droughts

---

[91] Tsikata, "Dealing with a Transnational Corporation," 3.
[92] Gitlitz, "The Relationship."

Fig. 2.2 Reduced water level at Akosombo (July 1998)

around the globe.[93] Although past droughts have affected power production, the 1997–1998 drought is arguably the worst in Ghana history because of its long duration.

March 23, 1998, marked the eve of the first visit to Ghana by a U.S. President. Bill Clinton arrived to witness the institution of the largest electricity rationing schedule in Ghana history. Under the new plan, electricity would be supplied for 12 out of every 24 h. Households would be cut to 50 % of normal power while businesses and industries received between 50 % and 70 %.[94]

Effects on the Household

Because of the power crisis, households were forced to look for alternative sources of light energy, like candles, lanterns, and rechargeable and battery-powered flashlights. A market survey conducted by the Ghana News Agency on the prices of some of these commodities in Accra, Ghana's capital, showed that increased demand for them led to price hikes and shortages. Some of the more affluent Ghanaians purchased private generators for their homes. Demand for

[93] Aggrey, Emily. 1998. El NiZo causes high energy prices (May 25, 1998), *Panafrican News Agency, Africa News Online,* http://www.africanews.org/west/ghana/stories19980525_feat2.html

[94] LCG Consulting. 1998. Ghana power crisis spreads along Gold Coast" (March 23, 1998), *EnergyOnline,* http://www.energyonline.com/Restructuring/news_reports/news/c23afr.html

generators increased, but market competition kept the prices stable. Generators with capacities ranging between 1.4 and 3.0 KVA ranged in price between $2,300 and $7,000.[95]

Ghanaian cost of living increased as a result of the power shortage. The shortages affected demand for imported household electrical appliances like televisions, stereos, refrigerators, and blenders. Similarly, the prices of Ghanaian manufactured goods and household food items increased. Even the price of ice doubled, increasing soda and beer prices at local drink bars. Many factories were forced to reduce their labor force to avoid economic losses.

Effects on Industry and Exports

As part of the electricity rationing schedule, industries were supplied with slightly more electricity than households. They received electricity up to 70 % of the time.[96] According to Mr. Emmanuel K.K. Hayford, of Ghana Customs, Excise and Preventive Services (CEPS), who had been watching the effects of the power crisis on industry, these provisions seemed to be working well for them. A more difficult endeavor was to estimate the real impact of the power curtailment on export and on the economy as a whole. Because of the special arrangements, most of the industries worked round the clock to make up for lost time. Many companies also purchased heavy-duty generators to supplement the electricity supplied by VRA.

Mr. Hayford commented that because of improper city planning, some of the industries established themselves within residential zones and vice-versa. Those industries situated in residential zones were relatively small in size and their levels of production were relatively low compared to those located within industrial zones. Their small size, combined with their unfortunate location within residential zones, which received electricity for only 12 h of the day, greatly reduced their productivity.

Since much of the power curtailment had negative effects only on smaller industries situated in residential zones, and since larger industries had intensified their work schedules to suit their power supply arrangements, one was "tempted to assume that this problem has not affected exports much," commented Mr. Hayford. The effect of power curtailment on export quantities was negligible. However, its effects were reflected in increased production cost, since many industries purchased diesel generators to supplement the power supply. This may have raised the price of exports from Ghana (in the case of industrially manufactured goods).

---

[95] Aggrey, "El Niño."
[96] LCG Consulting, "Ghana Power."

What Lies Ahead for Ghana?

Thermal Energy

The Ghana Generation Planning Study of 1985 identified combustion turbines as the most attractive power supplement to the existing hydroelectric system. A thermal combustion plant could be powered by light crude oil (LCO) or natural gas. Given the high availability and relatively cheaper cost of fuel, a thermal combustion plant could prove to be both economical and a constant source of power, since droughts could not affect generating capacity. A site was identified near Takoradi for the construction of a thermal generating plant at an estimated cost of $400 million.

In 1992, Acres International Ltd. of Canada recommended the construction of a 400 MW generating facility by 1997. The proposed plant was composed of a 300 MW combined-cycle plant and a 100 MW simple-cycle combustion turbine with associated transmission line expansion to tie it into the existing national grid. Following further analysis and June/July 1993 negotiations with the World Bank, the major funding agency, the project was re-dimensioned to 300 MW. The new proposed plant was composed of two 100 MW combustion turbines, each with a 50 MW heat recovery steam generator.

A detailed environmental assessment was performed to ensure that the project met the environmental requirements of the funding agencies. A detailed pre- and post-construction program covered the terrestrial ecology of the site and transmission corridor, ambient site air quality, noise "pollution" levels, and biological characteristics of the local marine environment. For example, the cooling water used by the turbines had to be within 2°C of the receiving water temperature before it could be returned to the ocean.

Accelerated by the power crisis and the need for electricity, the first 100 MW combustion turbine was completed and synchronized into the national grid in November of 1997, and the second 100 MW turbine on January 8, 1998. The turbines were online before the rest of the facility was constructed. On March 16, an explosion in the lower chamber of the turbine chimney took one of the 100 MW units out of service. It was quickly repaired and running in order to lessen the effects on the public. Much suspicion surrounded this explosion. Some blamed the accelerated nature of the construction and others blamed the U.S. contractor of using second-grade General Electric components to build the turbines, but VRA attests that new parts were used by their contractor to construct the turbines.

Thermal power supplemented the energy grid in Ghana, and many believed that it would remain a viable option for future expansion and development. Although the plant was constructed with a 300 MW capacity, the design was adaptable for future expansion to 600 or 900 MW. In February of 1998, CMS Energy Corporation (NYSE: CMS) of Dearborn, Michigan announced it had reached an agreement with the Government of Ghana VRA for the acquisition and expansion of the Takoradi Thermal Power Plant (TTPP) and development of further energy infrastructure projects in Ghana. It would become a 50 % partner in ownership and operation of the plant and also assist to double the capacity of the plant in an accelerated timetable. In 1997 and 1998, the thermal plant burned LCO, but the turbine design allowed for a clean switch to cheaper and cleaner-burning natural gas if and when it became more readily available.

Importing electricity

At June 1998 meetings of West African energy experts in Abidjan, the commercial capital of Ivory Coast, several alternatives were examined to deal with the power crisis which had then spread to Ghana's eastern neighbors, Benin and Togo.

Earlier in March of 1998, Benin Prime Minister Adrien Houngbedji and his Togo counterpart, Kwassi Klutse, met in Abidjan with officials from Compagnie Ivoirienne d'Electricite (CIE), Ivory Coast's national utility, asking for energy to replace cutbacks from Ghanaian power exports to their countries. Ivory Coast had imported electricity from Ghana for many years until natural gas reserves were discovered off their sea coast. The natural gas reserves, combined with modern, more efficient power plants, transformed Ivory Coast from an importer into an exporter of electricity. As power became more available, the distribution grid within the Ivory Coast developed, and the power demand increased, limiting its export potential. Ivorian sources warned that satisfying the power demands in Benin and Togo could result in shortages in Ivory Coast.

In order to ensure against future West African crises, Ghana had to cooperate with its West African neighbors to establish a secure power network. At the 1998 gold award symposium for the Economic Community of West African States (ECOWAS) in Lagos, Nigeria, Executive Secretary Lansana Kouyate announced plans to begin construction on the $260 million West African Gas Pipeline by the end of calendar year 1998.

For many years, the vast natural gas reserves trapped in the air above Nigeria's oil reserves were flared away to waste. During the 1998 power crisis, they were viewed as a viable solution and a potential safety buffer against future power shortages. The gas pipeline project followed a World Bank study showing that Nigeria's surplus gas could meet the energy needs of the West African sub-region if well harnessed. According to Kouyate, the goal of the West African Pipeline was to ensure that energy generation in the sub-region would be from gas by the year 2000.[97]

According to the plans, the underwater pipeline would extend from Nigeria along the West African coastline to supply natural gas to Ghana, Benin, and Togo. The gas pipeline project was expected to pipe 50 million cubic feet per day of Nigeria's natural gas to the three countries over 20 years, starting from 1999. According to project plans, the volume of gas piped to the countries would rise to 160 million cubic feet per day by the year 2018.[98] The West African pipeline could eventually supply natural gas to the thermal plant at Takoradi, reducing energy costs (from burning LCO) by more than 50 %.

---

[97] Ikeh, Goddy. West African gas pipeline takes Off 1998. *Panafrican News Agency*, 2 June 1998, http://www.africanews.org/west/stories/19980602_feat3.html
[98] Goddy Ikeh.

Hydroelectric power

Other sites for potential hydroelectric plants have been suggested along the Pra, Tao, White Volta, and Ankroba rivers. However, a dam (with an estimated capacity of 400 MW) at Bui, along the Black Volta River in the Brong Ahafo region, is under serious consideration. Future hydroelectric power would require substantial investment but at the same time provide a relatively clean source of power.

In a press release early in 1998, Ghana Minister of Mines and Energy, Fred Ohene-Kena noted that, depending on the feasibility and designs, Bui might generate between 100 and 200 or 400 MW.[99] If a 400 MW-producing dam were constructed, the backwaters would inundate parts of the Bui National Park. In 1998, Bui National Park was a protected area of guinea savannah extending about 1,800 sq. km. International environmentalists noted the Bole Game Reserve and nearby Bui National park as one of the last remaining, highly diverse West African rainforests.

The Volta River Authority performed extensive site studies of the area encompassed within the Bui National Park, which showed that the boundaries of the park were poorly defined and not well secured. Poachers, illegal farmers, and fishermen entered the land at will to take advantage of the available resources. About 383 km^2 of land (20 % of the National Park) would be flooded if the Bui Dam were constructed. As compensation, VRA proposed to secure the Game Reserve by establishing protected boundaries and hiring rangers to monitor the up keep and preservation of the entire area. With the construction of the Bui Dam would also come the establishment of a defined and protected National Park, with secured buffer zones surrounding the boundaries. The objective of these buffer zones was to better involve the local population in the protection of the park by developing activities (such as tourism, controlled hunting, and fishing) which would generate profit for the people in harmony with the protection of the park.

For the long-term plan of the Bui hydro project, the Swedish-American Company, SKANSA, expressed interest to build on a turnkey basis. SKANSA, which had many interests in southern and eastern Africa, had also shown interest in toll road construction in Ghana, and even had plans to start feasibility studies on the projects. In 1998 SKANSA was actively building pipelines for water from Kpong to Accra and they also expressed interest in the Kotoka International Airport improvement project and the Ambassador Hotel rehabilitation program in Accra. It established a Ghana office, which was also responsible for projects in Burkina Faso, Cote d'Ivoire and Nigeria.[100]

Some Other Options

In late 1994, a research nuclear reactor was nearing completion at Kwabenyan, near Accra. At that time, the Ghana Atomic Energy Commission (GAEC) also recommended the construction of another nuclear physics center in Kumasi at the University of Science

---

[99] Joy 99.7 FM, No more power outages for industries by July. *This Week's Stories* (May 23, 1998), http://www.joy997fm.com.gh/news2.htm.

[100] Joy 99.7 FM, No more power outages for industries by July. *This Week's Stories* (May 23, 1998), http://www.joy997fm.com.gh/news2.htm#

and Technology. They believed that, if properly researched and implemented, nuclear energy could provide a lasting source of emission-free power to meet all of Ghana's energy needs. But critics argued that Ghana did not have the proper infrastructure to deal with the possibility of a nuclear disaster resulting from an accident at a nuclear generating station. By 1998 VRA had not actively entertained the possibility of adding nuclear power to its power options. The push for nuclear power also suffered growing sentiment against the construction of new plants.

Solar energy was being used on an experimental basis. It was viewed as a possible way of electrifying rural regions outside of the power grid. Due to high capital costs, solar power had not surfaced as a viable option for wide-scale integration in Ghana.

Small, localized, and relatively cheap fossil-fuel plants were constructed at some locations in Ghana to supplement power demand. For example, VRA had a 30 MW capacity diesel plant at Tema, which operated during the peak hours of 1,700 GMT to 2,200 GMT.[101] Although these plants provided a temporary solution to localized problems, the challenges of ensuring future national power viability overshadowed prospects of further localized plants.

In the heat of the 1998 power crisis, Ghana faced important decisions to safeguard its future economic viability. In 1994, 1997, and 1998, water levels were not sufficient to power hydroelectric generators to meet Ghana's growing energy demands. This led to a nationwide electricity-rationing schedule, reduction in exported electricity to Togo and Benin, and extensive negotiations and monetary compensation to Valco.

Decision makers (a few of whom included the Ghana Department of Mines and Energy, VRA, and the Ghana Electricity Supply Company), needed to make practical, affordable, and sustainable choices for electricity in Ghana. The options included: (1) thermal energy, (2) importing electricity, (3) construction of additional hydroelectric dam(s), and (4) other options like nuclear energy, solar energy, and other fossil-fuel-powered plants and generators. If you were a consultant to the Ghana Department of Mines and Energy, what would you recommend?

President Clinton's 1998 visit to Ghana brought new spirit to United States and other multinational interests in Ghana. Many Ghanaians regarded the flood of companies coming to Ghana for power generation, among other reasons, as a benefit to Ghana. How will the lessons from Ghana's history and past experiences affect Ghana's dealings with these multinational interests? What steps must be taken to ensure that future agreements and projects are economically and environmentally sustainable?

Acknowledgments

Special thanks to Mr. R.O. Ankrah, engineer and executive director, Takoradi Thermal Power Plant Project, and family for their loving hospitality and assistance; Frank Ashon, systems administrator, VRA information networks; Agyenim-Boateng, manager, Engineering Personnel, fisheries expert, and historian; Emmanuel Antwi-Darkwa and

---

[101] Panafrican News Agency. Ghanaians told to conserve power. *Africa News Online*, 23 August 1997, http://www.africanews.org/west/ghana/stories/19970823_feat1.html

Theophilus Sackey, civil engineers VRA Akuse; Owura K. Sarfo, manager VRA Engineering Department in Akuse; Erik N. Yankah, VRA executive director of Personnel, member 1982–1985 VRA-Valco Negotiations Team; Ricky Evans-Appiah and J. Amissah-Arthur, administrator and director, respectively, VRA Engineering and Design Department Akuse; K.K. Hayford, Ghana Customs Excise and Preventive Services; Esther Riverson, Ph. D, Ghana Resettlement project specialist; John Riverson, World Bank; Albert Wright, World Bank, and former professor, University of Ghana.

Exhibit 1: Principal Agreements

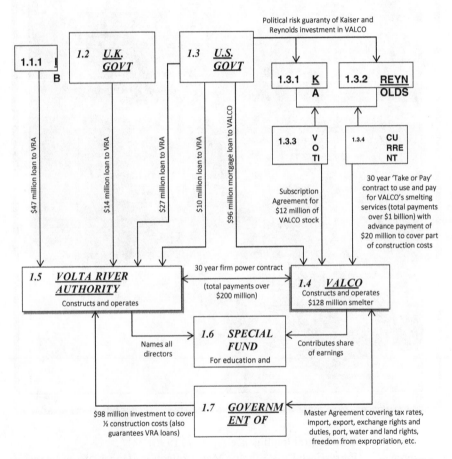

Schematic diagram of financing participants and principal agreements for the Volta River Project, executed on February 8, 1962 (Hart, 31)

[1] Morgan Guaranty Trust Co., Voting Trustee. If VALCO fails to build smelter, voting trustee replaces management until construction completed.

[2] First National City Bank of New York, Trustee. Handles all payments by Kaiser and Reynolds to VALCO, payment of VALCO expenses and taxes, and retains balance in New York.

Exhibit 2: Map of Ghana

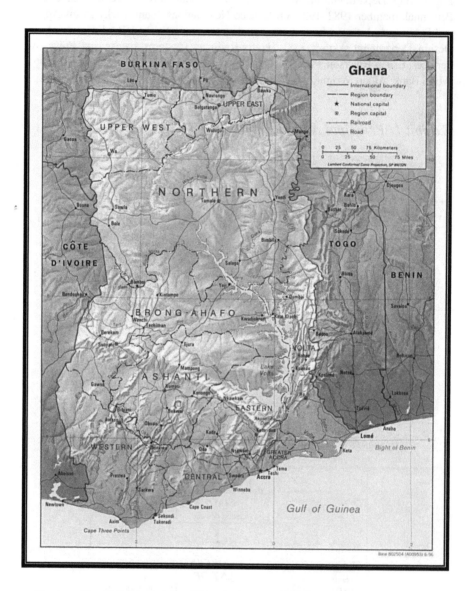

Produced by U.S. Central Intelligence Agency (1996)
Source: The Perry-Castañeda Library Map Collection. University of Texas at
Austin, http://www.lib.utexas.edu/Libs/PCL/Map_collection/ghana.html

Exhibit 3: Some Key Terms and Names

Alumina	A powder of refined bauxite that is smelted at high temperatures to form aluminum products.
Bauxite	A mineral ore containing aluminum oxide or hydroxides with several impurities.
Bui	A town in western Ghana. Potential site for a hydroelectric dam.
Burkina Faso	Ghana's northern neighbor. Previously called Upper Volta.
Gold Coast	Name given by first Portuguese explorers to the territory that is now Ghana. Became the Republic of Ghana after independence from Great Britain in 1957.
Impregilo	Italian contractor who constructed Akosombo and Kpong Dams.
Kaiser Edgar	American owner and founder of Kaiser Aluminum Corporation.
Kitson Albert (*later* Sir)	Director of the Gold Coast Geological Survey, discovered bauxite deposits near Mpraeso in 1914, and first proposed a dam at Akosombo.
Kpong Dam	A smaller hydroelectric plant downstream from Akosombo Dam, on the Volta River.
Master Agreement	The document outlining the negotiations and the terms governing the relationship between VALCO and VRA.
Nkrumah Kwame	African rights activist and Ghana's first elected president.
Rose Duncan	English engineer who had a keen interest in aluminum production.
St. John Bird Christopher	South African Engineer who worked with Duncan Rose to spur international interest for aluminum production in Ghana.
Takoradi Thermal Power Plant	VRA light crude oil/natural gas power plant constructed to supplement hydroelectric power from Akosombo and Kpong.
Volta Aluminum Corporation (VALCO)	A consortium of American aluminum companies including Kaiser (78 %) Reynolds (10 %).
Volta River Authority (VRA)	Ghana's statuary power provider.
Volta River Project	The name given to the association of the Volta River Authority (VRA) and the Volta Aluminum Corporation (VALCO).

Volta River Project Addendum – 2013

In the 14 years since this case's publication, the state of electricity in Ghana has made considerable progress on several fronts. Between 1999 and 2006, the Akosombo dam's turbines and generators were retrofitted with state-of-the-art technology, increasing the generation capacity from 912 MW to 1,020 MW. A third dam, on the Black Volta River at Bui, will add 400 MW of installed generation capacity and will complete construction in 2013.

The Volta River Authority and TAQA have recently completed funding to expand the 200 MW Takoradi 2 Thermal Power Plant, which will increase the installed capacity by 110 MW and convert it to a combined cycle unit. The Takoradi 3 Combined Cycle Thermal Power Project is currently under construction, and will provide a further 132 MW.

Though the Volta River Authority is exploring several solar and wind power options, perhaps the country's most exciting development is the 155 MW solar power plant, the continent's largest, due to begin construction near Aiwiaso in late 2013. Developed by Blue Energy, a UK renewable energy company, the photovoltaic plant will help the country's aim of increasing its renewable energy capacity to 10 % by 2020.

The government of Ghana had previously promised universal access to electricity for its citizens by 2020, but recently shortened the timetable to 2016, with the government bearing all costs of connection.

http://www.vra.com/

http://www.guardian.co.uk/environment/2012/dec/04/africa-largest-solar-power-plant-ghana

http://www.ghana.gov.gh/index.php/news/features/18845-ghana-to-attain-full-national-electricity-coverage-by-2016

http://www.ghana.gov.gh/index.php/news/general-news/19402-taqa-completes-financing-for-takoradi-2-expansion

Transforming Education in Rural Haiti: Intel and L'Ecole De Choix[102]

In the fall of 2011, John Cartwright was looking at a muddy construction site in Mirebalais, Haiti. Less than 2 years after a 7.0-magnitude earthquake devastated the country, Cartwright had traveled to this rural region of Haiti as part of a volunteer team of Intel Corporation (Intel) employees to support the installation of

---

[102]This case was prepared by Pauline J. Albert, Laura P. Hartrman, Crina Archer and Jenny Mead under the supervision of Patricia H. Werhane. Copyright©2012 University of Virginia Darden School Foundation. All rights reserved. One of the authors, Pauline J. Albert, worked for Intel between 1990 and 2002, and held a variety of communications and marketing positions in the U.S.

education hardware and software during the launch of a nonprofit school, *l'Ecole de Choix*[103] (Choix). Choix's vision was to transform the educational opportunities available to rural Haitian children. Computer literacy and computer-based educational tools were a significant element of Choix's objective to provide a quality education for its students, making the school a promising partner for Intel's Education Service Corps (IESC). If the mission of the IESC were strictly charitable, Cartwright's task would be daunting enough. But the infrastructure around him was still in postearthquake shambles. How would his team install computing platforms and train faculty and students without a completed building, let alone working electricity?

The challenges that Cartwright faced when Intel partnered with nonprofit organizations such as Choix were also informed by Intel's broader vision for the IESC program, which involved both business strategy and its corporate social mission. Julie Clugage, founder of the IESC, described these objectives in terms of a "triple win."[104] For projects to be successful, they had to result in a business "win": their execution had to be cost-effective, requiring limited financial investment by Intel, and their success should advance Intel's business strategy of raising the company's visibility and reputation in emerging market areas. The projects also aimed to produce a human resources "win" for Intel, as volunteer employees brought their enthusiasm and any new insights they had gained in the field back to the company after their IESC deployments. Finally, successful projects provided a "win" to nonprofit partner organizations and to the communities they served by providing high-quality learning technology tailored to local needs and sustainable over the long term.

The triple-win approach that Intel promoted with its IESC projects was an extremely promising idea, as the objectives were mutually reinforcing. But how was Cartwright to successfully implement this vision in Mirebalais, so that his efforts provided not only a sustainable benefit to the Choix students living in conditions of extreme poverty but also a return to Intel on the investment of its resources? Could Intel's integration of business and social strategy succeed in the context of postquake rural Haiti, where challenges ranged from exceptionally long construction delays and a lack of electricity to more entrenched obstacles such as the legacy of weak governmental support for education; crumbling infrastructure; and deep class, racial, and geographical inequalities?

At the beginning of this first visit to Choix, Cartwright wondered whether, at the conclusion of the trip, he would be able to report any success. This particular morning, he had to face the fact that he and his team might soon have to engage in a bit of construction work themselves if they were going to see any progress at all that week.

---

and Europe. During the early 1990s, she served as the technical assistant and speechwriter to Intel's cofounder Gordon Moore, as well as executive vice president and later president Craig R. Barrett. From 1999 to 2000, Barrett supported her in a K–12 education initiative to develop a web portal to help teachers teach math and science classes.

[103] "The School of Choice."

[104] Case writer telephone interview with Julie Clugage, May 24, 2012. All subsequent quotations attributed to Clugage, unless otherwise noted, derive from this interview.

Intel's Growth Strategy: Enabling the Next Generation

Intel's business strategy had long been focused on enabling the next generation of technology. During its 45 years in business, Intel had been a key driver behind the continuous, rapid march of technological progress. For average consumers, it was extremely difficult to comprehend the extensiveness of that progress. Innovation was often attributed to those with Star Trek-style visions of the future; few people realized how difficult it was to manufacture the components necessary to execute those visions. During the company's early years, Intel cofounder Gordon Moore predicted that engineers would be able to double the number of transistors in the company's devices about every 2 years.[105] The accuracy of Moore's prediction explained why personal computers powered by Intel microprocessors were considered obsolete about every 2 years. Sustaining this pace of transistor growth, however, had become more difficult due to the materials science and the cost of manufacturing the increasingly small components that drove many electronic devices, from parts of trains and planes to video games. By 2012, an Intel factory cost approximately $5 billion. While the 1971 Intel 4004 microprocessor executed 92,000 instructions per second, the contemporary Intel state-of-the-art Core processor could execute 92 billion. An individual whose typing speed had accelerated at that rate would be able to type Tolstoy's *War and Peace* in less than a minute. Even more dramatically, $1.00 bought about 37 transistors in 1971; it bought two million in 2011. If automobiles had progressed at this rate, a Porsche would cost $1.00 today.[106]

Manufacturing the microprocessor components was only the beginning of the challenge Intel faced. Intel's extremely complex microprocessors (sometimes described as the brain of the computer) required other components (e.g., chip sets, memory) and software that could take advantage of their capabilities. The relationship between these elements could be described in biological terms: the microprocessor was the seed, but for it to grow and prosper, it required an ecosystem. The vocabulary of a business ecosystem being analogous to an environmental system was not popularized until the 1990s,[107] but Intel had always known that it must support multiple layers of its respective business ecosystem to succeed in its business strategy. The original electronic component decisions that the hardware and software companies made were at the root of those product announcements and the competitive battles over new electronic gadgets.[108]

---

[105] "Moore's Law Inspires Intel Innovation," Intel Corporation website, http://www.intel.com/content/www/us/en/silicon-innovations/moores-law-technology.html. Accessed 15 June 2012.

[106] "40 Years of Intel Microprocessor Innovation, Following Moore's Law the Whole Way," Intel Corporation website, http://www.intel.com/content/dam/www/public/us/en/documents/promotions/Intel_40th_infographic_11-10-2011.pdf. Accessed May 2012.

[107] Moore, James F. 1993. Predators and prey: A new ecology of competition. *Harvard Business Review*, May 1993, 75–86.

[108] O'Brien, Kevin J. 2011. With new smartphones, high hopes for Nokia and Microsoft union. *New York Times*, October 26, 2011.

In the technology industry, as in many market areas in the twenty-first century global economy, business strategy was a lot more than simple competition between two companies making similar products. Growth was dependent on a firm's deep understanding of its unique competitive advantage[109] and the collaborative relationships it had established in the marketplace. For Intel to be successful, Intel sales engineers had to convince other engineers that its computer chips would run better on their hardware and software. An important design win in Intel's history occurred in 1981, when IBM selected the Intel 8086 microprocessor and Microsoft's operating system as the engine for IBM's entry into the personal computer industry. At the time, Moore and others thought that the PC would be used for little more than keeping track of recipes. Later, Moore laughed about his underestimation of that design win.[110] Revenue and high margins often depended on how quickly new technology "ramped" – that is, how quickly consumer products manufacturers adopted and sold their products to end users.

For decades, Intel had been invested in creating relationships across the entire computing industry. Its engineers were key players in the development of major industry standards such as videoconferencing on personal computers (using programs such as Skype), USB connectors, and wireless Bluetooth technology. Each of these technological innovations was invented in Intel labs and further developed in conjunction with industry standards. The higher the integration level of its products – the more smoothly components and software worked together – the faster Intel could ramp up the technology. In the 1990s, for example, Intel manufactured fully assembled personal computers and servers in its plants in Oregon and Ireland. The company was a significant player in producing fully assembled computers that were resold to distributors and often relabeled, in much the same way as a Procter & Gamble food manufacturer would produce products that might be sold under the Procter and Gamble name, or under the private label of a local grocery distributor. Such relationships between Intel and distribution vendors helped the computer industry grow faster.

It was to Intel's benefit to offer manufacturers prototypes that they could freely use to bring fully functioning products to market more quickly. For instance, at the January 2012 Computer Electronics Show, Intel demonstrated a "prototype" smartphone based on an integration of its Atom technology and the Android operating system. That prototype design became the basis of phones later sold by Motorola and Lenovo (the Chinese company that in 2005 acquired IBM's Personal Computer Division).[111] Lenovo had become bigger than Dell, which was not surprising given

[109] Porter, Michael E. 1985. *Competitive advantage: Creating and sustaining superior performance.* New York: Free Press.

[110] Sydell, Laura. 2012. Intel legends Moore and Grove: Making it last. NPR Morning Edition, April 6, 2012, http://www.npr.org/2012/04/06/150057676/intel-legends-moore-and-grove-making-it-last. Accessed 3 April 2013.

[111] "Our Company," Lenovo website. http://www.lenovo.com/lenovo/us/en/our_company.html. Accessed 1 June 2012; "Lenovo and Motorola Adopting Intel's Atom 'Medfield' SoC," TechPowerUp.com, January 11, 2012. http://www.techpowerup.com/158487/Lenovo-and-Motorola-adopting-Intel-s-Atom-Medfield-SoC.html. Accessed 30 May 2012.

Intel president and CEO Paul Otellini's comments in the company's 2011 annual report that "total PC purchases were higher in China than in any other country, followed by the U.S., Brazil, and Russia."[112] Increasingly, growth in the tech industry was achieved by creating or expanding markets for personal computing products in regions that were just beginning to join the technology revolution that had been underway for decades in countries such as the United States, Japan, and members of the European Union.

The implications of emerging markets in these regions were significant. In his groundbreaking 2005 book, C. K. Prahalad introduced the concept that there was opportunity for economic growth and innovation through selling to the "bottom of the pyramid" (BoP), a term that referred to the billions of people who lived on less than $2 per day. After Prahalad introduced this concept, many companies had sought to develop new markets in income-poor areas at the bottom of the economic pyramid. Importantly, as new markets emerged in developing economies, such as China and India, they often did not imitate Western models; acquiring market share required innovation to meet the specific needs of BoP producers and consumers.[113]

Thus, these growth opportunities were not without hurdles. In many cases, the business ecosystems required to address these markets did not exist and had to be created from scratch and tailored to the unique needs and challenges of the region. The material infrastructure and human resources required to sustain a business ecosystem, such as the system of vendor relationships that Intel depended upon to move from microprocessor to consumer product, might be lacking. In addition to the difficulties of building an ecosystem capable of supporting complex and shifting relationships between product design, manufacture, and distribution, growth opportunities were inherently limited in regions that suffered from high levels of poverty, and within communities that did not have the basic economic, logistical, and educational resources needed to benefit from new computing technologies and products.

China and India had a growing middle class, but poverty in countries such as Haiti could seem intractable. And in spite of this growing middle class, there were millions in China, India, and other swiftly developing countries who remained in abject poverty. Capitalism had helped create this emergent middle class, but the question of how to improve the lot of the poorest of the poor remained under debate. Some who studied poverty alleviation had come to the conclusion that philanthropic approaches dependent on NGOs, while certainly well meaning, were not sustainable over the long-term and, therefore, failed to produce significant, community-level changes. The effectiveness of new models, new ecosystems, and new kinds of business partnerships in alleviating poverty was becoming increasingly well documented.[114]

---

[112] Intel Corporation annual report, 2011.

[113] "Grow grow grow: What makes emerging-market companies run," *Economist*, April 15, 2010, http://www.economist.com/node/15879405. Accessed 1 April 2013.

[114] Werhane, Patricia H., Scott P. Kelley, Laura P. Hartman, and Dennis J. Moberg. 2009. *Alleviating poverty through profitable business partnerships: Globalization, markets, and economic well-being.* New York: Routledge.

Although Intel Corporation made its money primarily from selling individual components, its short-, medium-, and long-term success was based on its deep understanding of the ecology of both computer and competitive business systems. Intel had immense experience developing strong business ecosystems and its decision to use this experience in fostering effective educational systems reflected the company's view that quality education was a crucial engine for economic growth in emerging markets.

Intel's Programs to Transform Education

Intel had always supported the communities in which it manufactured products, and its values had included its desire to be a "great place to work"[115] almost since its inception. Like many large corporations, Intel supported employee volunteerism and matched employee donations to educational institutions, but its efforts in education went far beyond those of most large companies. A company fact sheet stated, "Over the past decade alone, Intel and the Intel Foundation have invested more than $1 billion and Intel employees have donated close to 3 million volunteer hours toward improving education in more than 60 countries."[116] The company considered investment in global education a strategic imperative not only for making the world a better place but also for growing the total addressable market (TAM) for electronic products based on its technology. Although 2.3 billion people were online by the end of 2011, "70 % of the total households in developed countries had Internet, whereas only 20 % of households in developing countries had Internet access."[117] In the late 1990s, Intel introduced Intel Teach, a program to support K–12 teachers in developing the skills to appropriately integrate computers into their teaching of math and science. Supporting over 10 million teachers in 70 countries, the Intel Teach program "improve[d] teacher effectiveness through professional development, helping teachers integrate technology into their lessons and promoting students' problem-solving, critical thinking, and collaboration skills."[118]

Expanded efforts in support of K–12 education were part of the legacy of Craig Barrett, who served as Intel's fourth chairman from 1998 to 2005. Barrett considered investments in education as a form of enlightened self-interest; he reasoned that

---

[115]"Life at Intel: Our values," Intel Corporation website, http://www.intel.com/lifeatintel/values/. Accessed 15 June 2012.

[116]"Intel Education Initiative: Empowering Tomorrow's Innovators," Intel News Fact Sheet. http://download.intel.com/newsroom/kits/education/pdfs/Intel_Education_FactSheet.pdf. Accessed 31 March 2013.

[117]International Telecommunication Union, "Key Statistical Highlights: ITU Data Release June 2012," http://www.itu.int/ITU-D/ict/statistics/material/pdf/2011%20Statistical%20highlights_June_2012.pdf. Accessed 30 March 2012.

[118]"Intel Teach Program Worldwide," Intel Corporation website, http://www.intel.com/about/corporateresponsibility/education/programs/intelteach_ww/index.htm. Accessed 15 June 2012.

Intel's future products and innovations, and even its long-term sustainability, depended on a well-educated populace of both future employees and technology users worldwide. He proposed that companies such as Intel had an important role to play in education advancement, since "information and communications technology (ICT) can transform education."[119] In Barrett's view, "ICT has the power to trigger a shift from knowledge acquisition, which limits learning to rote memorization and parroting back facts, to knowledge creation, which involves 'learning how to learn.' The latter cultivates skills that are vital for today's knowledge economy, including critical thinking, collaboration, analysis, problem solving, communication and innovation."[120]

Intel's overlapping social and business commitments to strengthening the knowledge economy exemplified the strategy of "shared value."[121] According to Porter and Kramer, "The concept of shared value can be defined as policies and operating practices that enhance the competitiveness of a company while simultaneously advancing the economic and social conditions in the communities in which it operates. Shared value creation focuses on identifying and expanding the connections between societal and economic progress."[122]

Intel's fastest-growing markets were in countries with newly developing knowledge economies, such as China. Increasingly, emerging market governments had identified education as a key factor for building sustainable growth. Similarly, companies such as Intel were proposing that, in the current global economy, competitive advantage was not based on one's ability to beat out the competition by selling more of the same product. Rather, market share was won through relationships developed at all levels of the value chain, creating a vested interest in community development. One extra year of schooling could result in a 7 % increase in aggregate labor productivity.[123]

The Education Market Platforms Group (EMPG) and the Intel Learning Series Products

Intel's primary business involved the sale of semiconductor components, but over its history, the company had focused on bringing total system solutions to the marketplace. In the 1980s, solutions meant helping manufacturers with manuals

---

[119] Barrett, Craig R. Commentary, Forbes.com, January 23, 2008, http://www.forbes.com/2008/01/22/solutions-education-barrett-oped-cx_crb_0123barrett.html. Accessed 30 March 2012.

[120] Barrett.

[121] Porter, Michael E., and Mark R. Kramer. 2002. The competitive advantage of corporate philanthropy. *Harvard Business Review,* December 2002, 56–68; Porter, Michael E., and Mark R. Kramer. 2011. Creating shared value: how to reinvent capitalism – and Unleash a wave of innovation and growth. *Harvard Business Review*, January 2011, 62–77.

[122] Porter and Kramer, 2002.

[123] Coulombe, Serge, and Jean-François Tremblay. 2006. Literacy and growth, *Topics in Macroeconomics* 6(2): 34. Retrieved from http://www.sba.muohio.edu/davisgk/growth%20readings/10.pdf. Accessed 3 April 2013.

and engineering support to design Intel products into cars, automation equipment, and traffic lights. In the 1990s, the focus became personal computer motherboards, systems, and development of innovations needed to grow the industry, such as Ethernet, USB, and Bluetooth, as well as enterprise system solutions through its consulting services. In the twenty-first century, the company had enabled technology growth by building prototypes (such as the Android smartphone) and creating programs that supported the distribution of educational technology and content worldwide.

EMPG, initially called the Emerging Markets Platform Group, was conceived in November of 2004. Engineers and social scientists based in China were sent to regional offices in Bangalore, Cairo, and São Paulo to explore how technology might be used to support people in these markets. For example, based on the ethnographic research it conducted in India, the team came up with a product called the Community PC that could be used as a kiosk in community centers to help locals get items such as government permits.[124] Products such as these had been known to substantially reduce corruption, which was often a problem in emerging markets.[125] Most of EMPG's initial products helped Intel learn more about the implementation of technology in different markets, but they did not lead to volume component sales. In a number of these emerging countries, however, governments were interested in expanding technology in schools. Consequently, education was selected as the volume market to which EMPG could dedicate itself with greater focus, and by 2011 the department's name had been changed to Education Market Platforms Group – the same acronym, but with a more focused target market.

By 2006, Intel had developed an initial prototype of a ruggedized netbook called the Intel Classmate PC. In 2007, it announced the product as a reference design from which manufacturers could build their own product. More importantly, Intel began to build an ecosystem, called the Intel Learning Series, by developing an alliance program that by 2012 included over 500 companies that sold software, hardware, peripherals, and services to the education market. Since 2007, the company had supported the distribution of over ten million Classmate PCs worldwide. Most had been sent to places outside of the U.S.: over two million in Europe, the Middle East, and Africa; almost 150,000 in Thailand; 4,000 in Japan; four million in Latin America; 9,600 in China; and 152,600 in North America.[126]

Many of the Classmate PC manufacturers were small companies, but in 2011, Lenovo and Samsung signed on as alliance partners to produce designs "compliant" with Intel Learning Series designs. In the software arena, partners included companies such as LEGO, which produced robotics kits to support the teaching of math

---

[124]Unruh, Greg. 2011. Intel emerging market platforms group. Thunderbird School of Global Management (2011), 14.

[125]Prahalad, C. K. 2005. *The fortune at the bottom of the pyramid: Eradicating poverty through profits*. Upper Saddle River, NJ: Pearson Education/Wharton School Publishing.

[126]"Education Around the World – Intel Education Solutions," Intel Corporation website, http://www.intel.com/content/www/us/en/intel-learning-series/world-wide-deployments.html?wapkw=education+series. Accessed 1 July 2012.

and science, and Waterford Institute, a nonprofit with 35 years of expertise in supplementing traditional English literacy instruction with technology-based learning. While some of these global alliance partners were not household names in the U.S., they were significant players in their local markets, providing local language educational software, and peripherals such as whiteboards, science probes, microscopes, and other technological tools for enhancing the quality of education. Intel had identified a unique core of Education Solution Providers (ESPs) who brought together all the elements required to service a particular local environment. These were complete educational solutions that incorporated tools for teachers and tracking of students' progress. In 2012, EMPG promoted three reference design systems: a "clamshell" Classmate PC that opened and closed like a traditional laptop, a convertible Classmate PC with a touch screen that swiveled into tablet mode, and a new education tablet announced in 2012 called Studybook. Manufactured to Intel specifications, the systems were then able to use alliance software that had been optimized to work smoothly on these tailor-built systems. The manufacturers and resellers determined the final price to the customer, but the 2012 pricing of the computers, depending on the country, model, and volume purchased, was in the $200 to $500 range per device.

Enter the Intel Education Service Corps (IESC)

Within this ecosystem, the Intel Education Service Corps (IESC) provided a "specialized sales force" of Intel employees like John Cartwright to serve the unique needs of NGO customers, such as Choix, in Haiti. Julie Clugage, the founder of IESC, described the goal of EMPG as providing the "catalyzation" for the ecosystem of software and hardware partners, education providers, and NGOs. Before joining Intel in 2002, Clugage spent four years working for the World Bank and the Inter-American Development Bank in Washington, DC, as well as two years at a teacher-training high school in rural Guatemala. After getting her MBA from University of California, Berkeley, she joined Intel and rose to the position of chief of staff for the VP of corporate affairs, where she supported Intel's corporate social responsibility efforts in education as well as Intel's relations with govern- mental development agencies and NGOs.[127] In 2009, Clugage transitioned to EMPG to work with alliance partners throughout the world in providing Intel-based education solutions.

Clugage discovered that her colleagues in other departments were interested in getting involved with these global educational initiatives. Inspired by this employee interest in participating in EMPG's support of educational efforts in emerging markets, she conceived of the IESC, which drew volunteers for EMPG projects

---

[127]"Meet the Bloggers – Julie Clugage," Intel Corporation CSR@Intel website, http://blogs.intel. com/csr/authors/. Accessed 2 Aug ,2012.

from a pool of Intel employee applicants. It took months of negotiating, but Clugage won the support that she needed to launch the IESC program in August of 2009. The mission of IESC was embodied in the "triple-win" outcome goal: cost-effective visibility and reputational benefits for Intel in emerging markets, benefits to employee job satisfaction and skills development, and increased availability of quality education in target communities.

Clugage was excited to have received 80 applications for 10 available slots during the first week of the program's life: "It's sort of like starting the Intel version of the U.S. Peace Corps, with a focus on using our technical and human resources to improve the quality of global education. It has been a dream of mine for about five years now, so it really was an occasion to do a little dance outside my gray cube when we launched this program."[128] Employee enthusiasm for the opportunity to participate in this program was reflected in the e-mails and applications Clugage received during the launch: "In 19 years at Intel, I have never been so excited about a potential opportunity;" "This program is so cool! I'm so proud to work for Intel;" "Thanks for taking such a bold approach in these turbulent economic times."[129]

As of November 2012, the IESC had supported 39 projects, sending 207 volunteers to 16 countries. 1,000 teachers and administrators and 7,500 students had been directly trained, and 45,000 more were slated to benefit from these ongoing projects. In addition, IESC project teams had distributed 1,400 Classmate PCs. These outcomes represented the contribution of $4 million from Intel in the form of pro-bono labor. Each project involved sending four to six Intel employees into a developing nation to provide support for the integration of Intel Classmate PCs in schools. NGOs, such as World Vision, CARE, Save the Children and others, were brought together with allied hardware and software vendors to form a nexus of business and social organizations within an ecosystem tailored to the site-specific needs of the local institutions served by Intel's education products. In addition to the project with Choix in Haiti, the IESC had partnered with many local NGOs on projects in Africa, Asia, and South America (see Exhibit 1 for examples). IESC deployments were not conceived as one-off projects. The aim was to bring every project to the point of local sustainability, which involved different levels of commitment at each site. Six different teams went to Vietnam over a 3-year period (2010–2012), for example, although the goal was that each project would "graduate" and become self-sustaining after approximately three visits over a 1- to 2-year period.

Project team members had to secure their manager's approval for the 2-week "in the field" deployment as well as a 4- to 8-week, part-time preparation and training period, which was a challenge in Intel's intense and results-oriented culture.[130]

---

[128]Clugage, Julie. "Announcing the Intel Education Service Corps," Intel Corporation CSR@Intel website September 3, 2009, http://blogs.intel.com/csr/2009/09/announcing_the_intel_education/. Accessed 3 April 2013.

[129]Clugage.

[130]Johnson, Cory. 2012. Intel: An engineering culture. *Bloomberg Businessweek* video, 2:14, May 15, 2012, http://www.businessweek.com/videos/2012-05-15/intel-an-engineering-culture. Accessed 30 March 2013.

Thus, not only did the employee have to be motivated, but his or her manager and teammates also had to be willing to support this effort. Teams were made up of employees from around the world who brought a variety of skills to the project. Valued skills for a particular site might include experience with computer hardware and software, teaching, local languages, or cultural knowledge of the country being supported. During the estimated 40 h of preparation and training, team members met over the phone and with their client to solidify equipment requirements and perform as much testing of the actual configurations (combination of hardware and software) to be deployed as possible. The planning stage was followed by 2 weeks of actual in-country experience, and an additional 2 weeks after the trip, during which members spent 10 h preparing a project debrief. The team had to summarize what went well, what challenges remained, and what recommendations it had for the NGO, for EMPG employees, and, if relevant, the next IESC team.

Intel was clear about its guidelines for the local NGO partners selected for IESC support. These partner organizations had to purchase the necessary technology infrastructure (Intel did not donate equipment for IESC projects), outline a clear description of the scope of work or project needs, and provide assistance in identifying providers for local lodging, meals, and transportation, as well as on-the-ground guidance for the Intel volunteers. Intel's human resources department funded the volunteers' travel expenses, which represented about 90 % of Intel's out-of-pocket costs. Employees often shared rooms, and it was not uncommon for volunteers to sleep on the floor or even in tents in rural locations without hotels. The Intel volunteers were primarily tasked with providing technical assistance, training, and support in defining the scope of work.

It was not easy to be selected to become a member of the IESC. Cartwright noted that Intel selected its "best and brightest" for these projects. During the July 2012 selection cycle, 326 Intel employees completed the application. The IESC staff selected roughly 90 of these applications for interviews and 40 were selected for assignments to take place between September and November. Thus, only 12 % of those who applied were ultimately selected as IESC volunteers, a lower admissions rate than many of America's top business schools.[131] Clugage reported that IESC volunteers typically returned to work excited and transformed. The teams formed new relationships and bonds with Intel people from many different countries who had varied cultural and life experiences, as well as with students, teachers, and NGO representatives from around the globe. For example, Dr. Joya Chatterjee, deployment manager for EMPG, spoke with enthusiasm about convincing a 15-year old in her native India that he could go to college someday. Chatterjee concluded her video story by saying that she "found the soul of Intel" in her work with IESC.[132]

---

[131] Sheedy, Kelsey. 2012. 10 business schools with the lowest acceptance rates. *U.S. News & World Report*, March 15, 2012, http://www.usnews.com/education/best-graduate-schools/the-short-list-grad-school/articles/2012/03/15/10-business-schools-with-the-lowest-acceptance-rates. Accessed 30 March 2013.

[132] "Dr. Joya Chatterjee at Upgrade Your Life III," YouTube video, 0:34, posted by "channelintel," July 18, 2011, http://www.youtube.com/watch?v=4j2SqDbuVpc. Accessed 3 April 2013.

Gary Shaye saw the potential for a match between Intel's strategic objectives in education and emerging markets and Haiti's educational needs, which had intensified in the wake of the 2010 earthquake. Shaye had worked with Intel as an NGO client previously, in Bolivia, and was now the country director for Save the Children in Haiti. By chance, he had also met Laura Pincus Hartman, the founder of Choix, when seated next to her on a plane from Port-au-Prince, Haiti to Miami, Florida. Hartman had been exploring options for Choix's technology solutions and training, but had encountered hurdles with other programs that did not provide training and education on a long-term basis. Shaye introduced Hartman to Clugage, and the two women quickly discovered a congruent vision. Both Choix and Intel were interested in promoting twenty-first-century skills through technology, with the aim of revolutionizing education. Clugage determined that Choix was a good fit with IESC's program requirements, and in turn, Intel offered the services and support, through IESC, that Hartman had been unable to find elsewhere. The question that remained was whether the partnership that Intel and Choix envisioned could be implemented in Haiti.

Haiti: Land of Mountains

In front of Haiti's National Palace in Port-au-Prince stood a statue named Nèg Mawon (Creole for "brown man") designed to represent the spirit of the proud Haitian people who fought off slavery to gain their freedom. In one hand, Nèg Mawon held a conch shell used to call escaped slaves to meetings and a machete used to cut sugarcane and fight off the French. In his other hand was a handcuff and broken chain. In 1492, Columbus claimed the island of Hispañola for Spain, but over the next several centuries the French and Spanish fought to control the large island, which eventually consisted of two distinct and independent democratic countries: Haiti and the Dominican Republic.

By the middle of the sixteenth century, an indigenous population (called Tainos) of approximately one million had dwindled to a few hundred survivors. Many had died from working the gold mines, while others perished from diseases caught from their Spanish landlords. When the gold mines were depleted, Spain lost interest in the territory, ceding the western part of the island to the French in 1697. The French named its territory Saint-Domingue, and it soon became the center of the infamous triangular trade route: manufactured goods went from Europe to Africa, where they were exchanged for slaves, who were then brought to Saint-Domingue and other Caribbean countries. The slaves worked the sugarcane fields, and the processed sugar and rum were then sold back to Europe.

By the end of the eighteenth century, of a population of 519,000 people, 87 % were slaves, 8 % were white, and 5 % were freed men.[133] The island, producing

---

[133] Helen Chapin Metz, ed., A Country study: Haiti. In *Dominican republic and Haiti: Country studies* (Washington, DC: Federal Research Division, 2001), http://lcweb2.loc.gov/frd/cs/httoc. html#ht0101. Accessed 3 April 2013.

approximately 40 % of the world's sugar, had become one of the richest colonies in the world.[134] The members of the colonialist culture developed lavish lifestyles, and cruelty to slaves was accepted practice; slave insurgencies were common. After many years of fighting for liberation from their oppressors, the slave population fought off Napoleon's armies in 1804. The island became the first black republic in the Western Hemisphere, and the only country created by a successful slave revolt. Jean-Jacques Dessalines, a former slave turned general who led the revolt, renamed the country Haiti from the Taino word meaning "land of mountains."[135]

The country's first constitution forbade whites from owning land and decreed that all Haitians, both mulattoes and blacks, were to be called "blacks." The children of unmarried French planters and female slaves had gained their freedom much earlier under *Le Code Noir* (the Black Code).[136] Adopted under Louis XIV, the code defined the status of slaves in the various French colonies. Lighter-skinned Haitians freed prior to 1804 grew up speaking French and saw themselves as superior to *les nouveaux libres* (the newly free), who had gained their independence through the Dessalines-led revolution. The sugar plantation system collapsed, and this "emergent peasantry" in the rural areas remained illiterate, while the more literate plantation owners moved to the cities and emerged as Haiti's ruling class.[137]

In the early nineteenth century, the Vatican and the United States refused to recognize Haiti as a free nation. The Vatican's lack of recognition limited the Haitian state's ability to establish a solid education system, since Catholic religious orders were a major source of formal education in that era. Other factors affected the stability of Haiti's development. Between 1843 and 1915 (the year that the U.S. began a Haitian occupation), 22 different heads of state led Haiti's government. For 19 years (1915–1934), Haiti was a protectorate of the United States. The period of American occupation was characterized by stability, with significant improvements in public health, economic development, and basic infrastructure such as roads, bridges, and telephone service. But much of this activity was based in and around Port-au-Prince, resulting in increased centralization of the economy in urban Haiti. Additionally, order was established and maintained "largely by white foreigners with deep-seated racial prejudices and a disdain for the notion of self-determination by inhabitants of less-developed nations," a situation that was deeply resented by the majority of Haiti's mulatto and black citizens.[138]

Class and racial conflicts persisted after the Americans left, and two light-skinned presidents were elected between 1935 and 1946. At this point, student protests

---

[134]Dash, J. Michael. 2001. *Culture and customs of Haiti*. Westport, CT: Greenwood.

[135]Dash, 2, 6.

[136]The Black Code itself did not allow for the mistreatment of slaves, and it was in many respects ignored. It outlined that slaves could not be raped – and if they were, they were to be married and freed. Families could not be separated. If freed, slaves became French citizens. These laws were considered by some scholars to have been progressive for their time.

[137]Dash, 7.

[138]"Occupation of Haiti (1915–34)" GlobalSecurity.org Military page, http://www.globalsecurity. org/military/ops/haiti19.htm?&lang=en_us&output=json. Accessed 16 April 2013.

forced the president into exile and the military stepped in, orchestrating an election in which the emerging middle class of blacks from the northern region brought François Duvalier to power as president.[139] In 1957, Duvalier was elected on a pro-black nationalist platform, with strong support from the military. His early paternalistic attitude toward supporting those living in poverty and ill health gained him the name "Papa Doc." Duvalier violated the constitution to run for reelection in 1961, which he won by "an official tally of 1,320,748 votes to zero."[140] He proceeded to declare himself "president for life" in 1964. Upon Duvalier's death in 1971, his 19-year-old son, Jean-Claude – who would come to be known as "Baby Doc" – took over as president.

Though largely choosing to leave day-to-day governance to others, "Baby Doc" Duvalier's regime was initially received positively by many Haitians, as well as by foreign observers.[141] In 1971, the United States restored its aid program to Haiti, which had been severed during the period of the elder Duvalier's rule. Over time, however, "Baby Doc" Duvalier lost domestic and international support as a result of corrupt practices – which included "drug trafficking, pilferage of development and food aid, illegal resale and export of subsidized oil, and manipulation of government contracts" – as the country deteriorated into deeper poverty.[142] In 1986, threatened by riots and widespread popular discontent, and pressured by the United States, "Baby Doc" escaped to exile in France.[143]

After a period of provisional governments, Jean-Bertrand Aristide, an outspoken former Catholic priest and critic of Duvalier, won 67 % of the vote in the 1990 election, which was deemed free and fair by international observers.[144] Early on, Aristide attempted to dissipate the army's power and to collect back taxes from the country's elite. He was ousted by a military coup after only 7 months, however. Because of severe repression and deteriorating economic conditions, thousands of Haitians tried to escape by boat to the coast of Florida. During 1991 and 1992, the U.S. Coast Guard rescued more than 40,000 Haitians from the sea; in all likelihood, thousands more drowned. For two and a half years, the United States and the United Nations imposed economic sanctions. Eventually, in return for amnesty, the junta agreed to step down, allowing U.S. troops to enter Haiti and return Aristide to power in September of 1994. When Aristide stepped aside after the conclusion of his term in 1995, his prime minister, René Préval, won the ensuing election.

---

[139] Metz.

[140] Metz.

[141] Metz.

[142] "Haiti's History," PBS Frontline/World website, December 13, 2007, http://www.pbs.org/frontlineworld/rough/2007/12/haiti_belos_sonlinks.html. Accessed 30 March 2013.

[143] At the time of preparation of this case study, the ends of the Aristide and "Baby Doc" Duvalier stories had not yet been written. Both former leaders returned to Haiti in the aftermath of the earthquake. The Haitian justice system is ill-equipped to deal with their return. See Laurent Dubois, Haiti: *The Aftershocks of History* (New York: Metropolitan, 2012); Paul Farmer, *Haiti: After the Earthquake* (New York: PublicAffairs, 2011).

[144] PBS.

By 2000, corruption in Haiti, along with human rights violations and election fraud, had halted development assistance from other countries. A disputed election in 2001 returned Aristide to power, but political turmoil, violence, and a breakdown of government institutions followed. Haiti suffered a deep recession from its loss of foreign aid and protests ensued. In 2004, armed rebels demanded Aristide's ouster and the U.S. military airlifted him to safety. United Nations peacekeepers, led by American forces, established an interim government until elections for president and the National Assembly were held in early 2006. The elections were not without controversy, and some claimed fraud; but a majority re-elected Préval. On January 10, 2010, when the 7.0-magnitude earthquake struck Haiti, Préval was still serving as president, and the United Nations's mission became exponentially larger.

As these numerous political and military power struggles unfolded across two centuries of Haiti's national history, rural peoples were particularly disadvantaged. In the early twenty-first century, 80 % of Haitians lived below the poverty line, unemployment was estimated to be over 40 %, and more than half of the government's budget came from outside sources. In 2009, the World Bank forgave more than $1.0 billion of the country's debt through the Highly-Indebted Poor Country initiative. Michel Martelly, elected to the presidency in April of 2011, campaigned on a pledge to initiate greater foreign investment to make the country more self-sustainable.

The State of Education in Haiti

The January 2010 earthquake devastated Haiti, a country that was already the poorest in the Western Hemisphere. While 380,000 people were still living in tents as of 2012,[145] initially there were 1.5 million displaced from their homes out of a population of about 10 million. The severity of damage caused by an earthquake was tied to both the density of the population and the quality of a location's buildings. In the case of Haiti, the severity was enormous. There were 230,000 reported dead in the tragedy; by comparison, the 1989 earthquake of similar magnitude in San Francisco resulted in 63 fatalities.

The education sector, like nearly all aspects of life in Haiti, was deeply affected. Indeed, it was difficult to speak accurately of the state of education in Haiti by reference to pre-quake data, and postquake data was unavailable in many relevant areas. Haiti had struggled to provide basic primary education prior to the 2010 earthquake, falling significantly short of achieving the state's aim of universal educational access. Many of the challenges that Haiti faced in delivering quality basic education to all of its children, while exacerbated by the quake, had roots in entrenched problems that predated the 2010 disaster. As the government acknowledged in its March 2010 Post-Disaster Needs

---

[145]Sontag, Deborah. 2012. Earthquake relief where Haiti wasn't broken. *New York Times*, July 5, 2012.

Assessment (PDNA) report, "Overall, the Haitian education system already presented deficiencies before the earthquake that made it unfit to contribute to socio-economic development."[146]

Education Challenges Before the 2010 Earthquake

The constitution of the Republic of Haiti (1987) "guarantees the right to education," declaring that the state and its territories "must make schooling available to all, free of charge, and ensure that public and private sector teachers are properly trained."[147] Primary schooling and free access to "classroom facilities and teaching materials" were compulsory formal rights for all elementary-age children. The primary school completion rate, however, was estimated at 20 % in 1991.[148] The government initiated a 10-year education plan in 1997 with the goal of achieving universal access to education.

A decade later, the Ministry of Education reported progress toward this goal, with an estimated 67 % of Haitian children completing primary education.[149] Approximately 400,000 children from ages 6 to 11 remained without access to basic education, however. Few of Haiti's primary schools were state-funded public institutions, reflecting a trend of increasing privatization of education. In the mid-1980s, private schools represented approximately 60 % of Haiti's schools; during the 1990s, this number had increased to nearly 75 %[150]; and by the mid-2000s, between 80 % and 90 % of Haiti's schools were privately run, with many charging tuition fees that represented a significant entry barrier for low-income students. The Ministry of Education's census reported that more than three-quarters of these private schools did not have the required license.[151] Of the population of enrolled primary school students, 30 % did not stay beyond third grade and 60 % abandoned schooling by sixth grade.[152] Despite the evident challenges to primary school access, however, there remained "a strong social demand for education among Haitian

[146]Adams, Anda, and Rebecca Winthrop, The Re-foundation of Haiti: Building a strong base with education. *Brookings Institution website*, March 23, 2010, http://www.brookings.edu/research/opinions/2010/03/23-haiti-education-winthrop#_ftnref6. Accessed 30 March 2013.

[147]"National Constitutional Provisions – Haiti," Right to Education Project website, http://www.right-to-education.org/country-node/349/country-constitutional. Accessed 31 March 2013.

[148]UNICEF, Division of Policy and Practice, Statistics and Monitoring Section, "Education Statistics: Haiti," May, 2008, http://www.childinfo.org/files/LAC_Haiti.pdf. Accessed 30 March 2013.

[149]Woolf, Laurence. Education in Haiti: The way forward. Inter-American Dialogue website, September 26, 2008, http://thedialogue.org/page.cfm?pageID=32&pubID=1605&s=Education%20in%20Haiti:%20the%20way%20forward. Accessed 30 March 2013.

[150]Salmi, Jamil. Equity and quality in private education: The Haiti paradox. The World Bank, LCSDH Paper Series no. 18, May 1998, http://www.hopeforhaiti.com/uploads/world_bank.pdf. Accessed 30 March 2013.

[151]Lunde, Henriette. Youth and education in Haiti: Disincentives, vulnerabilities and constraints. *Fafo*, 2008, http://www.fafo.no/pub/rapp/10070/10070.pdf. Accessed 29 March 2013.

[152]"UNICEF Humanitarian Action: Haiti in 2008," UNICEF Humanitarian Action Report 2008, http://www.unicef.org/har08/files/har08_Haiti_countrychapter.pdf. Accessed 29 March 2013.

families as evidenced by the high percentage of household income spent on schooling – approximately 15 % per child."[153]

In 2007, Fafo, a Norwegian nonprofit organization, conducted an extensive qualitative research study in which it interviewed Haitian families with school-age children to better understand the incentives and disincentives to education access.[154] The study documented families struggling to raise sufficient money to send their children to school, and reported high barriers that interfered with children's ability to progress from one grade to the next. Some of the major issues identified by the study were cost, the constraints of the rural agricultural economy, the quality of teaching, and poor physical infrastructure.

The Fafo study reported that while the mandated cost of public school was set at $2.50 per year, families were also required to pay for their children to take the state-mandated exams at the end of fourth, seventh, and ninth grades. Children frequently dropped out because families were unable to pay these fees or because they failed the exams and became discouraged over the prospect of repeating the same grade. Public schools were overcrowded, and though prohibited from dismissing students because of low performance, the schools frequently did so due to capacity issues. While students were required to have promotion exams at the end of fourth, seventh, and ninth grades, many schools administered tests more frequently, requiring that parents pay test fees, which resulted in the cycle of repeated grades noted above. Elite private schools for students from high-income families could be found in the major cities, but there also existed so-called "lottery schools" on most city street corners. The nickname for these lower-quality private schools was derived from both the small lottery stands on many street corners and the assumption that children had about the same probability of graduating as they did of winning the national lottery.

The quality of teachers and instruction also contributed to the challenges facing the Haitian education system prior to the earthquake. The majority of teachers lacked training, with most having only completed a few more grades than the students whom they were teaching.[155] During the Duvalier era, many educated Haitians left for the United States, Canada, and Europe. The difficulty of training and retaining qualified teachers, especially in rural areas where pay rates were lower, was one of the biggest challenges the Fafo report identified in improving the education sector.[156] NGOs such as the United Nations Educational Scientific and Cultural Organization (UNESCO) provided teacher training, but reported that once teachers become qualified for better paying positions, they often relocate to cities and better opportunities than teaching.[157]

---

[153] United States Agency for International Development, Haiti: Education Overview, 2006, http://web.archive.org/web/20071017050613/http://www.usaid.gov/ht/education.htm. Accessed 30 March 2013.

[154] "About Fafo," Fafo website, http://www.fafo.no/english/hist/abo-Fafo.html. Accessed 15 June 2012, and Lunde.

[155] Lunde.

[156] Lunde.

[157] "UNESCO's Education Priorities in Haiti," UNESCO website, http://www.unesco.org/new/en/education/themes/planning-and-managing-education/policy-and-planning/single-view/news/unescos_education_priorities_in_haiti/. Accessed 30 March 2013.

The Fafo study found that obstacles to access to basic education were particularly steep in rural areas, where the density of schools was much lower than in urban areas, and the agricultural economy did not generate enough income for many families to cover the cost of attending a local school. During the rainy season, poor infrastructure contributed to attendance problems, given that some students, especially those in higher grades, had to walk for up to two and a half hours to get to a school. Suffering scarce resources, families might select the oldest or the brightest from among their children to send to school, but issues such as fees, lack of shoes, or requirements to work in the fields resulted in few children completing fourth grade.[158] In addition, many rural teachers stated that they had to find supplemental work in agriculture to make a living, reducing their teaching availability during harvest season.[159] The challenges to school access increased for upper grade levels. More than a quarter of rural households did not have an upper-grade-level school within 15 km, and therefore, as the 2008 study stated, "While more than 40 % of the children in and around Port-au-Prince continue to seventh grade, less than 10 % of the children in rural areas do."[160]

The Haitian government itself recognized that the overall quality of education was often inadequate or lacking in relevance in the areas identified by Fafo's research.[161] A study by the U.S. Agency for Economic Development (USAID) and the Haitian Institute for Education,[162] as well as a strategic plan developed by the Haitian Educational Ministry,[163] highlighted the aforementioned issues, but they also described problems with the content and delivery methods predominant in Haitian education. Many Haitian schools were using methods that had not changed in 50 years. There was an emphasis on rote learning and regurgitation that had been shown to discourage the development of strong critical thinking and analytical skills.[164] Teachers lacked tools, books, and the ability to accommodate different modes of learning, such as the use of experiential and applied learning strategies. In 2009, fewer than 40 % of Haitians had access to electricity and only 8 % used the Internet,[165] limiting the resources available in many homes and classrooms.

Language skills also constrained academic success for many Haitians. Though Haitian national exams were administered in French, teachers were often Creole

---

[158] Lunde.

[159] Lunde.

[160] Lunde.

[161] Lunde.

[162] The American Institutes for Research and L'Institut Haïtien de Formation en Sciences de l'éducation (IHFOSED), "Les institutions de formation initiale des enseignants du fondamental et du secondaire en Haïti," August 2007, http://pdf.usaid.gov/pdf_docs/PNADK047.pdf. Accessed 30 March 2013.

[163] Ministère de l'Éducation Nationale et de la Formation Professionnelle (MENFP), "Bulletin d'information du Ministère de l'Éducation Nationale et de la Formation Professionnelle," March 2012, http://www.eduhaiti.gouv.ht/PDFs/journal_menfp.pdf. Accessed 30 March 2013.

[164] Lunde.

[165] World Bank, Data by Country: Haiti, http://data.worldbank.org/country/haiti#cp_wdi. Accessed 31 March 2013.

speakers who were poorly educated in French. Haitian Creole was a combination of seventeenth-century French and a variety of African dialects. Creole became an official language as a result of the 1987 revisions to the Haitian Constitution, but its orthography was not formalized until 1979, and it remained far from standardized. Consequently, the vast majority of people in Haiti spoke Creole, but few wrote or published formally in the language. French was the official language of government, the courts, street signs, and all educational testing, despite the fact that many people, particularly in rural areas, neither spoke nor wrote proficiently in French.[166] Both Creole and French were considered official languages, but they were unequal in status. For the most part, French was the language of the elite in Haiti, and English was increasingly the language of global commerce spoken by NGO leaders and high-level government officials. Creole was the language of the majority of low-income Haitians. According to some scholars, the exclusive use of French in the classroom resulted in socioeconomic discrimination against Creole speakers who faced a high bar to educational access as a result of French-only educational practices.[167]

Strike and Aftermath of the 2010 Quake

The January 2010 earthquake devastated the already-fragile Haitian education system. Approximately 38,000 students, 1,347 teachers, and 180 school system employees were killed. More than 4,000 school buildings were destroyed, as well as the Ministry of Education building itself. At least half of the country's 15,000 primary schools and 1,500 secondary schools were badly damaged. First Lady Elizabeth Préval stated in a March 2010 speech at George Washington University that the quake and its aftermath was a "nightmare" that left at least 1.5 million students without access to education.[168] Other estimates placed the number of children displaced from schools at 2 million. First Lady Préval voiced a desire to go beyond restoring Haiti's schools to the conditions prior to the disaster:

'The government should guarantee free education to all the children enrolled in the schools,' Préval said. 'This will be our first demonstration for the dignity and respect for the Haitian community, and the pain that has been brewing since January 12. I understand that many schools have been damaged from the earthquake, but I urge the government to do whatever necessary to bring children back to school as soon as possible.'[169]

In May 2010, President Préval "gave the Inter-American Development Bank (IDB), [Haiti's largest multilateral donor] a mandate to work together with Haiti's

---

[166]Dash.

[167]Luzincourt, Ketty, and Jennifer Gulbrandson. 2010. Education and conflict in Haiti: Rebuilding the education sector after the 2010 earthquake. *United States Institute of Peace Special Report 245*, 2010, http://www.usip.org/files/resources/sr245.pdf. Accessed 31 March 2013.

[168]Cahn, Emily. Haitian first lady seeks change Amid reconstruction. *GW Hatchet*, March 11, 2010, http://www.gwhatchet.com/2010/03/11/haitian-first-lady-seeks-change-amid-restoration/. Accessed 31 March 2013.

[169]Cahn.

Ministry of Education and National Education Commission to prepare a major reform of the Haitian education system."[170] According to the plan, Haiti's private schools would remain privately run, but would be publicly subsidized with support from several international organizations partnering with the IDB to provide grants totaling $500 million in the first 5 years.[171] Private school funding would be contingent upon schools meeting certification requirements that would increase in stringency over time. Also included in the ambitious plan was a modernization of the curriculum, training programs for the country's teachers, the construction of at least 625 new primary schools, a tripling of the number of public schools. Upon election in 2011, Martelly pledged to continue support of the education reform agenda.

In the 2 years after the earthquake, a vast array of international and domestic organizations, as well as the IADB-led partnership and the Haitian government, had worked to improve education conditions. The Ministry of Education completed its first census in nearly a decade, reporting that by mid-2011, Haiti had 16,072 schools – a significant increase from prequake estimates – 44 % of which were located in urban areas and 56 % of which were in rural areas.[172] Of the total number of current schools, 88 % were privately run and 12 % were public. There were now more children in school than before the earthquake.[173]

Progress had been slow, however. On issues of school health, UNICEF reported that the most pressing issue facing the Ministry of Education was "the multiplicity of actors with different and sometimes contradictory points of view. Scattered interventions were characterized by duplication and wasting money."[174] Infrastructure remained a significant obstacle. Electricity was a greater challenge in 2012 than it was a year earlier.[175] Two years after the earthquake, a World Economic Forum (2012) report concluded that Haiti's information technology infrastructure was the weakest of the 142 countries included in its study. Other challenges to implementation of education reform included a slow rate of pledged donor funds reaching Haiti, party opposition within the Haitian legislature, and limited coordination between state and local governments and between the state and civil society.[176]

---

[170]"Haiti Gives IDB Mandate to Promote Major Education Reform," Inter-American Development Bank (IDB) news release, May 15, 2010, http://www.iadb.org/en/news/news-releases/2010-05-15/haiti-gives-idb-mandate-to-promote-major-education-reform,7150.html (accessed March 31, 2013).

[171]"Haiti's Schools," *New York Times*, August 17, 2010.

[172]http://www.eduhaiti.gouv.ht/PDFs/journal_menfp.pdf.

[173]Press Conference by Deputy Special Representative of Secretary-General for Haiti, United Nations website, November 29, 2011. http://www.un.org/News/briefings/docs/2011/111129_Haiti.doc.htm. Accessed 31 March 2013.

[174]"UNESCO in action: Working together for Haiti," UNESCO Bureau of Field Coordination report, 2010. http://unesdoc.unesco.org/images/0019/001905/190539e.pdf. Accessed 31 March 2013.

[175]"The ease of doing business in Haiti," The World Bank and International Finance Corporation (IFC) website, 2012, http://www.doingbusiness.org/data/exploreeconomies/haiti. Accessed 31 March 2013.

[176]Cohen, Marc J. Haiti – The slow road to reconstruction: Two years after the earthquake. Oxfam International website, January 10, 2012, http://www.oxfam.org/en/policy/haiti-slow-road-reconstruction. Accessed 9 Nov 2012.

Research by the World Bank asserted that each additional year of education had the potential to increase an individual's income by 10 %. In the aggregate, good education offered to the entire population could translate into a 1 %-per-year increase in Gross Domestic Product (GDP). The World Bank's study extrapolated that "[o]ver a 75-year horizon, a 20-year reform yields a real GDP that is 36 % higher than would be with no change in educational quality."[177] The link between a good education system and a country's prosperity could not be overemphasized. While there were many opinions on how to improve educational results in Haiti, there was little doubt that quality education was a key to economic growth and prosperity.

L'Ecole de Choix in Mirebalais, Haiti[178]

In 2006, a group of former students from Mirebalais established the Foundation for the Technological and Economic Advancement of Mirebalais (FATEM), a tax-exempt nonprofit (501c3) organization. FATEM's mission was "to be a catalyst for sustainable change to benefit the residents of Mirebalais and surrounding areas." Its projects included the rebuilding of schools, hospitals, libraries, and infrastructure to support Mirebalais's 75,000 residents, with the aim of erecting these structures to much higher, more sustainable specifications.[179] FATEM established Choix in 2011 after it was determined that the most significant area of need in Mirebalais postquake was sustainable elementary education for children in conditions of extreme poverty.

Laura Pincus Hartman was the Vincent de Paul Professor of Business Ethics in DePaul University's Department of Management as well as special assistant to the president for Haiti initiatives. As part of its mission, DePaul University had long supported poverty alleviation throughout the world and had a distinct focus in Haiti; but activities increased exponentially after the 2010 earthquake. Hartman had spent a considerable amount of time in Haiti over the previous 5 years doing work for DePaul. When it appeared that Choix was becoming too large a project for FATEM to manage with all of its other activities, Hartman established the School of Choice Education Organization, an Illinois nonprofit corporation that took over management of Choix. Interestingly, the seed money for building the

---

[177] Hanushek, Eric A., and Ludger Wössmann, The role of education quality in economic growth. World Bank Policy Research Working Paper 4122, February 2007, http://www-wds.worldbank.org/external/default/WDSContentServer/IW3P/IB/2007/01/29/000016406_20070129113447/Rendered/PDF/wps4122.pdf. Accessed 31 March 2013.

[178] Mirebalais was a rural commune in Haiti's Centre Department, located approximately 60 km (37.2 mi.) northeast of Port-au-Prince, the capital. Despite the close proximity, the drive could range from 90 min to 4 h, depending on traffic and weather.

[179] "About FATEM," FATEM website, http://www.fatem.org/about-fatem. Accessed 31 March 2013.

school, which opened its doors in October 2011, came from the players of online games. Mark Pincus, Hartman's brother, was the founder of Zynga and the visionary behind Zynga.org, which provided gamers with the opportunity to buy virtual goods while playing online games such as *Farmville* and *Mafia Wars*. The proceeds from these virtual goods were contributed through Zynga.org to NGO partners such as FATEM, as well as the World Food Programme and Save the Children. Since the inception of Zynga.org in 2009, gamers had contributed more than $10 million, $3 million of which went to Haiti to support a variety of projects, including l'Ecole de Choix.[180]

Hartman's vision was to build a school that provided a quality education for children living in extreme poverty – a school with a mission not only to change their lives and those of their families, but also to deliver a leadership-based education that motivated those children in turn to change the lives of their fellow Haitians. The school's curriculum was focused on developing leadership and communication skills, and with the goal of building these skills while affirming "[the students'] individual dignity through the choices they make." See Exhibit 2 for Choix Mission and Values. The Choix education was based on the sense that education was a right, not a privilege, but one that was coupled with a "responsibility to ourselves, to our communities and to our society."[181] The school's founding values highlight role modeling, responsibility, inclusiveness and respectfulness, as well as fun. Initially serving prekindergarten to fourth grade students, the school was committed to following its 183 students through to the twelfth grade. As the oldest students graduated, new prekindergarten students were admitted, allowing the school to maintain six grade levels at all times and a constant student body size until funding for additional grade levels was secured.

Choix's administrators recognized that good nutrition was important in learning, and the school purchased its meals through the United Nations World Food Programme so the children could be fed while at school. An additional major aspect of the Choix strategy was the decision to employ only qualified teachers (university degree and teacher certification) and to pay them a living wage. Choix had an ambitious program to provide students with a trilingual education in Creole, French, and English. The choices that Choix had made in order to develop and launch a school with a viable chance of success in making a difference in the lives of rural youth in Haiti made Choix a promising partner for Intel's IESC program. When viewed in the context of Haiti's history and its current educational system or, more accurately, lack thereof, Choix's mission stood out as a fine-tuned effort to address directly some of the most deeply entrenched barriers to opportunity that faced children in rural Haiti in the twenty-first century.

---

[180]"About Zynga's Haiti initiatives," Zynga Inc. website, http://www.zynga.org/initiatives/haiti.php. Accessed 15 May 2012.

[181]"Vision and values," L'Ecole de Choix website, https://ecoledechoix.org/values. Accessed 1 May 2012.

John Cartwright's Visits to Haiti's l'Ecole de Choix

In many ways, Cartwright was uniquely positioned to meet the unexpected challenges facing his IESC team upon their arrival at Choix in September 2011 to provide support for the school's launch. Cartwright grew up on a farm in California, becoming the man of the house at only 13 years old, when his father died. He and his sister helped his mother to run the farm, and Cartwright became a jack-of-all-trades. He built his own house and one for his mother in a rural area of California. He learned a lot about plumbing from his father-in-law, who ran a large plumbing business on Long Island in New York. Cartwright was humble, yet eager to share his skills. He exemplified Intel's can-do culture and spoke with pride about his experience first as a green-badge (contractor) in 1992, then a blue-badge (full-time employee) in 1997. In 2012, he was a full-time IT manager in the company's Supply Network Capability.

Cartwright's application to join the IESC team that would be deployed in fall of 2011 was inspired by his 17-year-old son, who gave up a significant amount of an earlier summer vacation volunteering at an Easter Seals camp for seriously disabled children. He was excited to be selected for his first choice, traveling to Haiti to support the installation of Intel Classmate PCs in time for the opening of Choix in October 2011. Cartwright got to know his five colleagues over the phone during their 4 weeks of preparation for the trip. They came from various parts of the United States, Costa Rica, and Ireland. All had worked in other countries, and Cartwright was the only team member who did not speak French. Cartwright eventually referred to one team member, Jean-Marie Erie, as his "adopted brother." Erie had a doctorate in materials science and engineering from the University of Florida. As part of his job at Intel Arizona, he worked on the packaging for the Atom chip, which was the microprocessor component driving the Intel Classmate PC.

Born in New York City, Erie moved to Haiti with his parents and lived there from 1982 to 1998 before returning to the United States and Canada to complete high school and university. Didier da Costa worked for Intel in Ireland, but she loved languages and was of French and Portuguese descent. Luke Filose, a former Peace Corps volunteer, had worked in 10 different African countries. Filose was brought into EMPG by Clugage in 2011 to manage the IESC program, so he was assigned to the Haiti team as a teacher trainer to get firsthand experience on the program that he later administered. Silvia Jenkins had worked for Intel in Costa Rica for 14 years, and this was to be her first trip to Haiti. Michael Wiggins had been with Intel for 3 years, and worked in human resources in Arizona, but as an international business major at the University of Illinois, he had lived in Paris and Montpelier, France. He also had experience volunteering in Mexico and in the Czech Republic.

Cartwright's preparatory work before traveling to Haiti involved testing the Waterford Early Learning software on a classroom server manufactured by Critical Links that would be used to support learning, networking, and administration. The testing was critical because this combination of hardware and software from allied vendors had not been used before. He reported having had to "beg, borrow, and steal lab space" to perform his pretravel tests, but that was actually the easy part of the installation effort at Choix.

Cartwright carried the server into Haiti in his luggage, and his colleague Filose took nearly half a mile of Ethernet cable in two 30-lb boxes, leveraging frequent flyer status accumulated from his travels to Africa. The Intel IESC team landed in Port-au-Prince, Haiti, and was greeted by the marching band that serenaded arrivals at the earthquake-damaged airport, which was being housed in a converted warehouse. When Cartwright and his colleagues arrived in Mirebalais to begin installation and training at Choix, however, the school's building was still under construction and there was not yet electricity. Cartwright noted, "It could only be described as a muddy mess." The unexpected construction delay became a blessing in disguise, however, providing Cartwright with an opportunity to discover that the contractor was using the wrong kind of power supply, and that the wiring was being put in backwards. Cartwright's experience in building his own house came in handy, and he and Erie became consultants to the local construction crew. Erie relayed Cartwright's advice on basic wiring to the crew. The crew appeared to follow Cartwright's suggestions, but Erie told him that they still bad-mouthed him behind his back, evincing the class struggles common in Haiti.

The four other members of the team were initially idle, since they needed power to begin training the teachers. They quickly adapted, however, and moved the teacher training to a hotel in town. Cartwright and Erie stayed on-site getting the power supply, a cooling system for the server, and then an antenna for the Internet installed during the first week. Demonstrating their can-do attitude and creativity within the cost limits of IESC deployments, Cartwright and Erie hired local workers to dig trenches and were then able to install the Internet wiring themselves. The result was a wired network installation with a total cost of $300, far less than the $3,000 quoted by a local vendor for this service. The job was not easy, however: Cartwright sent Choix's principal to Haiti's best hardware store in the capital city for a voltage regulator to protect the equipment from power surges, but the regulator the principal returned with was dead on arrival. Unfortunately, Cartwright noted, it was not rare in Haiti to discover that ostensibly new products purchased off the shelf were actually used or damaged products that had been packaged to appear new. Cartwright added, "I don't think that [the principal] ever got his $100 back." Somehow, the team adapted to each challenge in its path, finding alternatives when its original plans were thwarted by unexpected developments.

While all these electrical issues were transpiring, parents kept dropping by, begging for their child's admission to the fancy new school. It broke Cartwright's heart when he sent them to the school principal, since he knew that all 183 students had already been selected. The policy at Choix was to have no more than 30 students in each of the six grades, to ensure that all had the best chance possible to learn. Cartwright observed, however, that the principal apparently did not do a good job of "firewalling the classroom size," and found that he was no longer there when Cartwright traveled to Haiti for a second visit in March 2012. There was not yet security on-site, so every night Cartwright and his teammates carried the server, Classmate PCs, and other equipment (approximately 45 boxes) back to their hotel where it would be safe. Cartwright lost 20 lb during the 2-week trip. He noted, "This is Intel; we do whatever it takes to delight our customers," echoing the company's mission statement to "[d]elight our customers, employees, and shareholders by relentlessly delivering the platform and technology advancements that become essential to the way we work and live."[182] To the IESC team, a customer in Mirebalais, Haiti, was just as important as a multimillion-dollar client on Wall Street in the United States. Indeed, central to the IESC philosophy was the tenet that its local education partners were not – and were not to be treated as – the recipients of charitable aid, but were Intel customers and deserving of full-service customer care.

The 2nd week of Cartwright's initial visit was much more exciting, since the building was completed and the teachers, school administrators, and students arrived for further training in the Choix computer lab. In contrast to most schools in Haiti, where teachers had little more than a sixth grade education themselves, the teachers and administrators at Choix were highly educated and most were trilingual, speaking and teaching in English, French, and Creole. By the time the students arrived, the school was Wi-Fi enabled, and the IESC crew had provided initial training to the teachers and all 183 Choix students. The teachers were equipped with computers and had basic training on how to support the students.

The Intel team members returned to their respective home countries, but the festival and dedication ceremonies in early December were an exciting display of what was possible when talented people worked together with hopes for a better Haiti. Just a few months after the school opened, it posted YouTube videos of the fourth graders speaking English and telling the world about their hopes and dreams. Each child chimed in with his or her aspirations, "I want to be a nurse, a teacher…a doctor…a police woman…a model, an architect, an engineer, an agronomist."[183] L'Ecole de Choix was under way.

The Postmortem and John Cartwright's Second Trip to Haiti

The team's postmortem report highlighted the formidable accomplishments of its 2 weeks in Haiti, including the installation of 35 Classmate PCs and eight teacher laptops, along with training for six teachers, five administrators, and 183 students. With no complaints about many unexpected challenges, it also included a number of recommendations for follow-up trips by future IESC teams, such as more training for the lab director and written policies for maintaining the equipment. In addition to further IESC deployments to bring Choix to the point of "graduating" to sustainability, the school needed more local support. Arrangements were made for getting additional direct support from Critical Links and Waterford Institute.

[182] "Quality and reliability – Intel executive perspectives," Intel Corporation website, http://www.intel.com/content/www/us/en/quality/executive-perspectives.html. Accessed 3 April 2013.

[183] "Dreams and aspirations of our Choix Fourth Graders," l'Ecole de Choix video, 1:02, December 16, 2011, https://www.ecoledechoix.org/content/videos#dreams. Accessed 31 March 2013.

The postmortem report included pictures of the students and teachers working on the new equipment, and it was clear that these students were excited about the opportunity being afforded to them at Choix. As Filose highlighted in his posttrip blog post, "In a country where less than one in three children finishes the sixth grade, Choix was an ambitious project addressing an enormous need. And the excitement was palpable. Before our classes, students wrapped around the building waiting to be admitted into the classroom, and other children and parents crowded outside the windows to catch a glimpse."[184] When Filose thanked several of the Intel Learning Series alliance members who provided discounted or free software, the impressive list included BrainPOP, British Council, LEGO, PASCO, and Skoool. com, in addition to the Critical Links education appliance. The software working seamlessly on these systems was critical to the English language immersion at Choix. Filose reported that by the end of the week the young children were "rapping" the English alphabet.[185]

The second trip to Choix was slated for March of 2012. Intel usually sent a completely new team of volunteers for follow-up projects to selected sites, but in the case of Choix, Cartwright was able to get his division to support him for a second trip. He actually used some of his Intel-provided sabbatical time, but his preparatory time in Oregon was fully supported by his coworkers and by Cartwright's willingness to go the extra mile. Clugage and Filose were now wondering whether Cartwright had created an innovative model for the future, with the overlap of one team member to facilitate project continuity.

Cartwright's second group of four teammates traveled from Amsterdam, California, Massachusetts, and New Mexico, and represented a similarly diverse global perspective. Yvonne Ntem, from Folsom, California, was born in Ghana and raised in Ivory Coast, and Nancy Bardel, a process engineer from New Mexico, was born and brought up in Port-au-Prince, Haiti. Anne Mieke Driessen traveled to Haiti from Amsterdam but did business development in education for the Benelux countries (Belgium, Netherlands, Luxemburg) and had also lived in Germany and the United Kingdom. Cartwright reported that one of the major learning experiences on these projects was that one was not only working with people from all over the world and learning to work with cultural differences but that the typical team stages of forming, storming, norming, performing, and adjourning[186] transpired extremely efficiently. Everyone walked away with new friendships within Intel as well as a deep sense of how privileged they were to have been members of the Intel Education Service Corps. Despite the exhausting work, they found that their participation re-energized their commitment to Intel, and often resulted in becoming engaged in additional volunteer work in education.

---

[184]Filose, Luke. IESC Haiti: Intel and Zynga give kids permission to learn. Intel Corporation website, October 19, 2011, http://blogs.intel.com/learningseries/2011/10/19/iesc_haiti_intel_and_zynga_giv/. Accessed 31 March 2013.

[185]Filose.

[186]Tuckman, Bruce W., and Mary Ann C. Jensen. 2010. Stages of small-group development revisited. *Group Facilitation: A Research and Applications Journal* 10 (2010): 43–48.

Cartwright described the second trip as "less geeky and more student-focused." The Critical Links server worked from October 2011 to February 2012, but the team learned during the trip preparation that it was no longer working properly. The technical tasks included resuscitating, rebuilding, and restoring the Critical Links EA100 server; reimaging the Classmate PCs; providing technical services for the teacher laptops; upgrading the wireless and wired networks, including printers and scanners; upgrading the Waterford Early Learning (WEL) software; installing eBeam interactive whiteboards; and retraining on educational software and content including Waterford, Mythware, BrainPOP, Khan Academy, LEGO, and PASCO.

Cartwright brought a server assembled from various components that he gathered through contacts at Intel. Cartwright built the system the prior month to test if Waterford's latest software release would work on a new version of the Critical Links EA100 platform. The server he built was nearly identical to the latest EA100 with a few modifications to enhance the system performance. After validating that the new server ran better than the previous version, Cartwright packed up the server as the temporary standby for the failed Choix system and the parts needed to also upgrade the failed system. The new box became the school's network and Waterford application server for the first week while the team repaired and then completely rebuilt the school's EA100. The team also fixed the power supply issues that caused the server failure, replaced broken headsets and cables, and performed basic maintenance, such as cleaning out the computer closet. They extended the wireless network to the classrooms and administration building to improve connectivity for everyone. Company representatives from PASCO also joined Choix via Skype, as they wanted to share their products to support the school's educational mission. PASCO sold digital microscopes, probes, and supporting software that could be connected to the Classmate PCs in support of life, earth, and physical sciences courses.

Most important, the IESC team spent time working in the lab with students, setting up a disciplined way for the students to come into the lab in small groups and sign in by selecting their picture on the lab's Classmate PCs. The team saw that, since the server went down, the lab time had become unstructured and that the equipment had been not been fully utilized. With the server repaired and some new procedures put in place, each student could log in and be led directly to where he or she had been working in the previous session. Teachers were kept apprised of student work on their systems, so they knew with what skills individual students might be struggling and could provide additional help. Cartwright reported that the "change [between the first and second IESC team visits] was like night and day, and I am optimistic that the new systems (both mechanical and human) will remain in place."[187]

The school was only using a fraction of the computers' capabilities, but Cartwright was excited about future possibilities. He already had ideas for how to streamline and improve the server installation process in the future to avoid some of the

---

[187] Case writer telephone interview with John Cartwright, May 17, 2012.

difficulties he had to overcome at Choix. Still, Cartwright acknowledged that he had "no perfect answer" to the question of how Choix's server would be supported if new problems arose moving forward. Though a local IT company had committed support, its ability to support a school hours away from the capital city had proven to be limited. Ideally, Choix would eventually be able to sustain its technology without Intel's support, but that was not the case in 2012.

Cartwright had been changed by his trips to Haiti. After spending the previous 15 years in Intel's IT organization, he was now exploring a position with Intel's EMPG organization to do more to help underserved children by providing them with educational opportunities they did not have. He was already making plans with his wife to perform school volunteer work in emerging markets after he retired from Intel. These plans were not immediate, though, as he had two children in college, and his third child would soon be a freshman in college. While retirement and full-time classroom volunteering might be years away, Cartwright was actively preparing for that next adventure. While on his second sabbatical at Intel during the summer of 2012, Cartwright and his family spent 6 weeks volunteering at Choix and various schools in Kenya. Cartwright was able to learn from the educational opportunities the students had at Choix and, through reengineering the application and hardware system, deliver similar reading, math, and science programs to schools in Kenya with less infrastructure than was needed at Choix. For Cartwright, this appeared to be just the beginning of delivering opportunity through education to children who had so few opportunities in their lives.

What Next for Intel's Partnership with l'Ecole de Choix?

In 2012, Choix celebrated its first anniversary. Thanks to many supporters, including Hartman and the Intel team, it was built and sustained for its first year, but questions remained. Had the IESC Choix project achieved success in its mission? Would Choix be able to sustain its mission in the midst of the current economic climate in Haiti? Would it prove sustainable for Intel and its education partners to support technology in a rural part of Haiti?

Since its creation in 2009, IESC had proven its ability to provide a high level of service to its NGO clients and create meaningful experiences for Intel's employee volunteers. Two major questions remained in Filose's mind. The first concerned the sustainability of the model from an alliance and support perspective. The second involved the scalability of a skills-based volunteer program.

In the developing world, it was all too common to encounter the problem of "white elephant" projects, in which well-meaning NGOs, development agencies, and, often, corporations contributed resources to projects that were not adequately supported or properly designed from the outset. IESC pointed out that its focus on sustainability and its program pillars – including the requirement that NGOs purchase the equipment and the provision of follow-up support teams – were intended to avoid such problems.

IESC deployments were set up as "lighthouse projects," in the sense of acting as beacons that worked to draw the attention of allied companies to the viability of integrating social responsibility and business goals in the area of education. Intel Learning Series alliance members were asked to make donations and give preferential pricing on their products and services to make them affordable to NGOs or as a promotional deal to increase visibility for its solution. For example, in 2011, LEGO Education donated 50 of its WeDo Robotics kits for deployment on IESC's 2012 projects. These kits retailed for roughly $240 each, making this a donation valued at $12,000.

"Is LEGO getting its money's worth?" Filose asked himself.[188] He did his utmost to promote their generosity in blogs and Twitter messages about the projects, but he worried that at some point, alliance members would want to see follow-on sales in order to continue making such donations. "One thing I've learned at Intel is that companies have a limited ability to sustain donations."

Another aspect to sustainability that IESC and its NGO clients had to consider was the ability to provide technical and pedagogical support to make the projects successful over the long term. The technical skills needed to fix problems ranging from crashed servers to virus-infected PCs were not easy to find in rural parts of the developing world. While Intel's alliance partners were typically generous with their time in supporting technical issues, there was a practical limit to what one could do from thousands of miles away. Additionally, from a pedagogical perspective, Intel fully understood the challenge placed on teachers when computers were put into their hands and the hands of their students. Filose thought about how he could better prepare IESC volunteers to train teachers during their assignments, and how intermediary check-ins through Skype, e-mail, and cell phones could help teachers during the 6–12-month gaps between IESC team visits.

With regards to Filose's second challenge of scalability, he noted that he was currently running IESC as something of a "one-man band" (supplemented by volunteer support from IESC alumni), screening applications, interviewing candidates, and training and mentoring volunteers to prepare them for their assignments. But increasing interest from business units, which could sponsor a team-building experience for their employees at a cost of only $15,000 to $20,000 per team, resulted in an increasing number of projects. When Clugage began the program, IESC ran a biannual cycle of five teams per round. When Filose joined in 2011, there were six teams, and in the second half of 2012, he managed eight projects.

"I probably spend about 20 h on each project over a two-month period from the discussion of the scope of work with the NGO to the debrief after the team returns," Filose said. The work included many activities, such as updating the volunteer application, behavioral interview guidance, and scoring rubric; creating and

---

[188] Case writer telephone interview with Luke Filose, November 2, 2012. All subsequent quotations attributed to Filose, unless otherwise noted, derive from this interview.

managing interview committees; updating and delivering virtual and face-to-face training; and responding to volunteer queries from the field. "The extra 40 h from two projects may not sound like a lot over two months," Filose said, "but IESC is just part of my job." He also managed other engagements with NGOs that were not always related to IESC assignments.

Intel's employee base contributed 1.1 million volunteer hours in 2011.[189] IESC volunteers contributed an average of 130 h during their preparatory, deployment, and postmortem phases of the project, meaning that in 2011, the 55 IESC volunteers contributed roughly 7,150 h, or half of 1 % of Intel's total volunteer hours.

Was this the best use of a full-time Intel staff member with an MBA (like Clugage, Filose went to Berkeley)? Filose thought so. "While IESC and other skills-based volunteer programs may never scale up to the level of our other volunteerism programs, there's an incredibly powerful effect on motivating other employees at Intel." In effect, Intel leveraged IESC as a kind of "special forces" volunteering effort. In an update to employees in July 2012, Intel Director of Worldwide Sales Greg Pearson highlighted IESC as one of Intel's best and most promising initiatives. Employees returned from their assignments to blog, hold brown-bag lunches to share their stories, and convince their colleagues to apply for the program or simply volunteer in their local communities.

In 2012, IESC had also proven its ability to support larger education technology deployments managed by ministries of education, in addition to its NGO partners. These deployments were of high strategic business value to Intel because, in many countries outside of the United States, schools were equipped with technology through a centralized process controlled by the national government.

In November of 2012, the IESC experimented with a new model of support, sending teams to support Ministry of Education deployments consisting of approximately 1,000 Classmate PCs in more than 20 schools in Namibia and the Seychelles. In both cases Intel and its partners had already installed the equipment and delivered professional development training, including the Intel Teach program to teachers. At that point, IESC was then invited to visit a subset of model schools to work closely with teachers to practice their skills, develop additional techniques for employing technology in the classroom, and then share those skills with teachers from the other schools in the deployment.

Filose saw this model expanding over time, due to its ability to scale indirectly to more teachers and students than deployments focused on a single school. In addition, this model excited Intel's business development managers around the globe, who saw IESC as a way to provide extra support to their most valued customers within ministries of education.

Could Intel continue to expand this unique program given limited human resources and the challenges of bridging the gaps between the first world and the realities of countries such as Haiti?

---

[189]Intel Corporation Corporate Responsibility Report, 2010, http://csrreportbuilder.intel.com/PDFFiles/CSR_2010_Full-Report.pdf#page=58 . Accessed 31 March 2013.

Exhibit 1: Transforming Education in Rural Haiti: Intel and L'Ecole De Choix

IESC Projects: Countries and Clients

Country	Clients
Bangladesh	Save the Children, BRAC
Bolivia	Save the Children
Ecuador	Fundación Nobis
Egypt	CARE
Ethiopia	Worldwide Orphans Foundation
Haiti	L'Ecole de Choix
India	CARE
Kenya	Orphans Overseas, Free The Children, Rusinga Island Trust
Namibia	Ministry of Education
Rwanda	World Vision
Senegal	World Vision
Seychelles	Ministry of Education, University of Seychelles
Tanzania	World Vision
Uganda	BRAC, Maendeleo Foundation
Vietnam	Orphan Impact
Zambia	World Vision

Source: Intel Corporation.

Exhibit 2: Transforming Education in Rural Haiti: Intel and L'Ecole De Choix

L'Ecole de Choix – The School of Choice
    Vision and Values

Our Vision

L'Ecole de Choix is anchored by the principle that a quality education provides individuals with the fundamental tools to affirm individual dignity through the choices they make. Choice and autonomy grant us our dignity; and it is that dignity that assures each of us the very heart of our humanity, both in the way we are responsible for ourselves, as well as for the communities in which we live. It is in this way that education becomes the pathway to our humanity.

Our Values

L'Ecole de Choix is located in Haiti, managed by both a Haiti-based and U.S.-based team, with advisors representing cultures from around the world. Integrated into the culture of Choix are those values that represent the most effective traits from all of our educational environments. These values include vital civic ideals such as leadership, responsibility, inclusivity, and respect for one another and for education as a whole.

Each Member of The Choix Community is a *Leadership Model* for each Other

As the Choix facility is designed to be a model from a physical perspective, the behavior of each individual within our community is a model for each other. We act in ways that would be acceptable if everyone in the Choix community acted in that manner. One of the tenets of the Choix facility is its mixed age, cross-program and inter-generational environment. The adults and older students shall always feel the burden of serving as a role model while the younger students shall always feel the burden of living up to high standards.

Each Member of the Choix Community is *Responsible* for Each Other

The Choix community is a model of responsibility and accountability. Since we treat others as we would have them treat us, we maintain a responsibility for our community members, we care about their well-being and trust that they shall care about us.

Choix Community Members are *Inclusive and Respectful* of Individuals and of Difference

Within our community, difference shall be celebrated as an extraordinary value, recognized for the benefit it can bring to our environment, and the breadth of learning that it represents. Individual opinions shall be sought and heard; and space for debate and challenge will be a core priority in the education process. It is the policy of l'Ecole de Choix not to discriminate against applicants, students or staff on the basis of race, color, national or ethnic origin, religion or sexual orientation.

Choix Community Members *Honor Education* as a Privilege while also Recognizing the *Responsibility* it Brings

In Haiti today, an education such as l'Ecole de Choix is unlikely for many Haitians and thus should be treated with respect, as the truly precious value that it represents. Moreover, as learning occurs, the growth in capacity for the students brings with it a growth in responsibility to use that learning to choose, to act, to make a change. With these abilities come responsibilities and Choix has significant expectations of its students.

Learning At Choix is the *Most Fun* a Kid can have with Her or His Day!

Not despite the above values, but because of them, the environment at Choix will be one where students cannot wait to arrive at school each day! It will be a place of change, of inspiration, of excitement and bewilderment, of fascination and new ideas. Learning will be an adventure that each student will take in discovering what her or his mind can do when challenged, the choices that become available to you when you dream, and the excitement in these infinite possibilities.

Choix Will Serve as a *Paradigm*

Choix is a paradigm both for the Mirebalais educational network, initially, and for educational institutions throughout the region with respect to both the quality of education it delivers as well as its strong pedagogical methods. At all levels, its quality and processes shall bolster the Vision stated above and further inspire them to be open to limitless possibilities, to follow their dreams and to become constructive, contributing citizens.

Source: "Vision and Values," L'Ecole de Choix website, https://ecoledechoix. org/values. Used with permission.

Transformational Gaming: Zynga's Social Strategy (A)[190]

In January 2009, Mark Pincus, founder and CEO of Zynga Game Network, one of the world's most successful and popular social gaming companies, had lunch with his sister, Laura Hartman, DePaul University business ethics professor. Hartman described their lunch conversation as a possible tipping point of a new direction for Zynga:

> Mark had reached a point in his career where he was ready…to move forward with a greater impact on the world in terms of what role Zynga would play, because Zynga was really a culmination of a lot of his business efforts. So we had lunch, and both of us brainstormed about what that could look like. Mark had been thinking about this for a long time, about what to do and how to place his social vision into practice. Our backgrounds and experiences complemented each other because I had spent years working with corporations, trying to encourage them to do something. So it came together.[191]

---

[190]This case was prepared by Laura P. Hartman, Jenny Mead, Danielle Christmas and Patricia H. Werhane. Copyright©2012 University of Virginia Darden School Foundation. All rights reserved.

[191]Case writer interview with Laura Hartman, Chicago, March 19, 2010; unless otherwise indicated, all subsequent attributions derive from this interview.

Although these ideas had been germinating with Pincus for some time, his discussion with Hartman was the initial step in an effort to build a new brand of corporate social strategy. But the stakes of this social strategy, tied up as they would be in the nonprofit partners with whom Zynga wanted to develop relationships, were equally linked to the company's preexisting corporate strategy. For this young and unabashedly successful company, Pincus's proposed new social strategy would be an intentional tangent from what Zynga had done overwhelmingly well – develop highly profitable interactive social games. Pincus's challenge was to see whether he could develop similarly profitable synergies between social gaming and nonprofit partners that were making a broader social impact. Was it possible for one company to develop a strategy that would both be profitable and engender social change?

Zynga and the Revolution in Social Gaming

Mark Pincus founded Zynga[192] in 2007, long after multiplayer online games had emerged in the 1980s and become mainstream through Xbox LIVE in 2002. But Zynga revolutionized social gaming. With the increasing popularity of social networking platforms such as Facebook, Myspace, Bebo, and LinkedIn, developers saw an opportunity to test a new concept. Zynga's social games allowed people to connect with their friends through an online, interactive environment without the need for consoles such as the Xbox. Players engaged in activities as diverse as harvesting crops, slicing apples, and playing poker and strategic (and virtual) "board games" and could encourage and assist friends with gaming goals by sending virtual gifts or leaving messages and by inviting nonparticipating friends to join. Although the games could be played synchronously, social games allowed for asynchronous playing in which, most of the time, games were not played in real time. The game sites did not charge a fee to play, so the games could be played continuously for no cost at all. Alternatively, players could opt to pay for items or could participate in activities that would allow them to earn points or rewards with which they could then purchase certain items.

According to Zynga's vice president of business development, Hugh de Loayza, the average players "go to spend time within social networks – and not a lot of time at that. You're going to come in for 5–10 min to see what your friends are doing, play for a few minutes, and you're off."[193]

---

[192]Pincus named the company after his late American bulldog, Zinga.

[193]Chang, Victoria, and Haim Mendelson. 2010. Social games, EC39. Stanford, CA: Stanford Graduate School of Business.

Mark Pincus and Zynga's Development

After receiving his MBA from Harvard Business School, Pincus cofounded a series of Internet start-ups, including the social networking site Tribe Networks and the software service-based companies FreeLoader and SupportSoft, the first of which he sold for $38 million in 1995 and the second of which went public in 2000. He was also an early investor in successful Web 2.0 initiatives including Napster and Facebook. When he launched Zynga in January 2007 in an old potato chip factory in San Francisco, Pincus brought his entrepreneurial interest in social networking to bear on his experiences with casual games and Facebook's flexibility and used the Facebook platform as a foundation for code. He believed someone needed to answer the question, "What am I going to do while I'm hanging out on Facebook?" Pincus developed his first Zynga game, Texas Hold 'em (later called Zynga Poker), and had 400,000 monthly active users in just 4 months, even as he refined and optimized Zynga's monetization potential.[194]

By January 2008, Zynga had 27 employees and was known for its innovative social networking approach to classic games such as poker and Risk.[195] By November of the same year, the company had grown to 150 employees and had received an infusion of cash from various backers, including the venture capital firm Kleiner Perkins.

The Closing Analysis

Just as Pincus began the January 2009 dialogue with his sister, the media started a round of speculations about Zynga's worth that culminated in estimates of up to $5 billion by July 2010.[196] As Mark Pincus sat in his office at the end of January, weighing his interest in a new kind of social strategy against the arguments of Zynga's studios and vice presidents, he was forced to confront the stakes of making the wisest and most effective decision for Zynga's present and future shareholders. Given the company's success, his corporate strategies had worked thus far; Pincus was tasked, then, with bringing this same wisdom to his decision about whether to expand Zynga's fulfilled mission to include a new kind of social engagement.

---

[194] Chang and Mendelson.

[195] Stone, Brad. 2008. More than games, a net to snare social networkers. *New York Times*, January 15, 2008.

[196] Hopkins, Curt. 2010. Google's stealth investment in game Co Zynga exceeds $100 million. *ReadWriteWeb*, July 11, 2010, http://www.readwriteweb.com/archives/googles_stealth_investment_in_game_co_zynga_exceed.php. Accessed 5 April 2011; see also, Dean Takahashi, "Could Zynga Really Be Worth $5 Billion?," *VentureBeat*, April 6, 2010, http://venturebeat.com/2010/04/06/could-zynga-really-be-worth-5-billion/. Accessed 5 April 2011.

Transformational Gaming: Zynga's Social Strategy (B)

In June 2009, Mark Pincus's already highly successful company Zynga, whose employees now numbered over 700, introduced FarmVille. FarmVille would later reach 780 million users a month, posting the highest monthly active users (MAUs) in the industry.[197] The most popular social game in the industry with as many as 30 million players per day,[198] Zynga's FarmVille asked players to build virtual farms in which they planted and harvested crops, bought and tended to animals, and furnished their farms with buildings and other "decorations," such as fences and hay bales (Exhibit 1). Players invited friends to be their FarmVille neighbors through their Facebook social network accounts. Once connected, they could send gifts of animals and other items, fertilize their neighbors' crops, and support award-based farming projects through the Co-Op feature launched in April 2010. FarmVille, like all of Zynga's social games, was free, but players could spend real money in the game to buy specialty items in the market, accelerate their rates of farm growth, "level up" (access higher levels in the game), or make the game easier to play. Game developers referred to this transformation as the "monetization" of the gaming experience, in which users opted to purchase, invest, donate or otherwise convert real currency to virtual currency through the gaming platform.

Like other social games, FarmVille's most valuable segment of the market demographic included players – primarily women and older adults – disinclined to access other gaming platforms.[199] Pincus accounted for the market's shift in virtual gaming development strategy in this way: "Gaming is a fundamentally social experience – not a single-player experience and not a technology experience. We are bringing gaming back to its roots."[200]

When measured by user volume, Zynga was the largest social gaming company, followed by competitors Playdom and Playfish. Zynga had a diverse portfolio of games; its other top games included Mafia Wars, Zynga Poker, Café World, FrontierVille, YoVille, FishVille, and PetVille.

The Formalization of a New Social Strategy: Zynga.org

The ideas that had inspired siblings Pincus and Hartman for much of their lives, and which they had discussed during their 2009 lunch, evolved over that following year

---

[197]Cashmore, Pete, 2010. FarmVille surpasses 80 million users. *Mashable Social Media*, February 20, 2010, http://mashable.com/2010/02/20/farmville-80-million-users/. Accessed 27 Sept 2011.

[198]Coelln, Eric von, How farmVille broke through 30 million daily active users. *EVCin: All About the Data Around Marketing, Social Media, Games, and More* (blog), February 19, 2010, http://www.voncoelln.com/eric/2010/02/19/how-farmville-finally-broke-through-30-million-daily-active-users/. Accessed 4 July 2011.

[199]Bagga, Atul. 2009. Online gaming: Takeaways from think tomorrow today conference. *ThinkEquity*, May 19, 2009.

[200]Bagga, Atul. 2009. Social games: Interview with the CEO of Zynga. *ThinkEquity*, February 24, 2009, http://www.avalon-ventures.com/news/social-games-interview-with-the-ceo-of-zynga. Accessed 1 July 2011.

into concrete plans regarding international partnerships: a new intracompany sector called Zynga.org. Although this project would not formally launch until fall 2009, the company had, in the spring of that year, entered into two partnerships. In May 2009, the YoVille studio of San Francisco-based Zynga had established a community partnership with the San Francisco Society for the Prevention of Cruelty to Animals (SF SPCA). The company described the partnership on its website:

> Through our virtual social goods program, YoVille players can adopt a dog or cat wearing an SF SPCA vest. Every virtual adoption results in a $2 donation to the SF SPCA nonprofit, which protects and cares for dogs and cats in need. Since launching the initiative in the spring of 2009, YoVille players have raised more than $90,000 for the cause.[201]

Although the SF SPCA partnership did not conform to Zynga.org's focus on global issues or its intention to rotate partnerships after a particular tenure, it worked well because it was a local partner. Because the YoVille studio wanted to participate in Zynga.org's core Haiti mission, which would come about later that year, without sacrificing the SF SPCA relationship, Zynga.org's directors managed the situation of studios' running multiple campaigns. They had to analyze each team and game, in terms of how they monetized and what the dollar per use was, to understand whether they could handle more than one campaign. One of the goals was to avoid donor fatigue while making sure that the different franchises[202] were able to handle more than one campaign.

The company's commitment to preexisting partnerships was also reflected in the Mafia Wars studio's relationship with the Huntington's Disease Society of America (HDSA). Zynga's contributions specifically focused on the HDSA's Coalition for the Cure, a research program composed of scientists from around the world who had made key discoveries surrounding Huntington's disease and who were developing therapy treatments.

Although Zynga.org grew organically over the following months to represent a particular mission and direction, these campaign partnerships – YoVille with SF SPCA and Mafia Wars with HDSA and, later, also with Fisher House, among a few others – proceeded successfully, notwithstanding the variance from Zynga. org's specific mission. These were based on preexisting plans, special circumstances, and/or unique links to franchises. Given the high value Zynga.org placed on meaningful and lasting partnerships, preexisting relationships were given precedence over mission congruence.

Zynga.org strove to proceed with the highest possible levels of integrity and knowledge and by using its partners' expertise to the fullest possible extent. Because of Hartman's established relationships with two grassroots organizations in rural Haiti, among others, the co-directors and Pincus decided to make use of these connections in focusing the nascent dot-org's efforts; a significant breadth of knowledge and

---

[201] "YoVille," *Zynga.org*, http://www.zynga.org/initiatives/sfspca.php. Accessed 1 July 2011.

[202] "Franchises" and "studios" both referred to those separate divisions of the company responsible for a particular game. For example, within the company, the Zynga team that developed and supported FarmVille was interchangeably referred to as "a franchise" or "a studio."

expertise about the subject matter became one of the team's core criteria for Zynga. org in choosing partners. Pincus reflected on what such a partnership might look like, given the organizations' focus on families and self-reliance, and which Zynga franchise would be most compatible with these particular organizations.

Because FarmVille represented Zynga's largest user base, it was the natural platform for Zynga.org's official launch. Although the company had engaged in community partnerships before the creation of Zynga.org, FarmVille would be the first venue in which the company considered using this emerging social strategy on a macro scale while serving Zynga.org's developing mission.

Moving Forward

The plan started to take shape. Virginia McArthur, director of operations for Zynga. org and one of Zynga's executive producers, and Hartman proposed to the FarmVille team an innovative strategy whereby the users would be offered a limited-time, special-edition item within the game: "Sweet Seeds for Haiti." Through FarmVille, Zynga would contribute 50% of all proceeds from the sale of these seeds ($5.00, in this case) to two Haiti-based causes: Fonkoze and FATEM (a microfinance initiative and an educational and school-meals program, respectively). The studio conducted the necessary coding in-game and Zynga.org initiated its first live launch on October 1, 2009 (Exhibit 2). The campaign was met with an exceptionally positive reception among its user community and throughout the media.[203]

During this start-up period, the Zynga.org directors began to develop criteria that would help with the decisions they would have to make on a daily basis. These criteria addressed issues such as the organizational focus on worldwide rather than solely domestic challenges in determining which causes or recipients to support. Following the success of the original Zynga.org campaign, this had become particularly important. The success of that first campaign in October 2009 led to an influx of requests from various organizations to partner with Zynga. Having these articulated standards helped the directors with the difficult task of turning away organizations doing meaningful and urgent work and provided a satisfactory explanation for the rejected partner.

---

[203] For examples of user and media coverage, see: Ashby, Alicia. 2009. FarmVille's sweet seeds raise $487K for charity. *EngageDigital* (blog), October 20, 2009, http://www.virtualgoodsnews. com/2009/10/farmvilles-sweet-seeds-raise-487k-for-charity.html ("Zynga's Sweet Seeds for Haiti promotion in FarmVille may in fact be the single largest amount of money raised for charity through sale of specific virtual goods to date."); Takahashi, Dean. 2009. Zynga's FarmVille gamers donate to Haiti's poor via virtual goods. *VentureBeat*, October 20, 2009, http://venturebeat. com/2009/10/20/zyngas-farmville-gamers-donate-to-haitis-poor-via-virtual-goods; Nash, Adam. 2009. Farmville economics: Sweet seeds are almost genius...," *Psychohistory: The Personal Blog of Adam Nash* (blog), October 5, 2009, http://blog.adamnash.com/2009/10/05/farmville-econom- ics-sweet-seeds-are-almost-genius; Gunnin, Lucinda, Farmville's sweet seeds for Haiti charity event underway. *Associated Content from Yahoo!*, October 8, 2009, http://www.associatedcontent. com/article/2262915/farmvilles_sweet_seeds_for_haiti_charity.html. Accessed 4 July 2011.

Zynga.org made a deliberate choice to differentiate itself as a separate unit within Zynga, rather than as staff within each studio, in order to maintain sustainability and to reinforce its core mission. The company needed strong metrics to prove that its dot-org partnerships and campaigns were truly successful.

The metric assessment, accompanied by other nuances of implementation and back-end evaluation, were at the center of McArthur's position as operations director. Hartman's role, as the director of external partnerships, was to establish a rigorous vetting process in connection with due diligence to manage these newly formed relationships and to participate on the ground once the projects were in the implementation phase so as to ensure that the ultimate recipients received a true benefit. It was crucial to identify partners who, by virtue of size, could accommodate this kind of field-level participation and assessment. Given Zynga's mission of "connecting the world through games," it became vital that Zynga.org's organizational partners and all resulting campaigns would have a significant impact on fund recipients.

As Zynga.org evolved and focused on its own sustainability, the directors continued to refine these core criteria – to focus interests and efforts – and to articulate more-specific criteria for potential partners. With its scale and its ability to provide users a pipeline to the concrete use of funds raised (e.g., soon after the first launch, FarmVille players could access periodic updates about the application of funding), Zynga.org could focus on its chosen values: children, families, and education.

As Hartman dealt with the external criteria for the selection and validation of partners, McArthur had to negotiate reasonable internal expectations in the selection of franchise partners. With more than 20 game studios active at various times, Zynga ran games that ranged from those in beta mode, to just-launched games that were struggling to go viral, all the way to the industry giant FarmVille, which had almost 60 million MAUs in July 2010.[204] When assessing how and when to introduce a possible Zynga.org campaign, McArthur noted that the key question for a potential Zynga franchise partner was whether the partner had enough resources within its game to support it. Together, the directors established a benchmark of games with one million daily active users for the introduction of a Zynga.org campaign; this threshold limited the base of potential Zynga.org franchise partners to FarmVille, YoVille, FrontierVille, Mafia Wars, FishVille, PetVille, Zynga Poker, and Café World.

The relationships between franchises and their potential partners developed organically from the implementation of these criteria. For example, following the success of Zynga.org's Sweet Seeds campaign, Pincus forwarded an e-mail to the co-directors introducing Water.org, a nonprofit committed to providing clean drinking water to developing countries, which seemed precisely appropriate for the FishVille studio. Water.org presented as a potential partner organization that allowed for manageable scale, proved thematically relevant to the franchise, and was salable to the user from an operational and content-based perspective. Moreover, the

---

[204]"App Leaderboard. 2010. AppData: Independent accurate application metrics and trends from inside network, July 31, 2010, http://www.appdata.com/leaderboard/apps?metric_select=mau. Accessed 6 July 2011.

compatibility of the Water.org partnership with the preestablished Haiti partnership supported Zynga.org's evolving goal of making the biggest impact possible by establishing a centralized theme and centralized effort. Its mission was fulfilled, at least in part, by the fact that a user of both FarmVille[205] and FishVille could, by connecting these efforts, be sufficiently confident to contribute in both games with this increased impact in mind.

Expectations

Bim Majekodunmi, producer of FarmVille, joined Zynga in September 2009, less than a month before Zynga.org's first in-game launch. The expectation that Majekodunmi join that studio, maintain its success, and simultaneously sort out the orientation of the Zynga.org project in the studio's roadmap, raised an important challenge in this synergy: There had been no question that Zynga's exponential growth imposed a continuous challenge for both existing staff as well as for new employees to adapt quickly. By integrating the Zynga.org social strategy into the company's mission, Pincus risked distracting these employees from the already arduous and high-stakes task of learning and implementing Zynga's standards for success. In his first week, Majekodunmi had to incorporate the first Zynga.org campaign, Sweet Seeds, into Farmville. Barely knowing his colleagues and under time pressure, Majekodunmi said, made it difficult to get this Zynga.org campaign going online.[206]

Even Pincus wondered whether the Zynga.org strategy would be successful in the long run because of the question of economic sustainability from the studios' perspectives. If any venture, such as a studio, would be measured based on traditional bottom-line metrics, Zynga would have to consider the impact of a Zynga.org campaign on those metrics. Pincus was concerned not only about questions surrounding motivation, but also about the perspective of Zynga's leadership, which was responsible for setting company-wide, rather than studio-level, goals. Several of Zynga's vice presidents and managers were skeptical of the Zynga.org concept, fearing that it would not be sustainable and could possibly cannibalize other revenue. In general, however, the various teams' genuine excitement about the project mitigated any potential conflict or disorientation.

---

[205]FarmVille was the franchise partner for FATEM and Fonkoze during the fall 2009 Zynga.org campaigns, Sweet Seeds for Haiti I and II. For more information, see Zynga.org, http://www. zynga.org. Accessed 6 July .

[206]Like other social games, FarmVille was played in real time, allowing online users to sign in at their convenience and, through personal avatars, work on their unique simulated farms. Because the game was always available, studios had to "go live" with new features and market items without a lapse in availability. This raised the stakes for Majekodunmi's understanding FarmVille's culture in order to introduce a game-appropriate item the first time around that would launch the brand-new company-wide social strategy.

Implementation

With Zynga.org and its specific focus on implementing social changes through the sale of virtual social goods established, the social vision that Pincus and Hartman had discussed over lunch in January 2009 was on its way to becoming reality. It was time for implementation, and projects in earthquake-torn Haiti would be Zynga.org's first venture.

FATEM and Fonkoze: The Partners and Their Context

Haiti in brief: politics, economics, and demographics[207]

As a nation born of African slave revolt and the poorest country in the Western hemisphere, Haiti shared the island of Hispaniola with the Dominican Republic and had a dynamic political, demographic, and economic narrative (Exhibit 3). The former Saint Domingue had seen political upheaval since its founding in 1659.[208] The 20th century presented a series of challenges for the country. From 1915 to 1934, the United States occupied Haiti in an effort to manage civil unrest. The U.S. presence was not universally welcomed. It was during this time that the United States also played a role in dismantling the constitutional administration, which caused conflict with the Dominican Republic. From 1934 to 1956, a territory dispute with the Dominican Republic led to the Parsley Massacre of 20,000 Haitian laborers stationed in the country. In 1957, the newly elected Dr. Francois Duvalier initiated the hereditary dictatorship that kept him and his son in office until Jean-Claude Duvalier, or "Bebe Doc's," overthrow and the adoption of a new constitution in 1986. The 1990 election of former priest Jean-Bertrand Aristide launched a new use of paramilitaries, which was followed by the election of his former Prime Minister, Rene Preval. In 2000, Aristide returned amid new claims of human rights abuses.

After four hurricanes near the end of the first decade of the twenty-first century, followed closely by one of the strongest earthquakes to hit the area in the past 200 years, in 2010, Haiti found itself struggling for a future. Eighty percent of its population lived below the poverty line. And although economic investment had begun to return after the U.S. Congress passed the Haitian Hemispheric Opportunity through Partnership Encouragement (HOPE) Act, which allowed for some U.S. free trade, insecurity prevailed. In late 2010, the Haitian government was sustained by pledges of international assistance that would be slow to materialize.[209]

---

[207] Charles Arthur, *Haiti in Focus,* Interlink Publishing Group, January 18, 2002. This guide, in conjunction with the CIA's biweekly updated *2010 World Factbook,* is the source of the information contained in this section.

[208] The Spanish, under Christopher Columbus, had taken control of the island from its natives in 1492 and their rule lasted until the French took over in 1659.

[209] Johns, Joe, and Maryanne Fox. 2010. Most countries fail to deliver on Haiti aid pledges. *CNN World,* July 15, 2010, http://www.cnn.com/2010/WORLD/americas/07/15/haiti.donations/index. html; *2010 World Factbook,* CIA, https://www.cia.gov/library/publications/the-world-factbook/ geos/ha.html. Accessed 30 July 2011.

Haiti's national demographic complicated its portrait. The population was concentrated in urban and coastal areas, particularly in the capital of Port-au-Prince, where Haiti's principal industry – agriculture – was not truly viable, which contributed to the dismal per-capita income and to the unsafe and unsanitary conditions that resulted from its geographical concentrations. Haiti's immense deforestation, brought on by logging operations and unsound agricultural practices, among other things, was a severe problem affecting land productivity and infrastructure, and fuel sources.

Zynga.org's Inaugural Partners

Zynga's Haiti partnerships soon became the cornerstone of Zynga.org's implementation. The first Zynga.org campaign launched on October 1, 2009, within the FarmVille game and offered players sweet potato seeds that did not wither in exchange for the equivalent payment of $5.00. Half of all proceeds from the "Sweet Seeds for Haiti" campaign went to two partner organizations: FATEM and Fonkoze. A second Sweet Seeds campaign ran in November, benefiting these same organizations.

FATEM

In April 2006, a group of Mirebalais, Haiti, expats, living in Boston, developed a plan for an organization that would give back to the community that nurtured them. FATEM was organized to be a catalyst for long-lasting positive change in the Mirebalais community by providing educational opportunities, technology training, and strengthening the community's capacity to improve its social, economic, and environmental conditions (Exhibit 4). Once the group formalized the organization's structure, the members articulated their vision:

> We have always envisioned a region where all residents will be gainfully employed, and where children have access to quality education that allows them to compete on a global scale, made possible in part by the power of the Internet.[210]

To this end, FATEM's central project in 2010 was its partnership with Zynga in the creation of a K–12 educational institution with a focus on quality education, income generation, and financial literacy. FATEM's leadership wanted this community center to serve as a model for its own educational network of schools, as well as for other educational institutions throughout the region.

> [This community] is in dire need of a K–12 school that can be used as a reference…to raise the standard in local education. In addition to the usual 14 classrooms, the school shall have a well-equipped technology and computer room/language lab, necessary teaching tools and supplies, and, most importantly, a safe and comfortable environment that [facilitates] learning. Part of our budget will support…the salaries of trained teachers who can stimulate the children's appetite for learning and make it fun for them.[211]

---

[210]Hartman, Laura. "FATEM: Vision and mission statement," e-mail to the case writer, May 28, 2010.
[211]FATEM: Vision and Mission Statement.

Starting with the May 2010 Sweet Seeds Zynga.org campaign, all campaign moneys raised went entirely toward the construction of FATEM's K–12 school, *L'École de Choix*, or the School of Choice (Exhibit 5).[212] (For a video of this evolution and the resulting project, please see http://www.youtube.com/watch?v=9qejcsWvLAk.)

Fonkoze

In 1994, a cohort of 32 Haitian community leaders responded to Haiti's challenging economic circumstances with a plan. Fonkoze founder Father Joseph Philippe was concerned that "although a majority of poor people in Haiti knew how to organize themselves politically, they knew nothing about how to organize themselves economically."[213] These leaders answered this need by designing a bank built by and for Haitians living in conditions of extreme poverty. Not only was the organization one of the few truly grassroots microfinance institutions in Haiti, but it was also Haiti's largest with more than 40 branches covering every region of the country. As a part of Philippe's vision "to provide the means for all Haitians, even the poorest, to participate in the economic development of the country," Fonkoze established its target group as women, because "women are the backbone of the Haitian economy and the doorway into the family unit."[214]

When former Washington, DC, management consultant Anne Hastings decided to join Philippe in Fonkoze's formation, she was promptly named director and, as the head of the bank's nationwide community network, oversaw an exponential expansion of the bank's accessibility and client base. By July 2010, Fonkoze would be serving more than 45,000 women borrowers, most of whom lived and worked in the countryside of Haiti, and more than 200,000 savers. Fonkoze's primary function had been to organize solidarity groups, small groups of women who, through shared mentorship and oversight, pursued literacy, health care, and business skills as they worked with Fonkoze to apply for small to medium-size loans. As the bank continued to grow its membership and measure its long-term impact (Exhibit 6), it began offering to borrowers additional services including currency exchange; money transfers, or remittance services; literacy, business skills, women's health, children's rights, and environmental protection education; and life and credit microinsurance.

One of its most successful programs, and a tie-in to the virtual livestock available in FarmVille, was its *Chemen Lavi Miyò* (CLM), in Haitian Creole, the Road to a

---

[212]Zynga.org, "Sweet seeds for Haiti campaigns," http://zynga.org/initiatives/sweet-seeds.php. Accessed 4 July 2011.

[213]Fonkoze, "Who we are: Our history; the context," http://www.fonkoze.org/aboutfonkoze/whoweare/ourhistory.html .Accessed 30 July 2011.

[214]Fonkoze. 2010. A bank the poor can call their own: A history of Fonkoze – Haiti's alternative bank for the organized poor. www.fonkoze.org/docs/fonkoze_history.pdf. Accessed 31 July 2010.

Better Life. This introductory-level individual development program was designed to meet the most vital needs of those living at the lowest levels of poverty in Haiti:

> It accompanies them with training, one-on-one supervision and encouragement, confidence building, and other services like health care and home repair. It protects clients as they move forward along a two-year road from abject misery until they have their own functioning microenterprise and are ready to enter a microfinance program.[215]

The first step of CLM involved the delivery of an asset to the participant: a chicken (an egg-layer), a goat (a milk-producer), or a small amount of funds, depending on a discussion with the participant and her capacity at the time she entered the program. From there, the Haitian and her family would begin to build their future.

After successful autumn campaigns with its two inaugural partners, Zynga.org expanded its reach, with the United Nations World Food Programme (WFP), through a cross-game holiday promotion that established a foundation for what had become one of Zynga.org's most enduring relationships. With seven separate campaigns leading up to a comprehensive launch in October 2010 in honor of World Food Day, Zynga players had been able to make a significant contribution through micropayments to the WFP's private-donor strategy.

Other partners since Zynga.org's inception have included Fisher House (helping military families), the National Audubon Society (for Gulf Coast clean-up efforts), and Water.org (in connection with water, health, and sanitation in Haiti).

The Original 50/50 Profitable Partnership Model

At Zynga.org's inception, McArthur and Hartman had to determine how to apportion funds raised through its campaigns. What should be the percentage split between the recipient organization and the partnering studio? After much consideration by the Zynga.org co-directors, and after evaluating alternative models of corporate giving, the company originally settled on a 50-50 split. That gave the model more of a partnership feel and seemed sustainable in the business. Although they later opted to go well beyond, it was this critical balance that the co-directors sought to be both intraorganizationally justifiable as well as externally market-sustainable.

The co-directors examined a variety of corporate-social-strategy models in connection with many widely known corporate humanitarian campaigns. For instance, some corporations maintained completely separate foundations for their giving operations, such as Salesforce.org and Google.org. Other corporations partnered with the (RED) initiative, a network organized for the purpose of eliminating AIDS in Africa (Exhibit 7). According to the (RED) fact sheet:

> (RED) works with the world's best brands to make unique (PRODUCT) RED-branded products and direct up to 50% of their gross profits to the Global Fund to invest in African

---

[215]Fonkoze, "Who we are: How Fonkoze works; Fonkoze's fight against poverty," http://www.fonkoze.org/aboutfonkoze/whoweare/howworks.html. Accessed 31 July 2010.

AIDS programs. (RED) is not a charity or "campaign." It is an economic initiative that aims
to deliver a sustainable flow of private sector money to the Global Fund.[216]

The variability in corporate-giving models had led to confusion over Zynga.org's
50-50 strategy, particularly following its campaign to raise funds immediately
following the January 2010 earthquake. In an effort to provide disaster relief as
quickly and as significantly as possible to those in desperate need, and because
Zynga was already on the ground in Haiti, the firm decided to temporarily offer
100 % of all proceeds from a brief five-day launch for that singular purpose. But this
slight detour, although well intended, led to misunderstandings.

In an attempt to place Zynga within the matrix of corporate contributions, Brazilian
newspaper *Folha* published a chart comparing Zynga.org's percentage of giving
with other high-visibility corporations with long-term humanitarian campaigns.[217]
The chart, entitled "How Companies Pledged in Relation to Sales of Products Linked
to Humanitarian Campaigns," clearly demonstrated that Zynga had far surpassed all
the others examined, other than McDonald's, which it met at 100 %. Other corporations considered included Dell, Motorola, Starbucks, Gap, and Apple.

In another turn of events, for its September 2010 Sweet Seeds campaign to fully
fund L'École de Choix, the school it was supporting in Mirebalais, Zynga shifted
back to the 100 % contribution level and also reported 100 % contributions by
Facebook from its Credits receipts.[218]

Zynga.org and its Sweet Seeds partners had expressed satisfaction with the
clear and mutually beneficial terms of their partnerships, and the company had
turned over funds raised to the organizations quickly after they had been contributed.
This was as much a sign of Zynga.org's growing efficiency as it was an extension of
its commitment to produce immediate and concrete impact with and for its user base
and ultimate recipients.

Monetization and Reputation Management

In addition to monetizing through direct payment for in-game virtual goods and
virtual social goods, Zynga and other social-gaming companies had used lead-
generation offers, allowing users to sign up online for deals, such as text-message
subscriptions or video rentals, in exchange for game credits. Players who were not
able to or preferred not to spend money on the site for Zynga "cash" had the option
of responding to these offers instead, and these lead-generating transactions then

---

[216] (RED), "What is (RED)?," http://www.joinred.com/pdfs/(RED)%20Fact%20Sheet.pdf. Accessed
4 July 2011.

[217] Kanno, Mauricio. 2010. Doações Não Devem Depender de Lucros, diz Especialista Sobre
'FarmVille,' *Folha Online*, March 24, 2010, http://www1.folha.uol.com.br/folha/informatica/
ult124u711295.shtml. Accessed 4 July 2011.

[218] These "credits" were a virtual currency that the site's visitors could use to purchase – via credit
card and PayPal, among others – "virtual" goods offered in any of the games or applications.

monetized players who might otherwise not have provided revenue in the traditional pay-to-play model. This form of monetization came under scrutiny in fall 2009, only a few weeks after the October 1 launch of Zynga.org's Sweet Seeds campaign, when Michael Arrington published a scathing critique in *TechCrunch* of Zynga's lead-generation practices in the much-discussed article, "Scamville: The Social Gaming Ecosystem of Hell."[219] While lead-generation offers generally were considered relatively benign, Arrington accused Zynga of accruing as much as one-third of its income, with the tacit support of Facebook, by knowingly working with scam advertisers who would place deceptive offers. Arrington claimed that the offers would manipulate users into downloading software and accepting pricey, recurring mobile subscriptions, both of which were constructed in a way that prevented the average user from easily removing them.

As critics and users joined in the challenge, Zynga had a quick turnaround time on its reply; Pincus responded by immediately announcing in his November 2, 2009, blog post that the company would remove from the site all mobile offers of any kind, that it had already terminated its relationship with its principal cell-phone-subscription offer provider, and that it planned to screen all lead-generation offers moving forward before placing any new ones on the site.[220] Arrington was not satisfied, though, and on November 6, 2009, he answered Pincus:

> Zynga CEO Mark Pincus said earlier this week that he intends to make sure his company's games don't include scammy offers in the future…But what he didn't say in that blog post is that Zynga has been scamming users from the beginning quite intentionally as part of their revenue model.[221]

Arrington was armed with Pincus's own words; he linked his article to a video of the CEO speaking at a Startup@Berkeley bar mixer in which Pincus explained his early strategy, saying he "funded [Zynga] myself but did every horrible thing in the book…just to get revenues right away…We did anything possible just to get revenues so that we could grow and be a real business."[222] Pincus was perfectly willing to eat his words. "I didn't mean to be so crass," he said, sighing. "But I was talking in a bar." He later clarified, "I respect companies that build a service that can scale and make a lot of money."[223]

---

[219] Arrington, Michael. Scamville: The social gaming ecosystem of hell. *TechCrunch*, October 31, 2009, http://techcrunch.com/2009/10/31/scamville-the-social-gaming-ecosystem-of-hell/. Accessed 9 Nov 2010.

[220] Pincus, Mark. My take on Zynga and CPA offers. *Markpincus.com* (blog), November 2, 2009, http://markpincus.typepad.com/markpincus/2009/11/my-take-on-zynga-and-cpa-offers.html. Accessed 9 Nov 2010.

[221] Arrington, Michael. Zynga CEO Mark Pincus: 'I Did Every Horrible Thing in the Book Just to Get Revenues'. *TechCrunch*, November 6, 2009, http://techcrunch.com/2009/11/06/zynga-scam-ville-mark-pinkus-faceboo/. Accessed 9 Nov 2010.

[222] "Zynga CEO Mark Pincus: 'I Did Every Horrible Thing in the Book Just to Get Revenues.'"

[223] Hendrickson,Matt. 2010. Why you should love the most hated man on facebook. *Details*, May 2010, http://www.details.com/style-advice/tech-and-design/201005/mark-pincus-facebook-mafia-wars-farmville-zynga. Accessed 9 Nov 2010.

Under separate circumstances, and long after Arrington's articles and the revival of the Berkeley video, the company's relationship with its principal platform, Facebook, became strained. Facebook suspended Zynga's brand-new game, FishVille, for a few days on claims of advertising violations.[224] Facebook explained that its decision was unrelated to Arrington's article; and all seemed to have been settled since the two companies announced a five-year deal to work together.[225] Social-gaming insiders noted that each organization faced significant challenges at the time; Facebook was confronted by claims of privacy violations, while both Zynga and Facebook were subject to several lawsuits specifically related to the issues of online offers, later dropped entirely.[226]

In February 2010, Pincus was interviewed by CNN and "acknowledged not being vigilant enough with the automated ads that appeared on Zynga games during the company's early days."[227] Pincus explained, "[w]e were playing Whack-A-Mole. Every time we found one of these or got a complaint, we would take them down. Eventually…we realized we had to take a much more aggressive stance than a normal website."[228] While the simultaneity of the Zynga.org launch with the "Scamville" crisis posed strategic challenges during the start of a new and developing social strategy, the overlap was absent from media analyses of the company through November and December 2009. More specifically, as a part of its public relations strategy, the company chose not to capitalize on the Zynga.org venture in support of reputation management.

The special nature of Zynga's social strategy forced Pincus, Hartman, and McArthur to consider shareholder accountability, producing measurable benefits in exchange for those resources directed toward extra-corporate purposes. Their decision to avoid engaging Zynga.org during the time when Zynga was taking the greatest public heat over the Scamville article was not necessarily a black-and-white one. Later, Pincus questioned whether avoiding publicity at that time had been the best strategy.

---

[224] Arrington, Michael. 2009. Zynga's FishVille sleeps with the fishes for Ad violations. *TechCrunch*, November 8, 2009, http://techcrunch.com/2009/11/08/zyngas-fishville-swims-with-the-fishes-for-ad-violations/. Accessed 9 Nov 2010.

[225] Holly Sanders Ware, "Facebook, Zynga Bury the Hatchet," *New York Post*, May 19, 2010, http://www.nypost.com/p/news/business/facebook_zynga_bury_the_hatchet_7c40mXaPBzAnkJTepwohlN. Accessed 9 Nov 2010.

[226] Swartz, Jon. 2009. Lawsuit says Ads in social games are scamming players. *USA TODAY*, December 7, 2009, http://www.usatoday.com/money/industries/technology/2009-12-07-games07_ST_N.htm; Ryan Tate, "Facebook Named in Federal Class-Action Suit over Scammy Zynga Ads," *Gawker*, November 19, 2009, http://gawker.com/5408472/facebook-named-in-federal-class+action-suit-over-scammy-zynga-ads. Accessed 9 Nov 2010.

[227] Gross, Doug. The facebook games that millions love (and hate). *CNN Tech*, February 23, 2010, http://www.cnn.com/2010/TECH/02/23/facebook.games/?hpt=Sbin. Accessed 9 Nov 2010.

[228] Gross.

In January 2010, Pincus was voted Crunchies CEO of the Year by a group of Silicon Valley's most influential blogs.[229] As a part of his acceptance speech, Pincus said of Zynga.org's most recent fundraising campaign, "It opened my eyes to the potential of social gaming and how we'll see virtual goods raise amazing amounts of money for great causes in a scalable way."[230] As he further invested Zynga's resources into its evolving social strategy, the company's growth and reputation set up the firm for the possibility of increasing media attention. Pincus would have to determine whether and how Zynga.org could intervene in the media discourse before future assaults and how the project might contribute to the most effective PR strategy once Scamville-like campaigns had already happened.

Exhibit 1: Transformational Gaming: Zynga's Social Strategy (B)

Zynga's FarmVille

Source: Laura P. Hartman. Used with permission.

---

[229] "Every year, Silicon Valley's biggest blogs (including us) put together the Crunchies, an event where the tech community puts the spotlight on the best entrepreneurs, startups, and investors." Kim-Mai Cutler, "Crunchies: Zynga's Mark Pincus Sees a Future for Socially Conscious Virtual Goods," *SocialBeat*, January 8, 2010, http://social.venturebeat.com/2010/01/08/zynga-social-virtual-goods/. Accessed 9 Nov 2010.

[230] Cutler.

Exhibit 2: Transformational Gaming: Zynga's Social Strategy (B)

Sweet Seeds for Haiti

Source: Zynga. Used with permission.

Exhibit 3: Transformational Gaming: Zynga's Social Strategy (B)

Map of Haiti

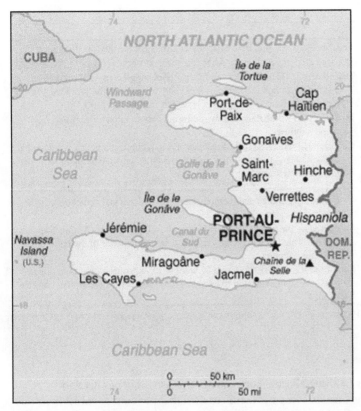

Source: *2010 World Factbook,* CIA, https://www.cia.gov/library/publications/the-world-factbook/geos/ha.html. Accessed 1 July 2011.

Exhibit 4: Transformational Gaming: Zynga's Social Strategy (B)

FATEM'S Projects
  Past Projects

Month	Project
October 2006	Contributed to the purchase of 15 street lamps for the city of Mirebalais
June 2007	Donated 20 pairs of shoes to ASM, the local soccer team
October 2007	Distributed 5,000 notebooks and other school supplies to rural school children; through the Learn to Read and Write program, provided 140 children (Haitian gourdes) HTG1,250 as tuition assistance[231]
October 2007	Inaugurated a Mirebalais weekly radio show about citizen rights and responsibilities
April 2008	Collaborated with ASTAM (Association des Techniciens pour l'Avancement de Mirebalais) to install new and improved street signs throughout the city and facilitate traffic
July 2008	Joined forces with OPAJEC (Organisation des Paysans et des Jeunes du Centre) to build a small computer lab for students and professionals to conduct research
August 2008	Supported an initiative to train 185 agricultural, community health, veterinary, and construction technicians/agents to serve the needs of the region in multiple domains
August 2008	Supported REFAM (Rezo Fanm Mibalè) in its exposition of woman-made products and its mission to encourage and foster the development of area women

Source: FATEM, "Programs and Projects," http://www.fatem.org/programs-and-projects (accessed October 22, 2011).

Future Projects

- Help build or renovate all rural community schools within our network
- Implement cybercafés/computer labs in each of the four communal sections (districts) of Mirebalais.
- Initiate efforts to integrate computer literacy in primary and secondary school curricula throughout the region.
- Hold regular computer literacy seminars for "IT Teachers," selected from all primary and secondary schools in the Mirebalais area.
- In collaboration with local residents, implement agricultural and farming projects designed to help more parents become self-sufficient by boosting their income so they can afford to support their children's education.

Source: Laura Hartman, "FATEM: Vision and Mission Statement," e-mail to the case writer, May 28, 2010.

---

[231] The exchange rate on June 2, 2010, was HTG39.5030 to (U.S. dollars) USD1.00.

Exhibit 5: Transformational Gaming: Zynga's Social Strategy (B)

L'École de Choix, Mirebalais, Haiti
   EDUCATION => AUTONOMY => CHOICE => DIGNITY => HUMANITY

Executive Summary

FATEM, Mirebalais's community organization, along with local representatives, global NGOs and others, have broken ground on an extraordinary K–12 school and community center, intended from its inception to meet the most pressing and critical needs of those living in extreme poverty in Haiti, with a focus on quality education, income generation and financial literacy.

Key Distinctions

Our Educational Program Seeks To Prepare Students To Be Socially Responsible Leaders For Tomorrow.

   K–12 academic track had an emphasis on language proficiency in English, French and Creole in all grades, technology instruction, teacher training and curriculum coordination (partners Nova Southeastern University, DePaul University and Francis W. Parker School).

   Our After-School Programs Provide A Holistic Response To Community Needs.

   "Plas ti Moun"-style youth center with a focus on psycho-social development, including education surrounding the arts, culture, handicrafts, new technologies, athletics, academic support services, and preventative health care education. English-as-a-second-language, literacy, financial literacy, as well as work skills training programs for adolescents and adults.

   The after-hours program "works" for Mirebalais! We are partnering with Global sourcing firm Samasource, which will provide micro-technology jobs to workers within the facility during the 11:00 p.m.–7:00 a.m. shift.

   Our Construction Plans Create Long-Term Jobs And Will Be Locally Responsible.

   Sourcing decisions for school construction will intentionally strive to support and even help to create new jobs in the local community through long-term renewable contracts for those supplies that will need to be purchased on a continual basis. Sourcing priorities will be sustainable, ecologically responsible, responsive to the environment for natural cooling and shade, and designed to be hurricane- and earthquake-resistant.

   We Are Working In Solidarity With Our Community.

   The local community is a full partner in the construction, creation and development of L'École de Choix.

   The land was contributed by the municipality for the construction and local leaders, including Mirebalais Mayor Lochard Laguerre, the Prefect of Bayasse (its precise location) and the Senator of the Central Plateau Edmonde Supplice Beauzile, are involved in the process.

L'École de Choix Represents A Multi-Faceted Partnership.

Additional partners include World Food Programme and Haiti's prestigious Bureau de Nutrition et Développement in connection with the school meals program, and Water.org with regard to the water management.

L'École de Choix was designed from its inception to serve as a *replicable* paradigm of public–private partnerships, established to serve its (broadly construed) community with educational and economic resources.

Our Vision

L'École de Choix is anchored by the principle that a quality education provides individuals with the fundamental tools to affirm individual dignity through the choices they make. Choice and autonomy grant us our dignity; and it is that dignity that assures each of us the very heart of our humanity, both in the way we are responsible for ourselves, as well as for the communities in which we live. It is in this way that education becomes the pathway to our humanity.

Our Values

Each Member of the Choix Community is a *Leadership Model* for each other

As the Choix facility is designed to be a model from a physical perspective, the behavior of each individual within our community is a model for each other. We act in ways that would be acceptable if everyone in the Choix community acted in that manner. One of the tenets of the Choix facility is its mixed age, cross-program and inter-generational environment. The adults and older students shall always feel the burden of serving as a role model while the younger students shall always feel the burden of living up to high standards.

Each Member of the Choix Community is *Responsible* for each other

The Choix community is a model of responsibility and accountability. Since we treat others as we would have them treat us, we maintain a responsibility for our community members, we care about their well-being and trust that they shall care about us.

Choix Community Members are *Inclusive And Respectful* of Individuals and of Difference

Within our community, difference shall be celebrated as an extraordinary value, recognized for the benefit it can bring to our environment, and the breadth of learning that it represents. Individual opinions shall be sought and heard; and space for debate and challenge will be a core priority in the education process. It is the policy of L'École de Choix not to discriminate against applicants, students or staff on the basis of race, color, national or ethnic origin, religion or sexual orientation.

Choix Community Members *Honor Education* as a Privilege while also Recognizing the *Responsibility* it Brings

In Haiti today, an education such as L'École de Choix is unlikely for many Haitians and thus should be treated with respect, as the truly precious value that it represents. Moreover, as learning occurs, the growth in capacity for the students brings with it a growth in responsibility to use that learning to choose, to act, to make a change. With these abilities come responsibilities and Choix has significant expectations of its students.

Learning at Choix is the *Most Fun* a Kid Can have with Her or His Day!

Not despite the above values, but because of them, the environment at Choix will be one where students cannot wait to arrive at school each day! It will be a place of change, of inspiration, of excitement and bewilderment, of fascination and new ideas. Learning will be an adventure that each student will take in discovering what her or his mind can do when challenged, the choices that become available to you when you dream, and the excitement in these infinite possibilities.

Choix Will Serve As A R*eference* for both the FATEM educational network, initially, and for educational institutions throughout the region with respect to both the quality of education it delivers as well as its strong pedagogical methods. At all levels, its quality and processes shall bolster the Vision stated above and further inspire them to be open to limitless possibilities, to follow their dreams and to become constructive, contributing citizens.

Sources: Jacky Poteau and Laura Hartman, "L'École de Choix, Mirebalais, Haiti," July 2010, http://wiki.squeakland.org/download/attachments/2097378/Ecole+de+Choix+Brochure+v5.pdf?version=1&modificationDate=12867572 83000; L'École de Choix, "Key Distinctions" and "Vision and Values," http://www.ecoledechoix.org/ (accessed February 7, 2012) Used with permission.

Exhibit 6: Transformational Gaming: Zynga's Social Strategy (B)

Fonkoze's Key Statistics[232]
  Key indicators as of Dec 31, 2009

	Fonkoze financial services	Fonkoze: the foundation	Consolidated
Number of branches	24	17	41
Portfolio outstanding	$7,099,297	$1,607,651	$8,706,948
Percent female (solidarity loans)	100 %	98 %	99 %
Number of active loan clients	32,409	12,935	45,344
Savings balance	$11,028,456	$3,320,731	$14,349,188
Number of savings accounts	143,121	55,619	198,740

Key Literacy Indicators

	2000	2001	2002	2003	2004	2005	2006	2007	2008
Clients completing basic literacy training	1,904	1,075	2,219	2,332	3,610	3,586	4,278	13,345	11,003
Clients completing business skills training	458	616	1,040	1,167	3,138	3,764	1,898	7,590	8,665
Clients completing health training						219	954	3,450	1,949

Progress since Inception

	Number of depositors	Total value of deposits	Number of loan clients	Value of loans outstanding	Number of branch offices	Number of employees
1996	193	1,175,801	110	348,515	1	9
1997	3,444	3,273,342	1,542	5,158,185	11	52
1998	5,134	9,878,735	2,607	7,038,578	15	101
1999	7,900	18,820,335	2,834	10,235,763	15	118
2000	13,260	38,646,349	4,794	21,135,636	16	130
2001	20,854	66,923,566	8,416	23,614,213	18	170
2002	32,000	115,228,058	10,000	42,397,213	18	225
2003	53,013	163,091,418	24,990	113,308,168	18	247
2004	69,057	194,866,736	28,183	185,871,012	20	313
2005	94,342	321,597,487	31,090	255,279,288	26	486
2006	119,118	361,498,800	43,689	366,003,832	30	552
2007	158,857	415,650,851	49,959	404,837,729	33	710
2008	190,269	515,107,088	54,204	481,520,887	39	765
2009	198,740	602,942,815	46,344	365,859,841	41	743

Data source: Fonkoze, "Key Statistics," http://fonkoze.org/aboutfonkoze/keystatistics.html. Accessed 4 July 2011.

---

[232] All amounts are in Haitian gourdes. The exchange rate on June 2, 2010, was HTG39.5030 to USD1.00.

Exhibit 7: Transformational Gaming: Zynga's Social Strategy (B)

(RED) Initiative Giving Models

- Bugaboo Strollers donates 1 % of all company proceeds.[233]
- Nike donates 100 % of the proceeds from the sale of (PRODUCT) RED items.[234]
- Gap, Inc. donates 50 % of the proceeds from the sale of (PRODUCT) RED items.[235]
- Armani donates 40 % of the gross profit proceeds from the sale of (PRODUCT) RED items.[236]
- Converse donates between 5 % and 15 % of the net wholesale price from the sale of (PRODUCT) RED items.[237]
- Apple donates $10 of the proceeds from the sale of (PRODUCT) RED items.[238]
- Hallmark donates 8 % of the net wholesale sales from (PRODUCT) RED items.[239]
- Starbucks donates between $0.05 and $1 of the proceeds from the sale of (PRODUCT) RED items.[240]

---

[233] Bugaboo (PRODUCT)[RED], http://www.bugaboostrollers.com/web/guest/learn/bugaboo-red. Accessed 7 Feb 2012.

[234] Nike(RED), "See the Impact," http://www.nike.com/nikeos/p/red/en_US/impact. Accessed 7 Feb 2012.

[235] "Gap (PRODUCT) RED Showcases Company's Ongoing Commitment to Social Responsibility," Gap Inc. press release, October 13, 2006.

[236] Tschorn, Adam, Rose Apodaca, and Samantha Conti. 2006. RED brigade: Gap, Armani to battle AIDS; musician and activist Bono Launches PRODUCT RED campaign to raise funds for treating disease around the World. *Daily News Record*, January 30, 2006.

[237] . Converse, "Converse (PRODUCT RED)," http://www.converse.com.sg/products/116554.asp. Accessed 7 Feb 7 2012.

[238] "Apple Announces iPod nano (PRODUCT) RED Special Edition: Portion of Proceeds Contributed to the Global Fund to Fight AIDS," Apple Inc. press release, October 13, 2006, http://www.apple.com/pr/library/2006/10/13Apple-Announces-iPod-nano-PRODUCT-RED-Special-Edition.html. Accessed 7 Feb 2012.

[239] Hallmark (PRODUCT) RED COLLECTION, http://www.hallmark.com/online/red/. Accessed 7 Feb 2012.

[240] (Starbucks) RED, "Buy (STARBUCKS) RED. Help Save Lives.," http://red.starbucks.com/red/default.aspx. Accessed 7 Feb 2012.

Chapter 3
Health

Introduction

The insufficient availability of healthcare facilities and medicines perpetuates poverty, particularly when curable diseases are involved. The problem is particularly serious with HIV/AIDS in Sub-Saharan Africa where, even in 2013, 40 million people are infected. Another deterrent to health is the lack of clean water, a phenomenon that plagues many developing countries. In this chapter we will include three cases of companies that work to address the issues of health access, HIV/AIDs, and clean water.

Novartis, the third largest pharmaceutical company in the world, established The Novartis Foundation for Sustainable Development, and it has been working in a district in Tanzania for almost 50 years. It has developed clinics, a hospital that also trains clinicians, a leprosy sanatorium, a malaria prevention program, and with Tanzanian government partners, health insurance and microlending programs in five area villages. These programs are highly successful in alleviating recurring malaria infections and in providing needed health care to that region. The aim is to create sustainable programs that will be independent of Novartis, but that has not yet been achieved.

The Female Health Company (FHC) is a small for-profit company that has the only effective female condom. Through a series of learning experiences it now markets to women in over 100 countries, so that women can be protected from HIV-infected partners.

Proctor & Gamble (P&G), a large global corporation found itself, through an acquisition, in possession of a water purification product, PŪR. Unable to compete with Brita in the United States market, it formed a non-government organization to distribute this product in parts of Africa where the water is particularly polluted and dirty. P&G has also been able to create jobs for local people who sell these purification packets to their neighbors and friends, who trust them more than strangers when they describe the importance of this form of water purification.

P.J. Albert et al. (eds.), *Global Poverty Alleviation: A Case Book*, The International Society of Business, Economics, and Ethics Book Series 3, DOI 10.1007/978-94-007-7479-7_3, © Springer Science+Business Media Dordrecht 2014

All of these cases illustrate what companies and NGOs can do to improve health in blighted communities. Each organization uses its particular expertise to improve health in remote areas. Each is a model for what other companies can do with their expertise to improve health and health access. Even if one is a cynic, what these organizations are doing is improving the health of communities, and thus the health of potential workers and the viability of new markets.

The Novartis Foundation for Sustainable Development: Tackling HIV/AIDS and Poverty in South Africa (A)[1]

In 1998, sociologist Kurt Madörin from the Swiss-based NGO *terre des hommes schweiz*[2] approached Klaus Leisinger and Karin Schmitt of the Novartis Foundation for Sustainable Development in Basel, Switzerland. There was an acute problem with orphans in sub-Saharan Africa, he told Leisinger, Novartis president and executive director, and Schmitt, director of foundation affairs and special projects. With one or both parents dying from AIDS, many African children were left vulnerable to homelessness, exploitation, abuse, violence, starvation, and other dangers. There were more than 8 million AIDS orphans in Africa, a number expected to reach 42 million by 2008.[3] Being an orphan often meant being a social outcast, and orphaned children were more likely to fall into greater poverty. At the time, there was no effective solution for dealing with the crisis; these parentless children were either put into orphanages, if available; lived on the streets; or were taken care of by an NGO, which gave them food, shelter, and clothing. The result often was deep psychosocial trauma for the orphans, which no group was equipped to handle. Madörin wanted to develop a program that would help the orphaned children of Africa deal with this psychosocial trauma. He wanted to start in Tanzania, where the number of orphans who had lost both parents had risen from 71,100 in 1992 to 174,400 in 1998.[4] A pilot program in Tanzania would help him assess the feasibility and effectiveness of such a program. But he needed financial and other assistance. Madörin asked Leisinger and Schmitt if the Novartis Foundation could help. They agreed to consider

---

[1] These cases were prepared by Jenny Mead under the supervision of Patricia H. Werhane. Copyright©2008 University of Virginia Darden School Foundation. All rights reserved.

[2] *terres des hommes schweiz* focused on the health, social care, and rights of children worldwide.

[3] Nelson, Benjamin F. "Global Health: The U.S. and U.N. Response to the AIDS Crisis in Africa," *U.S. General Accounting Office Testimony* (February 2000): 2. http://www.gao.gov/archive/2000/ns00099t.pdf. Accessed 12 Sept 2007.

[4] "Number of AIDS Orphans Rapidly Increasing in Sub-Saharan Africa," *Reproductive Health Matters* 11, no. 22 (2003): 193.

the proposal, although Novartis, one of the largest pharmaceutical companies in the world, did not manufacture or sell any HIV/AIDS-related products.

The HIV/AIDS Crisis

As the close of the 20th century approached, the 20-year-old AIDS crisis had ravaged many developing countries. Particularly hard-hit was sub-Saharan Africa, called by some the "global epicenter"[5] of the crisis. Of the estimated 33.4 million people living with HIV/AIDS worldwide in 1998, 22 million of them were in sub-Saharan Africa. Already, in this area, 12 million had died and life expectancy had plummeted from 62 years to 47. See Exhibit 1 for 1998 worldwide HIV/AIDS statistics and comparisons. Although the AIDS crisis was obviously a worldwide issue, the scale of the epidemic in Africa made "its repercussions qualitatively different from those in other parts of the world."[6] Because HIV transmission in African countries occurred primarily through heterosexual contact, AIDS was considered a family disease.

Of particular concern, and cited in a sobering 1997 U.S. Agency for International Development (USAID) report called "Children on the Brink," was the number of orphans (or "children affected by AIDS," as the specialists preferred) the pandemic created. The statistics for Africa were deeply disturbing: AIDS had accounted for 16 % of the deaths that orphaned African children in 1990, but estimates were that the proportion would be 68 % by 2010.[7] The USAID report forecast that by the year 2010, 40 million to 42 million children worldwide, primarily in Africa, would be without one or both parents because of HIV/AIDS. The results of being orphaned, the report continued, would include severe emotional distress, malnutrition, no health care, and a lack of identity. These orphans also would face a variety of painful futures including child labor, no education, loss of inheritance, destitution, forced migration, and a vastly increased exposure to HIV infection. Historically, the worldwide percentage of orphans was around 2 %, but predictions for 2010 were as high as 17–25 %. In addition to the devastating physical effects (e.g., starvation and abuse), of great concern also was the psychosocial trauma these orphans were experiencing.

Previously, the "orphan" problem in African countries was mitigated by the fact that children who lost their parents were taken in by other family members:

---

[5] http://www.thebody.com/content/world/art33120.html. Accessed 25 April 2007.

[6] Foster, Geoff. 2002. Supporting community efforts to assist orphans in Africa. *New England Journal of Medicine* 346(24): 1907.

[7] Foster, 1907.

The extended family was the "safety net."[8] But AIDS had overburdened and weakened this informal social structure by increasing the number of orphans, reducing the number of caregivers, and damaging the overall safety net. Paradoxically, "the effectiveness of the traditional African social system in absorbing millions of vulnerable children has contributed to the complacency of governments and agencies in addressing the orphan crisis."[9]

Novartis

Novartis was the product of a record-breaking 1996 merger between "two Swiss giants of the pharmaceutical world"[10] and long-time competitors, Ciba-Geigy and Sandoz. The histories of the companies that formed Novartis in 1998 dated back to the 18th and 19th centuries. In addition to pharmaceutical products, Ciba-Geigy produced, among other things, pesticides, photographic products, eye care items, and synthetic plastics and resins. Sandoz specialized in pharmaceutical products, various industrial-use chemicals, infant and diet foods, and distribution of agricultural raw materials. Both companies had also acquired a number of U.S. biotech and genomics companies (Sandoz had a large stake in both Genetic Therapy and Systemix; Ciba-Geigy in Viagene and Chiron), although profits from these were not expected until at least 2006.[11] The merger, announced in early 1996 and officially sanctioned by the U.S. Federal Trade Commission in December of that year, was a seismic transaction, worth more than USD30 billion.[12] It took many people by surprise because the two companies had long been competitors, although their physical locations' being just across the Rhine River from each other allowed them to "stare into each other's labs from buildings on opposite banks of the river that flows through Basel."[13]

The merger made Novartis the second-largest drug company after Glaxo Wellcome. At the time, in the mid-1990s, mergers of large pharmaceuticals were understandable due to the difficult times for drug companies in general. Not only were the new drug pipelines "lackluster," but "[i]mportant drugs lose their

---

[8] Foster, 1907.

[9] Foster, 1907.

[10] Freudenheim, Milt. 1996. Merger of drug giants: A new image for corporate Switzerland. *New York Times*, 8 March 1996, D1.

[11] Moore, Stephen D. 1996. Novartis Leaps last regulatory hurdle. *The Wall Street Journal*, 18 December 1996, B11.

[12] According to Freudenheim, this was the third-largest deal at that time, following Mitsubishi Bank's acquisition of the Bank of Tokyo for USD33.8 billion and Kohlberg Kravis Roberts's deal for RJR Nabisco for USD30.6 billion.

[13] Moore, Stephen D. and Philip Revzin. 1996. Challenge for Novartis Lies in the lab. *Wall Street Journal*, 30 July 1996, B8.

profitability with age. Prices drop as similar, me-too drugs are approved."[14] And perhaps most importantly, "Patent protection for the original groundbreakers eventually runs out, and prices decline even further."[15] The patent on Voltaren, Ciba-Geigy's enormously popular and profitable antiarthritis drug, was on the verge of expiring.

The name Novartis was derived from *novae artes*, Latin for "new skills" and, according to the Novartis Web site, "reflects our commitment to bringing new health care products to patients and physicians worldwide."[16] In 1997, its first full year as a new company, Novartis did well: Total sales were up by 9 % to (Swiss francs) CHF31.2. Net income had grown by 43 % to CHF5.2 billion, and operating cash flow saw a 31 % increase to CHF4.7 billion.[17] To reduce costs, the company had trimmed 9,100 employees, primarily through "natural fluctuation and early retirement" and, in the case of job redundancy, "offered severance packages that reflect our commitment to social responsibility."[18] The company had spun off some of its divisions, including Ciba-Geigy's specialty chemical unit (textile dyes, pigments, and polymers), choosing instead to focus on its Gerber products (Sandoz bought the baby-product business in 1994), pharmaceuticals, agricultural chemicals, and its over-the-counter medications such as Tavist, Ex-Lax, Gas-X, and Maalox. By the end of 1997, Novartis was competing "head-to-head" with Glaxo Wellcome, and had introduced five new products: Migranal, a migraine preventative nasal spray; Foradil, for asthma; Femara, a treatment for hormone-dependent cancer (e.g., breast cancer); Apligraf, a human skin regenerative biotechnology product; and Diovan, a hypertension drug.[19] Novartis was not involved in research and development of HIV/AIDS medicines, but its health care effort included fighting leprosy, malaria, and tuberculosis. See Exhibit 2 for company financial information and Exhibit 3 for the 1995 percentage of pharmaceutical world market share.

Origins of the Novartis Foundation for Sustainable Development

Development aid and humanitarian assistance had been a tradition of several Basel-based companies and started in a small Tanzanian location in 1949. At the request of the local bishop in Ifakara, zoologist Rudolf Geigy, an expert in pathogens and tropical diseases, visited Tanzania to see if he could devise a solution for the malaria, sleeping sickness, river blindness, and other diseases that ravaged the community. Using an improvised laboratory, Geigy studied ticks, fleas, and other regional

---

[14] Freudenheim

[15] Freudenheim.

[16] http://www.novartis.com/about-novartis/company-history/index.shtml (accessed 04 November 2007).

[17] Novartis Operational Review 1997, 4.

[18] Novartis Operational Review 1997, 4.

[19] Bale Communications Inc., "Novartis Looking To Be the Biggest," *Adnews Online*, 18 December 1997.

insects. Eventually, the Rural Aid Centre was established in 1961, with financing by the Basel Foundation for Assistance to Developing Countries. This foundation was the creation of the former Ciba, Geigy, Sandoz, and companies based in Basel, which Geigy recruited for continued support. Geigy's firm belief was that "aid should have a sustainable impact and … be more than the distribution of charity,"[20] which became the credo of the Novartis Foundation.

In the early 1970s, the chairman of Ciba-Geigy, just recently formed from the merger of J. R. Geigy AG and Ciba, asked a young graduate student, Klaus Leisinger, to outline a working set of guidelines for an international company doing business in Africa. What Leisinger came up with, said Novartis's Karin Schmitt, was legendary for that time. "He had some very funny and courageous ideas," said Schmitt. "He felt you should Africanize the companies, that the local CEOs should be African."[21] In addition, Leisinger's paper emphasized selling solutions, not just products. The result was an "unequivocal" set of guidelines and obligations for doing business in a poor country. From Leisinger's paper emerged an Africa Policy, which then became a Corporate Policy for the Third World. At the same time, Novartis established a Third World Staff Unit, followed by a Third World Committee, which then, in 1979, became the Ciba-Geigy Foundation for Cooperation with Developing Countries on the basis that "the company did not content itself with declarations, but actually put its principles into practice."[22]

The purpose of the organization, according to its founding document, was to promote development of the poorest countries in the Third World, primarily by collaborating in agriculture, health care, and education, with the ultimate purpose of fostering self-help and providing aid in the event of a disaster. In 1990, this purpose was amended and "scientifically based analyses" and "consultations and information on development policy issues" were added to the list of resources to be made available. The objective of the foundation thus became three-pronged: consulting on development policy inside and outside the company, engaging in dialogue about development policy and human rights, and using its knowledge and insights in development projects.[23]

Schmitt emphasized that although the then Ciba-Geigy had a tradition of philanthropic work, the emphasis really was on achieving sustainable results. "You can give just money away," Schmitt said, "but that was never the purpose." Although Ciba-Geigy did give charitable donations, the company took development assistance very seriously. "You don't just throw money into things, make a nice publication, make photos, and make public relations with it, but you really build up something." The Novartis Foundation's charitable efforts were never designed to build markets where there are none because, as Schmitt said, that might lead to a conflict of

[20] "Success Through Perseverance and Patience: The History of the Novartis Foundation is One of Continuity Over 25 Years," 19, http://www.novartisfoundation.org/platform/apps/Publication/get-fmfile.asp?id=652&el=543&se=634215889&doc=14&dse=1 . Accessed 17 July 2007.

[21] Karin Schmitt (Novartis), interviewed by Jenny Mead, April 4, 2007, Darden Graduate School of Business Administration, Charlottesville, Virginia.

[22] "Success Through Perseverance and Patience," 20.

[23] "Success Through Perseverance and Patience," 21.

interest between the company's commercial efforts and its interests in Third World country development. Its Leprosy Fund worked closely with governments, the World Health Organization (WHO), and nongovernmental leprosy organizations to address the sociocultural problems as well as medical needs of those suffering from leprosy in countries such as India, Sri Lanka, Madagascar, and Brazil.

The foundation staff was small, but its activities were wide and varied. There was, according to Schmitt, think tank and publication work.

> We work very much academically on issues like corporate citizenship and business ethics; but we were also greatly interested in green biotechnology, population policy "with a human face," and other broader issues of social and political relevance. We also take a scientific approach to our assistance programs, so that we really can disseminate knowledge in a form that is acceptable to the most different circles of stakeholders – to academia but also to lay people, but also to people who are working in development to governments to others.

Experimenting in Tanzania

What Madörin proposed doing in Tanzania had in a similar fashion already been tried out independently in Zimbabwe, where the HIV/AIDS orphan crisis was also severe. Stefan Germann, a Swiss aid worker who was at the time with the Swiss Salvation Army, had just founded the Massiye Camp, primarily to help develop the coping capacity of children affected by HIV/AIDS, and to focus on psychosocial support and life-skills development for orphans and other vulnerable children. Madörin wanted to do his work in a very remote rural area of Tanzania, where NGOs rarely go, because he thought if his concept could work there, it would work everywhere.

This type of project inevitably would have a modicum of controversy, with some questioning why an organization would focus on the psychosocial issues of children rather than their material needs. The answer, according to Madörin, was that giving children food and clothing was no longer enough. There was a "causal relationship between death, poverty, and alienation, resulting in grief, anger, and antisocial behavior."[24] If left unaddressed, Madörin contended, this "failure to support children to overcome this trauma will have very negative impact on society and might cause dysfunctional societies, jeopardizing years of investment in national development."[25] Nonetheless, Madörin's proposal was unusual and did not fit the normal profile of suggested programs to combat the effects of AIDS in Africa. Novartis also did not manufacture any HIV/AIDS medical products, leading some to question why the company would even consider addressing this particular problem. Novartis and its foundation did have the choice of many worthwhile opportunities to address crises in developing countries, whether or not related directly to its products. In addition to AIDS, there was leprosy, malaria, and tuberculosis, and although Novartis had addressed these health crises with various

---

[24] Germann, Stefan, Kurt Madörin, and Ncazelo Ncube. 2001. Psychosocial support for children affected by AIDS: Tanzania, and Zimbabwe. *SAFAIDS* 9(2): 11.

[25] Germann et al., 11.

programs, in this case, the company decided to support a project that tried to approach, in an innovative way, a real socioeconomic need of vulnerable children. The idea was to develop "good practices," proof of the concept, and a sustainable program. Novartis also wanted to make all lessons learned in this process and implementation available to interested donors worldwide.

Exhibit 1: The Novartis Foundation for Sustainable Development: Tackling HIV/AIDS and Poverty in South Africa (A)

Worldwide AIDS statistics – 1998

Region	Adults and children living with HIV/AIDS	Adults and children newly infected with HIV	Adult infection rate
Sub-Saharan Africa	22.5 million	4.0 million	8.0 %
North Africa and Middle East	210,000	19,000	0.13 %
North America	890,000	44,000	0.56 %
Latin America	1.4 million	160,000	0.57 %
South and Southeast Asia	6.7 million	1.2 million	0.69 %
East Asia and Pacific	560,000	200,000	0.068 %
Australia and New Zealand	12,000	600	0.1 %
Western Europe	500,000	30,000	0.25 %
Caribbean	330,000	45,000	1.96 %

Source: "AIDS Epidemic Update: December 1998," UNAIDS Joint United Nations Programme on HIV/AIDS

Exhibit 2: The Novartis Foundation for Sustainable Development: Tackling HIV/AIDS and Poverty in South Africa (A)

Novartis AG 1997 Financial Information (all figures in CHF millions)

Summarized consolidated income statements

For the years ended 31 December 1997 and 1996	1996	Pro forma 1997
Sales	31,180	26,144
Cost of goods sold	−9,847	−8,414
Operating expenses	−14,550	−12,803
Operating income	6,783	4,927
Financial income/expense, net	120	−83
Taxes and minority interests	−1,692	−1,207
NET INCOME	5,211	3,637

Summarized consolidated balance sheets

	31 Dec. 1997	1 Jan. 1997
ASSETS		
Long-term assets		
Tangible fixed assets	**11,589**	11,534
Other long-term assets	**6,069**	4,912
Total long-term assets	**17,658**	16,446
Current assets		
Inventories, trade accounts, receivables, and other current assets	**15,684**	15,273
Marketable securities, cash, and cash equivalents	**18,486**	18,527
Total current assets	**34,170**	33,800
TOTAL ASSETS	**51,828**	50,246
EQUITY AND LIABILITIES		
Equity		
Share capital, net	**1,370**	1,377
Reserves	**25,431**	22,187
Total equity	**26,801**	23,564
Liabilities		
Long-term liabilities		
Financial debts	**3,611**	5,254
Deferred taxes, other long-term liabilities, and minority interests	**4,360**	3,892
Total long-term liabilities and minority interests	**7,971**	9,146
Short-term liabilities		
Financial debts	**7,465**	6,722
Trade accounts payable and other short-term liabilities	**9,591**	10,814
Total short-term liabilities	**17,056**	17,536
Total liabilities and minority interests	**25,027**	26,682
TOTAL EQUITY AND LIABILITIES	**51,828**	50,246

Source: Novartis operational review, 1997, 29

The Novartis Foundation for Sustainable Development: Tackling HIV/AIDS and Poverty in South Africa (B)

Developing a Pilot Program

The increasing problems of millions of HIV/AIDS orphans and the perceived necessity of an innovative and creative solution to tackle the psychological, social, and economic needs of vulnerable children tipped the scales in favor of accepting Kurt Madörin's proposal: Klaus Leisinger and Karin Schmitt of the Novartis Foundation for Sustainable Development gave Madörin the go-ahead for setting up a pilot program in Tanzania to address the psychosocial needs of children who had lost parents to AIDS. With the financial help of the foundation as well as the Swiss Agency for Development and Cooperation (SDC), Madörin traveled to Kagera, Tanzania, where approximately one-third of children had lost one or both parents to AIDS.

His pilot program was called "Humuliza" (a Kihaya word meaning "consolation"). The two stated goals of Humuliza were to (1) develop practical instruments to enable teachers and caregivers to support orphans psychologically, and create a supportive environment for children affected by HIV/AIDS; and (2) develop children's capacity to cope with the loss of their caregivers in an effort to enhance their resilience.[26]

Madörin discovered that the orphaned children in Tanzania faced daunting challenges: surviving on their own, caring for younger siblings and sometimes grandparents, and no money for food, clothing, or school fees. Many were forced to leave school and work in the fields to survive. Many fell prey to drug traffickers and prostitution. In addition to the physical challenges, many of these children experienced "a loss of emotional security and confidence as the world around them collapsed."[27]

Using his background as a sociologist, Madörin began developing model approaches designed to stabilize children both psychologically and socially. In the Humuliza program, the focus was on encouraging children's development, self-confidence, and survival skills. Key to accomplishing this was teaching the orphans to cope with their grief and loss. Children were also taught to "cultivate life skills, develop goals, build self-esteem, learn through play, provide peer care, and manage the stigma associated with HIV/AIDS."[28] In Madörin's models, children could describe their feelings and their emotions, and act out these feelings in many ways, including by crying. Through talking, the children were better able to work out their trauma. Madörin's therapeutic approaches included many different exercises. In one, for example, children collected stones and put them in a bag, which symbolized how heavy their emotional burden was.

A key component of the program was creating groups of children and teenagers in which they would help each other to cope and survive on their own and not end up in orphanages. The emphasis was on helping them get back to community life. The children eventually would help the elders around them; in turn, the elders would care for the youth. These children learned survival mechanisms such as how to grow food and how to take care of themselves physically. At the same time, they were able to stay in school; the Novartis Foundation paid the school fees. A nine-person professional local team provided support. There were agricultural courses, English classes, and self-defense classes for girls. A mobile farm school was established and there was a bank offering microcredit loans, and financial assistance for those in dire need. Over several years, older children began leading the organization and supporting the younger ones. The program grew; manuals for adult caregivers and teachers were prepared, children were taught to help each other cope, and teachers and other adults associated with the program were trained in counseling distressed

---

[26] http://www.humuliza.org/index.php?option=com_content&task=view&id=1&Itemid=1. Accessed 20 Aug 2007.

[27] Novartis, "Regional Psychosocial Support Initiative: Bringing Hope to AIDS Orphans," 4.

[28] http://www.humuliza.org/.

children. At the same time, awareness of the problems of AIDS orphans was raised through radio programs. And "self-managed youth organizations were created, so that orphans could experience friendship and mutual help."[29]

Creation of REPSSI

After several years of successfully working with children in Tanzania, Madörin and Stefan Germann of the Salvation Army Zimbabwean camp wanted to expand and broaden the program and export it to other African countries. They believed that a collective approach to dealing with AIDS orphans – such as creating a knowledge bank – would be extremely useful in transferring their knowledge and experience to new countries where help was also desperately needed. Using their experience in Tanzania and Zimbabwe, Madörin and Germann wrote up a model psychosocial program; it was translated into other languages and made available on the Web. Humuliza soon caught the interest of larger organizations, including UNICEF and UNAIDS.

In October 2000, Madörin presented his program in a workshop at Massiye Camp. The creation of a Regional Psychosocial Support Initiative (REPSSI) occurred in 2001 at a psychosocial support (PSS) "Think Tank" meeting whose attendees included providers of support to AIDS orphans, various aid organization representatives, scientists and doctors, and also children and young people. The goal was to combine the different approaches of various relief agencies in the area, and to increase awareness among these agencies of concepts of PSS. Initially, REPPSI was just a "loose" initiative, but two organizations, the International HIV/ AIDS Alliance and the Southern Africa AIDS Training Program (SAT) were brought in. These two NGOs, in collaboration, became the governing umbrella for REPSSI. The organization as a whole also committed to the goals outlined in a June 2001 U.N. General Assembly Special Session on HIV/AIDS, with particular emphasis on the articles relating to children both orphaned and made vulnerable by the pandemic. See Exhibit 1 for Novartis Foundation financial information. The costs of the Humuliza and REPSSI programs were projected to be approximately USD500,000 per year, about 7 % of the foundation's overall budget.[30] See Exhibit 2 for UNGASS AIDS commitments involving children and AIDS.

But a stable donor community was necessary. In March 2002, the Novartis Foundation along with SDC and the Swedish International Development Cooperation Agency banded together to provide this support. The organization recruited staff members and "then grew at breathtaking pace," until it became clear that it was unable to keep up with the constantly increasing demands. The management team

---

[29] http://www.humuliza.org/.

[30] For more detailed information about the Humuliza Project, see http://www.humuliza.org/index. php?option=com_content&task=view&id=1&Itemid=1. Accessed 04 Nov 2007.

had to learn to set priorities, while the donors had to appreciate that the managers needed additional professional support.[31] Also, in May 2002, the REPSSI initiative became a regional technical psychosocial support capacity-building program. The aim of the program was "to improve and scale up psychosocial assistance for CABA [children affected by AIDS] in East and Southern Africa through partner organizations."[32]

Those working on the initiative, however, needed an organizational structure, defined logistics, and contracts and legal protection. In short, the initiative needed an organizational developer. In addition, REPSSI needed to be based in a safe and stable location, allowing the program to grow, endure, and flourish. Because of political problems in Zimbabwe, the initiative, which was then based there, had to move elsewhere. The Novartis Foundation and the other organizations involved had to assess different countries and determine which one would be the best headquarters for REPSSI, and they had to focus on creating a strong and effective organizational operation.

Exhibit 1: The Novartis Foundation for Sustainable Development: Tackling HIV/AIDS and Poverty in South Africa (B)

Budget 2007 of the Novartis Foundation for sustainable development (in CHF)

Think tank activities and networking	1,000,000
Health projects	6,200,000
The fight against Leprosy	890,000
Preventive and basic health	3,710,000
Access to treatment	1,600,000
Human rights and knowledge management	700,000
Administration	1,858,000
Total budget 2007	9,758,000

Plus product donations for Leprosy, Tuberculosis, and Malaria in the order of magnitude of CHF10 million

---

[31] http://www.novartisfoundation.org/page/content/index.asp?Menu=3&MenuID=237&ID=526& Item=44.6. Accessed 27 Aug 2007.

[32] "History of REPSSI," www.repssi.org/home.asp?pid=31. Accessed 20 Aug 2007.

Exhibit 2: The Novartis Foundation for Sustainable Development: Tackling HIV/AIDS and Poverty in South Africa (B)

United Nations General Assembly Special Session on HIV/AIDS
  AIDS Commitments, Articles 65–67.

Children Orphaned and Made Vulnerable by HIV/AIDS

Children Orphaned and Affected by HIV/AIDS Need Special Assistance

65. By 2003, develop and by 2005 implement national policies and strategies to: build and strengthen governmental, family and community capacities to provide a supportive environment for orphans and girls and boys infected and affected by HIV/AIDS including by providing appropriate counselling and psycho-social support; ensuring their enrolment in school and access to shelter, good nutrition, health and social services on an equal basis with other children; to protect orphans and vulnerable children from all forms of abuse, violence, exploitation, discrimination, trafficking and loss of inheritance;
66. Ensure non-discrimination and full and equal enjoyment of all human rights through the promotion of an active and visible policy of de-stigmatization of children orphaned and made vulnerable by HIV/AIDS;
67. Urge the international community, particularly donor countries, civil society, as well as the private sector to complement effectively national programmes to support programmes for children orphaned or made vulnerable by HIV/AIDS in affected regions, in countries at high risk and to direct special assistance to sub-Saharan Africa;

For a complete list of articles from the Declaration of Commitment on HIV/AIDS published by the U.N. General Assembly Special Session on HIV/AIDS (June 25–27, 2001) see http://www.un.org/ga/aids/coverage/FinalDeclarationHIVAIDS.html.

Exhibit 3: The Novartis Foundation for Sustainable Development: Tackling HIV/AIDS and Poverty in South Africa (A)

Percentage of pharmaceutical World Market share in 1995

Top 33 %	
Glaxo Wellcome	4.7 %
Novartis (Ciba and Geigy)	4.4 %
Merck	3.5 %
Hoechst Marion Roussel	3.5 %
Bristol-Myers Squibb	3.1 %
American home products	3.0 %
Pfizer	2.9 %
Johnson & Johnson	2.9 %
Roche pharmaceuticals	2.8 %
SB	2.5 %
Balance: 66.7 %	

Source: Reuter, "Sandoz-Ciba Merger Hailed as World's Biggest," *The Financial Post* (Toronto), 8 March 1996, 5

The Novartis Foundation for Sustainable Development: Tackling HIV/AIDS and Poverty in South Africa (C)

REPSSI: Growth and Evolution[33]

The donors jointly commissioned Ernst and Young to conduct a risk assessment of how REPSSI could be brought to other African countries both legally and effectively. The original initiative had to be transformed into an organization, and a host country had to be chosen to implement the program. South Africa, where the HIV/AIDS problem and its effects on children seemed the most severe, was chosen. Johannesburg became the headquarters of REPSSI, with branches in 13 countries. Schmitt recalled that serendipitously, at that juncture, she was approached by the head of the Novartis international human resources division, who offered to help with human resource and organizational development and finance management for the new venture.

Representatives from Novartis human resources traveled to South Africa to assess all the gaps and weaknesses in the organization. To strengthen the program,

---

[33] Karin Schmitt (Novartis), interview by Jenny Mead, April 4, 2007, Darden Graduate School of Business Administration, Charlottesville, Virginia. (Unless otherwise noted, all Schmitt quotations in the case are from that interview.)

Schmitt said, "They drew together not only our resources, but specialist organizations like coaches, organization builders, finance management people." At the same time, they worked with universities, including Harvard, to build and strengthen REPSSI.

First Annual Review

In 2003, REPSSI had its first annual review in which it emerged that there was a need for stronger planning and reporting processes, and for REPSSI to operate in a results-based management framework. In the early months of 2004, REPSSI team members underwent intense training, and the ensuing "Results Chain" was developed to enable the organization "to work toward achieving long-term positive impact in the lives of children affected by AIDS in East and Southern Africa."[34]

Novartis Foundation Philosophy

An organization's ability to make progress in development in other countries, as several decades of experience had proved, hinged on the domestic political and economic conditions in partner countries. This justified the increasing international demands on the governments of developing countries for better governance. For the same reasons, many people and organizations were acknowledging the need for a trade policy favoring poor countries through a genuinely free world market (at least theoretically).

Sustainable development could only take place, the Novartis Foundation believed, by overcoming obstacles to this development. The need for changes aimed at overcoming such obstacles might have seemed obvious, given the widespread destitution in developing countries. But the foundation believed that a pragmatic development policy could not afford to wait for these changes to occur and obstacles be diminished before implementing strategies designed to alleviate poverty. The Novartis Foundation, Schmitt said, sought "to promote practical development measures that take account of existing conditions, and to take immediate action wherever we see the best potential for implementing our concept of sustainable development."

The less room there was for maneuvering with regard to poverty-oriented development strategies at the higher level of political action, Schmitt explained, the greater the intrinsic value of poverty alleviation projects at the local level. She said the foundation was aware that its development work could not have any direct impact on the conditions shaping the national or international framework. "Questions of this type require discussions well beyond the project level – between policymakers for the donors and recipients in the public sector, in the context of bilateral governmental consultations and multilateral coordinating committees such as the World

---

[34] "History and Background of REPSSI," http://www.repssi.org/home.asp?pid=31. Accessed 1 Sept 2007.

Bank Consultative Group." Ideally, such discussions would result in the formulation by the donors of explicit allocation conditions, with the aim of intentionally changing the existing framework. For these reasons, Schmitt said, the Novartis Foundation normally restricted itself to measures that focused on the grass-roots level. The foundation did not regard development assistance as an alternative to political solution nor as a purely charitable form of philanthropy. Schmitt said:

> We make a continual effort to ensure that our decision-making processes reflect a developmental perspective by focusing on criteria that allow us to expect the maximum effectiveness and sustainability from the collaborative work we undertake. The criteria relate to the conditions that can have a substantial influence on the success and effectiveness of a project or program.

Schmitt enumerated the elements that projects and programs supported by the Novartis Foundation should have[35]:

- Maintain a direct relation to poverty – focusing on developing neglected productive resources in disadvantaged population groups (rather than focusing, for example, on expanding existing potential without clearly linking such expansion to the target population);
- Take account of the core problems in the developing country concerned (rather than focusing on problems of little relevance). Core problems were those that posed the greatest obstacles to economic and social development.
- Take account of a partner country's potential for development (rather than initiating work when the potential for development is low).
- Take account of the partner country's experience (rather than making commitments in areas where previous experience had been rather problematic, or the foundation had little expertise);
- Take account of the partner country's priorities (rather than pursuing priorities in which the partner country had no interest);
- Take account of the conditions for achieving a goal, and for the effectiveness and sustainability of an intervention (rather than making an effort where the pressure of problems was great but the conditions unfavorable);
- Take account of the need for external assistance (rather than choosing areas of development in which the country concerned was capable of self-help);
- Take account of other donors' commitments. (In negative terms: Avoid duplicating the efforts of other donors; in positive terms: Determine whether other donors' commitments could be effectively complemented to achieve synergistic effects);
- Take account of the amount of resources available to the foundation (because this determined the extent and the focus of the contribution the foundation could make in solving a significant problem).

Despite all attempts to be objective and to reason from a developmental perspective during the selection process, in the final analysis, determination of priorities always required evaluations (of core problems, development potential, conditions, willingness of the partner to pursue development, etc.) by Novartis's project

---

[35] Schmitt emphasized that this list of criteria was not complete; the degree of specification in Novartis's criteria for development work was too extensive to catalogue in this case.

managers. These priorities often varied greatly in terms of the resources they required. But a specific level of funding, Schmitt emphasized, was never the starting point for a development priority. Complementary situations, however, were often created. For example, support for a psychosocial counseling program or project for African children orphaned by AIDS might have been a priority when it contributed to solving a locally significant development problem, even if the program's activities required a minimal budget and involved primarily information and educational efforts. Novartis was guided by the overriding aim that the effectiveness and impact of the resources it committed to problem-solving could be improved by concentrating on the priorities in each case. All the development activities underwent independent evaluations to assess their degrees of effectiveness, which facilitated a continual learning process and allowed Novartis to replicate successful approaches.

Schmitt emphasized the incremental approach that the Novartis Foundation took. Whether it's "leprosy, malaria, or AIDS, one actor can hardly do anything. So the foundation comes in, starts with a small initiative like Humuliza in Tanzania, and finds ways to make the impact bigger." The Swiss and Swedish governments supported the program. They provided funds, while the Novartis Foundation, in addition to the funding, provided organizational development assistance. For the biggest influence the foundation focused on building the capacity of the organization and consequently advancing the whole field of psychosocial care for AIDS orphans.

The philosophy behind helping children, whether in South Africa or in countries such as Sri Lanka with its civil war, or in Gaza, Schmitt said, was to reach them at a very early age:

> I believe in supporting early childhood development and youth development. This is the most important thing if you want to have sustainable development. You have to break the vicious circle because children who grow up in violence, who grow up with abuse, are incapacitated for their whole life. They simply repeat the circle.

Medical and physical care is vitally important, she said, but so was looking at what's happening inside children. "It's like a volcano, and this volcano breaks out sooner or later," she said. "The number of those children growing up in these circumstances is simply enormous and it's growing."

Schmitt emphasized taking an almost scientific approach to complex problems to imbue the programs with credibility. At the same time, even the most complex problems, she said, had to be presented in a simple way. "As a single actor, you're just one little mosaic stone in the huge picture of mosaics," Schmitt said. "But other actors bring in the other mosaic stones." REPSSI was an organization that shared this philosophy and worked hard to realize mutual principles in their program work.

Types of Cooperation

The foundation's development assistance took two main forms: supporting projects and programs and contributing to small projects and shared initiatives.

Project and Program Assistance

More and more of the resources devoted to development were allocated to programs. Whereas projects consisted of individual health development measures and were limited in terms of duration and funding, program assistance involved several coordinated measures. For example, programs focused on a region or a particular population group (such as AIDS orphans). The programs and projects concentrated on activities that directly addressed the basic needs of the poor and disadvantaged. Ecological aspects and approaches enhancing the position of women in society received special attention.

Technical Cooperation

Wherever it was necessary to strengthen a local project partner by improving its functional capacities – as was particularly the case for REPSSI – financial and technical cooperation were required. In the area of technical cooperation, Novartis provided advisors, trainers, specialists, consultants, and other experts; it also offered training and further education of local specialists and managers in developing countries.

Cofinancing with Other Donors

Novartis considered cofinancing along with other bilateral and multilateral donors to be an appropriate instrument for supporting complex projects and programs (again, such as REPSSI). The advantages of cofinancing included joint pursuit of common development aims, combined experience and financial resources, and division of labor. But the foundation was careful to observe its own criteria for development cooperation in all such cases. By doing so, the foundation would be free to initiate additional program activities if and when necessary or desirable even if other donors might choose not to participate in these programs. The foundation looked specifically for activities and project elements that would continue after its own involvement ended; to achieve this goal, the foundation introduced a project module with performance-based funding.

Small-Scale Projects

In addition to projects and programs, in exceptional cases, Novartis also supported small-scale projects that required rapid, effective assistance to promote self-help. The measures that seemed the most worthy of support in this regard were those which would be successful only if they were rapidly implemented, and which could not be financed by local agents qualified to execute them (such as churches). These small-scale projects were not meant to have any direct connection with other projects being supported by the foundation, and they had to consist of self-contained measures that did not result in continuing obligations.

REPSSI in 2006

By 2006, REPSSI, through its various organizations and institutions throughout sub-Saharan Africa, had touched the lives of more than 300,000 orphans. It had worked at various times with more than 140 aid organizations. The collaboration had, in particular, been extremely successful in "transferring best practices in labor management, leadership, and financial skills."[36] Many of the services provided for the NGO by businesses and universities were pro bono. REPSSI continued to grow as 2006 came to a close and, with management stretched thin, those involved with REPSSI looked once again to Novartis's corporate human resources as well as the foundation itself to guide them to greater growth.[37]

REPSSI goals were also, according to Novartis, in line with the eight Millennium Development Goals (MDGs), established by the United Nations in 2000 and to be achieved by 2015. The MDGs were a summary of the actions and targets outlined in the Millennium Declaration, adopted by 189 nations and signed by 147 heads of state and governments during the September 2000 U.N. Millennium Summit. These goals were to

1. "eradicate extreme poverty and hunger
2. achieve universal primary education
3. promote gender equality and empower women
4. reduce child mortality
5. improve maternal health
6. combat HIV/AIDS, malaria, and other diseases
7. ensure environmental sustainability
8. develop a Global Partnership for Development"[38]

Building Leadership Skills

In 2006, as the growth of REPSSI outpaced some of the team's own management capabilities, Novartis's corporate human resources offered to provide leadership and management training. The knowledge and skills Novartis could transfer to the

---

[36] Novartis, "Regional Psychosocial Support Initiative: Bringing Hope to AIDS Orphans in Africa," 2, http://www.novartisfoundation.org/platform/content/element/1172/Bringing_Hope.pdf. Accessed 24 Aug 2007.

[37] In addition, by 2006, the Novartis Foundation had been involved in a number of other projects including: improving access to leprosy services in Sri Lanka (1989–2006); integrated health care project in Mali (2001–2005); community development program in Sri Lanka (2000–2005); organization and community development in Brazil (1993–2004); support for youth training centers in Tanzania (1998–2002); rural women's project in Bangladesh (1992–96); and empowerment of women in Gaza (1992–1996).

[38] For more information about the Millennium Goals, see http://www.un.org/millenniumgoals. Accessed 17 Jan 2008.

REPSSI staff would build the organization's long-term effectiveness as the leading authority in psychosocial support in southern and eastern Africa. The leadership of Novartis South Africa also became active in coaching, training, and providing consultative support.[39]

The Novartis Foundation, REPSSI, and Novartis corporate learning identified specific areas for leadership development and agreed on a midterm strategy:

- Reviewing REPSSI HR policies and procedures
- Providing training in basic leadership skills for the REPSSI team
- Establishing project management skills to support the planned growth of REPSSI
- Developing business acumen for the REPSSI leadership team to manage growth and build increasing independence from the group's funding partners
- Improving REPSSI's communications strategy

Motivation and Creative Partnerships

Internally, Schmitt said, the corporate citizenship efforts helped motivate employees and brought particular satisfaction as well as a new dimension to the work of those who participated directly (such as Novartis's corporate HR department's and Novartis South Africa's involvement with REPSSI). Employees had an opportunity to address a significant social need as individuals and as part of a larger team. Because of the REPSSI case, Novartis employees in 2007 set up an "expert pool" intended to offer specific skills needed in development programs. They would focus on not only the foundation, but also would work with other NGOs and organizations involved in development assistance. Schmitt said a direct benefit of this employee involvement was better retention and recruitment for the company. Employees and others were aware that the foundation, by involving itself early in the AIDS orphan problem, not only demonstrated a clear sense of corporate social responsibility, but also enhanced its role beyond merely providing funds. The foundation gained a reputation as a leader in developing pioneering programs and initiatives particularly with U.N. organizations and other NGOs. The foundation's work, said Schmitt, simply "exemplifies how social problems can be tackled through creative partnerships."

By 2007, the project was financially secured for another three years by the Swedish Development Agency (SIDA), the Swiss Development Cooperation (SDC), the Novartis Foundation for Sustainable Development and other donors. The Novartis Foundation's goal was to make REPSSI the "implementing agency of choice" for such programs and securing long-term financing through expanding the donor base.

---

[39] The cost of this particular venture was not readily determined because the Novartis corporate human resources department put it together and paid for it. By 2007, approximately 500 man-hours and 10 airfares from Switzerland to South Africa had been attributed to this program.

Procter & Gamble: Children's Safe Drinking Water (A)[40]

In 1995, Procter & Gamble (P&G) scientists began researching methods of water treatment for use in communities facing water crises. P&G, one of the world's largest consumer products companies, was interested in bringing industrial-quality water treatment to remote areas worldwide, because the lack of clean water, primarily in developing countries, was alarming.[41] In the latter half of the 1990s, approximately 1.1 billion (out of a worldwide population of around 5.6 billion)[42] people lacked access to clean drinking water or sanitation facilities. An estimated six million children died annually from diseases, including diarrhea, hookworm, and trachoma, brought about by contaminated water.[43] One report estimated that "about 400 children below age five die per hour in the developing world from waterborne diarrheal diseases"[44] and that, "at any given time, about half the population in the developing world is suffering from one or more of the six main diseases associated with water supply and sanitation."[45]

Procter & Gamble[46]

The Procter & Gamble company dated back to 1837, in Cincinnati, Ohio, when William Procter and James Gamble, married to sisters, started a soap and candle business with $3,596.47 each. By 1859, P&G sales reached $1 million, the company had 80 employees, and it was supplying the Union Army during the Civil War. Gamble's son, a trained chemist, created an inexpensive white soap in 1879 that they named "Ivory" from the biblical phrase "out of ivory palaces." Ivory soap became one of the first nationally advertised products. In the late 1880s, during a time of labor unrest throughout the country, P&G developed a pioneering profit-sharing program for factory workers, giving them a stake in the company.

---

[40] These cases were prepared by Laura P. Hartman, Justin Sheehan, Jenny Mead under the supervision of Patricia H. Werhane, Copyright © 2008 by the University of Virginia Darden School Foundation, Charlottesville, VA. All rights reserved.

[41] "Safe Drinking Water," P&G Health Sciences Institute, http://www.pghsi.com/pghsi/safewater (accessed 15 February 2008).

[42] U.S. Census Bureau, International Data Base, "Total Midyear Population for the World: 1950–2050," 16 July 2007, http://www.census.gov/ipc/www/idb/worldpop.html. Accessed 28 Feb 2008.

[43] Hawkes, Nigel and Nigel Nuttall. 1995. Seeds offer hope of pure water for the developing world. *The Times* (London), 15 September 1995.

[44] Gadgil, Ashok. 1998. Drinking water in developing countries, *Annual Review of Energy and the Environment* 23:254.

[45] Gadgil, 254.

[46] "Our History," P&G Web site, http://www.pg.com/company/who_we_are/ourhistory.jhtml. Accessed 15 Feb 2008.

By 1890, P&G sold more than 30 different types of soap. The company also set up one of the first product research laboratories in the United States. In 1911, P&G developed Crisco, the first all-vegetable shortening, less expensive and considered healthier than butter.

In 1915, P&G built its first manufacturing facility outside the United States, in Canada, and established its chemicals division to formalize research procedures and develop new products. In 1919, Procter revised its articles of incorporation to include the directive that the "interests of the Company and its employees are inseparable." The 1920s saw several marketing innovations: P&G's Crisco was the sponsor of radio cooking shows; the company created a market research department to study consumer preferences and buying habits; and the company developed a brand management system.

As the twentieth century progressed, P&G rolled out a number of new and eventually successful products and expanded its product lines through regular acquisitions of well-known and long-standing consumer brands as well as lesser-known products that showed considerable development potential. Products included: Camay (1926); Dreft, the first synthetic detergent intended for household use (1933); Drene, the first detergent-based shampoo (1934); Tide detergent and Prell shampoo (1946); Crest, the first toothpaste with fluoride (1955); Charmin toilet paper (a 1957 acquisition); Downy fabric softener (1960); Pampers (1961); Folgers coffee (a 1963 acquisition); Pringles Potato Crisps, named for a street in Cincinnati (1968); Bounce fabric softener sheets (1972); Always feminine protection (1983); Liquid Tide (1984); Vicks and Oil of Olay (separate 1985 acquisitions); Pert, a combination shampoo/conditioner (1986); Ultra Pampers and Luvs Super Baby Pants, thinner than traditional diapers (1986); Noxell, whose products were CoverGirl, Noxzema, and Clarion (a 1989 acquisition); Febreze, Dryel, and Swiffer, introduced and distributed globally in 18 months (1998); Iams canine products (a 1999 acquisition); and ThermaCare air-activated HeatWraps (2002).

Along the way, P&G celebrated its 10th anniversary in 1937 with sales of $230 million, then its 150th anniversary in 1987 as the second-oldest company among the 50 largest *Fortune* 500 companies. P&G created its first division, drug products, in 1943, and in 1978, introduced its first pharmaceutical product, Didronel (etidronate disodium) – a treatment for Paget's disease. P&G was also a leader in environmental and solid waste prevention practices. In 1988, Germany's retail grocers called P&G's refill packs for liquid products, which reduced packaging by 85 %, the invention of the year. In the early 1990s, the company began using recycled plastic for more and more of its products, and in 1992, it received the World Environment Center Gold Medal for International Corporate Environmental Achievement. P&G was also recognized for its affirmative action programs by the U.S. Department of Labor, in 1994, with its Opportunity 2000 Award for commitment to instituting equal employment opportunities and creating a diverse work force. In 1998, P&G began to implement Organization 2005, designed to "push the often slow-moving P&G to innovate, to move fast with product development and marketing and with this, grow revenues, earnings, and shareholder value."[47]

---

[47] Marguerite Nugent, "P&G CEO Sees Transformation in Five Years," Reuters News Service, 12 October 1999.

The Global Water Crisis

As the twentieth century came to a close, there was general agreement that the characteristics of a developed country included "[i]mproved longevity, reduced infant mortality, health, productivity, and material well-being."[48] But none of these was easily attainable unless the country had a supply of safe, drinkable water and a successful means of disposing of the household and industrial waste that often contaminated the drinking supply in developing countries.

Many of the deaths attributed to contaminated water were preventable, if a product that sanitized water was paired with effective systems of education and distribution. Most of the communities without access to clean water sources lacked the infrastructure to build large municipal water treatment facilities; often, if these facilities existed, they were hard to maintain. Inhabitants of these areas used wells or local surface water for bathing, drinking, and cooking. In addition, animals (both domesticated livestock and those that were wild) frequented the water sources, contaminating them with their feces. Heavily populated areas in some countries were susceptible to natural disaster, which often produced safe-drinking-water crises. Floods, monsoons, and earthquakes often led to the contamination of local water sources when "large runoffs of silt and clay [ran] into the catchment areas of municipal water supplies, which overwhelm[ed] routine sedimentation and filtration methods"[49] and overwhelmed efforts to obtain and then to distribute safe water.

The metal contaminants in water could impair the mental development of children who drank it. The main diseases that resulted from contaminated water included:

- Diarrhea, which occurred when microbial and viral pathogens existed in either food or water. Diarrheal diseases were the big killer and, if they did not result in death, brought about malnutrition and stunted growth in children, because the diseases left the body unable to absorb important nutrients long past the period of the actual diarrhea.
- *Ascaris, Dracunculisis*, Hookworm, and *Schistosomiasis* were caused by infestations of different kinds of worms. Ultimately, people suffering from them experienced disability, morbidity, and occasionally, death.
- Trachoma, which was caused by bacteria and often resulted in blindness.

In addition to the deaths and physical illnesses caused by unsafe drinking water, there were larger economic consequences. These included "economic and health costs of about 10 million person-years of time and effort annually, mostly by women and girls, carrying water from distant, often polluted sources."[50] Entire households suffered financially when the primary breadwinner became ill. Boiling water as a purification technique was time-consuming, often eating up hours each day that could better be spent raising crops as food or, for children, attending school. In short, a shortage of safe drinking water could stunt the growth of a community just as it could stunt the growth of sick and malnourished children.

---

[48] Gadgil, 264.

[49] Gadgil, 264.

[50] Gadgil, 256.

The Search for a Solution

In the mid-1990s, a number of companies, such as Mioxx Corporation, Innova Pure Water, Pall, CUNO, Millipore, Ionics, and Clorox's Brita, were already in the water-purification business. Their products covered a range of needs, including household, municipal, and military. As the global water access crisis grew, however, there was greater pressure to address the needs of developing countries though new water sanitation products and the alteration of existing technology. Crucial to the success of any water purification program was developing effective models for distribution and combining them with effective education about the use of potential products. A successful program would feature a product that could offer:

- Inexpensive, on the spot, or "point-of-use" treatment;
- Ease of use, requiring no more than simple educational demonstrations;
- Potential to fit into a long-term, sustainable distribution system flexible enough to be utilized in disaster relief efforts.

With a long history of scientific research and innovation in health, hygiene, and nutrition, P&G, with more than 200 scientists, considered ways the company could address the safe-drinking-water crisis as the millennium approached. The United Nations was drafting its Millennium Development Goals, which would be presented for resolution by the General Assembly in 2000. Included in the draft document was a 2015 goal to cut by half the world population that currently did not have access to safe drinking water. Although P&G had a vast array of successful products, the company did not offer anything that involved water purification, either domestically or in developing countries where poverty, lack of infrastructure, and inaccessibility of remote communities made the prospect of cleaning up the water more difficult.

Procter & Gamble: Children's Safe Drinking Water (B)

In 1999, P&G purchased – through the acquisition of Recovery Engineering in a $265 million deal –PUR Water Filtration System, a point-of-use water filtration system. Harvard graduate and entrepreneur Brian Sullivan had founded Recovery in 1986, and by 1999, the company had 550 employees, annual sales of $77 million (in 1998),[51] and was the number-two water filtration product in the United States behind Clorox Company's Brita.[52] Sullivan said that his company's mission had

---

[51] P&G had sales of $38.1 billion and net earnings of $3.76 billion in 1998.

[52] In the first quarter of 1999, PUR had 21.2 % of the market, compared with Brita's 66.2 %, and had gained 49% of the market in the month of July 1999, according to Susan E. Peterson, "Pretty Price for Recovery Engineering," *Minneapolis Star-Tribune*, 27 August 1999, 1-D.

always been "to solve the world's drinking water problems"[53] and that P&G's marketing clout would help expand sales of the product globally. PUR products had only been distributed domestically, and Sullivan said that "it would take us a long time to have a global impact.... The technology ... is very powerful, with fantastic potential, and it's something that can best be leveraged under the umbrella of a global consumer products firm."[54]

This was a new product category for P&G, said a spokesperson, but – referring to the company's detergent, hair- and skin-care products – "we've been in the water management business for a long time... We've learned a lot about water – how to manage it well – so there is some synergy."[55] With this acquisition, P&G took a huge first step toward supplying drinkable water to areas throughout the world.

Development of PUR

The PUR water filtration system used a combination of the flocculant iron sulfate, an agent that caused particles suspended in water to bind and form sediment, and calcium hypochlorite (chlorine), a disinfectant. After acquiring the product, P&G began to develop and expand it. Over the next several years, the PUR product line included home faucet mounts, refrigerator pitchers and dispensers, portable water bottle systems, and eventually, optional flavor packets that created gallons of clean, flavored water through specialized pitchers. P&G also began to experiment with a small point-of-use purifier: small sachets of flocculant-disinfectant. These sachets were approximately the size of a "pack of coffee creamer" and could "suck out dirt, bacteria, and parasites from 10 l of water."[56] They were simple and easy to demonstrate, as well as inexpensive to produce, affordable to purchase (approximately $0.10 a unit), and easy to distribute. The user would mix a small packet of powder in a container of water. After stirring, the contaminants separated out and fell to the bottom of the container as visible sediment. These contaminants included "dirt, pesticides, toxic heavy metals, such as arsenic and lead, as well as bacteria, viruses and protozoa that [were] resistant to chlorine alone."[57] P&G called this system PUR Purifier of Water.

---

[53] Peterson.

[54] Peterson.

[55] Peterson.

[56] Coolidge, Alexander. 2003. P&G water purifier aids third world. *Cincinnati Post*, 19 June 2003, B6.

[57] Procter & Gamble Press Release, "New P&G Technology Improves Drinking Water in Developing Countries," 24 April 2001, http://www.pginvestor.com/phoenix.zhtml?c=104574&p=irol-newsArti cle&ID=628966&highlight=. Accessed 25 Feb 2008.

Strategic Partnerships

In 2001, to combine "a wide range of health care research into one research institute,"[58] and broaden its philanthropic reach, P&G created the Procter & Gamble Health Sciences Institute (PGHSI), which was "dedicated to identifying, developing, and using leading health care technologies in the development of effective products for both the developing and developed world."[59] PGHSI partnered with the nonprofit International Council of Nurses (ICN) and the U.S. Centers for Disease Control and Prevention (CDC) to improve the technology for use in developing nations. The Switzerland-based ICN, a federation of 124 national nurses' associations that represented millions of nurses globally, had made universal access to clean water a priority, with the following statement:

> ICN believes that the right to water is non-negotiable. Secure access to safe water is a universal need and fundamental human right; an essential resource to meet basic human needs, and to sustain livelihoods and development....
>
> ICN also believes that with commitment and political will by governments and others, clean and safe water can be made accessible to all people at low cost using appropriate technology.[60]

The Atlanta-based CDC was part of the U.S. Department of Health and Human Services. Its Safe Water Systems (SWS) program was "a water quality intervention that employ[ed] simple, robust, and inexpensive technologies appropriate for the developing world."[61] This intervention involved point-of-use treatment of contaminated water, safe water storage in containers, and behavioral techniques to educate the affected populations about the importance of, among other things, hygiene and proper use of water storage vessels.

In April 2001, at the CDC's annual Epidemic Intelligence Service Conference, PGHSI unveiled its small sachets of flocculant-disinfectant, or what it called PUR Purifier of Water. Between 2001 and 2003, the strategic partners conducted part of the PUR development process in parts of Guatemala and Haiti that suffered from a lack of clean drinking water. The studies they carried out tested the utility of PUR in large-scale water relief programs. After several years of testing, an impact study linked the use of four-gram sachets of PUR to a significant decrease in the occurrence of diarrhea. The 20-week study that comprised more than 600 families linked the use of PUR sachets to a 25 % decrease in instances of diarrhea among children

[58] "Global Joint Program Partners," Health Communication Partnership, http://www.hcpartnership. org/Partners/gjpp.php . Accessed 25 Feb 2008.

[59] "Mission," P&G Health Sciences Institute, http://www.pghsi.com/pghsi/mission/. Accessed 25 Feb 2008.

[60] "Universal Access to Clean Water," ICN Position Statement, 1995, http://www.icn.ch/pswater. htm. Accessed 25 Feb 2008.

[61] "Safe Water System," Centers for Disease Control and Prevention, http://www.cdc.gov/safewater/. Accessed 25 Feb 2008.

younger than two.[62] The *American Journal of Tropical Medicine and Hygiene* published an article, based on the studies in Guatemala, about the success of PUR in significantly reducing diarrheal illness in children. In January 2003, the *Journal of Water and Health* published an article called, "Evaluation of a New Water Treatment for Point-of-Use Household Applications to Remove Microorganisms and Arsenic from Drinking Water," also describing the efficacy of the PUR system. PUR not only removed microbial contaminants, but also heavy metal contaminants such as chromium, lead, arsenic, and nickel.

At that point, P&G had spent $20 million developing PUR,[63] although it claimed that the product was "a social marketing breakthrough rather than a commercial initiative."[64] With glowing reports about the water purifier, various nonprofits began purchasing and shipping it all over the globe. The International Rescue Committee in 2003 shipped 350,000 packets to Iraq, where fighting had destroyed or damaged many of the water systems. Relief agency AmeriCares delivered more than a million PUR sachets to Sudanese refuges in Chad. In 2003, the product had been used in Botswana, Malawi, Liberia, and Zimbabwe as well.

Children's Safe Drinking Water

With the success of PUR Water Filtration System, PGHSI and its partners created the Children's Safe Drinking Water (CSDW)[65] campaign in 2003. But there were obstacles to expanding the program effectively in developing countries and to persuading people in target water crisis areas to use it, so PGHSI needed seasoned strategy and expertise. PGHSI found that Population Services International (PSI) and the Aquaya Institute were organizations that were both experienced in the methods of social marketing and disaster relief planning.

Population Services International (PSI)

Founded in 1970 as a nonprofit organization focusing on family planning and reproductive health, PSI expanded to operate programs promoting oral rehydration therapy and HIV awareness in the developing world. PSI utilized social marketing

---

[62] Crump, John A., Peter O. Otieno, Laurence Slutsker, Bruce H. Keswick, Daniel H. Rosen, R. Michael Hoekstra, John M. Vulule, Stephen P. Luby. 2005. Household based treatment of drinking water with flocculant-disinfectant for preventing diarrhoea in areas with turbid source water in rural western Kenya: Cluster randomised controlled trial. *British Medical Journal (BMJ)* 331; 478, published on-line July 26, 2005. http://www.bmj.com/cgi/reprint/331/7515/478. Accessed 19 Feb 2008.

[63] Coolidge, B6.

[64] "Financial Express: P&G May Test Waters With PUR," *Financial Express*, 26 May 2004.

[65] "Children's Safe Drinking Water," Procter & Gamble, http://www.pg.com/company/our_commitment/drinking_water.jhtml. Accessed 25 Feb 2008.

models to promote products that could improve health conditions for the poor. The PSI approach to social marketing "engaged private sector resources and used private sector techniques to encourage healthy behavior and make markets work for the poor" and focused heavily on combining measurable results and private-sector operational efficiency.[66] This often included finding members of target communities to act as contacts for the program and to sell the water treatment systems. These local contacts had access to potential end users, understood local customs, and would be more likely to achieve product acceptance. PSI used performance metrics and review processes to create a level of operational efficiency comparable to a successful for-profit corporation. The organization operated water treatment programs in 23 countries, and used the social marketing model for successful distribution of PUR water treatment sachets in five countries.[67]

Aquaya Institute and PURelief

The Aquaya Institute offered consulting services to organizations planning and implementing safe water programs. It conducted original research on the technology, distribution systems, and impact of safe water programs. Supported by the Procter & Gamble Fund, the institute began developing a geographic information system that would help create sales strategies for communities reliant specifically on surface water. The Aquaya Institute joined the Johns Hopkins University School of Public Health to investigate methods of marketing and distributing PUR in Indonesia in 2004 with funding and support provided by the Procter & Gamble Fund. The program expanded after the December 26, 2004 Asian tsunami, which greatly exacerbated existing water shortages. P&G joined local government organizations, as well as leading nongovernmental organizations (NGOs), to provide disaster relief in the form of PUR treatment. Indonesians in disaster areas received a portion of 15 million sachets of PUR, saving thousands of lives. Later, in 2007, the Aquaya Institute joined PSI in a PUR distribution program in Kenya.[68]

With the help of PSI and the Aquaya Institute, P&G expanded the use of PUR to many developing countries. P&G also worked with other organizations and nonprofits, including the Johns Hopkins University School of Public Health, CARE, UNAIDS, WHO, and UNICEF in supplying and distributing the water purification product. See Exhibit 1 for a description of travels made by PGHSI Executive Director Greg Allgood, to various regions around the world to observe the implementation of and response to the PUR product.

---

[66] "About PSI," Population Services International, http://www.psi.org/about_us. Accessed 21 Nov 2007.

[67] In 2006, PSI estimated that it had treated over 8.6 billion liters of water, averted 4.1 million cases of diarrhea, and prevented 6,000 child deaths that year. "Water/Child Survival: Safe Water and Diarrheal Disease Control," http://www.psi.org/child-survival. Accessed 18 Dec 2007.

[68] "Aquaya to Assist PSI in Community Targeting for the Social Marketing of PUR in Kenya," Aquaya Institute press release, http://www.aquaya.org/news.php#010807. Accessed 4 Dec 2007.

The Economics of PUR

Many of the PUR programs operated either on partial cost recovery, where the user paid only for the product and donor funds subsidized other program costs, or – in the case of emergencies, such as the Asian tsunami, flooding in Haiti, or cholera epidemics in Africa – as fully subsidized free distribution. In general, each PUR sachet was provided to relief or NGOs at a cost of $0.035, but program costs also included "transport, distribution, education, and community motivation."[69] Most often, sachets were sold at product cost recovery for $0.10 each, which translated to $0.01 per liter of treated water.

PUR Expands Globally

In June 2004, P&G's PUR Purifier of Water won the International Chamber of Commerce (ICC) World Business Award in support of the Millennium Development Goals. This was part of the first annual worldwide business awards to "recognize the significant role business can play in the implementation of the UN's targets for reducing poverty around the world by 2015." P&G's Children's Safe Drinking Water program went on to win other awards: the Stockholm Industry Water Award (2005), the Ron Brown Presidential Award for Corporate Leadership (2007), the EPA Children's Health Excellence Award (2007), and the Grainger Challenge Bronze Award 2007). Throughout the Children's Safe Drinking Water program from 2003 to 2007, P&G had sold the sachets at no cost, made no profit on PUR sales, and donated programmatic funding to some of the projects. Between 2003 and 2007, 85 million sachets of PUR, treating 850 million liters of water, had been distributed globally in emergency response or sold through social marketing projects. With the help of its various partners, PGHSI had made the product available in 23 countries.

Procter & Gamble: The Search for Safe Drinking Water (C)

Blogging from Borneo[70]

In 2005, industrial toxicologist Dr. Greg Allgood, executive director of Procter and Gamble's Health Sciences Institute (PGHSI), began a blog to tell the story of his travels through the tsunami-ravaged regions of Southern Asia. The December 26, 2004, tsunami killed hundreds of thousands of people and created water shortages throughout the affected areas, leaving millions without access. As part of PGHSI's

---

[69] "Household Water Treatment Options in Developing Countries," Centers for Disease Control, January 2008, http://www.ehproject.org/PDF/ehkm/cdc-options_pur.pdf. Accessed 15 Feb 2008.

[70] Source: Greg Allgood blog at http://childrensafedrinkingwater.typepad.com/pgsafewater/2007/11/boiling-in-born.html. Accessed 20 Nov 2007.

Children's Safe Drinking Water Program, Allgood assisted in providing safe, clean drinking water to regions that had lost the ability to maintain the sanitation of water sources in the wake of the disaster. Along the way, Allgood worked to educate the people of each region about the dangers of unsafe drinking water. Over the next 3 years, Allgood's travels would take him from Sri Lanka to Pakistan, India, parts of Africa, Vietnam and, in late 2007, into Indonesia.

In November 2007, Allgood and representatives from Aquaya Institute, a research and consulting NGO and the Dian Desa Foundation, a well-established Indonesian nonprofit, entered the Indonesian region of Borneo. The trip was organized to promote safe water education in rural parts of the island and to investigate local acceptance of water treatment products. Experiencing the region's torrential downpours, Allgood and his team covered miles of rain-battered roadways, reaching the town of Batulicin and nearby villages. There they offered demonstrations of the PUR Water Filtration System.

Allgood joined a local PUR distributor, Heini, to tour nearby villages and demonstrate the water sanitizing properties of the product. Heini, a local, was chosen by the Dian Desa Foundation to assist Allgood and Aquaya Institute's Jeff Albert in documenting the acceptance of PUR by regional consumers. Using water taken from a river nearby, Heini's demonstrations convinced a number of locals to begin using PUR to sanitize their drinking water. Unfortunately, many potential PUR consumers had difficulty accepting the product, preferring instead to use decades-old purification techniques.

In a community along the route, Allgood watched locals pulling water from irrigation ditches. The water looked clear, but Allgood worried that it was contaminated nonetheless. Surprisingly, villagers preferred the taste of the unpurified water to sanitized water in a blind taste test. When members of his crew paused to join men from the village at a local mosque, they participated in ritual absolution before prayers. "They wash and cleanse their mouths from the irrigation ditch water," Allgood worried, "and I hope they don't get sick from it."

To demonstrate the product, Heini would draw 10 l of water in one or more vessels from a contaminated local source. After reiterating the threat posed by unsafe water, Heini introduced a single sachet of PUR powder to each vessel, often inviting locals from the audience to participate in the treatment process. After stirring the water for 5 min, they allowed it to sit for another 5 min as the formerly turbid water visibly cleared. When the water was clear, they poured it into another vessel through a piece of cotton fabric, and allowed it to sit for another few minutes before drawing the now purified water into several clear cups. The audience was invited to comment on the clarity and flavor of the water.[71] Reactions varied greatly in each region in which PUR was introduced, as hesitant locals experienced a totally new flavor of water. Reluctance to stray from traditional sanitation methods and familiar flavors would become a major hurdle to acceptance of PUR in some areas.

---

[71] A video of a typical PUR product demonstration, produced by members of the nonprofit, Other Paths, may be seen at http://www.youtube.com/watch?v=mij0-3hBKs8&feature=related (accessed 25 February 2008).

Local Networks

The final stop in Allgood's tour of Borneo was a village that had only recently been introduced to PUR. The village, located in a swampy region where the well water was saturated with mud, had a tradition of boiling drinking water. Residents had a mixed response to PUR; some preferred to keep old habits of boiling, and others warmed up to the relative ease of cleansing water in this novel way. One villager, a tea and snack merchant named Sutyami, had been using PUR for a week. She was hesitant to use the product at first, but chose to test it to save time and money. Boiling, her habitual method of water sanitation, was expensive and time consuming. She agreed to become a local distributor of PUR, and began selling the sachets alongside her regular wares. Like many other distributors in rural areas, she made a good local contact to provide the sachets to her community, and also generated extra income from selling them. With assistance from programs such as PGHSI's Children's Safe Drinking Water, local distributors like Heini and Sutyami have been able to create sustainable water safety outlets for their communities, bringing affordable safe water practices to those most in need.

The Female Health Company (A)[72]

As a biochemist, activist, and entrepreneur, Mary Ann Leeper wanted nothing more than to slow if not halt the spread of HIV/AIDS. Though massive public health efforts targeted at gay men had begun to slow the spread of disease among that population, statistics indicated that, between 1992 and 1995, the number of women with the disease had begun to rise. A female-controlled method for HIV/AIDS prevention had been discussed at the 1987 World AIDS Conference. Since then, Leeper had found an inventor who had designed one – a female condom. She persuaded him to work with her to perfect the design, and she ushered the product through a tortuous U.S. Food and Drug Administration (FDA) approval process. As the president of the Chicago-based Female Health Company (FHCO), she had successfully faced many business challenges, including most recently a major restructuring of the company, but none prepared her for what she confronted now.

Knowing that a female condom would be a tough sell, Leeper had sought the best advertising and PR help for the product launch in the U.S. private and public sectors.[73] It was obvious to both Leeper and the big-name firms that a novel product such as a female condom would take time to catch on. But the consumer and public

---

[72] This case was prepared by Lili Powell and Gerry Yemen.©2013University of Virginia Darden Foundation. All rights reserved.

[73] The public sector included public health agencies, city and state health departments, university health centers, and nonprofit health care advocacy groups such as Planned Parenthood. The words "private" and "commercial" are used interchangeably to include all non-public-sector businesses and organizations.

response to the new product was not at all what they expected. It was 1996, and after spending years and millions of dollars on the female condom's product development and launch, the company was operating on seriously depleted resources. Leeper spent a lonely winter weekend in her office on Michigan Avenue. She kept thinking, "Here we are with a revolutionary, lifesaving, and important product that is not moving off the shelves and is costing big dollars to promote." On the verge of giving up, the question for Leeper now was how to respond to what she was hearing.

The Spread of HIV/AIDS in the United States

AIDS (acquired immunodeficiency syndrome) was first recognized in the early 1980s. By the early 1990s, the virus that caused AIDS – HIV (human immunodeficiency virus) –was found all over the world. The nature of HIV/AIDS and cultural norms accounted for the higher incidence in women. Women's anatomy and traditional sexual roles made them more vulnerable to contracting the disease. HIV/AIDS could also be spread to the children of HIV-infected women, either during childbirth or through breast milk. Therefore, preventing HIV/AIDS in women meant preventing it in their children too.

The U.S. Centers for Disease Control and Prevention (CDC) revealed alarming statistics on HIV/AIDS in the United States:

- Between January 1985 and December 1996, 581,429 persons with AIDS had been reported to the CDC.[74] This figure almost doubled from the 1993 cumulative total (361,164).
- Children represented 7,629 cases (or 1 %) and women represented 85,500 cases (or 15 %). In 1996, women represented 20 % of adults/adolescents reported to be living with AIDS.[75] This figure was greater than the proportion in any previous year.
- In the United States, HIV-related death had the greatest impact on young and middle-aged adults, particularly racial and ethnic minorities. In 1996, African-American adults and adolescents exceeded the percentage of whites with the disease for the first time. Many of these young adults likely were infected in their teens and twenties.

From Concept to Market

The male condom had been shown to be effective at reducing the risk of spreading HIV/AIDS, but it had a major drawback– use of a male condom required the man's compliance, if not consent. Like health and human rights activists who for years urged scientists to develop safe, reversible, female-controlled contraceptives

---

[74] These statistics should be interpreted with caution because collection of demographic and risk information varies among states.

[75] U.S. CDC, *HIV/AIDS Surveillance Report* (1994): 6, no 2, http://www.cdc.gov/hiv/pdf/statistics_hivsur62.pdf. Accessed 1 May 2013.

(for pregnancy prevention), Leeper thought a similar device that protected against HIV/AIDS and other sexually transmitted diseases should exist.[76]

When Leeper began her quest, she worked for FHCO's progenitor, Wisconsin Pharmacal, a company that manufactured and marketed a wide variety of specialty chemicals and branded consumer products. Originally trained as a biochemist, Leeper had years of experience bringing products to market in the United States. Leeper saw her opportunity to do something about the spread of HIV/AIDS when she heard about the female condom, invented by Danish physician Lasse Hessel. The product was already available in a few European countries, but Leeper convinced Hessel to let her firm develop his device for the North American market.

The hope was that if the FDA approved the female condom, most countries around the world would ultimately approve it. An agreement was signed in October 1987 for Leeper to develop the product to meet FDA criteria. Hessel, through his company later called Chartex International, developed the manufacturing processes and ironed out the bureaucratic details necessary to allow multicountry distribution of the female condom. A U.S. patent was obtained on April 5, 1988.

Under Leeper's watchful eye, the company pursued the preclinical and clinical studies necessary to develop the female condom for worldwide use. Near the end of 1988, Leeper was convinced the product met FDA requirements and scheduled a final approval, without knowing that a major, and somewhat ironic, wrinkle lay ahead. Unbeknownst to Wisconsin Pharmacal, the National Women's Health Network (NWHN) had, at the same time, filed a petition with the FDA. NWHN persuaded FDA regulators to use stricter criteria to evaluate all new condoms, male and female. As Leeper recalled:

> The petition was aimed at the new models of male condoms that only covered the glans— not just female-controlled condoms. The result of the NWHN action was that the FDA held an advisory committee meeting at which it decided that the female condom was so different and that it addressed such a critical disease that it should be classified as a Class III medical device and therefore undergo even greater scrutiny. This classification placed the female condom among products such as heart valves and other implants that addressed other life-threatening diseases, in contrast to previously developed male condoms that were Class II. Approval of our product now looked as remote as the moons of Jupiter.
>
> Being placed in Class III meant we had to file a premarket approval (PMA) for medical devices. This is similar to a new drug application (NDA). PMAs require extensive safety and efficacy studies – very different from what new male condom manufacturers, at the Class II level, would have to do. They would file a simpler form called a 510k (premarket notification). PMA studies cost millions more dollars and took many more years of work to complete. Class II male condoms had never been tested to the extent that we had to test the female condom.

The new classification criteria resulted in costly, extensive, and time-consuming research projects at Wisconsin Pharmacal. But 5 years later, Leeper's persistence was rewarded when the FDA finally approved marketing and distribution of the female condom as a Class III medical device. Wisconsin Pharmacal began making plans to begin limited distribution in the summer of 1993.

---

[76] Gilbert, Lisa K. 1999. *The Female condom (FC) in the US: Lessons learned.* University of Idaho.

The Product and Its Launch

Having passed the FDA approval process, the female condom was now ready to be introduced to the U.S. market. The product itself was made of a sheer, non-latex, polyurethane material and shaped as a sheath with flexible O rings on each end (see Exhibit 1). While the female condom transferred heat, the plastic used was extremely strong and impermeable to temperature changes, humidity, and oil- or water-based lubricants. More importantly the sheath was impenetrable to various viruses and bacteria that caused sexually transmitted diseases (STDs) such as trichomoniasis, cytomegalovirus, herpes virus, hepatitis B virus, OX174, and HIV. The condom's uniqueness lay in the control it gave women to protect themselves against STDs as well as unintended pregnancies.

The results of market research were mixed. As Leeper said, "For every complaint we got, there was an equal amount of positive feedback. No one really knew how the consumer was going to judge the product." The product had many perceived benefits when compared to other prophylactics and contraceptives. The device did not require health care services to fit, prescribe, refill, insert, or remove; it had no systemic (hormonal) side effects for the user; it did not require partner consent because it could be inserted well in advance of sexual activity and therefore was less disruptive to intercourse; it was not necessarily obvious to the male partner, and was odor- and taste-free. There were, however, some notable obstacles; the device was aesthetically unusual, was difficult for some to insert, produced discomfort or reduced sensation for some users; and occasionally became dislodged. Some partners even objected to using it.

Wisconsin Pharmacal prepared to distribute the female condom in both the public sector and on the commercial market. By the end of 1993, the female condom was available in the public sector, where physicians and public health care providers were the customers who would be responsible for recommending the product to end users. Broad-scale commercial distribution was initiated 9 months later.

Product branding and marketing targeted women's empowerment and positioned the product as an alternative to the male condom. The female condom sold under the trademark "Reality." Ads for Reality used the tagline "Count on Yourself"; its intention was to encourage women to feel empowered to protect themselves (see Exhibit 2). In supermarkets and drug stores, Reality was shelved with other personal care products. The packaging included directions and a toll-free customer information number. Female condoms came in boxes of three or six, priced at about $7.50 and $15.00, respectively. Leeper recalled those early days:

> We had hired a high-profile publicity firm to handle public relations and a New York ad agency to design the overall campaign. The initial mailing promotion to physicians cost well over $250,000; the sales rep promotion averaged $1 million per month. Advertising to the consumer was in the multi-million-dollar range. Plus, of course, there were big retainer fees to keep the advertising and PR firms on board.

The product launch to the public sector progressed slowly but on track. A lot of education for public health workers and end users was needed. It was a new method, so the way it was offered was important. Presentation had to be favorable for the product to be accepted both by providers and potential users.

As for the commercial introduction, directly to consumers—that was a different story. Even the market research did not foretell what would happen.

Despite the hefty costs, the whole campaign flopped. Within six weeks of the national launch that fall, I knew we were in for a struggle. Most of the typically white, affluent young women we were trying to reach simply did not hear the message. Intellectually, they thought it was a good idea to be able to protect themselves, but emotionally, in the heat of the moment, forget it—safe sex stayed outside the bedroom! These young women really did not recognize that they were at risk of getting an STD, let alone the possibility of being infected with HIV and ultimately dying from sex.

As an added bonus to our dilemma, the media jeered at the female condom. Numerous jokes and embarrassed laughter littered the pages of women's magazines. Something had to be done.

What Now?

Leeper didn't yet fully understand why the commercial target market wasn't using Reality. So to understand what was happening, Leeper went to the sources that she knew mattered most – the people who were interested in using (and already using) the product. Through conversations with employees who answered the consumer information line and listening into calls, Leeper's picture of Reality's target market began to change. Inquiries and calls were coming from all kinds of women – and men! – not just young, white, affluent women. Many mentioned that they had heard about the product from a friend. A larger-than-expected portion of the responses came from women of color. Some of the women and men were in long-standing relationships or were married. Often the questions this diverse group of callers asked were not about the product, but about how to suggest using the female condom to one's partner. The overwhelming commonality was that these people already believed that they were at risk.

Next, Leeper investigated what might be happening in public clinics. After several conversations, Leeper realized how dependent the female condom's acceptance was on an important gatekeeping audience.

> During my initial contact with public health counselors, I discovered that they were mostly young white female adults who, for the most part, could not imagine themselves using the female condom. I heard comments like it was too odd-looking, and it seemed to be more of a gimmick than a lifesaver. I was concerned that their attitude might translate into reluctance to recommending that their clients use the female condom.

Weighing what she had heard, Leeper began to wonder how she could take a different approach. Something was needed; after all, using a female condom was a little more personal and sensitive than buying a new brand of soap.

Exhibit 1: The Female Health Company (A)

Female condom

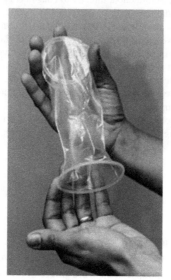

Source: All exhibit images are used with permission from The Female Health Company.

Exhibit 2: The Female Health Company (A)

Count on yourself campaign

1st US Campaign

PERCEPTION:

If he doesn't use male latex condoms, she has no protection against STDs, including AIDS, and from pregnancy.

REALITY:

Now she has the means to protect herself.'
The REALITY® Female Condom.

New REALITY helps prevent STDs, including AIDS, and unintended pregnancy. The REALITY Female Condom is a highly effective barrier to HIV, as well as to a particle that is smaller than the Hepatitis B virus²—the smallest virus known to cause an STD.

In clinical trials, when REALITY was not used correctly or consistently (typical use), the contraceptive failure rate at 6 months was 12.4%.³ When REALITY was used correctly and consistently (perfect use), the failure rate was 2.6%.³ (See adjacent page for details.)

The REALITY Female Condom: Now she has the means to protect herself.'

For additional information call 1-800-635-0844.

REALITY®
FEMALE CONDOM
Make it her reality.

The Female Health Company (B)

On an early fall day in 1996, Mary Ann Leeper listened intently while Daisy Nyamukapa, manager of the HIV/AIDS Coordination Programme for Zimbabwe's Ministry of Health and Child Welfare, explained why she had called. Over 30,000 Zimbabwean women had signed a petition demanding that the government bring Leeper and her company's product, the female condom, into their country. As president of The Female Health Company (FHCO), based in Chicago, Leeper was stunned by Nyamukapa's extraordinary request. Then again, Leeper had developed a talent for listening to her supply chain customers and end users. This request was bound to be another trial by fire, yet again testing Leeper's and FHCO's abilities to adapt to a complex set of new audiences. Based on her recent experience in developing an entirely new approach to marketing the female condom, Leeper had a newfound appreciation for the cultural and communication-intensive nature of her company's product. But the challenge would be worthwhile if they could reach a population that desperately needed the product.

Perception Meets Reality

After a very long process leading up to the product launch, Leeper was disappointed that the first attempt to promote the female condom in the U.S. commercial and public sectors missed the mark. But there were even more immediate concerns. In 1995, after spending years and millions of dollars on the female condom's product development and launch, Wisconsin Pharmacal's board of directors approved a plan to restructure the company. All its assets and liabilities, except those related primarily to the female condom, were transferred to a newly formed subsidiary,[77] which was sold to an unrelated third party later that year. Next, Wisconsin Pharmacal renamed itself The Female Health Company (FHCO), and in February 1996, it acquired the female condom's inventor's firm – Chartex – which included the female condom's London-based manufacturing facility. (See financial data in Exhibit 1.) In the end, the newly named FHCO's sole business now consisted of the exclusive manufacturing, marketing, and sale of the female condom.

With the reorganization behind her, Leeper was determined to turn the business around and gain public acceptance of the company's important product. The manufacturing facility had an annual capacity of 60 million units, and Leeper estimated that she needed to sell 14 million units a year just to break even. To accelerate U.S. commercial sales, Leeper redefined the promotional strategy and advertising message based on what she had learned about the diversity among people who were interested in the female condom and the qualities of the relationships that enabled its use. Leeper acted decisively: "I got rid of the big-name firm, brought the campaign in-house, hired a designer down the street whose work I admired, and set up a telephone database to do my own research."

Listening to users' feedback, FHCO redeveloped its product advertising message and repositioned the female condom. Leeper explained:

> The advertising focus changed to center on communication between partners, shifting the emphasis from women to both sexes. We used slogans such as: "Safer sex just got better" and "Feeling is believing." We showed a loving couple – lovers who cared about each other – not a casual relationship (Exhibit 2). We drew upon some of the questions people were asking on the phone and answered them in the ad campaign. Most of the ads were print, but in some rare markets, such as Austin, Texas, local television affiliates allowed us to run television ads.
>
> The new campaign was a great success; the database phone calls increased tenfold. We had four telephone lines installed to try and handle the nearly 1,200 calls a day we were getting. Interestingly, we noted a pattern. The majority of the calls were from people who were already concerned they were at risk, mostly people of color, particularly females. The rest of the calls were from men aged 40 to 45, which was a surprise.
>
> This information hit me like a lightning bolt. I realized there were people out there who really understood they were at risk. I needed to shift more emphasis to the public sector where women cared about the issue and their own personal health. They would recognize the product's benefit.

---

[77] The subsidiary was named WPC Holdings.

The Public and Commercial Sectors[78]

Based on what she was hearing, Leeper drew FHCO's attention to the public sector. Key customers in the public sector included public health agencies, city and state health departments, university health centers, and nonprofit health care advocacy groups such as Planned Parenthood. The company also shifted focus from mass advertising in the commercial market to directly addressing the public health communities in several major metropolitan areas. Leeper described the new approach:

> We picked nine major U.S. cities: Atlanta, Baltimore, Boston, Chicago, Philadelphia, Los Angeles, New York City, San Francisco, and Washington. We launched in each city where we met with key health officials for a press conference announcing the availability in the public and nonprofit clinics.
>
> While this time period should have been exciting, I was still uneasy with the reaction. Some women on the street seemed interested in the product, but counselors at the outreach clinics were just not receptive. It was almost like they did not want to be bothered. So I finally realized that in the public sector, I had to sell not just the product but also sell clinic workers on why and how they should introduce the female condom to potential users. I found that clinic workers needed help on reaching out to potential users, and both groups needed to be educated about the product.

Executives at FHCO decided that teaching counselors and health care providers how to talk about the female condom was going to be their responsibility. Leeper understood that if health care providers didn't think they would use the female condom, their clients would never learn to accept the product. So they got busy working on materials to present to the public sector. Leeper tried to anticipate questions and situations that clients and customers may have encountered and then addressed each one. The FHCO team designed brochures that were specifically targeted to different audiences, including these:

- *How To Use* was a visual-only brochure for non-literate or non-native-English-speaking groups.
- *Inserting the female condom...easier than you think* was a pamphlet designed for audiences that were unfamiliar with basic anatomy.
- *Reality Female Condom* in Spanish was for Spanish-speaking customers.
- *The Female Condom: A contraceptive choice* was appealing to customers who were looking for a contraceptive option with the added benefit of STD prevention.
- *The Female Condom: Safer sex just got better* was meant for those that understood the need for contraception but not the safer sex issue. This handout encouraged clients and their partners to think about dual protection.
- *What Is Reality?* was intended for the commercial audience to build the brand while showing the product's benefits.

The plan was to have master copies of each pamphlet available for health care providers. FHCO brochures were purposefully not covered by copyright laws so

---

[78] The words "private" and "commercial" are used interchangeably to include all non-public-sector businesses and organizations.

that agencies could make and distribute as many copies to patients or clients as they wanted. As Leeper recalled:

> I had to develop a whole new communication program – a step-by-step program. The public-sector campaign amounted to a "train the trainers" program designed to teach the counselors so they, in turn, could help their clients. This approach seemed to generate acceptance and satisfied users.

The training model included a section on how to talk to men about the product. It also addressed the reluctance some females had approaching their partner about using the female condom. Women needed to have the ability to convince their partners that it was in their mutual interest to have safer sex without changing the basis of the relationship or the intimacy of the moment. Negotiating for safer sex was not always an easy task. FHCO materials suggested including men in counseling or introducing the condom in group sessions – this offered a friendly setting where women could share information, ideas, or apprehensions with their partners and each other. The company also recommended role-plays and real-life testimonials be worked into counseling.

At the same time, Leeper had not given up on the commercial sector, and she realized that commercial advertising could help demand in the public sector as well. FHCO focused its efforts by doing intensive test marketing in a single city. Leeper remembered:

> We chose Austin, Texas, as a test market and decided to do everything we could in that particular city. In Austin we did regional advertising in a cross section of magazines: women's, men's, and unisex. We did billboards, radio, and television advertising. There were posters on the outside of buses, inside bus depots, and in subway stations. We did a three-month blitz in Austin that cost us $350,000. And we could not keep the product on the shelf. The whole experience indicated that we could get the safer sex message across, but we just could not afford to do it on a national basis!

Given its financial constraints, FHCO targeted a narrower audience elsewhere, focusing on college and university campuses. Actress Drew Barrymore also agreed to act as a spokesperson and gave her time gratis to get the message of safer sex to young people.

Going International

Daisy Nyamukapa's call gave Leeper the last nudge to forge ahead into international markets. She remembered:

> Our plan was to move our U.S. public-sector approach into the global market. I toyed with the idea of a global strategy several years earlier when discussion of a female condom first came up at the 1987 World AIDS Conference. When we became an international company with the purchase of Chartex, I began negotiations with the joint United Nations Programme on HIV/AIDS (UNAIDS) and the WHO. On World AIDS Day in December 1996, FHCO signed an agreement with UNAIDS and WHO to make the female condom available in developing countries at a special rate of 38 British pence (about $0.68) apiece; they, in turn, would help with the announcement and overall advocacy of the product. At that time, we

sold a female condom for $2.50 in U.S. drugstores and $0.90 to the U.S. public sector, so at $0.68 apiece in developing nations, volume would be critical.

Here began a communications strategy beyond imagination. I had at least 25 countries identified as targets to get the message out. Women in those countries needed to learn about the female condom and what it could do to help them protect themselves. Somebody (who and how many I did not yet know) within each country had to learn that such a device as the female condom was available. We had to make sure they understood why it was important to them to have it be readily available. Then we needed to train counselors, distribute the product within their systems, and reach out to those who needed it the most. We discovered the most need was in villages and rural areas of sub-Saharan Africa.

The phone call from Zimbabwe presented the opportunity Leeper needed. She had learned many lessons in the United States by trial and error. The HIV/AIDS epidemic plaguing Africa made Leeper more determined than ever that the female condom was part of the solution. She just had to make this work.

Zimbabwe's History, Economy, and Geography[79]

To be effective in a new environment and market, Leeper had to investigate Zimbabwe's cultural context, starting with its history, economy, and geography. For the period prior to contact with Europeans in the 1800s, little written history of Zimbabwe survived. Archaeologists and historians pieced together the existence in the region of an advanced civilization and military organization with complex tribal movements. In 1890, Cecil Rhodes and his British South Africa Company used a military force to conquer the Shona territory and the Ndebele kingdom. The former kingdoms were established as a British territory called Rhodesia. By 1923, the colony had full self-governance under an administration controlled by European settlers. African voting rights were restricted, and from the start, white settlers made every effort to institutionalize their supremacy. In the years that followed, Shona and Ndebele peoples were unhappy with British occupation. They resented the loss of their land and cattle, their role as forced laborers, and other abuses that followed European dominance.

Over the years, several organized groups challenged colonial rule and some members attempted to work within political coalitions to institute change. But it was not until 1980 that the people of Rhodesia gained complete independence from British rule – accomplished through a grisly war among various factions. Under the leadership of Robert Mugabe, a new government was formed; it was recognized internationally as Zimbabwe on April 18, 1980. Since Zimbabwe became an independent republic, the ZANU (PF) political party has most often ruled.

The economy experienced a period of stagnation during the 5 years preceding independence and during the war. It experienced a brief recovery in 1980 and 1981,

---

[79] Sources consulted while researching this section include *Country: Zimbabwe, History* (Kaleidoscope. 2001); *Doing Business in Zimbabwe* (New York: PriceWaterhouse, 1995).

mostly due to international recognition and the lifting of international sanctions, but the new country was struck with a severe drought and recession from 1982 to 1984. A 4 % average growth rate was maintained until 1989 when the government introduced a 5-year Economic Structural Adjustment Programme (ESAP). Trade liberalization was introduced, but the country once more suffered from a severe drought in 1992 that devastated the economy and the ESAP. The economy slowly recovered and the GDP grew in real terms by almost 4 % by 1996. Zimbabwe's economy was mixed and very dependent on a symbiotic relationship between a strong and viable private sector and a welfare-orientated government.

Geographically, Zimbabwe was landlocked, but it was well-known for its rich supply of mineral and energy resources. Some of the world's finest deposits of chromate, asbestos, lithium ores, gold, nickel, copper, coal, tin, iron ore, limestone, platinum, pyrites, diamonds, and precious stones were found in Zimbabwe. Zimbabwe was about the same size as California (see Exhibit 3) and had a population of almost 12 million. The official language for governmental and business purposes was English. Approximately 19 % of the population spoke Ndebele and 77 % spoke Shona. The urban population (3.6 million) was vastly smaller than the rural population (8.2 million). The urban population was employed in the developed sectors of the economy and had varying levels of education and skills, while a large portion of the rural population was engaged in subsistence agriculture.

HIV/AIDS in Zimbabwe

Leeper soon learned that the global HIV/AIDS epidemic hit Zimbabwe especially hard, and the statistics were staggering. Here are a few:

- In 1994, the average age of life expectancy at birth was 62 years for females and 58 years for males.[80]
- During 1997, Zimbabwe had the highest percentage (25.8 %) in the world of people between the ages of 15 and 49 infected with HIV or suffering from AIDS.[81]
- Teenage girls suffered five to six times the infection rate of boys.[82]
- Women and children overwhelmingly represented most of the nearly three million HIV/AIDS infected Zimbabweans.
- In Harare, the capital of Zimbabwe, 32 % of pregnant women during 1995 were infected.[83]

---

[80] Compare that with 1994 U.S. life expectancy at birth for females (79 years) and males (72 years).

[81] Altman, Lawrence K. 1998. Parts of Africa showing HIV in 1 in 4 adults. *New York Times*, June 24, A-1.

[82] Cowley, Jeffery. 2000. Fighting the disease: What can be done. *Newsweek*, January 17, 38.

[83] Altman, A-5.

- In another town that lies between Zimbabwe and the South African border, 70 % of women attending prenatal clinics in 1995 were found to be infected.[84]

Zimbabwean women were especially susceptible to HIV/AIDS due to their economic and social dependence on men. Most Zimbabwean women were completely financially dependent upon men, and often sex figured into that dependence.[85] For example, Leeper recalled, "In Zimbabwe, women are totally dependent on men for their well-being. Most women do not earn money. The men bring in the money and help keep shelter over women's heads. It is an extremely traditional society."

In many African cultures, talking about sex was taboo.[86] Culturally, women were not expected to discuss or make decisions about sexuality.[87] Leeper knew that:

> Many men do not want to wear male condoms. They want free sex, not something that is physically binding. Other differences exist geographically; for example, in Zimbabwe, men prefer dry sex. So they want sex to be condom-free.
>
> Normally, women could not request or insist on using a condom or any form of safer sex or prophylactic protection. If a woman refused sex or asked her partner to use a condom, she often risked abuse because such a request was interpreted as an admission that she had been unfaithful.

Not using condoms, even in committed relationships, was also dangerous because it was culturally acceptable for married and unmarried Zimbabwean men to have multiple partners, that sometimes included sex workers; that increased the opportunity for the virus to spread (especially among young virgin females). At the same time, for daily survival, many women exchanged sex for material favors. They were not necessarily formal sex workers; rather, by necessity, they used informal sex exchange, particularly in poor settings, as a way of providing for themselves and their children.

Conclusion

Leeper wondered how much of what she had learned so far would apply in a new setting such as Zimbabwe. Given her experience, she knew that cultural differences would matter, but how? What could she anticipate now? Could she rely on the communication competency she had developed thus far? How could organizations such as UNAIDS and WHO help?

---

[84] Altman, A-5.

[85] "Women and HIV/AIDS," WHO Fact Sheet No. 242, June 2001, http://www.who.int/mip2001/files/2271/242-WomenandHIVAIDSforMIP.pdf. Accessed 1 May 2013.

[86] "Leaders: The Battle with AIDS," *Economist,* July 15, 2000, 17.

[87] "Women and HIV/AIDS."

Exhibit 1: The Female Health Company (B)

FHCO financial data

Income statement	
Period ending:	**30-Sep-96**
Total revenue	**$2,064,258**
Cost of products sold	$3,684,698
Gross profit	($1,620,440)
Operating expenses	
Research and development	$361,094
General and administrative	$2,987,839
Sales and marketing	$2,980,000
Royalty and exclusivity fees	N/A
(Loss) from operating	($7,949,913)
Nonoperating income (expense)	
Interest expense	($560,030)
Interest income	$106,708
Other, net	($252,607)
	($705,929)
	$3,357,316
(Loss) from continuing operations	($8,655,842)
Discontinued operations	
Income (loss) from operations and gain on sale	($4,461)
Net (loss)	**($8,660,303)**
Net income (loss) per weighted average number common shares outstanding	
Continuing operations	($1.31)
Discontinued operations	N/A
	($1.31)
Weighted average number of common shares outstanding	**$6,611,796**
Balance sheet	
Period ending	**30-Sep-96**
Current assets	
Cash and cash equivalents	$2,914,080
Trade accounts receivable	$457,226
Inventory	$967,398
Prepaid expense and other current assets	$370,555
Total current assets	**$4,709,259**
Other assets	
Prepaid royalties	N/A
Note receivable net of unamortized discount of $189,003	$810,997
Intellectual property rights	$1,089,578
Other assets	$194,032
	$2,094,547
Property, plant, and equipment	
Land and building	$1,222,511
Equipment, furniture, and fixtures	$3,710,683
	$4,933,194

(continued)

(continued)

Less: accumulated depreciation	($471,377)
	$4,461,817
Total assets	**$11,265,623**
Current liabilities	
Notes payable to stockholders	$1,956,670
Notes payable to bank	N/A
Current maturities long-term debt	$1,736,706
Trade accounts payable	$721,015
Accrued product returns and trade promotions	$635,000
Accrued royalty and exclusivity fees	N/A
Accrued expenses and other current liabilities	$533,668
Total current liabilities	**$5,612,959**
Long-term liabilities	
Long-term debt and capital lease less maturities	$477,296
Convertible debentures	$1,910,000
Other long-term liabilities	N/A
	$2,708,392
Stockholders' equity	
Convertible preferred stock	N/A
Common stock	$72,117
Additional paid-in capital	$32,864,572
Additional paid-in capital warrants	$508,500
Foreign currency translation gain	$83,850
Accumulated deficit	($30,584,775)
	$2,944,272
	$11,265,623

Cash flow	
Period ending:	**30-Sep-96**
Net (loss)	**($8,660,303)**
Adjustments to reconcile net (loss) to net cash (used in) operating activities	
Depreciation	$425,084
Amortization of debenture issuance costs	$4,278
Provision for doubtful accounts, returns, and discounts	$120,126
Provision for inventory obsolescence	$950,000
Gain on sale of holdings	($224,538)
Loss on disposal of equipment	$37,576
Issuance of stock, warrants, and options for services	$706,268
Amortization of discount on note received and interest earned on lease deposit	($29,703)
Amortization of discount on notes payable and convertible debentures	$166,570
Amortization of other assets	$250,000
Changes in operating assets and liabilities of continuing operations	
Receivables	$47,269
Inventories	$1,935,923
Prepaid expenses and other	$177
Accounts payable	($914,876)
Accrued exclusivity and royalty fees	N/A
Accrued product returns and trade	$635,000

(continued)

(continued)

Promotions allowance	
Due to stockholder	($19,795)
Other current liabilities	$498,407
Discontinued operations	N/A
Net cash (used in) operating activities	**($4,072,537)**

Data source: The Female Health Company 1996 annual report

Exhibit 2: The Female Health Company (B)

"Feeling is Believing" Campaign

Source: All images from FHCO. Used with permission

Exhibit 3: The Female Health Company (B)

Africa Map

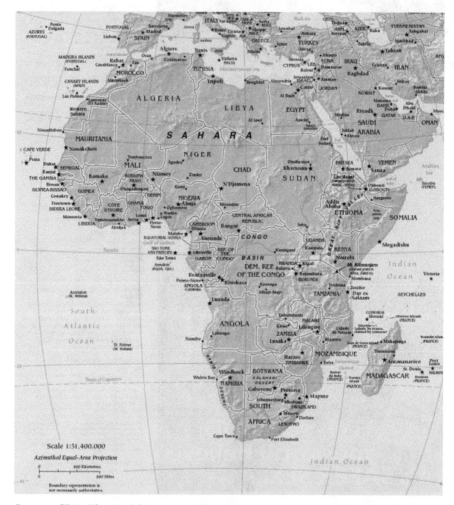

Source: CIA, *The World Fact Book*, http://www.cia.gov/cia/publications/factbook/reference_maps/africa.html. Accessed 6 April 2006

The Female Health Company (C)

As most firms followed the trend of global expansion, the company Mary Ann Leeper and her two partners had built was busy shifting its focus back to its domestic market, where it had started. The Female Health Company (FHCO) had built its brand and achievements on its global reach; by the end of 2012, Leeper and her colleagues had introduced the company's second-generation female condom (FC2) in 138 countries. Its product remained the only woman-initiated method that provided dual protection against unintended pregnancy and sexually transmitted diseases, including HIV/AIDS. The company, which by now had 144 employees, found itself trying to succeed once more in the domestic U.S. market.

Since 1996, Leeper had worked with international nongovernmental organizations and the global public sector (as well as governmental health ministries and private donors) to develop a web of relationships to help women in those areas hardest hit by AIDS. In introducing the female condom, the company had faced numerous barriers, including price point. Although Leeper and FHCO worked to keep costs as low as possible, the unit price of $0.90 offered to global public-sector agencies for the first-generation female condom (FC1) was too steep for many. So in 2005, FHCO introduced FC2, an equally effective alternative that was made from less expensive material and that cost less to manufacture. But unlike FC1, FC2 was for single use only; its unit price plummeted to $0.50, based on volume, and it became globally available (except in the United States).

The World Health Organization had given United Nations agencies the nod of approval to make bulk FC2 orders; in 2006, FHCO had its first profitable year. In addition, the extensive training materials and programs FHCO had developed to educate the public on how to use the female condom was made available digitally. As Leeper said, based on her early years of experience in introducing FC1 in the United States, "Instead of selling a product, FHCO was about selling a whole program – education on how to talk about and use the product and what it offered for women." Having overcome one of the biggest obstacles – price point – Leeper challenged the world to pay attention. She even titled one of the firm's annual reports *No More Excuses*.

Yet despite the product's global success and Leeper's stepping down as FHCO's president to become its strategic adviser, she was still asking a question she had in 1996: "Why is this revolutionary lifesaving product not moving off the shelves in the United States?"

From Reality to FC2

Developing relationships with public-sector agencies opened global markets for the company; coupled with the transition to FC2, FHCO started to turn a profit. The lower price and focus away from commercial sales increased gross margin and decreased sales and marketing costs.[88] By that time, annual condom sales worldwide had reached $34 million, and FHCO could produce through a single facility in Malaysia roughly 100 million units annually. In addition the company was publicly traded on the NASDAQ (see Fig. 3.1 for stock prices).

---

[88] The Female Health Company 10-K, 2012, 7–8.

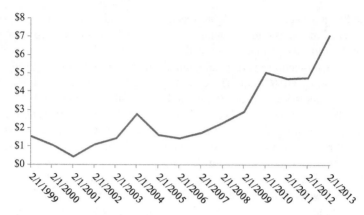

Fig. 3.1 FHCO stock price (Source: Yahoo! finance) (Prices adjusted for stock splits and dividends)

FHCO sold directly to major agencies, held no inventory, and produced product against orders. Orders tended to be large in volume from a small public-sector customer base (three large clients accounted for 85 % of total unit sales).[89] FHCO still had distribution agreements with some private-sector businesses to sell commercially, but that business was comparatively small. To avoid any currency issues, all FHCO transactions were all conducted in U.S. dollars or British pounds sterling.

Back Home in the United States

At the same time, there was growing international recognition of the feminization of the AIDS crisis and the fact that women had to have access to prevention methods. Yet one of the markets slow to show interest in FC2 was the United States. It wasn't until 3 years after it was available in places such as India and Brazil that the new, cheaper female condom was FDA approved and made available in the United States.

As FHCO increased its presence worldwide, the U.S. Centers for Disease Control and Prevention (CDC) issued alarming statistics. It warned that an HIV/AIDS epidemic was growing among *women* in the United States – especially among those of color (1 out of every 32 black females compared to 1 out of every 526 white females).[90] With a sense of urgency, FHCO applied locally what it had learned from the developing world – this time around, there would be no commercial efforts. Instead, FHCO sought partnerships across the United States with city and state public health clinics and nonprofits such as Planned Parenthood. The firm's "train

---

[89] FHCO 10-K, 2012, 5, 16.
[90] FHCO 10-K, 2012, 10.

the trainer" training and education materials, which it had developed for different audiences years earlier were key – the message was the same, but the channel choice changed to online.[91] According to David Holtgrave of the Johns Hopkins Bloomberg School of Public Health in Washington, DC, the FC2 prevention program *alone* saved more than $8 million in future health care costs (every dollar spent saved roughly $20). By 2013, the firm had made significant inroads in two large East Coast cities – New York City (with 1,001 locations) and Washington, DC. Good data, such as that from the CDC and health care researchers such as Holtgrave, were crucial for measuring outcomes – would the U.S. market finally catch on to the idea of the female condom?

Femy, Femidom, Reality, and FC2[92]

Nearly 30 years had passed since that winter day in Chicago when Leeper was almost ready to give up on the female condom. Now, FHCO was depending on the lessons of its global experience to bring relief to the epidemic facing the United States. Would the shift in approach work in the United States this time around?

---

[91] FHCO 10-K, 2012, 13.

[92] Femy, Femidom, and Reality are three of the patented names FHCO owned for its product.

Chapter 4
Environmentally Sustainable Projects

One of the challenges in the twenty-first century is to provide affordable environmentally sustainable products through engaging in sustainable projects. The cases in this chapter illustrate how that can be done in a variety of ways.

One of the ways to reduce poverty is to improve the infrastructure of a community, and as some of these cases illustrate, electricity is a key to improving the lives of people who have not had that available. The first two cases, Husk Power and Solar Electric Light Fund (SELF) work in very poor communities, communities that in the past have been neglected by state power companies, to provide electricity at low rates. Husk Power Systems is a very successful for-profit start-up company, started by former MBA students at the University of Virginia. SELF is a small NGO dedicated to providing environmentally sustainable solar power to remote communities in neglected and poverty-stricken areas. But both have the same mission – to improve the lives of communities through electricity in fiscally sustainable ways.

BHP Billiton is one of the largest mining companies in the world. Yet because of its mission to be environmentally sensitive as well as profitable, its smelting project in Mozal, Mozambique has set a precedent for other mining ventures that we hope will be emulated. The chapter ends with a study of Ecover, a small Belgian company that sells environmentally biodegradable (and even edible) soap products. These products are sold globally, including Whole Foods in the United States. Interestingly too, in keeping with its mission, Ecover's plant is completely self-contained requiring no outside energy or water.

Companies such as these provide role models for other companies. All except SELF are for-profit organizations, yet each is also, in its particular way, in the forefront of the global push for sustainable processes, projects, and products.

P.J. Albert et al. (eds.), *Global Poverty Alleviation: A Case Book*, The International Society   167
of Business, Economics, and Ethics Book Series 3, DOI 10.1007/978-94-007-7479-7_4,
© Springer Science+Business Media Dordrecht 2014

Husk Power Systems: Financing Expansion[1]

In Washington D.C., late April meant enjoying the cherry blossoms, but for Manoj Sinha and Chip Ransler, it was all about securing the future of their company – Husk Power Systems (HPS). They had just left their second meeting with Simon Pasternik, a partner at GreenPoint Partners and a potential investor. HPS needed $1.5–2.5 million of expansion capital to grow quickly beyond the small footprint it had established in northeast India. It aimed to provide electricity to millions of rural Indians in a financially viable way. With 10 "mini power plants" and a presence in 25 isolated Indian villages as of April 2009, the goal was to reach 350,000– 400,000 consumers in 400 villages by the end of 2011.

GreenPoint, a green-energy-oriented and emerging-markets-focused firm, was a great fit to finance HPS. During their first meeting, Pasternik concentrated on the usual drivers of investment decisions: EBITDA, operating margins, and the management team. This time, he carefully examined how the operations side of the business might affect the expansion plans and the ability to deploy that much capital. Pasternik grilled Ransler and Sinha on whether HPS had the capability, operational structure, and management team in place to meet the financial projections the business plan laid out.

Ransler and Sinha were certain HPS's business model was well suited for India's environment and that it capitalized significantly on obstacles unique to India. Ransler painted HPS's future as bright: It would be a dominant supplier of electricity to remote rural areas. The country's demographics and geography spoke loudly to the market size and to the potential entry barriers and operational challenges. Investors seemed to agree. GreenPoint was one of about a dozen funds that showed serious interest in investing in HPS.

But the problem lay in the financing terms different investors offered. HPS's growth plan was aggressive. And alternative revenue streams such as carbon credits were uncertain. Investors aggressively discounted for these risks, which significantly affected the equity stake they demanded. GreenPoint's offer at the second meeting was different from all prior pure (preferred) equity offers. In return for a $2.5 million capital infusion, GreenPoint asked for a convertible note security that would vest upon the next equity investment round.

Now the owners faced a different dilemma: Did this offer fit their business needs and ability to generate returns? How did it address their concern for potentially unfair company valuation by the investors? Should they take it?

---

[1] This case was prepared by Manoj Sinha, Chip Ransler and Elena Loutskina. Copyright © 2010 University of Virginia Darden School Foundation. All rights reserved.

Husk Power Systems

Husk Power Systems began as more of a hobby and a way of giving back to the community than an actual business venture. It was founded in 2007 by three college friends, Manoj Sinha, Gyanesh Pandey, and Ratnesh Yadav. Growing up in India, they all knew firsthand how uncomfortable it was living in small Indian towns with only 7–10 h of electricity during odd hours (e.g., from 2:00 a.m. to 6:00 a.m.) in a typical day. A strong desire to give back to the communities they grew up in led them to explore ways to provide power to those rural communities. They looked into a variety of potential energy sources. Jatropha biodiesel, a then-popular alternative energy source made from the seeds of the Jatropha plant, created problems related to food versus energy tradeoffs. Solar, wind, and fuel-cell options were too expensive or too difficult to operate and maintain. Finally, they looked into rice husks – a rice milling agricultural waste product – which proved to be a great fuel source. With a viable source identified, Pandey utilized his electrical engineering background to discover a method for generating electricity from the husks the cleanest possible way.

Although eager to start up their own power plant, the next step was to seek government approval. It turned out that in the Electricity Act of 2003, the Indian government removed the requirement of obtaining a permit to run a decentralized power plant. HPS could start its operations without jumping through bureaucratic hoops. At the same time, if a bigger corporation wanted to operate in the rural markets, it still had to obtain licenses from federal and local authorities. And foreign investors would face full tax implications if they remitted any dividends from India.

With $50,000 in total from all available sources including 401(k) accounts (probably a good investment given the financial meltdown in 2007–08) and several trial-and-error runs, the first power plant went live on August 15, 2007, in the village of Tamkuha in Bihar, India. Despite the nearest town being a mere 10 miles away, limited public transportation and challenging terrain made the village relatively inaccessible. The power plant served approximately 2,000 people (about 500 households) and was only the beginning for HPS.

That fall, Sinha headed to the United States to earn an MBA and partnered with Chip Ransler, a classmate at the influential southern business school they attended. Ransler immediately saw great potential in his friend's hobby business: The market's size and scope were enormous. The energy supply was sustainable and the growth potential was very attractive. Together, Sinha and Ransler created a business plan that portrayed an environmentally conscientious energy company capable of providing electricity to millions of rural Indians in a financially sustainable, scalable, and, most importantly, profitable way. Everything was on their side: the proprietary technology that cost-effectively converted rice husks into electricity, the almost dirt-cheap source of energy, and the underserved and almost unlimited market. This was not to underestimate the enormous business challenges the company faced in recruiting and training the right people and creating the market for electricity in rural areas – communities that had never seen electricity.

GreenPoint Partners

By private equity industry standards, GreenPoint Partners was a middle-aged firm. The firm raised its first fund in 2004, and in early 2009, it was in the stage of deploying the capital of its second fund. Pasternik was one of the firm's founders. Over the previous 6 years, he had successfully leveraged his investment banking experience, vast rolodex of large potential investors, and passion for the new green sector of the energy industry to invest in highly promising companies. Pasternik viewed HPS as an enormous opportunity albeit in a faraway place – rural India. He knew that to convince his partners and the investment committee that it was a good opportunity, the team needed to dig deeply into the key financial assumptions and see if there were any potential land mines.

Pasternik had 7 years' experience working with emerging-market firms. HPS was not the first company in India that GreenPoint had worked with. In fact, for an emerging market, India presented a lot of competition for GreenPoint. All reputable venture capital firms – such as Kleiner Perkins Caufield and Byers, Sequoia Capital, DFJ, New Enterprise Associates, Battery Ventures, and SAIL Venture Partners – had set up offices and were actively investing in India. Even with the global economic slowdown, venture capital flows to India continued to be strong with investments totaling $864 million in 2008, up 3 % over 2007.[2] With 1.1 billion consumers and a 450-million-strong middle class, India was a very large, very fast-growing, and hence, very attractive market. With the profitability of foreign investments in India at 19.33 % and the GDP expected to grow at an average annual rate of 8 %, everyone rushed to find their place in the market. India was expected to move from being the tenth-largest to the third-largest economy in the world by 2020.

Although it had a desire to invest in emerging markets, GreenPoint's main mission was to invest in clean technology (or "cleantech"). The sector had seen a dramatic increase in funding over the previous decade. Since clean technology was a rather broad definition, GreenPoint could invest in a wide variety of businesses: firms focused on new energy sources, energy efficiency, water conservation, and sustainable and innovative business models around energy efficiency for commercial buildings and homes.

In 2008, cleantech venture investments in China, India, the United States, and Europe totaled a record $8.4 billion, up 38 % from the $6.1 billion invested in 2007. It was the seventh consecutive year of growth in cleantech venture investing across the globe. The first quarter of 2009 was not as promising as 2008 had been; but it showed cleantech investments had held their ground during the economic crisis with venture investments of $1.0 billion across 82 companies.[3] Kleiner Perkins, Sequoia Capital, and other prominent venture capital firms created cleantech-specific

---

[2]Miller, Claire Cain. Venture investment climbs in India, China and Israel. *New York Times*, February 18, 2009. http://bits.blogs.nytimes.com/2009/02/18/venture-capital-investment-climbs-in-india-china-and-israel/. Accessed October 28, 2010.

[3]"Clean Technology Venture Investment Falls to $1 Billion in 1Q09," Cleantech Group LLC press release, April 1, 2009.

funds with hundreds of millions under investment. In addition, a new generation of funds was born. Good Energies, Khosla Ventures (led by renowned investor Vinod Khosla), and Climate Change Capital had sprung up to accelerate growth for the sector. GreenPoint featured prominently among these specialized sets of funds.

As of 2009, GreenPoint navigated the crowded waters of cleantech investments in emerging markets with success. With two companies in its portfolio and one successful exit via selling to another private equity fund, GreenPoint was considered an experienced player.

The Pitch

As Ransler and Sinha sought growth capital, they provided potential investors with a thorough overview of resources, opportunities, and innovation. They described their technology, their market, and their alternative revenue streams as clearly as possible.

A Unique Market

Traditionally, power in India was a complex and surprisingly unprofitable enterprise. In 2009, there was a 40 % electricity deficit in India; 480 million citizens (44.5 % of the population) were without access to reliable power. Even areas that were on the state electricity grid sometimes had power for only a few hours per day – and customers didn't know when they could expect power in their homes. Mumbai and Delhi were the only cities in a country of 1.1 billion people that had consistent and reliable 24-h power supply. Indeed, the Earth Institute at Columbia University characterized rural electrification in India as being in an "acute crisis"[4] – 125,000 Indian villages were "unelectrified," and not much had changed since that assessment.[5] Indeed, the Indian government had designated 18,000 rural villages as "economically impossible" to reach via conventional means.[6] That left roughly 30 million people without any promise of power and kept them in eighteenth-century living conditions without televisions, radios, refrigerators, or any other electrical gadgets enjoyed by most U.S. households. Electricity became a highly political issue in India; in an attempt to secure votes, officials frequently promised "free" power to rural customers. This practice led to immense inefficiencies and highly unprofitable electricity distribution even in the smaller metropolitan areas. Trying to reach rural communities was even more difficult.

---

[4] Vijay Modi, "Improving Electricity Services in Rural India," the Earth Institute at Columbia University, December 2005.

[5] Villages were identified as "unelectrified" if power was either available only to a minority of the population or was inconsistently available.

[6] Ghosh, Sonaton, Tuhin K. Das, and Tushar Jash. 2001. *Sustainability of decentralized woodfuel-based power plant: an experience in India*. Calcutta: School of Energy Studies, Jadavpur University.

The worldwide power market was valued at over \$6 trillion. India's power resources were large and growing at 6 % annually to support its population. India's rural power market was valued at \$102 billion in early 2009, 98 % of which comprised fossil fuel use.[7] Electricity consumption in India had more than doubled since 2000, outpacing economic growth. In 2008, the power sector consumed 40 % of primary energy and 70 % of coal use. This sector was the single-largest consumer of capital, drawing over one-sixth of all Indian investments over the previous decade. Despite these huge expenditures, electricity demand continued to outstrip power-generating capacity, leaving a 12 % electricity deficit and a 20 % peak power shortage.[8] The Indian rural power market (including the "Rice Belt") represented over 350 million rural Indians who used \$102 billion in power, a number that was growing at approximately 10 % annually. Using a conservative estimate and a modest increase in demand, HPS had the potential to claim roughly \$15 billion of this market over the following 5 years.

Government and private-sector attempts to provide electricity to villages had failed. Rural Indian villages were widely spread and small, making large power-plant implementations difficult and uneconomical. Power companies had to run long, inefficient transmission lines from distant coal-fired plants – losing an estimated 25–30 % of the power generated on its way to small villages of 500–3,000 people.

The power options that were available to rural villagers were costly and hence minimally used. Villagers needed power mainly for irrigation, cooking, and lighting. Portable diesel generators were relatively expensive to fuel, resulting in costs of \$0.30–0.35 per kilowatt-hour and thus confined to critical irrigation needs. Home lighting was limited to kerosene lamps. On average, 30–35 % of the total power distributed in metropolitan areas was stolen.[9] Once the electricity reached villages, some villagers stole it by "hooking in" to exposed power lines, some did not pay their bills, and some even stole miles of power lines, whose cabling was of high value in the metal commodities market.

A Unique Technology

Rice husks were a goldmine. According to the India Department of Agriculture, the amount of rice produced in India in 2007 was estimated to be 93 metric tons.[10] In order to decrease weight and volume for transporting rice to market, it was milled

[7]Hammond, Allen et al. The next 4 billion: market size and business strategy at the base of the pyramid. World Resources Institute, March 2007. http://www.wri.org/publication/the-next-4-billion. Accessed October 28, 2010.

[8]Pew Center on Global Climate Change, "Developing Countries & Global Climate Change: Electric Power Options in India," October 1999, http://www.pewclimate.org/publications/report/developing-countries-global-climate-change-electric-power-options-india (accessed October 28, 2010).

[9]Gregory, Mark. India struggles with power theft. BBC News, March 15, 2006. http://news.bbc.co.uk/2/hi/business/4802248.stm. Accessed October 28, 2010.

[10]"Rising Rice Production," Ministry of Agriculture, Government of India press release, November 30, 2007.

locally, leaving rice husks in the villages. For a small village of 2,000 people (90 % of whom were involved in rice cultivation), 1,500 t of milled rice produced around 250–300 t of rice husks. Those casings were discarded, either by burning them or leaving them to rot in the fields (which released harmful methane gas). Alternatively, HPS could purchase the waste and potentially secure 20–25 million tons of rice husks every year.

HPS's proprietary technology, developed by Yadav and Pandey and two key suppliers to the firm, converted each ton of rice husks into 760 kW of electricity supply. The process combined two technologies: a biomass gasifier and gas-fired generator set. Effectively, HPS created mini power plants that produced electricity that was then distributed to households and businesses via a small utility power grid. HPS distributed *prepaid* electricity using a point-to-point system that connected each household or business *directly* to the HPS station. This elaborate delivery system reduced the total default and theft rate to below 5 % (compared with India's national average default and theft rate of 25–30 %).

The HPS model relied significantly on collaboration with local *panchayats* (councils of elderly villagers). The 35–100-kW-h electrical plants were built at no cost to the villages. Relationships with the elders allowed for better fee collection, maintenance, and fraud management. HPS also entered into contracts with farmers to procure rice husks at a fixed rate. The firm employed three villagers at each plant site to operate the power plant, handle the raw materials, and conduct billing and collections. HPS escaped the fate of traditional power companies by providing decentralized power on-site using local labor and feedstock inputs. It targeted its mini power plant technology to villages in India's Rice Belt: the states of Bihar, West Bengal, Orissa, Uttar Pradesh, Madhya Pradesh, Andhra Pradesh, and Tamil Nadu. That represented roughly 25,000 rural villages without power but with a large supply of biomass for HPS. These villages, each with 2,000–4,000 people, were large enough to support a minimum of 35 kW of power. That way, HPS optimized village size for power consumption, created jobs, and bought inputs locally – all of which ensured profitability and a welcome market entry with right-size technology.

As of 2009, some of the rice mills and irrigation systems were run on power from small, portable diesel generators. The cost of this power heavily depended on oil prices, and in April 2009, they cost about $0.30–0.35 per kilowatt-hour. HPS offered the same product at $0.25 per kilowatt-hour to farmers and $0.15 per kilowatt-hour to villagers for domestic consumption. The higher power costs farmers and mills paid was offset somewhat by HPS's purchase of biomass from them.

There were three main sources of revenue for each power plant. The principal and most stable revenue source was households. HPS provided electricity to each household for only 8–10 h every day during the peak demand time (between 4:00 p.m. and 3:00 a.m.) and charged households $0.15 per kilowatt-hour based on their actual energy use. Although it was much higher than the prevailing wholesale rate of $0.08 per kilowatt-hour, it included all the costs and taxes and did not contain any hidden charges. HPS devised a basic package for each household that included two compact fluorescent lamps and an unlimited number of cell phone chargers (on average, villagers paid $0.25 each time they charged their cell phones). For this package, households paid approximately $1.75–2.00 a month and thereby saved approximately $2.00 per month by not having to use kerosene lanterns or diesel generator sets.

HPS also supplied power to small businesses such as video halls, rice mills, and small farms for irrigation. The price for such businesses was $0.25 per kilowatt-hour, which was 20–30 % less than the total fuel cost for diesel-based generators and pumps. Businesses usually consumed electricity in the morning, while house-hold consumption was concentrated in the second half of the day. HPS's ability to directly provide electricity as needed allowed it to maximize its plant utilization and minimize total capital.

By the end of 2008, a little over a year after launching its first successful plant, HPS designed and built four power plants sized from 35 to 100 kW and serviced customers locally with billing, collections, and maintenance. HPS's technological advancements resulted in reducing installation costs for each plant from $35,000 down to $27,000 in 2 years. The amount of time required to install one plant improved dramatically from 3 months to just 2 weeks. Further, refinements to rice husk acqui-sition, plant installation, payment collection, and accounting processes led to signifi-cant cost, resource (full-time manpower), and time savings. The installations of rice-husk gasification plants had gone from a total of three in year one to adding seven more in the first 4 months of 2009. At that point, Sinha and Ransler believed they had moved from "experimental mode" to "growth mode." They were confident in their Indian partners and their hiring strategies, and they had diversified to a point at which plant operations were averaging out to a fairly profitable enterprise.

Market Demographics

In the previous decade, India had been growing at a fast pace (6–7 % GDP growth); however, the growth had not been uniform across different parts of India. Although urban areas (metropolitan cities) experienced job growth and dramatic improve-ments in infrastructure, the gap between urban and rural areas grew wider in most Indian states. HPS operated in rural areas where roads were almost nonexistent. For example, it took Sinha and Yadav 17 h to transport power plant equipment from a supplier site to one of the installation sites located only 130 miles away. On the one hand, the lack of infrastructure became an entry barrier to other competitors. Any company with a desire to serve these areas would have to find people motivated enough to withstand harsh conditions. On the other hand, the lack of facilities in the villages created a hurdle for HPS to attract competent people to install and manage new power plants.

Aside from infrastructure issues, there were cultural considerations HPS had to overcome. As a result of 100 years of British rule in India, the Indian social system was very hierarchical. A strict caste system made doing business in rural India complicated because the hierarchical order established a few thousand years earlier was still practiced in some way or another. Hindus were divided into four main castes – Brahmins, Kshatriyas, Vaisyas, and Sudras – and there were over 10 subcastes. Brahmins were at the top of the hierarchy; people belonging to this caste were typically educated and did not work menial jobs. Such a system stifled any sense of ownership among employees.

To that end, HPS employed a unique strategy to move past recruitment and cultural issues. It recruited and trained local people who were motivated to change the conditions in their hometowns. The management team was innovative in creating job descriptions and selecting employees.[11] In addition, the company's partners visited the power plants regularly and assisted workers in day-to-day operations during these visits. By working together and assigning employees ownership of operational processes, HPS partners inculcated a sense of ownership among employees. Plus the company spent part of its income stream on local social causes such as education for needy children. These types of management practices created a high level of buy-in from employees.

Alternative Revenue Streams

Though not included in the business plan's financial projections, Ransler and Sinha actively explored alternative revenue streams that HPS could monetize within a couple of years. First, they looked into monetizing the rice husk ash (RHA), a waste product of the husk gasification process. Because gasified rice husks contained high levels of carbon and silica, RHA could be used in various applications including organic fertilizer, replacement for coal in stoves, and material replacement in cement production. In 2009, HPS successfully tested its RHA technology and distributed "incense sticks" (used in Indian households for worship purposes) to commercial operations in local markets. Eventually, Sinha and Ransler expected to sell RHA to concrete manufacturers and generate revenues of $100–600 per ton. Indian cement demand had risen 100 % over the previous 10 years and was expected to double again within 5 years. Indian rice production was 92 million tons in 2007, yielding approximately 21 million tons of rice husks, which could amount to 4 million tons of RHA. At a market price of $400 per ton (RHA prices ranged from $200 to $600), RHA represented an annual market opportunity of almost $2 billion.

Sinha and Ransler also recognized their firm's huge potential in the area of carbon offsets. HPS's production process was carbon-negative: The power plants released less carbon during operation than if they were not operating at all. The company's power plants used a renewable, sustainable feedstock (rice husks) that took carbon out of the air as it grew. Though the carbon was released back into the

---

[11] HPS faced a number of unexpected HR management matters. The company defined the operator as a person who not only ran the plant but also kept the equipment and plant area clean. Part of the job was to sweep the plant area with a broom. One of the operators was a Brahmin, so he refused to clean because he considered it to be against his caste conventions.

atmosphere when the husks were combusted, it still created carbon neutrality; this was preferred to using net-positive fossil fuels such as coal or oil, which only released carbon into the atmosphere. HPS also aided in replacing diesel used to power generators in villages and kerosene used to light homes. In addition, it prevented rice husks from rotting in fields and creating methane gas, which was 21 times more harmful to the atmosphere than carbon dioxide (CO_2). Effectively, the company was converting harmful methane gas to less harmful CO_2. As a result HPS earned carbon credit. With its negative carbon footprint, the firm planned to sell carbon offsets in the active carbon-trading markets.

HPS reduced CO_2 emissions by around 120 t per plant per year. That reduction could be translated into revenue of $1,350 in the form of carbon credits called certified emission reductions (CERs), which were not subject to any taxes in India. The market for CERs was dramatically increasing. In 2008, $126 billion in CERs were sold, up from $63 billion in 2007, and nearly 12 times the value in 2005. A total 4.8 billion tons of CO_2, the main greenhouse gas blamed for global warming, were traded in 2008, up 61 % from the 3.0 billion traded in 2007.

With help from a consulting firm called Emergent Ventures, HPS underwent the Clean Development Mechanism (CDM) certification process. The CDM certification allowed emissions-reducing companies based in developing countries to earn CER credits equivalent to one metric ton of CO_2. The company had to incur a total cost of $30,000 over a period of 15–18 months to get a Gold Standard certification. Given that HPS served customers at the bottom of the pyramid, it qualified for the Gold Standard. This certification allowed HPS to sell CERs in the open market at a premium price. The market rate in Europe for selling CERs generated in India ranged from $8 to $11 per CER. HPS qualified for about 100–125 CERs per power plant.

Funding Expansion

HPS's partners were concerned that the private equity investors were immediately discounting any numbers, and the firm's locations – in very rural parts of India – exacerbated the discounting. Valuing the firm at this nascent stage depended on a number of factors: growth in the number of power plants, each plant's profitability, the time each plant would take to break even, the increase in energy consumption in each village, the monetization of waste streams from the gasification plants, government subsidies, CER pricing, and the international partnership capabilities of the firm. It was a lot to account for, but the resulting valuation dictated the company share that investors would receive. After a number of attempted pitches and long hours spent with investors and foundations, Sinha and Ransler finally simplified their financial projections. The conservative financial projections contained only revenues from the projected plants and excluded any additional revenue streams. This simplified approach biased the bottom-line numbers down but eliminated the upper hand the investors had in arguing that the alternative revenue streams (e.g., carbon credits) were unproven and unlikely to be realized.

The financing structure GreenPoint offered resembled a convertible note. Sinha and Ransler now had to carefully evaluate whether this financing structure addressed their concerns. What were the financial implications of this offer? The founders knew this was only the first stage of raising funds for expansion and they planned to draw on them gradually Growing the business to its potential would require another $5–10 million in investments in 2012, and subsequent rounds were not out of the question. Were they on their way to diluting themselves out of their own business?

Solar Energy in Rural South Africa[12]

Despite the end of apartheid, South Africa was a country still plagued by widespread social inequalities between its white minority and black majority. Many of South Africa's whites resided in urban centers, while a good proportion of its black population lived in rural villages that lacked electricity. While 74 % of South Africans had electricity, 3.7 million of its citizens had no reliable electricity source. In rural (and predominately black) areas, only 15 % had access to grid electricity. Most of the electrification disparity between white urban and black rural residents could be attributed to differences in income. The black population had an average yearly income of $992 compared with $9,109 for whites. Additionally, electrifying homes in rural areas was more expensive. While urban access to the grid cost around $800 per household, rural residences incurred costs of $2,400. Such factors led the *Energy Economist* to report:

> Apartheid still haunts South Africa's energy economy. The country's emerging democracy has inherited two systems…The largely white affluent minority expect and receive electricity at the flip of a switch. Two-thirds of its black citizens have no electricity at all. Most live in uninsulated shacks, sweating in 30 °C plus temperatures in summer, shivering in winter, and breathing unhealthy air all year.[13]

Exhibit 1 shows South Africa and its neighboring countries, and Exhibit 2 includes information on demographics and the economy.

---

[12]The authors are grateful to Frank Hochmouth, University of Cape Town, and Will Cawood and Ben Cook, Solar Electric Light Fund, for their assistance in preparing this case study. This case was prepared by Scott Sonenshein under the supervision of Patricia H. Werhane. Copyright ©1997; 2013 University of Virginia Darden School Foundation. All rights reserved. Addendum was prepared by Tim Rolph.
[13]"South Africa Makes Some Decisions," *Energy Economist*, August 1996.

The Pilot Project

Faced with the millions of residents without electricity in South Africa, the Solar Electric Light Fund (SELF) decided to help out. SELF, a nonprofit company based in Washington, D.C., facilitated the introduction of photovoltaic (PV) power[14] into lesser developed countries, hoping to stimulate long-term, sustainable, independent PV markets and consequently provide a needed social good at low cost to the environment. SELF's goal of long-term, sustainable, independent markets reflected it's general philosophy that individuals were entitled to electricity only to the extent that they could pay for it. SELF did not donate technology but instead facilitated transactions between the end users of PV and the PV supplier. For example, SELF might secure low-interest loans for PV purchasers, educate communities about PV, or train installers; however, the end user ultimately paid for the electricity. Much of SELF's work was performed during the pilot project stage. During a pilot project, SELF targeted a limited area for solar electrification to demonstrate the feasibility of PV on a wider scale. SELF had instituted pilot projects in several countries including China, India, and Vietnam.

Will Cawood, a project manager for SELF, was given the assignment of leading the South African pilot project. Similar to its other projects, SELF needed to choose a specific area in South Africa to assess the feasibility of a countrywide PV electrification program that would hopefully provide the groundwork for the formation of independent PV markets throughout South Africa.

The Maphephethe Community

The Maphephethe region appeared to be the ideal location for the pilot project. The community of approximately 20,000 residents was on the east coast of South Africa and 80 km west of the city of Durban. The region's landscape was mountainous, making access to it difficult during the summer, especially when rainfall amounts reached averages of 1,000 mm/Pa. Besides a lack of electricity, the community did not have an adequate communication system, lacking both telephone wires and significant cellular phone coverage.

While the nearest power line was only 5 km from the village, neither ESKOM nor Durban Electricity, the utility companies responsible for conventional electricity in the region, had plans for extending the grid for at least 5 years. Since the villagers could only afford, at most, 100 kWh of electricity per month, grid extensions would require ESKOM or Durban utility to incur large initial expenses in a market with low demand for its service. Considering that it was doubtful that the utility companies would incur such costs to supply conventional electricity to the region

---

[14]PV power harnesses the sun's energy and transforms it into useable electricity.

in the immediate future, SELF's PV power seemed like a feasible alternative. Still before making a decision to proceed with the project in Maphephethe, Cawood needed to take some initial precautions.

Initial Precautions

The community's leadership was vested in a young chief who had brought peace to the region after his father's death. He had also been responsible for bringing fresh piped water to the community, thereby improving the standard of living while simultaneously creating jobs for its members. The chief had already made his views on electrification clear by noting on several occasions that his goal was to have electric lights in every cottage in his community. Because the cultural traditions of the community were strong, Cawood established a good relationship with the chief. Community members were skeptical of outsiders, but Cawood's relationship with the chief earned the project the necessary respect of community's residents.

After working with the chief, Cawood contracted with a group of researchers from the Energy and Development Research Centre (EDRC) of the University of Cape Town to assess the receptiveness of the new technology within the Maphephethe community. The team of researchers discovered that Maphephethe residents were aware of the technological capability of harnessing the sun's rays for energy, but most lacked specific knowledge of PV technology. Despite the residents' limited knowledge of PV technology, an EDRC survey concluded that over 80 % of them were keen about the concept of PV and eager to try the new technology.

While the residents appeared to be enthusiastic about getting PV power, they nevertheless remained ignorant of the specifics of the new technology. To increase the community's awareness of PV, Cawood decided to install a demonstration unit. With funding from South Africa's Department of Mineral and Energy Affairs, SELF installed a 225 Wp solar lighting system in the local courthouse. SELF installed the unit with some community members watching to educate them about PV and with a live presentation show how it worked. When these initial precautions taken, Cawood was ready to plan the project in greater detail.

Implementing the Project

Cawood decided to electrify approximately 75 homes in the village with 53 Wp units that cost around $550 each. While the 53 Wp units provided less energy than a conventional grid extension, they supported several lights and small appliances meeting some of the needs of the residents. The price of each unit was high for most community members, but Cawood arranged for financing and loans through the KwaZulu Finance and Investment Corporation (KFC). KFC provided 3- or 4-year loans to PV unit purchasers at an interest rate of 16.5 % and a minimum 10 % down payment. Loans for salaried workers were approved on the basis of their individual pay-slips, and these borrowers were encouraged to deduct loan payments directly from their salaries. For nonsalaried residents to get a loan, KFC deployed a field staff to ascertain how a potential borrower intended to pay it off.

As more individuals secured loans and were able to afford PV, Cawood hoped that an independent PV market with financial support from an independent loan market would develop. The next step then would be for SELF to leave the region, allowing loans to be presented to residents without external support. Cawood noted that "we hope this formula will...provide an answer for at least half of the 3.5 million South African families who have yet to receive electric service from the grid."[15] After six homes were electrified, an initial report arrived on Cawood's desk.

The Initial Assessment[16]

The initial report concluded that the PV units had reduced community residents' expenditures on energy, thereby preserving some of their scarce economic resources (Exhibit 3). Some households used PV to provide light so their children could read books and complete their homework at night. This PV use served to better educate the community as a whole and provided the foundation for long-term lifestyle improvements.

PV also replaced car batteries as the primary source of energy for some families in the region. Before the introduction of PV, residents needed to charge their batteries every 7–30 days. This task proved burdensome, especially considering the community's transportation infrastructure and its mountainous terrain. The charging stations were accessible only by bus, taxi, or car and required that the resident carry the 20 kg battery on foot from the main road to his or her dwelling (sometimes several kilometers away). Most families owned only one battery, so no electricity was available during the time it was away being charged (usually at least for one night). PV units allowed residents to have access to power all the time.

But the news was not all good. Although the lifestyle of the newly electrified residents was improving as their energy costs decreased, the report also discovered there was a distribution problem as only certain residents of the community were receiving the PV units. Most residents could not afford a PV unit, so it appeared that in Maphephethe the people who occupied places of higher status were empowered even more by the solar home systems (SHS) brought into the community. Individuals who had communal influence, such as the chief and the tribal courthouse secretary, and persons with permanent jobs, such as shopkeepers and teachers, were the purchasers of the PV units.

---

[15]Gorman, Michael E.. 1998. *Transforming nature: ethics, invention and discovery*, 271. Norwell: Kluwer.

[16]Frank Hochmuth, "Benefits and Impacts of SHS – A Case Study of Six Households," July 1996.

It was uncertain whether the PV technology would cause long-term disruptions to Maphephethe's socio-economic balance. Before the implementation of PV, all the residents – including the chief – lived relatively similar lives, residing in one-room, round, modest cottages. Technology might drastically alter this balance. One of the main advantages to the individual user of the PV unit was a savings in energy expenditures. Those in the high-status class who purchased the unit were saving on energy costs that the typical resident of Maphephethe incurred. This solidified the position of the upper class in the community. Additionally, since PV units allowed residents to extend their days, PV purchasers were also able to improve their social status by pursuing other work projects at night. For example, two of the six house-holds in the Maphephethe community operated manual sewing machines at night with the help of PV light.

While the electrification efforts in the Maphephethe community were helping to decrease the social inequality between whites and the largely nonelectrified blacks, they were also causing social stratification within the community. Would continuing the pilot project exacerbate this internal social divide in Maphephethe? Would expanding the project to other areas of South Africa result in similar internal social divides in other communities? Would abandoning the entire project prevent many rural communities of South Africa from reaching the twenty-first century with their white urban counterparts? As Cawood re-read the report, his boss telephoned him and asked when the remaining residences would be electrified.

Exhibit 1: Solar Energy in Rural South Africa

Map of South Africa and Neighboring Countries

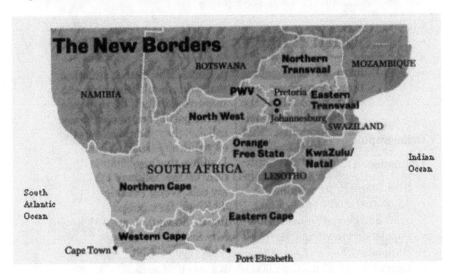

Exhibit 2: Solar Energy in Rural South Africa

South Africa Fact Boxes

General

Total Area: 1,219,912 sq kilometer
Land Area: 1,219,912 sq kilometer
(Slightly less than twice the size of Texas)

Climate: Mostly semiarid; subtropical along east coast; sunny days, cool nights

Terrain: Vast interior plateau rimmed by rugged hills and narrow coastal plain

Natural resources: Gold, chromium, antimony, coal, iron ore, manganese, nickel, phosphates, tin, uranium, gem diamonds, platinum, copper, vanadium, salt, natural gas

Land use:
- Arable land: 10%
- Permanent crops: 1%
- Meadows and pastures: 65%
- Forest and woodland: 3%
- Other: 21%

Environmental Issues: Lack of important arterial rivers or lakes requires extensive water conservation and control measures; growth in water usage threatens to outpace supply; pollution of rivers from agricultural runoff and urban discharge; air pollution resulting in acid rain; soil erosion; desertification; natural hazards: prolonged droughts

Electricity:
- Capacity: 39,750,000 kW
- Production: 163 billion kWh
- Consumption per capita: 3,482 kWh (1993)

Demographics:

Population: 41,743,459 (July 1996 est.)

- 0-14 years: 36% (male 7,578,639; female 7,428,123)
- 15-64 years: 60% (male 12,356,753; female 12,516,467)
- years and over: 4% (male 744,806; female 1,118,671) (July 1996 est.)
- Population growth rate: 1.76% (1996 est.)
- Birth rate: 27.91 births/1,000 population (1996 est.)
- Death rate: 10.32 deaths/1,000 population (1996 est.)

(continued)

(continued)

- Infant mortality rate: 48.8 deaths/1,000 live births (1996 est.)
- Life expectancy at birth: 59.47 years

Ethnic Divisions:
- Black 75.2%
- White 13.6%
- Colored 8.6%
- Indian 2.6%

Literacy:
- Total population: 81.8%
- Male: 81.9%
- Female: 81.7%

Economy:

Economic overview: Many of the white one-seventh of the South African population enjoy incomes, material comforts, and health and educational standards equal to those of Western Europe. In contrast, most of the remaining population suffers from the poverty patterns of the Third World, including unemployment and lack of job skills. The main strength of the economy lies in its rich mineral resources, which provide two-thirds of exports. Economic developments for the remainder of the 1990s will be driven largely by the new government's attempts to improve black living conditions, to set the country on a steady export-led growth path, and to cut back the enormous numbers of unemployed. The economy in recent years has absorbed less than 5% of the more than 300,000 workers entering the labor force annually. Local economists estimate that the economy must grow between 5% and 6% in real terms annually to absorb all of the new entrants, much less reduce the accumulated total.

- GDP: purchasing power parity - $215 billion (1995 est.)
- GDP real growth rate: 3.3% (1995 est.)
- GDP per capita: $4,800 (1995 est.)
- GDP composition by sector:
- Inflation rate (consumer prices): 8.7% (1995)
- Labor force: 14.2 million economically active (1996)
- By occupation: services 35%, agriculture 30%, industry 20%, mining 9%, other 6%
- Unemployment rate: 32.6% (1996 est.); an additional 11% underemployment
- Industries: mining (world's largest producer of platinum, gold, chromium), automobile assembly,
- metalworking, machinery, textile, iron and steel, chemical, fertilizer, foodstuffs

Source: *CIA Fact Book*, 1996.

Exhibit 3: Solar Energy in Rural South Africa

Energy Costs of PV

	HH no 1	HH no 2	HH no 3	HH no 4	HH no 5	HH no 6
Energy costs before SHS installed	R 66,42	R 240,72	R 140,05	R 244,57	R 164,21	R 114,73
Energy costs after SHS installed	R 28,00	R 172,80	R 87,00	R 100,00	R 62,75	R 66,60
Savings in energy costs (excluding SHS costs)	R 38,42	R 67,92	R 53,05	R 144,57	R 101,46	R 48,13
SHS costs[1]	R 36,00	R 36,00	R 36,00	R 36,00	R 36,00	R 36,00
Savings including SHS costs	R 2,42	R 31,92	R 17,05	R 108,57	R 65,46	R 12,13
Change in expenditure as perceived by the user	more	less	less	less	less	less
SHS installments	R 52,00	R 52,00	R 64,00	R 52,00	R 52,00	R 52,00

Savings on fuels as a result of the use of a SHS. All households in the sample do spend less money on energy than before, provided a calculation over 10 years is made. The monthly installments paid are given in the last row for comparison. Three of the users spend less money even if the monthly installment is included in the energy expenditure. Most users believe that they save money by using the SHS, and they seem to be right.

Note: Currency is in South African rand. There are approximately 4.5 per $US.

Source: Graph copied from "Benefits and Impacts of SHS—A Case Study of Six Households."

[1]Cost calculated on the basis of a useful life-time of 10 years. See "Evaluation of the SHS demand survey in Maphephethe," Frank Hochmuth, March 1996.

BHP Billiton and Mozal (A)[17, 18]

BHP Billiton, the world's largest diversified resource company at the start of the twenty-first century, did business in the fields of aluminum, energy coal and metallurgical coal, copper, manganese, iron ore, uranium, nickel, silver and

---

[17]This case is an authorized adaptation of the BHP Billiton socioeconomic case study, "Mozal: A Model for Integrating Sustainability Into Resource Projects," *BHP Billiton Sustainability Report 2005*, http://sustainability.bhpbilliton.com/2005/repository/socioEconomic/caseStudies/caseStudies38.asp (accessed February 29, 2008). The original case was condensed and slightly revised with the permission of BHP Billiton.

[18]This case was prepared by Jenny Mead, Laura P. Hartman and Patricia H. Werhane. ©2008. University of Virginia Darden School Foundation. All rights reserved.

titanium minerals, with interests in oil, gas, liquefied natural gas, and diamonds. In 1995, it began a feasibility study for building an aluminum smelter project in the Maputo province in southern Mozambique.

Mozambique was one of the world's poorest countries, emerging from 17 years of civil war in 1994 and making the difficult transition to a market-oriented economy. The country was hampered by fragile legal, financial, and health, safety, environmental, and community HSEC institutional structures and capacity. A limited number of people had the training and skills required for the project's construction and operational phases. Malaria was widespread and debilitating to the communities from which the plant would draw most of its work force; the disease was also a threat to attracting expatriate managers and skilled workers. HIV/AIDS was prevalent in the area, and infection rates were exacerbated by the influx of construction workers from neighboring South Africa.

Public services were bureaucratic, poorly equipped, and had limited capacity. Functions such as customs, immigration, public works, public health, port operations, and police would face challenges in coping with the magnitude of the project. Infrastructure such as roads, water supply, sewerage, and waste disposal was poorly developed and poorly maintained. Access to appropriate, affordable housing was limited. Most suitable development sites were occupied by concentrations of medium to large informally structured communities. High prices and poor quality of goods and services plagued local commerce and industry. In short, the area was limited in its capacity to satisfy the needs of a major project such as the proposed smelter.

BHP Billiton

BHP Billiton was committed to sustainable development and believed that social and environmental performance were critical factors in business success. The company's stated aim was to enhance the societal benefit of its operations and to reduce its environmental impact while creating value for many of its stakeholders. BHP Billiton believed firmly that sustainable development involved engaging and partnering with its community stakeholders to address the challenges associated with establishing resource projects and to share the benefits of success. Was this possible in Mozambique, given the nation's social and political challenges, the prevalence of malaria and HIV, and the weak infrastructure? Acknowledging that stakeholders had a role to play in achieving a successful and sustainable project, BHP Billiton adopted "Together we make a difference" as the slogan for this project.[19] The company called the project "Mozal." But would or could they be successful? And at what cost?

---

[19]Mozal Web site, "Governance and Ethics," http://www.mozal.com/gae.htm (accessed February 29, 2008).

Mitigating Financial Risk

An initial step in project development was to involve the International Finance Corporation (IFC), the private sector arm of the World Bank Group,[20] as a partner in phase 1. The IFC, whose mission was to reduce global poverty and improve lives by promoting a sustainable private sector in developing countries, provided a loan of US$120 million, its largest single investment in the nonfinancial sector. This helped mitigate financial risk and also facilitated loan syndication and promoted the project internationally. The IFC had robust environmental and social policies, as well as procedures and guidelines drawn from the World Bank Group. Requirements for strict compliance with the guiding principles gave assurance to other lenders and the host country that the project would achieve minimum standards relating to social and environmental impacts. To contribute to sustainable development, the company also had to put in place health, safety, environment, community, and socioeconomic initiatives, which were to be developed and implemented by the operation.

Even with IFC involvement, this was, at best, a corporate challenge and a very risky venture. How should BHP Billiton approach this multilayered project, or should it consider investing in smelters in other countries more hospitable

BHP Billiton and Mozal (B)[21]

The Mozal Aluminum Smelter: Project Profile

Designed as an advanced, cost-efficient plant, phase 1 of the Mozal project officially began in July 1998. At a budgeted cost of US$1.18 billion, it was to be the first major development in Mozambique in 30 years and the country's largest private investment ever. Phase 1 was successfully completed 6 months ahead of schedule and more than US$120 million under budget. The first aluminum was cast in June 2000, and the first ingots were exported in August of that year. In June 2001, phase 2 of the project – an

---

[20]The World Bank Group, often referred to as the World Bank, consisted of five different organizations. In addition to the International Finance Corporation, there was the International Bank for Reconstruction and Development, the International Development Association, the Multilateral Investment Guarantee Agency, and the International Centre for the Settlement of Investment Disputes.

[21]This case is an authorized adaptation of two BHP Billiton case studies: "Mozal: A Model for Integrating Sustainability Into Resource Projects," BHP Billiton Sustainability Report 2005, http://sustainability.bhpbilliton.com/2005/repository/socioEconomic/caseStudies/caseStudies38.asp; "Mozal Program Supports Small and Medium Enterprises in Mozambique." BHP Billiton Health, Safety, Environment, and Community Report 2003, http://sustainability.bhpbilliton.com/2003/caseStudies/cs_community30.html (accessed February 29, 2008). The original cases were condensed and slightly revised with the permission of BHP Billiton.

expansion – was started; its construction budget was US$860 million. The expansion of the smelter would double its capacity. It was completed in August 2003, 7 months ahead of schedule and US$195 million under budget.

From its earliest days, the project presented a number of significant challenges for BHP Billiton and its venture partners, Mitsubishi Corporation of Japan and the Industrial Development Corporation (IDC) of South Africa.

During the two construction phases, the project contributed more than US$160 million to the local economy, principally through the employment of Mozambican laborers and the use of local contractors and suppliers. Between 1998 and 2008, local spending grew to more than US$140 million annually. Mozal was one of the largest smelters of its kind in the Western world, producing more than 500,000 t of aluminum per year. In 2008, the operation employed more than 1,100 people.

Health and Safety Initiatives

In addition to caring for the health and well-being of its employees, BHP Billiton also worked with its host communities to set up programs focused on significant community health matters.

Malaria Prevention Programs

A baseline malaria survey conducted in southern Mozambique in December 1999 found that infection rates in the area surrounding the Beluluane Industrial Park, where Mozal was located, exceeded 85 %. The Mozal Community Development Trust (MCDT)[22] conducted a spraying program within a 10-km radius of the smelter and contributed funds to the Lubombo Spatial Development Initiative, a joint venture between the governments of South Africa, Mozambique, and Swaziland aimed at eradicating malaria in the region. MCDT also sent community members to training courses in manufacturing treated mosquito netting to help keep people from contracting malaria while they slept. The MCDT also provided sewing machines, insecticides, netting material, and consumables, and bought the initial batch of 1,000 bed nets.

After 3 years of intensive effort, the infection rate in the Beluluane area was reduced from 85 % to 18.6 %. During phase 1, the company had a peak of more than 9,000 employees; it established a malaria diagnosis and treatment facility at which it provided medical treatment to staff. The large number of expatriate workers with no natural immunity to malaria posed a major challenge. Thousands of cases were diagnosed, treated, and documented during phase 1. Analysis of those records steered the malaria management strategy toward awareness, early diagnosis, and prevention in phase 2, which resulted in significantly reduced malaria incidence.

---

[22] The Mozal board created the MCDT in August 2000 with the specific mission of facilitating projects and programs to improve the quality of life of the communities surrounding Mozambique's Beluluane Industrial Park.

HIV/AIDS Programs

The control of sexually transmitted diseases and opportunistic infections was an important strategy in the fight against HIV/AIDS. From 2001 to 2003, the MCDT sponsored the Total Control of Epidemic program, in which a group of 100 field officers educated approximately 200,000 people in the local communities of Boane, Matola, and Maputo on the dangers of HIV/AIDS and how to prevent it. Pivotal to the prevention of the disease was a person's knowledge of his or her HIV/AIDS status and management of behavior and health. Beginning in 2001, Mozal provided assistance for a Voluntary Counseling and Testing Center (VCT) in Boane, managed on behalf of the Ministry of Health by a Danish nongovernmental organization (NGO) called Ajuda De Povos Para Povos (ADPP). Eleven satellite units of the VCT were opened in Boane and Matola. Community leaders were trained to manage the facilities and provide counseling services and with the approval of provincial authorities, Mozal supplemented the stock levels of appropriate drugs at local clinics.

The Beluluane Public Health and Maternity Clinic

The local public health clinic, operated by the District/Provincial Health Directorate of the Mozambican Ministry of Health, served a community of about 18,000 people within a 10-km radius of the smelter. The MCDT provided the clinic with doctors' facilities, a laboratory, and three residences for staff, and constructed a maternity center within the facility. Initiatives further afield included the provision of a mother-and-child health care facility within the Matola health clinic, which served more than 300,000 people in the Matola municipality.

Environmental Initiatives

BHP Billiton decided early to focus on an integrated approach to the management of its social and environmental responsibilities. The IFC and the Mozambique Ministry of Environmental Coordination (MICOA) rigorously reviewed comprehensive social and environmental impact assessments. Subsequent environmental management programs provided the blueprint for the appropriate design of physical environmental aspects of the construction and operation of the plant, in line with BHP Billiton's philosophy of "Zero Harm"[23] to the environment. Regular monitoring and auditing, both internally and by external bodies (IFC and MICOA), provided a basis for correcting deviations and implementing continuous improvement processes. The

---

[23] Mozal Web site, "Governance and Ethics," http://www.mozal.com/gae.htm (accessed February 22, 2008).

environmental management programs included frequent public meetings as well as task force meetings; the task force was composed of environmental consultants, the contractors, and representatives from key government ministries, large state-owned enterprises, district administration, community groups, and Mozal.

Community Initiatives

According to BHP Billiton's Company Charter, an indicator of success was that its host communities valued the company's presence. From the outset, the Mozal initiative identified community needs and supported programs put in place to achieve sustainable outcomes for the community.

Relocation of Communities

The original site proposed for the smelter was densely populated, and construction there would have required the relocation of approximately 7,500 people. The social impact assessment led to selection of an alternative site, requiring the resettlement of 80 families and the provision of agricultural land for 910 farmers. The land, allocated to Mozal by the government of Mozambique, formed part of the Beluluane Industrial Park development. In September 1998, ACER Africa, a specialist resettlement consultant appointed by Mozal, drew up a Resettlement Action Plan. The government, with support and financing from Mozal, managed the relocation process in accordance with the World Bank Operational Directive on Involuntary Resettlement. Formal monitoring of the program over the years indicated that the quality of life of most of the affected people improved.

The Mozal Community Development Trust

The MCDT's development initiatives began in January 2001, with an initial annual budget of US$2 million, which increased each year. To achieve its mission, the MCDT defined four key policies:

- Align development initiatives with those of national, provincial, and local governments.
- Act as a catalyst and facilitator in establishing pilot projects that could be replicated (e.g., the IFC is funding the local replication of some projects).
- Form partnerships with stakeholders to achieve sustainable results.
- Involve relevant stakeholders from all levels of government, NGOs, communities, and the private sector, as well as Mozal employees.

The MCDT initiated approximately 200 projects and programs, with expenditures exceeding US$10 million.

Educational Projects

To overcome the lack of secondary education facilities in the region, the Nelson Mandela Secondary School was built, the first such school in the Mozal vicinity. The project was a joint initiative: Mozal provided funding, the local communities provided 10 ha of land, and the government managed the school's construction and operation. In 2008, the school was in its second year of operation; it accommodated 1,800 students, and there were plans to expand the capacity to 2,400 students. The total investment by Mozal would be approximately US$1 million. The MCDT also donated 41 computers to the school.

The primary school closest to Mozal was an abandoned house with no roof. A new school, constructed in two phases, included seven new classrooms, an administration unit, three staff houses, and sports facilities. Twelve other primary schools in the region were significantly upgraded, with improvements that included new classrooms, sports grounds, and water and electricity reticulation.

To build teaching capacity in the region, each year the MCDT supported the training of 40 teachers in new teaching methodologies and national curricula. Through the Look of Hope Project administered by the Ministry of Education, the MCDT donated 52,000 workbooks annually to disadvantaged children. The MCDT also funded new facilities at the Bilibiza Agricultural School in the northern province of Cabo Delgado, which had a population of more than one million. As more than 80 % of the population depended on subsistence agriculture, the school played a key role in helping to reduce poverty in the region.

Other initiatives included a community theater, construction of a new police station (as well as the purchase of four police vehicles), a road safety awareness campaign, sports events (e.g., an annual beach volleyball tournament), and cultural development (e.g., funding for theater groups and support of youth activities in art, sculpture, and handicrafts). Another community initiative involved developing and supporting various interaction channels between the community and BHP Billiton.

Socioeconomic Initiatives

The company believed that a stable, healthy, and supportive society facilitated the effective operation of its business. By contributing to the social and economic fabric of its host communities, the company hoped to create an environment in which its business could grow and, in turn, support sustainable development of the region.

Work Force Training and Development

To help ensure that Mozambican workers had the skills to execute their duties in a safe and productive manner, Mozal provided funding to establish local facilities for the training of mechanical and electrical maintenance and construction workers. Training at these centers, located in Maputo and Machava, was conducted in conjunction with the National Institute of Labour and Training (INEPF). The two facilities were able to operate autonomously starting in 2004. The Maputo center conducted courses in electrical and mechanical disciplines, and the Machava center provided training in bricklaying, plumbing, carpentry, painting, and welding. Several Mozambican industries recruited graduate trainees from the courses and sent technical staff to the centers for training. During the two establishment phases of the project, 9,846 Mozambicans received training in various construction disciplines; as a result, more than 70 % of the Mozal construction work force was local.

Other initiatives by Mozal to enhance employee competency and promote career opportunities included an Operators Development Program, Supervisory Capacity Building Program, "MY" Development Program (self-driven, competency-based training), Assisted Education Program (degree and postgraduate education), and a Graduate Development Program (GDP). Overseas assignments, to Brazil and South Africa, for example, were arranged for employees to prepare them for promotion.

Housing Project

BHP Billiton believed it was important to develop a residential area within the vicinity of the smelter. Many employees had difficulty buying homes, which affected work force stability and motivation. Under the Beluluane Land Use Management Plan established by Mozal, a site was selected and 96 houses constructed. An additional 96 homes were built in the second stage. Mozal managed the construction process, the procurement of materials, and the training of local enterprises to provide services.

Public Infrastructure

Through the Mozal project, the region was provided with significant public infrastructure, including roads and bridges, potable water, electricity, telephone service, sewage treatment works, housing units, and general amenities buildings. Mozal also funded the construction of a smelter import/export quay, infrastructure at the Matola port, and a modern landfill facility to handle hazardous waste from industries in the region.

Supporting Small and Medium Enterprises in Mozambique

During phase 1 of the Mozal project, the use of local contractors and particularly small- and medium-size enterprises (SMEs) was limited. To address this situation and boost local participation, BHP Billiton developed the Small and Medium Enterprise Empowerment and Linkages Program (SMEELP). Following a review of the Mozal 1 experience, it was clear that, if the expansion project was to succeed in involving local SMEs, a new methodology would have to be developed.

This imperative was reflected in the broader Mozal Empowerment Policy, which stated that "the management of the Mozal Expansion Project is committed to maximizing sustainable benefits to the local community using a combined strategy of development and use of local goods, services, and personnel, without compromising project objectives."

A commitment was made to

- maximize the use of local labor (more than 65 % Mozambican);
- provide skills training for local labor (train more than 3,800 workers in construction);
- actively encourage the use of local contractors;
- actively encourage the establishment of joint ventures between international and local contractors;
- allocate selected work packages solely for execution by local SMEs;
- promote SME training programs to enable local SMEs to be competitive and successful;
- establish systems for monitoring and reporting the project's empowerment progress.

The target for the total local spending, including SMEELP and all other forms of local expenditures, was set at US$80 million. Specific objectives were then established for the SMEELP, to facilitate the successful delivery of at least 25 SME contracts and the establishment of a sustainable SME training program.

To improve the likelihood of success of the program, the SMEELP was established as a collaborative joint venture between Mozal, the Africa Project Development Facility (APDF) of the International Finance Corporation (IFC), and the Centre for Promotion of Investment (CPI) of the Mozambique Government. After completion of the Mozal expansion project, the CPI planned to take over management of the program to ensure its sustainability. The methodology was designed to be suitable for any company wanting to successfully utilize local SMEs.

The key steps in developing an effective SMEELP were deemed as follows:

1. Creation of SME packages

   - Packages solely allocated to SMEs
   - Realistic scope in terms of size and complexity ensured
   - Sufficient backup time in case of failure provided
   - Standard packages, whenever possible, include SMEs.

2. Preassessment of SME capabilities

   - SMEs financial/technical capabilities preassessed
   - Capable SMEs recommended to the project by CPI
   - SME database established and periodically updated.

3. Training

   - Tender training (pre-tender): how to tender
   - Induction training (post-award): how to execute contracts
   - On-demand training: Quality Assurance (QA)/Quality Control (QC), Business Management, etc.
   - Training modules written and presented in local language, periodically updated.

4. Mentorship

- Custom-made mentorship plan for each SME
- Business mentorship: financial/commercial assistance
- Technical mentorship: on- and off-site technical assistance, including Safety, QA/QC, and Industrial Relations.

To help overcome the challenge of language differences and to facilitate the upgrading of SME infrastructures and technical standards, a dedicated bilingual empowerment coordinator was assigned to the SMEELP. The appointment also helped ensure the project's engineering, procurement and construction management (EPCM) contractor embraced the concept of SME participation. This was a major factor in the success of the SMEELP, with the EPCM contractor's team playing a key role in driving the project.

The program was successful, significantly increasing local participation during the construction of Mozal 2. The program, considered sustainable, was then used successfully in BHP Billiton's Hillside 3 expansion project in Richards Bay, South Africa. As of 2008, the SMEELP results included: creation of 27 SME contract packages; training for 36 SMEs; awarding of 28 contract packages (including one standard package) to 14 SMEs; successful delivery of 12 contract packages; no contract package cancelled; and allocating a total of more than US$5 million to SMEs.

Mozlink

The SMEELP program was extended under the name of Mozlink, which was also supported by the IFC and CPI. Through training and mentorship, Mozlink helped to build local capacity and increase business in Mozambique. Smelter operations relied on more than 200 Mozambican suppliers. Local spending exceeded 30 % of goods and services procurement (excluding major raw materials and electricity). An SME Development Centre was established to coach, train, and expose SMEs to best practices in supplying goods and services to the smelter and to measure ongoing performance improvements by registered SMEs in the areas of safety, maintenance, and financial and human resources management.

A knowledge-sharing and linkage Internet site was developed to provide information for SMEs about available packages, financing, best practices, tender procedures, and quality standards. The site allowed Mozal and other businesses to more easily locate SMEs. For example, a local supplier of brooms, which were previously imported from South Africa, was identified and used through Mozlink.

Small Business Development

A small- and microenterprise program was established to train women in the region in raising and selling chickens and eggs, carpet-making, and embroidery. Other initiatives included training farmers in cashew nut and other crop production. To provide an outlet for families participating in income-earning activities, the MCDT established the 80-stall Rhulani Market in the Beluluane area.

Capacity-Building in State Functions

Mozal, through provision of facilities, equipment, training, and facilitation, assisted state functions to improve service delivery. For example:

- Customs processes were streamlined at the Mozambique–South African border. Clearing times were reduced from days to hours. A new customs building at Mozal was fully equipped to manage exports from the operation.
- Transportation of abnormal loads was aligned with best practices through training and mentoring by professional load transporters and the donation of three escort vehicles.
- Town planners from the Department of Public Works and Housing received training in modern town-planning methodologies.
- Comprehensive training was provided to staff of the Ministry of Environmental Coordination on the operation of the hazardous waste facility.

Engineering Development in Mozambique

In October 2003, Mozal initiated a project aimed at raising the level of education of the country's engineers and technologists to international standards. International experts, relevant ministries, educational institutions, and other companies collaborated in a 3-year pilot project to strengthen the engineering faculty at the University Eduardo Mondlane in Maputo. In addition, a range of professional development courses was introduced and a broad-based computer-aided design training facility established. A registration system for engineers was also developed, based on global best practices. Mozal and BHP Billiton invested approximately US$300,000 in the engineering project.

Agricultural Programs

An Agriculture Development Program (ADP), recommended by the IFC, was implemented over a 4-year period, starting in 2000, to benefit farmers relocated from the Mozal site. Prior to the program, annual yields of maize were 300 kg per family. The ADP boosted yields five-fold, with a record average yield of 1,900 kg in 2002. Farmers were also supported in diversifying their crops to include drought-resistant crops using seed supplied by the MCDT. The 2004 harvests indicated that the scheme had the potential to alleviate poverty during drought. After severe floods in 2000 in the Boane district, a program was implemented to rehabilitate irrigation infrastructure, repair equipment, supply seed, improve access to markets, and provide training and mentorship. The program enabled the local farmers' association to again supply produce to markets and catering companies. In partnership with CARE International, the MCDT constructed 10 rural dams in the northern province of Nampula, helping to stabilize water supplies for agricultural development and domestic use and to minimize damage from heavy rainfall.

Mozal: Focusing on Sustainability, for Business and for the Community

Careful planning of the construction and operational phases of Mozal took into account all the challenges posed when investing in Mozambique. Since commencement, the project had complied with the environmental and social requirements of the IFC. Following phase 1, any gaps related to the values embodied in the BHP Billiton Charter and Zero Harm philosophy were addressed in phase 2. The entire project delivered significant achievements:

- Both project implementation phases were completed well under budget and ahead of schedule.
- Following good HSEC performance during phase 1, considerably better performance was recorded during phase 2 and the organization of operations.
- Harmonious industrial relations were exemplified by the phase 2 construction period, totaling 16 million work hours, when no days were lost due to industrial action.
- Operational performance ran at benchmark levels.
- The region and the country benefited from needs-based infrastructure, and social and community development projects.
- Ongoing projects and programs delivered by Mozal and the MCDT reinforced the principles of sustainable project implementation.

The IFC, in its publication *The Environmental and Social Challenges of Private Sector Projects*, stated that "Mozal has set a precedent for future projects in Mozambique. It illustrates the clear advantages of incorporating environmental and social issues early in a project, and reflects the approach and procedures IFC has been refining and putting in place to deal with environmental and social issues."[24] For BHP Billiton, the Mozal experience demonstrated that, when establishing a major resource project, it made good business sense to invest not only in the venture but also in the host community.

Ecover and Green Marketing (A)[25]

Ecover's mission is to be the pioneering example in sustainable social and economic development in the world. Ecover accepts that this challenge requires everyone to continuously go beyond known limits.

–Ecover Mission Statement

---

[24] Mahidhara, Ramamohan. 2002. *The environmental and social challenges of private sector projects: IFC's experience*, 40. Washington, DC: The International Finance Corporation.

[25] This case was prepared by Joel Reichart and Lisa Spiro under the supervision of Andrea Larson and Patricia H. Werhane. ©Copyright 1999 University of Virginia Darden School Foundation. All rights reserved. Addendum prepared by Tim Rolph. ©2013.

Depressed by the failure of his company that had manufactured private label detergents, Belgian chemist Frans Bogaerts was casting about for other business opportunities when a Swiss friend gave him a fortuitous recommendation: Why not create a detergent that would fulfill the environmental regulations recently enacted in Switzerland? Determined to come up with a formula for an environmentally friendly detergent, in 1979 Bogaerts set up a lab in a rented barn in Malle, Belgium. Whereas most detergents were composed of potentially dangerous ingredients such as petrochemicals and phosphates, Bogaerts developed a formula made from natural ingredients that posed far less environmental hazard. To signal the product's environmental friendliness, Bogaerts named both the brand and his company "Ecover," from the Latin for "environmental" and "green." As the company grew, it began to manufacture a range of biodegradable, "environmentally friendly" cleaning products for household and industrial use, including laundry detergent, bathroom cleansers, dishwashing liquid, and car wax. Initially Ecover products were primarily sold in health food stores, where they quickly attracted a large share of green consumers.[26]

By 1991, Ecover faced a crucial decision that could place it far from its humble beginnings in a barn: Should it invest in an expensive ecological factory that would allow it to meet its environmental principles and expand its production capabilities, or should it continue to aim for a limited segment of the market and keep operations small? Would expansion cause Ecover to compromise its green principles and destroy its future, or would growth allow the company to "go beyond known limits" in spreading its philosophy.

Company History

As a start-up company, Ecover set out to capture a specialized segment of consumers, those who shopped at health food stores. Until the 1980s, few health food stores had sold detergents, for both ideological and practical reasons. Not only were detergents regarded as potentially toxic chemicals, but also their packaging consumed large portions of valuable shelf space. With the development of Ecover and other "green" cleansers, however, health food stores moved into the detergent market; indeed, Ecover became the first detergent company to distribute through health food stores. Although this market was small and specialized, Ecover quickly established its dominance through its educational campaigns, becoming the recognized international leader in the green detergent industry. In 1986, the company was expanding so rapidly that operations were moved to an industrial park vacated by a failed oil trading company. By 1990, Ecover claimed 70 % of the health food market in Belgium, the Netherlands, the U.K., and Scandinavia, and 40 % in Germany and Austria.[27]

By the late 1980s, as Ecover began to establish itself more firmly, the company initiated a green "crusade" to alert consumers to the environmental risks posed

---

[26]Gunter Pauli, with Niraj Dawar and H. Landis Gabel, "Ecover," Fontainebleau, France: INSEAD, 1995, 2.

[27]Pauli, Dawar, and Gabel, 2.

by conventional detergents.[28] Rather than spending huge sums on advertising campaigns, Ecover sought to educate consumers and health food retailers about its practices and products through pamphlets, packaging, and informal communication. Even though Ecover disliked advertising, the company did sponsor an advertisement in Belgium warning that water pollution killed fish and fauna and touting its detergents for being safer for the environment. Although the advertising commission banned this ad for setting off consumer fear, it gained Ecover attention. Ecover also pursued more direct means of educating consumers, sending trailers throughout England, North America, Sweden, and Belgium with displays that cautioned people about the deleterious effects of conventional detergents on the environment. In addition, Ecover issued a manual explaining its key concepts, translating it into over half a dozen languages so that it could gain attention worldwide. By providing complete information about its ingredients on its packaging, Ecover let consumers know exactly what they were sending into the sewers and distinguished itself as one of the first detergent companies to offer such information. Most importantly, Ecover reached out to people working in the health food and environmental industries, publicizing its products and asking for feedback.[29] Indeed, Ecover contended that its active environmental campaigning established a climate that encouraged other green companies to take seed. Through word of mouth, Ecover developed both awareness and brand loyalty among green consumers, who were especially drawn by the environmental principles that Ecover espoused.

Environmental Principles

While conventional detergents include toxic chemicals and are suspected of having allergenic effects, Ecover developed unique formulas without these dangerous effects. According to Gunter Pauli, who served as Ecover's president and CEO from 1992 to 1994, "[Ecover's] people look at their work through the eyes of their children." Ecover promotes intergenerational equity by espousing five environmental principles that directly benefit the communities and markets where Ecover manufactures and sells its products.[30]

---

[28]Ecover itself uses the word "crusade" to describe its early campaigns to alert consumers to the dangers from conventional detergents and the benefits of its products. See "Marketing Policy," Ecover Web site, http://www.ecover.com.

[29]"Marketing Policy," Ecover website, http://www.ecover.com. Accessed May 11, 1999.

[30]Information about these principles is drawn from three primary sources: (1) Ecover internal documentation; (2) an in-class presentation by Gunter Pauli given at the University of Virginia Colgate Darden School of Business in Spring 1994; and (3) "Ecover's Five Commandments," World Paper, November, 1993, 3. In addition to his role at Ecover, Pauli has founded several companies, was founder and president of Worldwatch Institute Europe, created the European Service Industries Forum (a network of successful high-growth service businesses), and has authored numerous books and articles based on his experience as an entrepreneur, green economist, and Fortune 500 executive lecturer on sustainable development. In 1994, Pauli started the Zero Emissions Research Initiative at the United Nations University in Tokyo, which he continues to direct; for more information, see http://www.zeri.org.

Principle 1 – Biodegradability and Nontoxicity: Through biodegradation, organic materials are broken down and re-incorporated into the ecosystem. Practically all products will biodegrade given time; even plutonium will biodegrade in 100,000 years. The Organization for Economic Cooperation and Development (OECD) guidelines prescribe that a product is fully degradable when 80 % is degraded within 28 days. Ecover, however, argues that these guidelines and others like them are grossly insufficient, contending that industry needs to self-impose the strictest of rules governing the biodegradability of their products and wastes. Ecover practices what it preaches: 99.7 % of Ecover's washing powder will biodegrade within 11 days, and all of its products will biodegrade at least 98 % in 5 days.

One reason that many detergents take longer to biodegrade is that they employ a petroleum base, which may also pose risks to human health and the environment.[31] In contrast, Ecover uses natural renewable substitute ingredients wherever possible, and the company continues to review its formulations to determine where additional gains are feasible. Some of the organic ingredients used in Ecover's formulations include soap from vegetable oil, starch from potatoes or corn, derivatives from sugar, pits from citrus fruits, and essential oils from lemon grass and vinegar. By using natural ingredients instead of a petroleum base, Ecover "must invest between 300 % and 800 % more in the ingredients"; however, Ecover insists natural ingredients are well worth the cost, since they are renewable, biodegradable, and non-toxic.[32]

Many detergents contain phosphates, which enhance the performance of cleaning agents by emulsifying grease, softening water, and dispensing dirt. They also harm the environment. Through a process called eutrophication, phosphates spur the growth of algae that in large amounts can render a lake or river practically lifeless. Recognizing this risk, 30 % of U.S. states had banned phosphate-laden detergent by 1991.[33] Ecover's products have been phosphate free since its founding in 1979, and they contain none of the following commonly used household cleaner ingredients, many of which are known or suspected to be carcinogens or allergens and which degrade slowly in the environment:

- Chlorine Bleach
- EDTA (Ethylene diaminotetra acetate)
- NTA (Nitrilotriacetic acid)
- Sulfonates
- Sodium Metasilicate
- Optical Brighteners
- Synthetic Fragrances and Colors
- Polycarboxylates

By using natural ingredients, Ecover drastically reduces the toxicity of its cleaning products. A study by the Danish Consumer Organization indicated that "Ecover's

---

[31]Crace, John. 1998. Waste not, wash not. *The Guardian*, October 22, T14.

[32]*HOK Newsletter*, http://www.hok.com/sustainabledesign/newsletter/spring96.html, spring 1996, Accessed September 8, 1999.

[33]*Consumer Reports,* February 1991, Vol. 56, No. 2:105.

washing powder is 10 times less toxic than its nearest competitor and up to 15,000 times less so than the brand leader in the market."[34]

Principle 2 – Elimination of Tensio-Activity: Detergents contain surfactants, which are cleaning agents that reduce surface tension (or, to use technical terminology, show tensio-activity) and thereby make it possible to remove dirt. However, water surface tension is necessary to ensure the natural cycles of fresh-water biotic communities. If surface tension is reduced for too long, then aquatic and amphibious life will degenerate quickly. To prevent these deleterious effects, Ecover uses surfactants that degrade completely upon dilution or within 3 days. Ecover claims that the surfactants used in the most popular brands contain benzene components that persist in the environment.

Principle 3 – Reduced Consumption: Ecover embraces the idea of reduced consumption, a common tenet of environmentalism. To limit waste, Ecover provides consumers with detailed directions regarding the correct amounts of product to use given the hardness (mineral content) of a given community's water supply. For example, in areas with relatively soft water, such as the Pacific Northwest, 30 % less detergent is needed to achieve the cleaning results of communities that have hard water. (How many consumer product manufacturers actually recommend that one use *less* of their product?) Also, Ecover recommends washing with luke-warm or warm water, which significantly reduces the need for cleaning agents. Finally, the energy used to manufacture semi-organic detergents is much less than that used to manufacture chemical detergents.

Principle 4 – High Dermatological Quality: The occurrence of allergies has increased fivefold over the past 20 years, and many of the chemicals used in conventional cleaning products have been proven to cause, or are suspected of causing, allergies or skin irritations. Though many companies rightly claim that their ingredients have not been absolutely proven to be allergenic, Ecover points out that it has not been proven that they *do not* cause allergies. Ecover has eliminated all questionable ingredients, particularly optical brighteners (which are used to create an artificial "whiter-than-white" effect) and synthetic perfumes. The company also requires dermatological reports from its suppliers. In addition, Ecover has offered a prize of one million Belgian Francs for a research paper that shows the link between optical brighteners and allergies.

Principle 5 – Zero Emissions: Ecover aims to minimize the consumption of fossil fuels in its manufacturing processes, and it attempts to use as its raw materials either renewable resources or other companies' waste products.

Ecover at the Crossroads

By the end of the 1980s, both Ecover and the market for green detergents were poised for growth. Fueled by its success in the health food market, Ecover was expanding

---

[34] Van Den Broek, Guy. 1993. Green is not always the color of money. *Worldpaper*, November, 1993, 3.

rapidly, as it hired more employees and increased its production capabilities. Between 1985 and 1990, Ecover quadrupled its sales from BEF200 million to BEF800 million.[35] Ecover's management was also changing. In 1991, Herman Bogaerts, son of Ecover's founder, assumed ownership of the company, while Gunter Pauli, who had been hailed as a visionary thinker in ecological commerce, signed on as a member of the board of directors. With this new management team came ambitious plans to expand into new markets.[36] As part of these plans, Ecover began to convert the importers that had been selling its products abroad into joint venture companies.

However, Ecover faced both structural and ideological obstacles to its plans for expansion. Since 1987, Ecover had manufactured all of its liquid products at its own small factory in Belgium, but its washing powders were produced by a subcontractor. Whereas liquid detergents require little outlay of capital to produce, making powdered detergents demands greater expenditures. With a shortage of available funds, Ecover (like many other green detergent manufacturers) contracted out for its powders, which meant that it claimed a smaller margin for those products. Subcontracting also compromised the integrity of Ecover's products, since subcontractors, which worked most of the time for mainstream manufacturers, refused to clean or modify their machines for small batches like those needed by Ecover. As a result, Ecover feared that trace chemicals from other detergents would contaminate its products. Moreover, since the subcontractors' machines were geared to the large manufacturers, Ecover was limited in the innovations that it could pursue.[37]

To overcome these problems, Ecover was planning to build a factory that would allow it to enact its ecological principles and extend its production abilities. Although the company was rich in vision, it struggled with economic problems, making its plans much more difficult to implement. Prior to 1992, Ecover claimed only $42,900 in available capital.[38] If Ecover constructed an ecologically self-contained factory, it could expect to spend at least $4 million, while a more conventional factory would cost approximately half as much. With such limited resources, perhaps Ecover should hold off on expansion, or build a cheaper, more traditional factory. But Ecover believed that what they would call an "ecological factory" would reduce energy usage and minimize the waste of raw materials, thereby saving money. Moreover, such a factory would allow Ecover to further its commitment to the environment and might generate favorable publicity. By driving up its production abilities, Ecover could cut its costs, since it would be able to buy supplies in bigger quantities and produce greater volumes more efficiently.[39]

Along with economic difficulties, Ecover faced a potential ideological dilemma: In order to pay for the factory, Ecover would need to sell more of its products, which would require it to seek out space on supermarket shelves. To increase demand, Ecover would likely have to stimulate greater consumption and use advertising,

---

[35] 35 Belgian francs are equivalent to $1US. Gunter Pauli, "Ecover," Fontainebleau, France: INSEAD, 1995, 2.

[36] Ecover Web site, http://www.ecover.com/company/history.htm. Accessed March 23, 1999.

[37] Pauli, 6–7.

[38] Van Den Broek, 3.

[39] Rostler, Suzanne. Environmentally friendly products are costing less. *Orange County Register*, June 29, 1992, E1.

practices that many environmentalists opposed. In its efforts to reach supermarket consumers, Ecover would have to compete against the conventional detergent manufacturers, which wielded enormous advertising budgets and had shaped customer preferences for convenience and "whiter than white" brightness. Perhaps this move would transform the character of the company and cause it to dilute its environmental principles.

At this critical stage, Ecover confronted several crucial decisions: Should it continue with its plans to build a new factory, or should it maintain the old one? If it chooses to build a new factory, what kind should it construct – a conventional factory or an ecological one? How can it expand without abandoning its core principles and alienating environmentalists – its most loyal customers?

Ecover and Green Marketing (B)

This factory is only a drop of water. But this one drop of water, when we heat it well enough, becomes a lot of steam. And I do hope that we indeed will generate steam out of this place.

–Gunter Pauli, 1992 factory opening[40]

Despite the financial risks, Ecover went forward with its plans to build an ecologically self-contained factory. With limited supplies of capital, Ecover needed assistance to finance its new factory – Ecover borrowed 80 % from Kredietbank and paid for the rest through its cash flow.[41] In 1992, still confronting economic difficulties, Ecover agreed to a friendly takeover by Gunter Pauli, Ecover's president and CEO, and Group 4 Securitas, a Swedish multinational known as "the largest privately owned security services organisation in the world," each of which claimed 50 % interest in the company.[42]

Opened in Malle, Belgium, in 1992, Ecover's 57,000 square foot ecological factory indeed generated a lot of steam, with its innovative use of sustainable building materials and its adoption of environmentally conscious practices. However, in order to pay for this new showcase of environmental design, Ecover had to step up its marketing efforts and increase sales.

The Ecological Factory

Industrial factories are generally considered to be ugly, oppressive environments, but the beauty and grandiosity of the Ecover facility prompted one reporter attending the opening to say, "visitors might be forgiven for thinking they are inside a

---

[40] Ecover: Opening of the First Ecological Factory, Antwerp, Belgium, 21 October 1992. VHS tape. Green Light Communications, August 3, 1993.

[41] Pauli, Gunter. 1995. *Ecover*, 9. Fontainebleau, France: INSEAD.

[42] Group 4 Securitas website, http://www.group4securitas.com/. Accessed May 11, 1999.

modern day church or cathedral."[43] In planning the factory, Ecover applied the principles of organic architecture, where the laws of nature form the foundation of design. The entire factory, which was designed by Mark Depreeuw, was created as a closed-loop ecological system with a goal of zero emissions.[44] The only solid "wastes" issued from the building are the product and its packaging. Its innovative design included these highlights:

- The building was 100 % recyclable and biodegradable.
- The building was constructed from sustainably and locally harvested nonendangered inland wood and bricks made of coal-debris, clay, and sawdust instead of traditional cement, aluminum, steel, and glass. The use of these materials resulted in savings of 500 t of petroleum, one ton of "sour" gases, seven million liters of water, and nine tons of solid waste.
- The plant produced only 1,585 gal of wastewater a day, while a comparable factory in the United States typically released 25 times that amount. Wastewater was naturally purified through a biorotor (a revolving wheel that is encased in living organisms), then released to a reed meadow.
- The football-field-sized roof was covered with grass, which insulated in the winter. In the summer, water from the reed meadow was pumped onto the roof using windmill energy to provide evaporative cooling. (Vikings perfected this technique over 2,000 years ago.) The grass-covered roof also provided soundproofing.
- The factory maximized its use of natural lighting through light cupolas, glass walls, and proper orientation to the sun, cutting down on energy demands.
- The wall insulation was made from shredded and recycled paper.
- The office floors were made of vegetable-based linoleum.
- Wooden floors in the factory eliminated discomfort caused by cold feet, identified as a major source of industrial stress.
- Rather than demolishing the existing Ecover factory, the company remodeled it using ecologically safe materials.

With such innovative and expensive features, the factory cost twice as much to construct as an ordinary detergent facility. However, through the use of energy efficient processes, Ecover used one-third of the energy to make one ton of soap as Procter & Gamble, so that the extra expense would be recovered in 3 years due to decreased energy costs. The company estimated a "return on ecological investment" of 33 %, maintaining that "[t]he extra economic cost can be justified fairly easily, both at micro-economic level (less sick leave, less maintenance, lower water and energy consumption) and also at macro-economic level (no costs for the purification of wastewater by the government, no air pollution, no visual pollution)."[45]

---

[43]CNN, October 1992, reporting on the factory opening, excerpted in *Ecover: Opening of the First Ecological Factory, Antwerp, Belgium, 21 October 1992*. VHS tape. Green Light Communications, August 3, 1993.

[44]"AMP & Ecover: Different Green Business Practices, Both Profitable," Sustainable Business. com, http://www.sustainablebusiness.com/insider/feb99/1-greenbiz.html. Accessed May 7, 1999.

[45]"Ecover Manual Explains Ecological Factory," *Business and the Environment*, April 1, 1993; "The Ecological Factory," Ecover website, http://www.ecover.com/factory/factory2.html. Accessed May 7, 1999.

Ecover's factory attracted worldwide attention and quickly became a model of environmentally conscious manufacturing. Indeed, Ecover contended that its ecological factory made it unique as a green company, increasing its credibility and enabling it to claim added value. Ecover has been recognized as "the first ecological company (completely recyclable) factory in Europe."[46] The factory has become a tangible symbol for the company, used to convince customers "that they should choose Ecover as a reliable, high-quality ecological product."[47] Not only did the design of the factory minimize environmental harms, but it also raised the morale of the company's workers, who appreciated its use of natural lighting and wooden flooring. As Pauli argues, "You build a better environment for people and it encourages them. You have a lower staff turnover."[48]

Rather than monopolizing the knowledge and innovations that it developed in designing, building, and operating the factory, Ecover shares its expertise with similar companies. In 1993, Ecover published a manual detailing how to build and run an ecological factory. As Pauli wrote in the foreword to the manual, "Ecover, as market leader in the green sector, has a certain responsibility. Ecover knows that it is the first in this field, but hopes that it will not remain the only one. Ecover urged others to learn from its experience and improve on it."[49]

Green Marketing: Challenges and Opportunities

To pay for its new factory, Ecover needed to increase both production and consumption of its detergents. In determining how to make use of its increased manufacturing capacity, Ecover saw two possibilities: either it could become a subcontractor and produce detergents for other small companies, or it could cultivate a larger market by distributing to mainstream supermarkets. If it embraced the first option, Ecover would remain in the background rather than distinguishing itself as a leading green company, and its margins would probably be lower. However, if Ecover pursued a greater customer base, then it would place itself in direct competition with the big, well-funded detergent manufacturers.

Ecover had staked a secure position as a leader in a niche market, targeting ecologically conscious consumers who shopped at health food and specialty stores. Whereas many of these consumers were willing to make some sacrifices to protect the environment or their family's health, ordinary consumers expected that detergents would work quickly, make clothes "whiter than white," and be inexpensive. In order to distinguish itself from mainstream manufacturers, Ecover would need to promote its unique selling point – its benevolence toward the environment – yet at the same time would have to convince consumers that its products could perform as well as other comparably priced detergents. Since the natural ingredients that Ecover

---

[46]"Case Studies," *EMAS Tool Kit*, http://www.inem.org/inem/toolkit/case_studies2.html. Accessed May 8, 1999.

[47]"The Ecological Factory," Ecover website, http://www.ecover.com/factory/factory2.html. Accessed May 7, 1999.

[48]Quoted by Tom Walker, "Green for Growth," *The Times of London*, October 23, 1992.

[49]"Ecover Manual Explains Ecological Factory," *op. cit.*

employed for its products and packaging were more expensive than the petrochemicals used with mainstream detergents, consumers were paying on average 20–30 %
more. However, Ecover managed to cut costs and therefore prices by streamlining
distribution, avoiding expensive marketing campaigns, and cutting out unnecessary
ingredients.[50] Nevertheless, since large manufacturers wielded huge advertising budgets and claimed well-established brand loyalty, they posed a challenge to Ecover's
plans for expansion. Moreover, many consumers were unaware of the environmental
dangers posed by petrochemical-based detergents, and others needed to be persuaded
that such risks should lead them to change their buying behavior.

Still, the early 1990s seemed to be the perfect time for a company to pursue environ-
mentally-based marketing, because this period was predicted to be the decade of the
green consumer. A series of environmental accidents and reports increased customers'
concerns about the environment, motivating them to seek out products that promised
less harm to human and environmental welfare. Capitalizing on this new demand, in
1992 U.S. marketers brought out 575 new health and beauty products that proclaimed
their "naturalness."[51] Companies paid attention to marketing data that showed that consumers considered the welfare of the environment in making their purchases. For
instance, in a 1990 poll, 23 % of the 2,000 British consumers surveyed claimed that they
avoided purchasing from companies that had bad environmental records, while 40 %
said that they purchased goods made out of recycled materials, and 38 % claimed to buy
environmentally friendly detergents.[52] Yet often such stated preferences do not translate
into buying practices, particularly with cleaning products, where consumers have been
conditioned to expect a high level of convenience and artificial brightness. In 1990,
green products made up only 1 % of the market for detergents in Western Europe.[53]

Ecover's experiences in Britain, its largest market, illustrated the complex challenges and opportunities posed by green marketing.[54] In Great Britain, Ecover made
a surprisingly quick launch into the market after it won praise in *The Green
Consumer Guide*, a best-selling manual that advised consumers which products
were environmentally friendly. Energized by such good publicity, between 1989
and 1990 Ecover UK increased its earnings ten-fold, to £10 million. However, even
though Ecover had captured a significant proportion of the health food market, its
sales were quite small when compared to the large manufacturers. For example, in
August of 1992, Ecover held 1–1.5 % of the British detergent market, while Procter &
Gamble and Unilever each had 45 %.[55]

---

[50]Pauli, Dawar, and Gabel, 5.

[51]Denevy, Kathleen. Putting it mildly, more consumers prefer only products that are 'pure,'
'natural'. *The Wall Street Journal*, May 11, 1993, B1.

[52]Cairncross, Frances. 1995. *Green, Inc.: guide to business and the environment*, 183. London:
Earthscan.

[53]Pauli, Dawar, and Gabel, 6.

[54]"Will It All Come out in the Wash?" *Super Marketing*, April 10, 1992, 54(2). Ecover's strength
in the United Kingdom was due in part to the efforts of Robin Bines, director of Ecover's British
operation. From the 1960s to the present, Bines has been active in the British health food industry.
When he discovered Ecover in the 1980s, Bines recognized an important new product; soon he was
responsible for marketing the detergents in Great Britain.

[55]Wentz, Laurel. "Don't toss those old ads: Belgian detergent maker recycles rivals' commercials."
Advertising Age, March 2, 1992, 3.

Although it had succeeded with its niche strategy, Ecover aimed to cultivate a more generalized customer base by selling through supermarkets. To attract consumers, Ecover emphasized both what it had in common with mainstream detergents – low price and high performance – and what set it apart – systematic environmental benevolence. Ecover launched campaigns to inform consumers of the dangers of phosphates and petroleum-based detergents, and in so doing promoted its own ethic of protecting the environment.

Yet in its efforts to broaden its consumer base, Ecover confronted concerns that its products did not measure up to consumer expectations. As Ecover concept manager Peter Marchand explained, customers complained that Ecover failed to make clothes "whiter than white or brighter than bright" like conventional detergents, which used optical brighteners to create an artificial brightness.[56] Although Ecover could concede to consumer taste and add optical brighteners, by doing so it would dilute its own environmental principles. As UK managing director Robin Bines argued, "[The optical brightener] works by reflecting ultra-violet light. Whiteness is an illusion created by the advertising industry to represent cleanliness. People have been programmed into believing they need powerful cosmetic ingredients to look whiter than white."[57] Ecover maintained that besides being unnecessary, optical brighteners pose risks to human and environmental health.

While Ecover had to defend itself against criticisms that it was not enough like conventional detergents, the company also had to deal with mainstream manufacturers' efforts to market themselves as environmentally friendly. Forty-one percent of all household products brought out in 1991 claimed to be environmentally friendly, though many of these claims were based on superficial improvements. Too much hype can confuse and even turn off consumers, as Ecover discovered after the boom in green products in Britain between 1988 and 1989. As Stephen Jones, distributor for Ecover, commented, "Unfortunately, a lot of manufacturers have jumped on the eco-bandwagon in recent years, and a lot of consumers are getting a bit confused – not to say cynical, about it all. . . . the industry must make sure that it maintains an ethical approach. Integrity and quality are definitely what will count in the end."[58]

Despite Ecover's emphasis on integrity, consumer confidence in its products declined following the release of a report by the Consumers' Association claiming that green detergents were no better for the environment than regular ones.[59] Although Ecover and several environmental groups disputed the study, consumers were nonetheless discouraged from buying green, and Ecover's competitive advantage weakened.[60] Prompted by this study, supermarkets such as Sainsbury's began removing Ecover and related products from the shelves, convinced that there wasn't much difference between green and mainstream products. Nevertheless, Ecover insisted that it manufactured the best detergents, especially when the environment and human health were considered.

---

[56] Gupta, Udayan. Keeping the faith: first, there's the entrepreneur's vision; then success; but can the vision survive? *The Wall Street Journal*, November 22, 1991, R16.

[57] "Will It All Come Out in the Wash?" 54(2).

[58] Gray, Howard. How shelf space made ecover. *Marketing*, October 18, 1990, 26(2).

[59] The results of this study were later contradicted by a 1996 study at Sweden's Goetborgs University, which found that Ecover was non-toxic, with a toxicity 20 times lower than its nearest rival in Sweden. See Wise, Deborah. Make your Whites greener. *The Observer*, October 6, 1996, 13.

[60] Latham, Valerie. Testing green to the limit. *Marketing*, July 25, 1991, 18 (2).

206 4 Environmentally Sustainable Projects

By touting its ecological principles, Ecover believed that it could set itself apart and counter the chaos of the competitive marketplace. With all the hoopla and misinformation diminishing customer trust, Ecover promoted its integrity and openness: "While competitors cause total confusion in the market with their half-baked products and easy slogans, Ecover has always given priority to information campaigns, to the great satisfaction of both retailers and consumers. 'Communicate, don't irritate' is the watchword at Ecover. The company's policy attaches a great deal of importance to 'openness, information, and improving awareness.'"[61]

Ecover's Options

Advertising

In order to improve awareness and win a larger customer base in the United Kingdom, Ecover needed to develop an effective marketing strategy. But Ecover, along with many environmentalists, regarded advertising as "pollution, to a degree," since ads often encourage needless consumption and waste resources.[62] Moreover, Ecover executives condemned advertising as a sort of mental pollution, arguing that ads often made deceptive claims and used subliminal techniques to manipulate consumers to buy. With limited supplies of capital, Ecover had found advertising almost prohibitively expensive. If the company launched an advertising campaign, it might have to raise prices, which might make its products less competitive in the mainstream market. Previously Ecover had used relatively inexpensive educational campaigns, distributing pamphlets and setting up displays at stores.; however, Ecover was discovering that to reach mainstream consumers and compete against the dominant companies, advertising might be necessary. Should Ecover advertise? If so, what sort of marketing campaign should it launch? If not, how else could it gain consumer attention and confidence? In a larger sense, are commercial goals consistent with an environmental ethic?

Ecolabeling

In order to publicize its commitment to the environment without resorting to advertising, Ecover could pursue eco-labeling, a European Commission program to inform consumers about the environmental repercussions of products. Ecover discovered the benefits of this sort of publicity when the publication of *The Green Consumer Guide* stimulated consumer interest in environmentally friendly products. But ecolabeling was criticized both by environmentally-conscious and by traditional manufacturers, who wrangled over what standards to adopt. Fearful that ecolabeling would increase consumer confusion and place mainstream multinational corporations on the same

---

[61]Ecover website, http://www.ecover.com/company/history.htm. Accessed March 23, 1999.

[62]Chiat Day account executive David Abraham, quoted by Valerie Latham, "Testing Green to the Limit."

plane as small, environmentally friendly companies, Ecover was leery of embracing the system.[63] Would eco-labeling facilitate or impede Ecover's goals of educating consumers and increasing demand for its products?

Adapting to Consumer Tastes

A major impediment to Ecover's success in the mainstream market was its failure to make clothes "whiter than white." In order to overcome this obstacle, Ecover either had to give in to consumer taste by adding optical brighteners, or persuade consumers that such additives were unnecessary and dangerous. Given the low awareness of optical brighteners, Ecover might find it easier to add them to its supermarket line and emphasize other aspects of environmental production. On the other hand, perhaps it could win over more consumers in the end by sticking to its environmental principles.

Ecover and Green Marketing (C)

Ecover encountered an irony associated with its success: a number of other green or "not-so-green" products were emerging on the market, forcing the company to distinguish itself from challengers and pretenders. Although Ecover had initially condemned advertising as "pollution," the company decided that it needed to advertise so that it could increase awareness of its products and promote its ethical principles, which it regarded as its unique selling point.[64] But Ecover faced a key question: "how to advertise without producing yet more waste, how to get across the environmental message without creating more pollution in doing so?"[65] Rather than employing orthodox advertising techniques, Ecover resolved to find clever, principled ways to promote its product and at the same time to subvert conventional advertising. As Robin Bines, Ecover's U.K. director, remarked, "We don't agree with confusing consumers with half-baked claims"; therefore, Ecover's ads would be "funny, informative, and controversial."[66]

Recycling Advertisements

In collaboration with the British advertising firm Chiat/Day, in 1991 Ecover pioneered an advertising campaign that made recycling and environmental concern not only the message, but also the medium. For its advertising posters, Ecover recruited artists to create collages out of old ad posters, recycling for the sake of art and

---

[63] Nitall, Nick. Shoppers cross green products off their list. *The Times of London*, July 3, 1993.

[64] Latham, Valerie. Ecover turns to recycled posters for first ads. *Marketing*, August 22, 1991, 6.

[65] "Marketing Procedures," Ecover website, http://www.ecover.com. Accessed May 11, 1999.

[66] Latham, Valerie. Testing green to the limit. *Marketing*, July 25, 1991, 18(2).

commerce as well as the environment. At the end of the campaign, it "recycled" the posters once more by selling them, then donating 15 % of the proceeds to an environmental charity. According to Bines, "We liked the idea of recycled advertising because it cuts down on waste, but more importantly it gets the concept of recycling out to the public. It fit in so well with our environmental stance. And it gives us the opportunity to have a bit of fun."[67] Recycled posters were used not only in Britain, but also Antwerp, Belgium. Ecover continues to use these posters to advertise its products, posting digital images on its website (see http://www.ecover.com).

Pursuing a similar spirit of pastiche, the British TV spots for Ecover parodied black and white detergent advertisements from the 1950s, "subvert[ing]… patronising" ads for conventional detergents.[68] In one ad, a pitchman holds up a box of detergent manufactured by a competitor, but the Ecover brand is superimposed over the company's logo. The soundtrack is deliberately out of sync, as if to emphasize that the company is recycling ads and to reject the old stereotypes associated with cleaning. The announcer delivers a deliberately simple message: "All Ecover wants me to tell you is that it does a good job cleaning clothes with less impact on the environment." The commercials feature the slogan "Ecover washes righter," which calls attention to the activism of the company and the effectiveness of its product, as well as mocking conventional detergent manufacturers for claiming to get clothes "whiter than white."

Ecover continued its zany UK promotions in the fall of 1996, when it embarked on a campaign to persuade consumers to refill their Ecover bottles at refill stations across the country. Launched at Trafalgar Square, the campaign featured athletes riding "advercycles," tricycles decorated with advertising sails.[69] These human-powered vehicles were a pun on recycling and emphasized an ethic of reduced consumption and increased fun.

Marketing Principles

During its U.K. ad campaign, Ecover put its fundamental marketing principles into action. Aiming to provide information in an open and honest manner, Ecover bases its marketing on three central principles: "Communicate, don't irritate," Educate consumers in creative ways, and "Think globally, act locally."[70]

Communicate, don't irritate: Rather than manipulating consumers through meaningless slogans, Ecover makes available scientifically verified information about its products. To facilitate an open dialogue with its consumers, Ecover publicizes the ingredients of its products and their biodegradability. It also offers tours of its factory and publishes handbooks on ecological manufacturing.

---

[67] Wentz, Laurel. Don't toss those old ads: Belgian detergent maker recycles rivals' commercials. *Advertising Age*, March 2, 1992, 3.

[68] Hatfield, Stefano. Chiat day to recycle 50s films for ecover TV drive. *ASAP*, February 14, 1992, 7; Latham, Valerie. Ecover turns to recycled posters for first ads. *Marketing*, August 22, 1991, 6.

[69] "Refill Scheme Launched," *Manufacturing Chemist*, November 11, 1996, 14.

[70] "Marketing Policy," Ecover website, http://www.ecover.com. Accessed May 11, 1999.

Educate creatively: To help consumers make informed decisions about the products they use, Ecover educates them using a variety of imaginative techniques, such as clever advertising and publicity campaigns, road shows, and brochures. Educating consumers has become crucial to Ecover's mission as well as to its strategy for increasing its share of the market. As Gunter Pauli explained,

> [Ecover] didn't sell, we educated. We didn't compete on price, we competed on emotion. We took products that were utterly devoid of excitement – who cares about laundry detergent? – and made them something special.... Our factory didn't just supply cleaning products; its supplied education and entertainment – edutainment. That's what people are looking for today. They want products that reflect their values, and they want a good story. That's how you create a bond with customers.[71]

Think globally, act locally: Rather than mounting a unified international marketing campaign, Ecover initiates regional or local campaigns, targeting its messages to specific consumer groups.

The Ecolabeling Conundrum

Although European Union's ecolobeling scheme seemed to promise that Ecover would gain recognition for its ecological practices, the company refused to submit its products for testing. Ecover worried that the standards were too weak and that practically any product would be deemed "environmentally friendly." Discussing the dilemma facing green companies that are considering eco-labeling, T. E. Graedel and Brad Allenby explain, "The advantage of labeling systems is that they harness market forces and consumer preferences in the effort to achieve better environmental performance.... However, a potential disadvantage of the labeling programs is that unless their criteria are carefully chosen, environmentally suboptimal performance might be encouraged."[72] While mainstream firms wanted the criteria to focus on smaller reforms such as minimizing packing, Ecover favored taking into account the entire life cycle of detergents. Rather than an "all-or-nothing" system of labeling, Ecover pressed for a graduated label, which would create incentives for those companies with lower standards to move up the scale.[73] Disappointed when such efforts failed, Ecover helped to form the Environmental Detergent Manufacturers Association, a group of small companies that pledge that their products will meet basic standards of effectiveness, healthfulness, and minimal environmental impact.

---

[71]Butler, Steven. Green machine. *Fast Company*, June 1996, 112. Available online at http://www.fastcompany.com/online/03/gunterp.html. Accessed May 7, 1999.
[72]Graedel, T. E., and B. R. Allenby. 1995. *Industrial ecology*, 323. Englewood Cliffs: Prentice Hall.
[73]"EDMA," Ecover website, http://www.ecover.com/company/edma.html. Accessed May 7, 1999.

Compromising with Consumer Tastes

Although committed to expanding its share of the household cleaners market, Ecover refused to add optical brighteners to its products. Instead, Ecover included information about environmentally friendly products with its packaging, attempting to convert consumers to greater environmental consciousness and obviate their desire for the brighteners. Still, Ecover felt pressured to conform to consumer tastes in order to win a larger market.[74]

The Dilemma of Success

Offering an ecologically safe alternative in a traditionally "dirty" industry, Ecover experienced a 40 % growth in sales since its founding, with revenues of $35 m in 1994. However, as major manufacturers adopted green techniques, Ecover risked being choked out of the market that it helped to create. As Valerie Latham had predicted, "Selling a product because people like the ethical nature of your company, moving into the mainstream, and getting past the hype stage of environmentalism – all lay traps for companies like Ecover."[75]

Ecover seemed to have both succeeded and failed in Great Britain. On the one hand, its promotional campaigns have increased consumer awareness of detergents' environmental dangers and have led mainstream manufacturers to reduce the harms caused by their products. For instance, prompted in part by a desire to seem green, Lever decreased its packaging and cut down on the amount of water it uses in manufacturing its detergents.[76] Likewise, Procter & Gamble began selling detergents and fabric softeners in concentrated solutions, and they marketed refillable containers made out of recycled plastic.[77]

As conventional manufacturers touted their own environmental friendliness, Ecover found it difficult to win over mass-market consumers. By 1996, Ecover's sales in the U.K. had declined substantially, and many supermarkets had eliminated shelf space for its products. [78] While Ecover could claim a large part of the credit for raising

---

[74]Whether Ecover actually added optical brighteners to a line of detergents meant for grocery stores is a cloudy issue. In a 1991 article that appeared in *The Wall Street Journal*, Ecover executive Peter Marchand acknowledged that the company was using optical brighteners, justifying the decision by arguing: "We couldn't grow by selling products that customers don't want. But modifying what we do doesn't make us any less environmentally responsible" (Gupta, Udayan. Keeping the faith: first, there's the entrepreneur's vision; then success; but can the vision survive? *The Wall Street Journal*, November 22, 1991, R16). Yet Ecover emphatically denies ever using optical brighteners in any of its products. As Ecover employee Ludo Martens stated in an email dated June 28, 1999, "ECOVER HAS NEVER USED and WILL NEVER USE OPTICAL BRIGHTENERS" (correspondence with author).

[75]Latham, "Testing Green to the Limit."

[76]Wise, Deborah. Make your whites greener. *The Observer*, October 6, 1996, 13.

[77]Cairncross, Frances. 1995. Green, *Inc.: guide to business and the environment*. London: Earthscan.

[78]Gosling, Paul. 'Green consumers' give up trying to save the World. *The Independent – London*, April 21, 1996, 1.

concern about the environmental effects of detergents, it could not assert complete success in capturing new consumers and establishing a strong presence in the mass market. As Alison Austin, environmental manager for the supermarket chain Sainsbury, said, "Thanks to campaigning brands, like Ecover, the standard market has improved and narrowed the gap between regular and 'green' products. Some standard lines have improved so much that we decided to de-list some Green products."[79]

However, Ecover is continues to sell well in health food stores; according to a 1999 article, it claims "95 % [of the green market] in England and Holland, more than 50 % in Belgium and France, and 35 % in Germany. 20 % of the natural cleaners sold in the U.S. are made by Ecover."[80] Ecover sells its products in approximately 12,000 health food shops spread throughout Europe, Japan, and the United States, and its annual turnover is around $10.2 million.[81] In recognition of its achievement in environmentally conscious business, Ecover has received several awards, including the "Ecoproduit" award for green products from the French Ministry of the Environment (1989), the Oscar for exports from the Belgian Foreign Trade Office (1990), and the Global 500 Roll of Honour from the United Nations Environmental Programme (1993). Ecover demonstrated its social consciousness and earned credibility when it joined the Social Venture Network, which counts the Body Shop and Esprit as members.

Rather than regarding decreased demand in the mass market as a permanent setback, Ecover avers that it can attract customers through its innovative production processes, systematic vision, and ethically based marketing strategies. As Sharon Duguid, director of information and education for Ecover, argues, "Once the general public realizes that environmentally sound, high performance cleaning products are available at competitive prices, they will gladly opt for doing the right thing. The petrochemical line of detergents is at the end of its life cycle. Ecover is the beginning of a new life cycle for the environmental cleaning product industry."[82] Or is it?

Ecover 2013 Case Addendum

Since the writing of this case, Ecover has continued to expand its product line, now offering dishwashing detergents (in tablet, powder, and liquid form), hard surface household cleaners (in all-purpose, bathroom, floor, toilet and glass specialties), as well as other laundry products such as bleach powder, fabric softener, and stain remover.

---

[79] Swengley, Nicole. Why Sainsbury's are cutting back on 'green' lines. *The Evening Standard*, September 9, 1996.

[80] "Amp & Ecover: Different Green Business Practices, Both Profitable," *Sustainable Business.com*, http://www.sustainablebusiness.com/insider/feb99/1-greenbiz.html. Accessed May 7, 1999.

[81] "Case Studies," EMAS, http://www.inem.org/inem/toolkit/case_studies2.html. Accessed May 7, 1999.

[82] "'Green' Cleaning Products Begin to Reach Grocery Store Shelve in Some Northwest Cities," *Business Wire*, February 17, 1994.

Ecover acquired a second factory from an ecological washing agent brand, and having reached production capacity, built a second eco-friendly factory in 2007 in Northern France. Forty percent of the 10 million Euro project was devoted to extra measures to add ecological value. The factory has an insulating 'green roof,' uses rainwater for toilets and is run on green electricity.[83] The same year, Ecover generated 93 million Euros in revenue.[84]

In 2008, Ecover and its CEO, Mike Bremans, were chosen by *Time* magazine as one of 30 "Heroes of the Environment,"[85] and in 2010, Ecover was shortlisted for the European Business Awards for the Environment in the Process Category Surfactants, due to an innovative low-energy manufacturing process that uses natural and renewable materials.[86] In 2011, the company introduced a 100 % Plant Plastic bottle, which eliminates the need for petroleum-based plastics and uses plastic derived from sugarcane instead.

Though green cleaning products now account for over 3 % of the total household and laundry cleaner retail market,[87] Ecover faces substantially increased competition as Proctor & Gamble, Clorox, and others make increasingly larger pushes towards being eco-friendly, and Ecover's once-unique edge is lost in part due to European Union legislation that requires higher standards of biodegradability in detergents.[88]

In 2012, Ecover acquired Method Products, a San Francisco-based company founded in 2001 that, in 2006, *Inc.* magazine named the 7th fastest-growing private company in the United States. Method shares Ecover's commitment to the environment and sustainability, and combined, they generate $200 million in sales annually, making them the "world's largest green cleaning company."[89]

Also in 2012, Ecover forged its first entry into television marketing. Part of a 4 million Euro brand campaign, the "Feel-Good Cleaning" advertisement featured people dancing while accomplishing domestic tasks with the use of Ecover products, set to the James Brown song 'I Feel Good.'[90] The campaign also includes live marketing components, as well as a push on Ecover's social media networks.

---

[83] http://www.mikegolding.com/2007/05/ecover-opens-new-factory-in-france-2/

[84] http://www.time.com/time/specials/packages/article/0,28804,1841778_1841780_1841784,00.html

[85] http://www.time.com/time/specials/packages/article/0,28804,1841778_1841780_1841784,00.html

[86] http://ec.europa.eu/environment/ecoap/about-eco-innovation/good-practices/belgium/509_en.htm

[87] http://www.marketwire.com/press-release/us-market-green-household-cleaning-products-enters-forefront-consumer-consciousness-1265177.htm

[88] http://www.marketingweek.co.uk/could-the-days-of-market-domination-be-over-for-green-giant-ecover/2057452.article

[89] http://methodhome.com/wp-content/uploads/method_Ecover_Announcement_0904121.pdf

[90] http://www.marketingmagazine.co.uk/article/1110931/ecover-launches-4m-brand-campaign

Chapter 5
Environmentally Sustainable Processes

Environmental sustainability has become a focus for not only academics and scientists, but it is now at the forefront for most global corporations. In this chapter we present two exemplars of that corporate thinking. Baxter International has been working for some years in reducing is environmental footprint, with great success. Coca Cola, whose products are produced and sold worldwide, is an enormous user of clean water for its many beverage products, and it has recently embarked on a series of projects aimed at water conservation. Both of these companies are good examples of what forward-thinking companies can do without losing money. But we begin this chapter with another narrative, the story of Albina Ruiz, a Peruvian who saw a need for trash collection in the capital city of Peru, Lima, a need that was not being addressed by the city. Her story illustrates what one person can do to clean up the environment and provide jobs, even in a large city such as Lima.

Albina Ruiz and "Healthy City"[1]

As she walked each day to the National Engineering University, where she was studying industrial engineering, Albina Ruiz was horrified by what she saw around her in the streets of Lima, Peru. Trash was piled high, spilling into the streets and covering the sidewalks in many places. The smell was so bad that people covered their noses with handkerchiefs and scarves, yet Ruiz saw children playing in the garbage, clambering atop piles of debris as though they were forts. It was the late 1980s, and while Ruiz was aware that trash collection was a municipal task, it was clear that the job was, for the most part, not being done.

---

[1] This case was prepared by Jenny Mead under the supervision of Patricia H. Werhane. © Copyright 2013 University of Virginia Darden School Foundation.

P.J. Albert et al. (eds.), *Global Poverty Alleviation: A Case Book*, The International Society of Business, Economics, and Ethics Book Series 3, DOI 10.1007/978-94-007-7479-7_5,
© Springer Science+Business Media Dordrecht 2014

The research she had done into the problem made her all the more concerned. Sprawling mounds of uncollected garbage were a problem throughout Peru, but Lima's poorer areas were particularly hard-hit. In Cono Norte—a slum in northern Lima that was home to almost 1.5 million residents – an estimated 1,000 t of garbage were generated daily, less than half of which was being picked up by municipal workers.[2] Not only did that create health problems for city residents, but residents dumped the waste in rivers, thus contaminating the city's water supply. Foul odors and toxic fumes emanated from the piles of trash, which were breeding grounds for rats and diseases such as cholera. Poor and densely populated areas suffered the most because they had far more uncollected garbage than more affluent neighborhoods did. "The government in Peru," said Ruiz, "like in other countries, spends a lot of money collecting garbage, but it's only where the well-off live. In those neighborhoods, they collect garbage every day."[3]

Inspired in part by the massive amounts of waste she saw daily, Ruiz – the only female student in her class at the university – wrote her thesis on microenterprises and environmental sanitation in Cono Norte. She also organized her fellow students to pick up garbage from along the riverbeds and beaches. As she neared graduation, Ruiz began to formulate a plan as to how the city might deal with the trash and all its hazards.

The Plan

After graduating from the National Engineering University, Ruiz decided to tackle the problem of waste, starting in Cono Norte. Working alone initially, Ruiz started a microentrepreneurial enterprise in which she hired unemployed people in the community to pick up and dispose of garbage. She charged residents far less than the municipal rate – just $1.50 per month. To encourage participation, Ruiz devised a "wide array of creative marketing schemes – including special gift baskets – to entice families to use the services and, importantly, pay for them regularly and on time."[4] These efforts were successful, and piles of garbage both on and off the streets were greatly reduced. In her enterprise, Ruiz focused on enlisting women as managers of the entrepreneurial enterprises. In addition to collecting and processing waste, the enterprise expanded, and garbage was divided into recyclables (which the waste collectors sold) and compostable material. Garbage scavengers – or *recicladores* – had already combed the garbage for recyclables, but they did

---

[2]Profile of Albina Ruiz, Schwab Foundation for Social Entrepreneurship. http://www.schwabfound. org/sf/SocialEntrepreneurs/Profiles/index.htm?sname=117998. Accessed 7 Jan 2013.

[3]Erlich, Reese. 2005. Lima group recycles, while helping the poor. NPR Morning Edition, June 7, 2005. http://www.npr.org/templates/story/story.php?storyId=4683275. Accessed 7 Jan 2013.

[4]"Meet the New Heroes: Albina Ruiz," PBS.org, http://www.pbs.org/opb/thenewheroes/meet/ p_ruiz.html. Accessed 5 Jan 2013.

so with no physical protection (i.e., face masks and gloves) and for a pittance. Ruiz's enterprise changed that: she hired these people, paid them good wages, and provided them with protective clothing. Composting was encouraged; for example, unsold food from an outdoor market, instead of going into the trash, was gathered and composted by participants in Ruiz's program. The city of Lima would then buy and use the compost for trees and plants in city parks. One family earned over $160 a month – more than the minimum wage – by recycling paper.

Ciudad Saludable

For the first 15 years of her enterprise, Ruiz worked solo, consulting with government agencies (e.g., Peru's health ministry and environmental agency), various international programs (e.g., the Pan-American Health Organization), and industrial companies. In 2001, she founded a nonprofit organization – "Ciudad Saludable" (meaning "healthy city") – that continued the microentrepreneurial, community-managed model that had been so successful. Although it was community-based, Ciudad Saludable coordinated with local government agencies, including trash removal departments, to enhance the program. Over the next decade, the program expanded within Peru and beyond, to Colombia, Mexico, Brazil, and even India. Ruiz also created two new organizations – Peru Waste Innovations and Healthy Cities International – designed to encourage replication of the Ciudad Saludable internationally. The following were the goals and strategies of these organizations:

- "Influence in public policies to replicate the model of economic and social inclusion."
- "Promote the competitiveness of our social corporation that contributes to disseminate an alternative and successful model in the conventional market, with an economic and social sustainability and inclusion approach of the poorest."
- "Generate socially and environmentally responsible consumers, taking the national/regional/local government, businesses, the education sector, and social organizations as allies."[5]

By 2012, Ruiz's enterprise was vast – with over 1,500 waste collectors – and improving the lives of more than six million people in poverty-stricken areas. Ruiz and Ciudad Saludable were also responsible for the first legislation in Latin America to regulate the activities of waste recyclers and mandate recycling in Lima. Financial support came from a variety of NGOs as well as corporate partners, including PepsiCo, Kimberly-Clark, and Pluspetrol. International recognition came from a variety of organizations, including Ashoka,[6] the Schwab Foundation for Social

---

[5]"Profile," Ciudad Saludable. http://www.ciudadsaludable.org/en/profile/profile.html#vision. Accessed 6 Jan 2013.

[6]Ashoka was an organization that invested in social entrepreneurs.

Entrepreneurship,[7] the Skoll Foundation,[8] and Avina,[9] and Ruiz was featured in the PBS series "The New Heroes," as well as on NPR. Among other awards recognizing its environmental impact, Ciudad Saludable received the 2006 Dubai International Award for Best Practices to Improve the Living Environment, the 2006 Global Development Network Award, the 2007 Globe Energy Award, and the 2006 Bravo Latin Trade Award as Environmentalist of the Year in Latin America.

Despite all the successes, Ruiz and Ciudad Saludable were determined to expand their efforts, with an even greater international reach. Other countries, including the United States, were interested in implementing the model Ruiz had developed. Not only did Ciudad Saludable's programs promote cleaner and healthier cities and greater overall sustainability, but they increased the self-esteem of those participating. As Ruiz said, "Here in Peru, it's very common to look down on recyclers. To work with garbage is the most degrading kind of work. We work very hard so people don't see them as bad. They are recyclers helping the environment."[10]

A Case Study in the Evolution of Sustainability: Baxter International Inc.[11]

Introduction

On October 19, 1931 a small company, Don Baxter Intravenous Products, Inc., was incorporated in Delaware. Located in Glenview, Illinois north of Chicago the company's initial capitalization was 1,000 shares of preferred stock at a price of $100 per share, 1,000 shares of no par common stock and a reported initial workforce of nine individuals (Cody 1994). The company is now known as Baxter International Inc. In the early 1930s, Baxter was the first manufacturer of commercially prepared intravenous solutions. By 1939, Baxter had created a new medical product that would help put the company on the map: the Transfuso-Vac Container. This container made the long-term process of blood-banking a reality. The company's timely start and focused business strategy saw a solid growth in business. This changed

---

[7]The Schwab Foundation for Social Entrepreneurship promoted the advancement of sustainable social innovation globally.

[8]The Skoll Foundation had the stated mission of "driving large-scale change by investing in, connecting, and celebrating social entrepreneurs and the innovators who help them solve the world's most pressing problems." See http://www.skollfoundation.org/about/mission/.

[9]Avina was a foundation that worked toward sustainable development in Latin America.

[10]Erlich.

[11]This case was prepared by K. Kathy Dhanda, Department of Management, DePaul University, and originally published in the *Journal of Business Ethics*, Copyright 2012, volume 112 (2913), pp. 667–84. Reprinted by permission of the author and the Journal.

with the onset of World War II. With the imminent increase in demand for products that war brought to the health care and pharmaceutical industry, Baxter quickly grew and by 1947 had moved from its small initial operations in Glenview to a much larger facility in Morton Grove, Illinois. Three years later, the company opened its first manufacturing facility outside Illinois in Cleveland, Mississippi, and four years after that, the company opened an office in Belgium.[12]

The 1950s proved to be an important period for Baxter, not only because of its continued international expansion but also because of its acquisitions, which included Fenwal and Hyland Laboratories. In the 1960s, Baxter created its own sales team so that it no longer had to rely on outside sources. In 1961, Baxter stock was introduced to the New York Stock Exchange. Later in 1961, Baxter opened a research and pilot manufacturing facility in Round Lake, Illinois. In 1971, *Fortune Magazine* listed Baxter as one of the 500 largest American Corporations. With substantial growth, Baxter established a separate executive and administrative office north of Morton Grove, and in February 1975, Baxter moved to its new and current corporate headquarters in Deerfield, Illinois.[13]

The next 35 years proved to be a time of continuing business growth for Baxter. The corporation opened a plant in Singapore and eventually five manufacturing plants in China and three manufacturing facilities in India in order to manufacture goods for recipient Asia markets. Baxter also developed extensive manufacturing and support operations in Europe, Eastern Europe and North Africa. In 2000, Baxter created Edwards Lifesciences as a separate publicly traded entity focused solely on cardiovascular technologies. In the same year, Baxter created the Global Healthcare Exchange along with four other healthcare companies. Global Healthcare Exchange is an independent company that facilitates the exchange of relevant healthcare related information. One year later, Baxter acquired Cook Pharmaceutical Solutions.[14] During these decades of corporate change and development, Baxter was also developing some of the most innovative healthcare related technologies of its time. Not only did Baxter commercialize the artificial kidney machine, but it also created many home-based alternatives to hemodialysis, automated blood-cell separators and the first needleless system for IV therapy among others.[15]

By year-end 2011, Baxter had grown to $US 13.9 billion in sales and about 48,500 employees. Today Baxter manufactures health care products, primarily for patients with acute medical conditions, in 27 countries and sells products in more than 100 countries. Approximately 60 % of its sales come from outside the United States (Baxter Sustainability Report 2009).

---

[12] Baxter History, 2010, accessed November, 2010 at http://www.baxter.com/about_baxter/company_profile/history.html#2000

[13] For additional company-related historical, business, financial, environmental and sustainability information for Baxter International Inc. (Baxter), please refer to Baxter's Website, Annual Reports and Sustainability Reports

[14] Baxter International. (2009). Baxter Company Profile History. Retrieved from http://www.baxter.com/about_baxter/company_profile/sub/history.html

[15] Ibid.

At the first company visit on 3 Feb., 2010, the author interviewed Ronald Meissen to understand the history of the company. Dr. Meissen mentioned that most of the initial sustainability initiatives were put in place by William Blackburn, who was also interviewed on 18 Feb, 2010. Over the next few months, the author conducted follow-up interviews and made several other corporate visits. Other data sources included the corporate reports issued by the company, the media releases issued quarterly and other archival data of Baxter.

The work on Baxter International Inc. would be classified as descriptive and intrinsic. Using principles of grounded theory, the case study started without any propositions or hypothesis. Over a series of interviews and archival data collection, the history of the company and how it responded to the challenge of sustainability was recorded. As more documentation was gathered, the case study was updated and revised. The final case study was presented at the Vincentian conference and the paper was revised and updated to capture recent movements of the company up until October, 2012.

External Forces

Rachel Carson's book *Silent Spring* was first published in 1962. The publication of this book was an important catalyst that formed environmental awareness and led to eventual environmental regulation in the United States. *Silent Spring,* exhaustively researched and well written, was an attack on the indiscriminate use of pesticides (Carson 1962). It attracted immediate attention and wound up causing a revolution in public opinion on environmental matters. In 1969, President Nixon's Administration took action on the environmental front by setting up a Cabinet-level Environmental Quality Council as well as a Citizens' Advisory Committee on Environmental Quality.

On April 22, 1970 the first Earth Day celebration was held in the U.S., which brought 20 million citizens out for peaceful demonstrations in favor of environmental reform. Senator Gaylord Nelson (D-Wis.) and Congressman Paul McCloskey (R-Calif.) gave bipartisan sponsorship to the event. In December 1970, the U.S. Environmental Protection Agency (EPA) was formed and, beginning in the 1970s, it would issue many environmental regulations companies would need to address to deal with air, wastewater, hazardous and solid waste and other environmental-related issues.[16]

In the early 1970s, the United Nations (UN) also began to initiate a number of international environmental initiatives. The UN Conference on the Human Environment (also known as the Stockholm Conference) was held in Stockholm, Sweden in June 1972. This conference, the UN's first major conference on

---

[16]Lewis, J. 2010. The birth of EPA. http://www.epa.gov/history/topics/epa/15c.htm. Accessed Nov 2010.

international environmental issues, was attended by representatives of 113 countries, 19 inter-governmental agencies, and more than 400 inter-governmental and non-governmental organizations. At the conference, the United Nations Environmental Programme (UNEP), which is now the main environmental arm of the UN, was launched and the forum itself is widely recognized as the beginning of modern political and public awareness of global environmental problems.[17]

This case study breaks down Baxter's evolutionary path to sustainability into five distinct stages. Each of the stages was a response to emerging environmental challenges. The resulting actions, led by key and executive management, catapulted sustainability programs forward and, as the reader will learn, toward positive results.

Stage I: Initial Response to Growing Environmental Issues 1970–1985

From 1970 to 1976, Baxter's response to growing environmental requirements was managed by engineers within Baxter's Corporate Facilities Engineering group. In the beginning, the individuals involved in this subject had no formal environmental training. With mounting environmental regulations, in 1976, the department assigned a young engineer with some formal education specifically in the environmental area (B.S. and M.S. in engineering and a registered professional engineer) to assume this responsibility.[18]

In 1975, Baxter's visionary CEO William Graham believed global environmental issues would become more important and society's response would only intensify. He believed that Baxter ought to position itself to adequately respond to these challenges and address them in a more strategic manner. Mr. Graham's leadership set the direction of Baxter's environmental/ sustainability program for many decades. In recognition of this new reality, a top level Baxter committee called the Environment Review Board (ERB) was created. In late 1976, engineering and legal environmental experts were specifically hired to craft global environmental programs that could be undertaken to assure legal compliance with existing and newly anticipated regulations in order to properly control environmental risks and reduce waste. Ray Murphy, an attorney and an engineer, was the first Baxter environmental program leader (1977–1989). Others including Bill Blackburn, who was also an attorney and engineer, were involved in managing the program. In 1977, a formal Baxter Environmental Policy was developed, an Environmental Manual issued, a network of facility environmental coordinators established, site level environmental compliance audits started, and Baxter's first annual Environmental Conference was held.[19]

---

[17] UNEP. 2010. United Nations Environmental Programme. http://www.unep.org. Accessed Nov 2010.

[18] Blackburn, W. 2010. Personal Communication with author.

[19] Ibid. Baxter held an Environmental Conference for corporate, division and facility environmental staff annually for a number of years. In the late 1990s – early 2000s the forum was combined with health and safety personnel and held bi-annually through 2007.

By the early 1980s, the environmental engineering group, within Corporate Facilities Engineering, was comprised of an engineering manager and 3–4 environmental engineers. Ray Murphy in the Corporate Legal group had a small support team. Between 1976 and 1985, Baxter had established a very robust environmental compliance and risk management program, which was recognized both internally and externally for program excellence. The program, organized and deployed globally, fit in nicely with Baxter's overarching culture of maintaining high manufacturing and product quality standards in a strictly regulated environment, akin to the Food and Drug Administration (FDA). Reporting program activities regularly to Baxter's Environment Review Board helped to maintain program visibility and executive (including CEO) engagement and support, and executive recognition of facilities/individuals for outstanding achievement. *Here, we were thinking we had a great program, we were on top of the world. Little did we realize it was not enough.*[20]

Stage II: Business Growth Leads to Environmental Hurdles (1985–1989)

In 1985, Baxter acquired American Hospital Supply Corporation (AHSC), which had its corporate offices in Evanston, Illinois. AHSC included manufacturing operations and a very large distribution operation of medical products to customers, especially to U.S. hospitals. As a company, AHSC had revenues greater than Baxter and the number of AHSC facilities exceeded those of Baxter. Soon after the merger, for those involved in Baxter's environmental program, it became apparent AHSC's business culture and approach to environmental issues were much different from Baxter's. At the time of the merger, an environmental financial reserve of approximately $10 million was established to address anticipated and potential environmental issues associated with the acquisition.

Between 1985 and 1989, Baxter's corporate-level environmental legal and engineering staff became increasingly involved in AHSC environmental issues, including: underground fuel oil storage tanks permitting for regulated air emissions, the use of solvents and proper disposal of hazardous waste at off-site facilities, issues with property transfers (sales and acquisitions), asbestos surveys & abatement, and environmental compliance and risk management assessments. In this period, Baxter was increasingly drawn into "fire-fighting" actions with regards to environmental issues in many areas, such as air, waste water, and hazardous waste at a number of former AHSC sites.

In the 1980s, a new U.S. EPA Superfund law was being implemented, which required expensive cleanups, especially at sites that handled and disposed of hazardous waste, and often, such issues delayed large real estate transactions. At the same time, the EPA Toxic Release Inventory (TRI), which reported requirements, began disclosing information on the toxics that companies were emitting into the environment. During this time, newspapers frequently carried headlines on U.S. company

---

[20] Blackburn, 2010.

emissions, which raised community concerns - even though the companies were complying with environmental laws. As a result, Baxter was beginning to receive some unfavorable media publicity.

Although solid progress was being made in many areas, it was certainly stretching Baxter's environmental resources and detracting attention from Baxter's other sites and planned environmental initiatives. In 1988, a California news team broadcasted a live television news report showing Baxter's company name in front of a recent Baxter-acquired manufacturing facility south of Los Angeles, stating that this specific location emitted the largest annual quantity of toxic air emissions of any site in California's Orange County (Grad 1990). This newscast caught the attention of Baxter's environmental staff and senior management. Something needed to be done to strategically address Baxter's existing and possible future environmental issues.[21]

Stage III: Creating a Path Towards Sustainability (1990–1996)

One of the environmental consulting firms Baxter was using in the late 1980s and early 1990s was Arthur D. Little Inc. This firm was helping Baxter with environmental compliance site assessments, risk management, and advice on program development. At one point, a representative of this firm stated that if Baxter maintained a reactive type of environmental program it could expect environmental-related expenses and risks to generally increase over time. On the other hand, if Baxter were to invest more resources to implement a proactive global environmental program, future environmental-related expenses and risks should be expected to decrease and, in time, Baxter should realize a good return on this investment.

It was time to make a change. It was time to revisit Baxter's global strategic approach to managing global environmental compliance and risk issues and reassert Mr. Graham's environmental vision for Baxter. It was time to develop a much more robust environmental program – one which could respond to possible future challenges in a timely and efficient manner. Bill Blackburn and the company's environmental management team endorsed Arthur D. Little's suggested strategic approach – that is, Baxter should invest the needed resources to move from a reactive to a proactive global environmental program. This recommendation was presented to Baxter management and it was accepted. As a result, Blackburn was asked to lead this effort and the environmental program. Blackburn reported to the legal department and worked closely with Baxter's General Counsel. With the support of General Counsel, the legal department, and senior management, Blackburn served as the VP for Environmental Affairs from 1990 to 1996, and as the VP for Environmental, Health and Safety from 1997 to 2003.

First, Baxter needed to establish a new global Environmental Policy – one which stated Baxter would become a leader in respect to environmental issues.

---

[21] Ibid.

We needed to define what we are biting off. How do we put together a one-page policy that defines what we are committed to do?[22]

The team did not think Baxter's CEO would sign off on the first draft policy because it could have been viewed as inconsistent with Baxter's current status/challenges. Given this assessment, another provision was added to the policy in order to create an environmental program that would be *State of the Art* (SOA)[23] among the Fortune 500 companies.

The goal was to have this SOA environmental program defined and achieved at Baxter facilities in the U.S., Puerto Rico and Canada by 1993, and achieved at all remaining international locations by 1996. In addition, a new goal was included in the policy, which was to reduce air toxics 80 % (from 1988 to 1996).[24] The new direction would require the position levels of facility environmental managers to be re-evaluated. As a result of this review, some positions were raised and certain compensation levels increased to match site environmental responsibilities. New company environmental reduction goals, such as those related to solid and hazardous waste, air emissions, and packaging materials,[25] were established and widely communicated. Baxter management was very supportive of the program and signed the new Baxter Environmental Policy. Those involved understood that a relatively small initial investment should yield large scale long term gains – both financial and reputational.

In launching a new proactive environmental program, there was a need to get buy-in from the environmental representatives in each principal Baxter division to make it more democratic, and to help in the ultimate deployment of the program. After considering a few alternatives, a council of corporate and division environmental managers was formed. Next, Baxter needed to go through the process of defining what would be the new *State of the Art Standards* (SOA Standards). To accomplish this, the company studied the results of previous Baxter facility-level environmental compliance audits. Together, these audits identified the characteristics of facilities that were doing well in legal compliance, risk management and waste reduction. In the end, the corporate and division team came up with a list of 'best practices' that drove excellent environmental performance. Baxter's SOA Standards were built around these best practices. The new SOA Standards also included a progressive requirement that every Baxter site establish an active environmental outreach program with the community in which the site operated.

Arthur D. Little was brought in as a consultant to advise on what other multinational companies were doing to advance their environmental programs. This input helped the company refine the facility SOA Standards. The corporate and division

---

[22] Ibid.

[23] Baxter held an Environmental Conference for corporate, division and facility environmental staff annually for a number of years. In the late 1990s – early 2000s the forum was combined with health and safety personnel and held bi-annually through 2007.

[24] EPA defined air toxics emitted from Baxter facilities. Note that this goal was achieved by 1996

[25] Around 1998 +/– a Baxter energy efficiency (& associated energy-related greenhouse gas (GHG) emissions reduction) goal was established

teams concluded that these standards alone were not enough. SOA-type Standards needed to be developed at the division/business unit as well as corporate levels in order to dovetail with the new facility SOA Standards, so that there would be good alignment and shared responsibilities/accountabilities across the entire organization.

The various SOA Standards were established along with a scoring system designed to assess progress against the standards. Once the standards were completed, ongoing company environmental audits were used for the scoring and tracking of progress. Next, in a relatively short period of time, was the big challenge of hitting the 1993 and 1996 deadlines – which was in fact accomplished.

About the same time that Baxter was developing the new environmental policy and program that included the SOA Standards, a set of abbreviated environmental compliance audits were performed on several dozen facilities the company had recently acquired, and those results were compiled into a report. Blackburn was invited to share the results of these audits with the top 150 executives of the company. Upon hearing the presentation, Baxter's CEO Vernon Loucks was upset with these results and told his managers in no uncertain terms that improvement would have to be made *or else!*[26] Soon, the infrastructure for driving the new environmental program forward was in place – people knew what they needed to do, and the measurement of progress and the transparent communication of SOA scores were initiated. In addition, a more candid annual progress report on the environmental program was made available for the Public Policy Committee of Baxter's Board of Directors to review. The report contained informative graphs and charts, transparent in nature, explaining the number and nature of any environmental issues. This same information was also shared within the Baxter organization. The belief at that time was: *Light brings heat, which brings change.*[27]

The idea was that if the right goals, supporting metrics, good measurement, and progress report were provided in a transparent manner to each facility, division/business unit, and at the corporate level, then there would be internal and external pressure to address apparent issues. It was not so much about punishing people; it was more about recognizing the efforts and providing incentives to the plant managers and others whose operations were excelling – an approach of incentives rather than criticism and fear. In the end, top management support combined with clear expectations for performance (goals, measurement, reporting results), resulted in environmental performance taking off with enhanced compliance, better risk management, reduction in various wastes, an increase in environmental program savings, and positive environmental recognition for Baxter.

The next area of emphasis was at the international level. In the early 1990s, the company was in a domestic mentality and the next focus would be in the international space. With the help of regional meetings in different parts of the globe, the SOA Standards were modified so that these would be applicable internationally

---

[26] Balckburn, 2010.
[27] Ibid.

from a cultural perspective, while guaranteeing a common level of protection around the world for people and the environment. Culture played a very significant role. For example, there was a requirement that if an inspector got a wastewater sample, the sample was split in two – one part for the inspector, and the other part for the company to retain (and possibly analyze separately). In Japan, this requirement was considered insulting to the inspector, an affront that indicated that there was no trust. Keeping in mind the different cultural mind-sets, the standards were modified as required to make them more accommodating to the local needs and cultures.

In order to deploy the SOA Standards globally, regional environmental meetings were held in Southeast Asia, Europe and Latin America. This was a new area of focus for these facilities. For the most part, environmental laws outside the U.S. were weak at that time, and where laws existed, enforcement was not rigorous. A special senior management European Environmental Review Board was formed to drive the program in Europe, where Baxter had many facilities. There were numerous meetings of this Board – with questionable commitment by some members. Then one day, it all changed. At this particular meeting, the Plant Manager and environmental director of a Baxter manufacturing facility in Ireland told his fellow Board members that the SOA Standards were adding great business value and that they should continue to work on it. All of a sudden, the attitude shifted almost overnight, and implementation of the environmental standards across the region began to accelerate.

In 1992, Baxter began looking at reductions in packaging. For this, the company looked to the Germans and the Canadians, as those facilities were accomplishing the most in this area. Baxter held a summit, established a packaging task force, set goals, and reduced packaging significantly – ultimately saving the company roughly $35 million in costs.

Environmental Reporting and Environmental Financial Statement

An annual process was implemented for measuring specific performance (a report generated by all principal global Baxter locations) against all company goals, including environmental management systems and compliance assurance goals. Beginning in the early 1990s, Baxter began issuing first an internal, and next a public Environmental Report. Baxter was one of the first companies to measure and report its global energy usage and greenhouse gas emissions, beginning in 1996. In the late 1990s, Baxter's Environmental Report evolved into an Environmental, Health and Safety Report; this communication transitioned into an annual Sustainability Report by the end of the decade.

In 1994, Baxter developed a unique Environmental Financial Statement and subsequently published the statement in its annual public Environment Report. This financial statement summarizes all of Baxter's global environmental costs, savings, and cost avoidance due to its environmental initiatives. This Environmental Financial Statement (EFS), which continues to be published annually and is available on Baxter's website, has received considerable attention over the past 15 years, and has been featured in various publications. Overall through 2010, the EFS generally reflect that for about every $1 invested annually in a "proactive" global environmental program, Baxter receives a return of about $2 to $4. Arthur D. Little and Baxter management were correct. Not only is sound environmental corporate stewardship a responsible action to take – it simply makes good business sense.

Stage IV: Building the Framework for Sustainability (1997–2003)

In 1996, Baxter's environmental engineering group in Corporate Facilities Engineering, its environmental legal group in Corporate Legal, and its health and safety group in the Corporate Human Resources department were all brought together into one organization, which reported to Bill Blackburn (VP in the Legal group). A new Environment, Health and Safety (EHS) Policy was developed along with a new EHS Manual (Users Guide), from which all EHS Policies were compiled into an EHS Requirements Book. A new EHS organization in the regions/business groups and facilities was organized. Baxter's environmental compliance auditing program was expanded to an EHS auditing program. Previous separately-held annual environmental conferences and health and safety conferences were combined into unified EHS conferences – first annually, and then biannually. During this timeframe, Baxter pursued the implementation of the ISO 14001 environmental management standards, and set a requirement that all manufacturing and R&D locations should meet the ISO 14001 standards. Baxter's annual public Environmental Report became an annual Environment, Health and Safety Report.

> Earth Summit 1
> The UN Conference on Environment and Development, also known as the Earth Summit 1, took place in Rio de Janeiro, Brazil in June 1992… The central focus was the question of how to relieve the global environmental system through the introduction to the paradigm of sustainable development. This concept emphasizes that economic and social Progress depends critically on the preservation of the natural resource base with effective measures to prevent environmental degradation.[28]

By the mid-1990s, a group within Baxter's corporate EHS group was regularly discussing certain aspects of sustainability as well as the outcome of the 1992 UN Conference on Environment and Development (Earth Summit 1). This group realized the importance of sustainability/sustainable development, which was defined by a UN commission in 1987 as *development that meets the needs of the present without compromising the ability of future generations to meet their needs.* In 1997, Baxter's CEO Harry Kraemer signed the Ceres Principals (Ceres, 2010), and in the late 1990s Baxter was one of 22 companies that piloted the Global Reporting Initiative (GRI), which established international sustainability reporting guidelines.

In the late 1990s, Baxter also rejuvenated its energy management program, an important element of sustainability. Between around 1976 and 1986, Baxter had one

---

[28]www.eoearth.org/article/United_Nations_Conference_on_Environment_and_Development_ (UNCED). Accessed 3 Oct 2011.

point person coordinating energy management initiatives within the Corporate Facilities Engineering group. Back in the 1970s, there were a few OPEC (Organization of the Petroleum Exporting Countries) embargos and fuel prices had skyrocketed. Many corporations, including Baxter, formed teams to conserve energy and save money. However, by the mid-1980s, fuel prices had come down again. Baxter's centralized energy group was disbanded and energy management was relegated to divisions and business units to manage. Within a decade, energy prices were rising/volatile again, and the issue of global climate change was gaining more attention.

In 1998, a manager within Blackburn's staff joined with technical representatives of Baxter's largest U.S. manufacturing plant to organize a company-wide Energy Conference. This forum included many global engineering and energy management representatives, as well as a number of outside energy experts, including Amory Lovins from the Rocky Mountain Institute. Forum sessions were held on energy pricing, markets, and volatility. The facilities discussed best practices in energy management, and energy experts presented the latest energy technologies. By design, energy technologies and pricing issues were emphasized and the subject of global warming and climate change received only about half-an-hour of discussion at the end of the conference. In subsequent Energy Conferences, the climate change subject was given more attention.

An outcome of this Energy Conference was the need to again create a centralized energy manager position, which was accomplished. Subsequent energy audits indicated that there were good opportunities for savings with attractive returns on investment. Because of the financial aspect of the initiative, the finance group took an interest in energy management and prodded the organization even more. Agreements were made on Energy Reduction Goals and Programs to drive cost savings, and a new greenhouse gas goal was piggybacked onto those. In 2003, Baxter became 1 of the 13 founding members of the Chicago Climate Exchange (CCX), which was the world's first carbon cap and trading system. Over the years, as climate change has become more visible, Baxter greenhouse gas emission goals and performance has gained greater prominence both inside and outside of the organization.

In 1999, two members of the small EHS sustainability group presented the sustainability subject directly to Baxter's CEO at that time, Mr. Harry Kraemer. After some discussion, Mr. Kraemer soon issued a communication to Baxter's employees supporting this concept. With this endorsement by upper management, for year-end 1999 performance, Baxter's annual public EHS Report was renamed a "Sustainability Report." [Baxter's 2011 Sustainability Report (its thirtieth sustainability report prepared consistent with the GRI guidelines) was issued in June 2012.]

In 2003, Bill Blackburn, along with a number of other top executives, left Baxter due to a change in organizational structure and business direction. The following year, Baxter's CEO, Harry Kraemer, left the company. Joining the company in 2004 as the new CEO was Mr. Robert Parkinson, who was previously an executive within a university in Chicago, and prior to that had a long tenure with Abbott Laboratories. During the period from mid-2003 to year-end 2005, senior managers within Baxter's

EHS team managed the global EHS compliance and risk management program. Current initiatives were maintained (EHS teams, compliance and risk management systems, ISO 14001 standards, and reporting), new activities and partnerships were launched, and an EHS group continued to work on sustainability.

A Shift in EHS Reporting: From Legal to Manufacturing

From 1976 to mid-2003, the EHS organization, including certain legal experts, reported to Baxter's Legal group. With the organizational changes that occurred in mid-2003, the reporting responsibility of the EHS organization was switched from the Legal group to the Manufacturing group, with the exception of a few EHS individuals working on compliance assurance and legal issues,. The stated logic behind this organizational change was that because EHS was involved closely with manufacturing, this new change would provide greater alignment and synergy. Hence, the work that EHS was involved with began to focus more on cost containment/reduction and lean manufacturing – a different internal culture for EHS. The EHS legal team members provided independent oversight and engaged outside consultants to conduct EHS audits as required.

Stage V: Leadership Promotes Sustainability (2003–2012)

Starting in around 2003, the EHS sustainability team recognized that there were pockets of individuals and groups (for example, EHS, Energy Management, Packaging, Corporate Communications) working within Baxter to advance sustainability, but there was not enough traction needed to achieve the desired sustainability-related benefits. Sustainability had not appeared to have permeated the entire organization. Sustainability needed to be elevated, and momentum increased. In 2005, the concept of an executive-level Sustainability Steering Committee (SSC) was developed to accelerate the integration of sustainability throughout the Baxter organization.

> There was a need for an executive-level steering committee to help lead and integrate sustainability more into the organization and accelerate company sustainability programs and performance.[29]

In late 2005, Art Gibson was brought into Baxter as the new VP of EHS. In 2006 Mr. Gibson helped with the continuing discussion and proposed the formation of an executive-level Sustainability Steering Committee (SSC). In late 2006, the SSC concept was presented to the CEO, Mr. Parkinson, and he approved the formation of the SSC with nine initial executive members, plus a working group that would support the SSC.

---

[29] Meissen, R. 2010. Personal Communication with Author.

Prior to the first SSC meeting in early 2007, Professor Stuart Hart of Cornell University was engaged to attend all planned 2007 quarterly SSC meetings, to provide the Baxter executives with an overview of sustainability in business terms, and to facilitate sustainability-related discussions as required. In the first quarter and second quarter 2007 SSC meetings, Dr. Hart supported the SSC in learning about sustainability and defining nine high-level Baxter Sustainability Priorities. These Priorities, which represented Baxter's intended direction towards enhancing the companies' sustainability posture, were first presented to the public in Baxter's 2006 Sustainability Report, published in mid-2007.

Between mid-2007 and spring 2008, each member of the nine-member SSC championed one of the nine new Sustainability Priorities and coordinated a working team, which each member selected, to define a few specific 2015 goals to advance the specific Priority. Teams were encouraged to benchmark within and outside the healthcare industry to determine possible goal areas and best practices. In early 2008, the SSC reviewed and discussed many potential goals. After two quarterly meetings, the SSC and Baxter management approved nearly two dozen 2015 goals to support Baxter's Sustainability Priorities. These were first presented to the public in Baxter's 2007 Sustainability Report, published in mid-2008.

The Baxter executive-level Sustainability Steering Committee continues to meet quarterly to evaluate progress towards existing Sustainability Priorities and Goals, to gain knowledge on sustainability program and reporting trends (through external and internal presenters), and to consider new sustainability initiatives. Baxter's CEO Bob Parkinson typically attends one of the quarterly SSC meetings each year and provides his own insights and perspectives on the subject matter. Refer to the Appendix 3 for the Baxter 2009 Sustainability Priorities and Goals.

Sustainability helps contribute to long-term stakeholder value and it helps attract and retain key talent.[30]

Model of Shareholder Value

When Stuart Hart was consulting for Baxter, all the members of the SSC received a copy of his book entitled, *Capitalism at the Crossroads*.[31] As stated before, each member of the committee is generally responsible for one of the nine sustainability priorities in the Sustainability Report.

One of the models developed by Hart and Milstein was the model of *Shareholder Value*.[32] The vertical axis of this model represents time; this axis reflects the

---

[30]Parkinson, Bob, CEO in the Baxter Sustainability Report, 2011, accessed October, 2012 at http://sustainability.baxter.com/environment-health-safety/environmental-performance/energy.html

[31]Hart, Stuart. 2005. *Capitalism at the crossroads*. Upper Saddle River NJ: Pearson Education. (3rd edition 2010).

[32]Hart, S. and M. Milstein. 2003. Creating sustainable value,. *Academy of Management Executive* 17: 2.

organization's need to manage today's business while simultaneously creating tomorrow's technology and markets. The horizontal axis represents space; this axis reflects the organization's need to grow and protect the internal organizations capabilities, while simultaneously incorporating new external perspectives and knowledge. The concept is to balance the need to stay focused on core capabilities, while maintaining awareness of fresh, external perspectives. Utilizing both the time and space dimensions yields a matrix of four distinct areas: risk reduction, reputation, innovation, and growth, each of which being critical to the goal of generating shareholder value.

Sustainable Value Creation

The shareholder value model requires performance on multiple dimensions. In a similar vein, sustainable value is also multi-dimensional. A natural extension of the shareholder value model is the *Sustainable Value Framework*,[33] which is also built around the same two dimensions – time and space – from the Shareholder Value Model. In addition, this framework includes social and environmental challenges as well.

There are four sets of drivers that need to be considered for global sustainability. The first set of drivers relates to the negative impact of industrialization, namely: pollution, waste, and material consumption. The second set of drivers relates to the proliferation of civil society groups like NGOs, and their growing impact on society due to internet technologies, which allow the non-governmental organizations NGOs to quickly mobilize their members. The third set of drivers includes the emerging disruptive technologies, such as genomics, nanotechnology, biomimicry, renewable energy, etc., which have the potential to make energy- and material-intensive industries obsolete. The fourth set of drivers relates to the global concerns of increasing population, poverty and inequity arising from globalization (Fig. 5.1).

According to The Sustainable Value Framework, each **driver of sustainability** and its strategies and business practices correspond to a specific dimension of shareholder value.

For the lower left quadrant, organizations can create value by following a pollution prevention strategy to minimize emissions and waste. The immediate payoff is one of cost and risk reduction. Indeed, empirical evidence shows that companies pursuing pollution-prevention and waste-reduction strategies do reduce cost and increase profits.[34]

---

[33] Ibid.

[34] Christmann, P. 1998. Effects of 'best practices' of environmental management on cost advantage: The role of complementary assets. *Academy of Management Journal* 43(4):66–680. Sharma, S., and H. Vredenburg. 1998. Proactive corporate environmental strategy and the development of competitively valuable organizational capabilities. *Strategic Management Journal* 19(8): 729–753.

Sustainable Value Framework

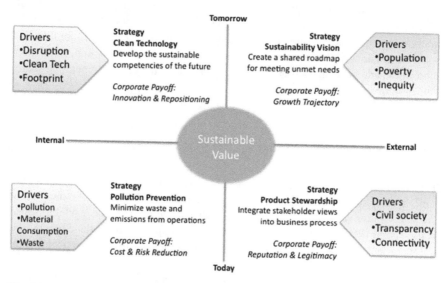

Fig. 5.1 Sustainable value framework

For the lower right quadrant, organizations can increase external confidence in their intentions and activities by constructively engaging stakeholders. The ideal strategy for a company would be to integrate stakeholder views into business processes in order to gain a payoff related to reputation and legitimacy. Some actions to take are cause-related marketing, life cycle management, industrial ecology, etc. As an example taken from industrial ecology, organizations can convert wastes from one operation into inputs for another operation. In 1997, Collins and Aikman Floorcoverings developed the capability to convert old carpet into new carpet backing. This product, ER3 (Environmentally Redesigned, Restructured, and Reused) has helped the company to obtain an increase in market share.[35] Another example is Nike: when faced with a growing backlash regarding its labor and environmental practices, Nike produced a turn-around by engaging stakeholders to address social and environmental issues.[36]

For the upper left quadrant, organizations would develop the sustainable competencies of the future for a resulting payoff related to innovation and repositioning. Future economic growth will be driven by companies that can engage in disruptive technologies in order to address the needs of the society. Firms that fail to lead in development and commercialization of such technologies are not likely

---

[35]Buffington, J., S. Hart, and M. Milstein. 2002. *Tandus 2010: Race to sustainability.* Chapel Hill: Center for Sustainable Enterprises, University of North Carolina.

[36]Hart and Milstein. 2003.

to be future market players (Hamel 2000). For example, BP and Shell are investing in solar, wind, and other renewable technologies; Toyota and Honda have incorporated hybrid power systems in their cars; GE, Honeywell, and United Technologies are investing in small scale energy systems; Cargill and Dow are developing biologically based polymers that will enable renewable feedstocks, such as corn, to replace petrochemical inputs in the manufacture of plastics. Another commendable example is that of DuPont, which transformed itself from a gunpowder and explosives manufacturer to a chemical company in late 1800s, and then transformed itself into a renewable resource company focused on sustainable growth in the 1990s.[37] Firms that invest in clean solutions pursue more novel approaches to long-term challenges and hence, create organizational structures that support the innovative process.[38]

For the upper right, organizations ought to create a shared roadmap for meeting unmet needs for a resultant payoff of a sustainable growth trajectory. In other words, firms that take the time to create a compelling sustainability vision have the potential to unlock future markets of large scale and scope. The common example is Grameen Bank, which opened a new pathway for business growth (Counts 1996). Another example of a multi-national corporation MNC is Hindustan Level Ltd. (HLL), which developed products specifically aimed at the rural poor in India and was able to provide affordable soaps and shampoos to this market (Balu 2002). As a result, more than half of HLL's revenues come from the customers at the bottom of the pyramid. In another example, HP has created a R&D lab in rural India to understand the needs of this burgeoning market. Other companies like Johnson & Johnson, Dow, DuPont, Coca-Cola, and Proctor & Gamble are attempting to leverage their skills to meet the basic needs of the world's poor.[39]

Application of Shareholder Value Model to Baxter

In 2007, Baxter's executive-level Sustainability Steering Committee evaluated, discussed and announced nine initial overarching "Sustainability Priorities," on which the company would focus (Baxter Sustainability Report 2009). These priorities represented a strategic direction toward which Baxter would move. The following year, goals for 2015 were established in support of the sustainability priorities. Refer to the Appendix for a detailed breakdown of these 9 priorities and 18 goals.[40]

Figure 5.2 presents the nine Baxter Sustainability Priorities in each of the four quadrants and highlights the priorities which appear most applicable to the specific quadrant. In some cases a priority, or a component of the priority, could apply to more than one quadrant. It appears that five of Baxter's nine current Sustainability Priorities relate to the lower left quadrant.

---

[37] Holliday, C. 2001. Sustainable growth, the DuPont way. *Harvard Business Review* 79(8): 129–132.
[38] Hart and Milstein. 2003.
[39] Ibid.
[40] Baxter Sustainability Report. 2009. Accessed December, 2010 at http://sustainability.baxter.com/

Strategy: Clean technology	Strategy: Sustainability Vision
9. Strengthen the Company's Commitment To Education, Especially Math and Science	8. Strengthen Access to Healthcare Through Product Development and Strategic Product Donations 9. Strengthen the Company's Commitment To Education, Especially Math and Science
Strategy: Pollution Prevention	Strategy: Product Stewardship
1. Promote a Safe and Healthy Workplace 2. Promote an Inclusive and Diverse Workplace 3. Promote Ethical Conduct and Legal Compliance 5. Drive Reductions in its Carbon Footprint 6. Drive Reductions in its Natural Resource Use	2. Promote an Inclusive and Diverse Workplace 3. Promote Ethical Conduct and Legal Compliance 4. Drive a Sustainable Supply Chain 7. Drive Enhanced Product Stewardship 8. Strengthen Access to Healthcare Through Product Development and Strategic Product Donations

Fig. 5.2 Baxter's sustainability priorities

From mid-2007 to spring 2008 Baxter's executive-level Sustainability Steering Committee worked to develop goals appropriate to each of the nine defined Sustainability Priorities. These "Sustainability Goals" were first presented in Baxter's 2007 Sustainability Report issued in mid-2008. Figure 5.3 presents the current 18 sustainability goals in the Sustainable Value Framework quadrant, which appears to be most suitable for the goal. Again, in some cases, a goal, or a component of the goal, could apply to more than one quadrant.

Where Does Baxter Go from Here?

Presently, Baxter International, Inc.

...develops, manufactures and markets products that save and sustain the lives of people with hemophilia, immune disorders, infectious diseases, kidney disease, trauma, and other chronic and acute medical conditions. As a global, diversified healthcare company, Baxter applies a unique combination of expertise in medical devices, pharmaceuticals and biotechnology to create products that advance patient care worldwide.[41]

---

[41] Baxter Website http://www.baxter.com/healthcare_professionals/products/.

Strategy: Clean technology	Strategy: Sustainability Vision
1. Promote a Safe and Healthy Workplace	1. Promote a Safe and Healthy Workplace
2. Promote an Inclusive and Diverse Workplace	2. Promote an Inclusive and Diverse Workplace
3. Promote Ethical Conduct and Legal Compliance	3. Promote Ethical Conduct and Legal Compliance
4. Drive a Green Supply Chain	4. Drive a Green Supply Chain
5. Drive Reductions in its Carbon Footprint	5. Drive Reductions in its Carbon Footprint
6. Drive Reductions in its Natural Resource Use	6. Drive Reductions in its Natural Resource Use
7. Drive Enhanced Product Stewardship	7. Drive Enhanced Product Stewardship
8. Strengthen Access to Healthcare Through Product Development and Strategic Product Donations	**8. Strengthen Access to Healthcare Through Product Development and Strategic Product Donations**
9. Strengthen the Company's Commitment To Education, Especially math and Science	**9. Strengthen the Company's Commitment To Education, Especially math and Science**

Strategy: Pollution Prevention	Strategy: Product Stewardship
1. Promote a Safe and Healthy Workplace	1. Promote a Safe and Healthy Workplace
2. Promote an Inclusive and Diverse Workplace	**2. Promote an Inclusive and Diverse Workplace**
3. Promote Ethical Conduct and Legal Compliance	**3. Promote Ethical Conduct and Legal Compliance**
4. Drive a Green Supply Chain	**4. Drive a Green Supply Chain**
5. Drive Reductions in its Carbon Footprint	5. Drive Reductions in its Carbon Footprint
6. Drive Reductions in its Natural Resource Use	6. Drive Reductions in its Natural Resource Use
7. Drive Enhanced Product Stewardship	**7. Drive Enhanced Product Stewardship**
8. Strengthen Access to Healthcare Through Product Development and Strategic Product Donations	**8. Strengthen Access to Healthcare Through Product Development and Strategic Product Donations**
9. Strengthen the Company's Commitment To Education, Especially math and Science	9. Strengthen the Company's Commitment To Education, Especially math and Science

Fig. 5.3 Baxter's sustainability priorities

Under the leadership of Robert L. Parkinson, Jr., the current Chairman, President and CEO, Baxter had 2011 sales of $US 13.9 billion and retained around 48,500 employees. Baxter's leadership over the past decade is unique in its ongoing efforts to advance sustainability. As Parkinson the CEO reports,

As global corporations increasingly play a greater role in addressing sustainability issues, they are changing how they operate in fundamental ways. Sustainability and profitability are not mutually exclusive. In fact, they are closely intertwined and reinforcing. The sooner we all recognize this, the better—for business and society.[42]

---

[42]Baxter Annual Report. 2011. Accessed 20 April 2012.

This belief in combining profitability and sustainability can be seen through Baxter's track record. According to Corporate Knights, for 2012 Baxter ranked at number 86 in its list of "Global 100 Most Sustainable Corporations in the World."[43] In addition, 2012 marked the eleventh year that Baxter was recognized as the Medical Products Industry Leader of the Dow Jones Sustainability World Index, and the fourteenth year that Baxter was listed in the Dow Jones Sustainability World Index (DJSI).[44] The Global Reporting Initiative (GRI) is an internationally recognized organization that has created a widely used sustainability reporting framework. This framework is largely made up of Sustainability Reporting Guidelines, the most recent installment of which is known as the GRI G3 Guidelines. The results of this type of economic, environmental and social reporting allow companies to systematically benchmark their performance. Additionally, because the GRI is such a well-respected system of reporting, having a high standing within the G3 framework helps consumers, investors and employees alike when assessing the moral standing of a corporation. According to Baxter's 2011 Sustainability Report, it stands at a level B- within the G3 guidelines, and Baxter is a GRI Organizational Stakeholder (OS).[45]

Baxter attributes many of its historical environmental risk reduction and cost-saving measures to helping improve/maintain its environmental standing. Baxter has been monitoring its annual environmental-related costs and savings through Environmental Financial Statements since the mid-1990s. By putting into effect methods agreed upon through this evaluation, Baxter was able to avoid many of its previous costs and consequently has improved its environmental standing as well as its financial standing.[46] Baxter's 2015 sustainability goals include a number of specific environmental goals, which are indexed to revenue with a 2005 baseline. These environmental goals include, reduce GHG from operations emissions 45 %, increase facility energy usage of renewable power to 20 % (of total), reduce energy usage 30 %, reduce water usage 35 %, reduce total waste generation 30 % and eliminate 5,000 metric tons of packaging.[47] It has yet to be seen whether Baxter will be able to achieve these lofty goals.

In general, Baxter has been decreasing its environmental impact both by conservation and utilizing renewable energy. Baxter employs numerous innovative methods throughout its many U.S. and internationally based facilities to conserve resources. For example, at one of its sites in North Carolina Baxter uses scrap wood chips (biofuel) from local lumber operations and furniture mills as input energy into a wood boiler to generate steam for building heat and sterilizing its products. More

---

[43] Global100.org. 2012. Global 100 most sustainable corporations in the World, 2012. http://www.global100.org/. Accessed 30 Jan 2013.

[44] Dow Jones Sustainability Index, 2012.

[45] Baxter Sustainability Report. 2011. Accessed October, 2012 at http://sustainability.baxter.com/environment-health-safety/environmental-performance/energy.html

[46] "Making Energy Conservation a Cornerstone of Sustainability". Baxter publication, pg. 35

[47] Ibid.

recently biofuel for boilers have been introduced at two Baxter facilities in India. Innovative projects such as this have contributed to Baxter's global energy conservation activities, "which, since 2005, have achieved cumulative savings of approximately $39 million on an annualized basis."[48]

According to Baxter's most recent 2011 Sustainability Report, the company is using increasing amounts of renewable energy for its global operations. The use of renewable energy contributes to multiple Baxter sustainability objectives, including the reduction of GHG emissions.

> During 2011, Baxter purchased 153,700 megawatt hours (MWh) of electricity generated from 100 % certified renewable power. This included 102,200 MWh for company operations in Europe (Austria, Spain, Switzerland, and the United Kingdom) and 51,500 MWh of certified renewable energy certificates (RECs) for U.S. operations. Baxter was recognized as the 29th largest corporate purchaser of renewable energy in the United States at year-end 2011 (Fig. 5.4).
>
> Beginning in 2007, Baxter has used various means such as electricity generated from certified renewable energy, carbon credits and carbon offsets to achieve and maintain "carbon neutrality" at its headquarters in Deerfield, Illinois, United States, and its facility in Cartago, Costa Rica. In both cases, at a minimum, the company offsets facility-related emissions from purchased electricity as well as fuel combustion on site. Beginning in 2012, all purchased electricity used by Baxter operations in Illinois, United States, approximately 80,000 MWh per year, will be generated from 100 % wind generated Green-e certified renewable energy.

Implications

Akin to Stuart Hart's title, it seems that Baxter may be at 'its own crossroads'. The work that the company has committed in order to be an environmental/sustainability leader is indeed impressive. In Newsweek's annual ranking of Green Companies, Baxter was ranked in the U.S. at No: 15 in 2010 and it jumped to No: 4 in 2011.[49] The Maplecroft Climate Innovation Index (CII) Benchmark (for 346 of the largest US companies) ranking for Baxter rose from #35 in Cycle 1 (2010), to #21 in Cycle 2 (2011) and then dropped back to #31 in Cycle 3.[50] However, this general success may be difficult to maintain. Given investor and NGO interest and media and public exposure, the bar of sustainability expectations appears to be moving up each year. Added to this fact is that there are more companies voluntarily joining or motivated to join the fray of so-called 'sustainable' or 'green' corporations. The combination of these representative factors makes the task of a company maintaining its sustainability performance daunting. This can be witnessed by the change of Baxter's

---

[48] Ibid.

[49] Newsweek Green Ranking 2010, Newsweek Green Ranking 2011. http:// www.baxter.com/press_room/features/2010/10_25_10_newsweek.html

[50] Maplecroff Climate Innovation Indexes, 2012. http://www.businesswire.com/news/home/20101215005218/en/Baxter-Advances-Science-Education-Haiti-Relief-Efforts

Strategy: Clean technology	Strategy: Sustainability Vision
15. By 2010, assess existing products for relevance to the "base of the pyramid" (developing economies) and identify high-impact, economically viable product opportunities. 16. Increase R&D investment from 2008 to improve access to healthcare for the "base of the pyramid"	15. By 2010, assess existing products for relevance to the "base of the pyramid" (developing economies) and identify high-impact, economically viable product opportunities. 16. Increase R&D investment from 2008 to improve access to healthcare for the "base of the pyramid" 18. Facilitate learning of math and science through biotechnology education for Chicago Public Schools teachers and students, and partner with other educational organizations to provide similar opportunities at other locations.
Strategy: Pollution Prevention	**Strategy: Product Stewardship**
1. Implement best-in-class programs designed to protect the safety and improve the health of employees 2. Create and sustain an inclusive culture... 3. Continue to champion internal and industry wide ethical sales and marketing practices 4. Reduce the carbon footprint of Baxter's U.S. car fleet... 6. Reduce Greenhouse gas emissions... 7. Increase facility usage of renewable power... 8. Reduce total waste generation... 9. Reduce energy usage... 10. Eliminate 5,000 metric tons of packaging materials... [Baxter savings] 11. Reduce water usage... 14. Identify new opportunities to replace, reduce and refine (3Rs) the use of animal testing.	2. Create and sustain an inclusive culture... 3. Continue to champion internal and industry wide ethical sales and marketing practices 5. Incorporate green principals into Baxter's purchasing program... 10. Eliminate 5,000 metric tons of packaging materials... [Customer benefits] 12. Implement two projects to help protect vulnerable watersheds or provide communities with enhanced access to clean water. 13. Incorporate the following elements as appropriate into Baxter's product stewardship programs... 17. Work with donor partners to develop and implement a strategic product donations plan beginning in 2010 that includes...

Fig. 5.4 Baxter's sustainability priorities

presence on some of the rankings. In years 2007 and 2008, Baxter was on the list of the Carbon Disclosure Project (CDP) Leadership Index, but has fallen off since then. For the list of "Global 100 Most Admired Companies in the World," Baxter's ranking was # 69 in 2010, fell to # 99 in 2011 and bounced back to # 86 in 2012.[51]

---

[51]Global100.org, 2012: Global 100 most sustainable corporations in the World, 2012. http://www.global100.org/)

With organizational sustainability performance increasingly scrutinized by independent and knowledgeable reviewers, will Baxter be able to maintain its standings?

What does Baxter need to do to ensure that this global sustainability innovation, momentum, and business benefits associated with this momentum, is maintained? How can a multi-national company continue to innovate in many respects, including in its supply chain, operations and products, to be at the forefront of sustainability leadership? Will the companies' trend of sustainability progress continue going up, slow down or tapper off? All these are questions Baxter leadership will need to reflect upon, innovation options evaluated and possible sustainability strategies considered as the world community strives "to meet the needs of the present without compromising the ability of future generations to meet their own needs."[52]

Acknowledgments

Two people were instrumental in gathering content for this case study. The first is Ronald Meissen, Ph.D., Senior Director of Sustainability, Corporate Environment, Health and Safety at Baxter. The second is William Blackburn, President of William Blackburn Consulting, Ltd., (WBC). Dr. Meissen was inordinately patient in his assistance with reviewing drafts of this case study and welcomed me to Baxter a few times. Mr. Blackburn helped me sort through the environmental/sustainability history of Baxter, especially during his tenure at the company. In addition, Milla Milojkovic helped with the final revisions of the paper.

Baxter Priority Sustainability and 2015 Goals – People

1. Baxter will Promote a Safe and Healthy Workplace	
2015 Goal	**2011 Progress**
Implement best-in-class programs designed to protect the safety and improve the health of employees that result in performance in the top three of industry peers.	Compared to 2010, Baxter improved its recordable case rate by 5% and its cases with days lost rate by 6%. However, the company's days lost rate rose by 20%. In 2011, Baxter launched a three-pronged approach to enhancing its safety culture and performance. In 2010, the most recent year data was available, Baxter's cases with days lost rate ranked third of industry peers.1 As part of the BeWell@Baxter strategy, the company offered free seasonal flu vaccinations to 98% of the global employee population during 2011.
2. Baxter will Promote an Inclusive and Diverse Workplace	
2015 Goal	**2011 Progress**
Create and sustain an inclusive culture where diverse ideas, backgrounds, experiences and perspectives are respected and valued.	All Baxter employees companywide completed training on how to contribute to an inclusive culture. Additionally, all employees were required to add an inclusion goal as part of their individual goals for the year. Also during the year, Baxter established two Business Resource Groups, "Building Women Leaders" and "Latinos@Baxter."
3. Baxter will Promote Ethical Conduct and Legal Compliance	
2015 Goal	**2011 Progress**
Continue to champion internal and industrywide ethical sales and marketing practices by:	In 2011, Baxter's major efforts in the United States focused on implementing a program to comply with the Physician Payment Sunshine Act. Outside the United States, Baxter enhanced its risk-based anticorruption education program by piloting an intensive anticorruption risk education session in the Asia Pacific region, in addition to the awareness and comprehensive training offered annually to employees who regularly interact with government officials and healthcare professionals.
• Implementing Baxter's enhanced U.S. Healthcare Compliance Program and International Anticorruption Program within the company	
• Working with U.S. and international trade associations, non-governmental organizations and governments to harmonize and enforce standards on financial interactions with healthcare providers that allow for appropriate education, research and dialogue on products and services and discourage improper incentives.	Baxter continued work with Eucomed and Advamed on a European approach to third-party anticorruption efforts, sharing Baxter's perspectives and helping to create a standard industry approach. Additionally, Baxter's China Ethics and Compliance team made progress with the China Association of Enterprises with Foreign Investment R&D-based Pharmaceutical Association Committee on advancing an industry-wide ethical sales and marketing code.

---

[52] World Commission on Environment and Development (1987). *Our Common Future*. Oxford: Oxford University Press. [The "Brundtland Report"].

Baxter Priority Sustainability and 2015 Goals – Operations & Products

4. Baxter will Drive a Sustainable Supply Chain

2015 Goal	2011 Progress
Reduce Baxter's U.S. car fleet greenhouse gas emissions per kilometer by 20% from 2007 baseline.	In 2011, Baxter's U.S. sales car fleet achieved a 4.1% reduction in greenhouse gas (GHG) emissions per kilometer driven compared to 2007.
Incorporate sustainable principles into Baxter's purchasing program with select 100 suppliers.	Baxter now embeds sustainability components into the purchasing, sourcing and supplier management process in nine countries, and conducted its third annual global supplier sustainability survey.

5. Baxter will Drive Reductions in its Carbon Footprint

2015 Goal	2011 Progress
Reduce greenhouse gas emissions 45% indexed to revenue from 2005 baseline.	In 2011, Baxter's net GHG emissions from operations equaled 717,800 metric tons carbon dioxide equivalent (CO2e), a 34% reduction compared to 2005 indexed to revenue, and an absolute decrease of 7%.
Increase facility energy usage of renewable power to 20% (of total).	In 2011, 19% of Baxter's energy use for operations was from renewable energy sources. Of this amount, 8% was from the use of biomass fuel and 11% was the renewable energy component of purchased electricity and RECs.

6. Baxter will Drive Reductions in its Natural Resource Use

2015 Goal	2011 Progress
Reduce energy usage 30% indexed to revenue from 2005 baseline.	In 2011, Baxter used 8,869 trillion joules of energy, a reduction of 24% compared to 2005, indexed to revenue, and an absolute increase of 7%.
Reduce water usage 35% indexed to revenue from 2005 baseline. To help achieve this, by 2010 evaluate potentially vulnerable watersheds associated with Baxter facilities and establish aggressive water conservation goals for high-risk areas.	In 2011, the company used 13.8 million cubic meters of water, a reduction of 33% compared to 2005, indexed to revenue, and an absolute decrease of 6%. Baxter's absolute water consumption increased by 4% from 2010 to 2011.
Implement two projects to help protect vulnerable watersheds or provide communities with enhanced access to clean water.	Baxter worked with two non-governmental organizations on proposals to protect watersheds and enhance sanitation in communities near manufacturing facilities located in water-stressed areas. The company expects to fund and implement both of these projects in 2012.

Baxter Priority Sustainability and 2015 Goals – Operations & Products

6. Baxter will Drive Reductions in its Natural Resource Use (Continued)

2015 Goal	2011 Progress
Reduce total waste generation 30% indexed to revenue from 2005 baseline.	In 2011, Baxter generated 70,700 metric tons of waste (including 65,000 metric tons non-hazardous and 5,700 metric tons regulated), a decrease of 11% compared to 2005, indexed to revenue, and an absolute increase of 26%. A product recall in the Europe, Middle East and Africa region resulted in approximately 9,400 metric tons of total waste in 2011, 13% of the 2011 global total. Excluding this waste, Baxter would have experienced a decrease of 23% compared to 2005, indexed to revenue, and an absolute increase of 9%.
Eliminate 5,000 metric tons of packaging material from products sent to customers from 2007 baseline.	Since the base year of 2007, Baxter has implemented projects that have reduced the amount of waste sent to customers by 4,300 metric tons, 86% of its goal.

7. Baxter will Drive Enhanced Product Stewardship

2015 Goal	2011 Progress
Further sustainable product design by identifying and minimizing life cycle impacts and proactively eliminating or minimizing known substances of concern in new products and packaging as feasible.	Baxter's XENIUM+ synthetic dialyzers became the second Baxter product to receive Carbon Footprint certification from the Carbon Trust. Baxter has continued the global marketing rollout of FLEXBUMIN [Albumin (Human)] – the first and only albumin in a flexible, plastic container – which is the world's first medical product to receive Carbon Footprint certification from the Carbon Trust (in 2009, re-certified in early 2012).
Identify new opportunities to replace, reduce and refine (3Rs) the use of animal testing.	Baxter is committed to enhancing animal welfare through the 3Rs — replacement, reduction and refinement. In 2011, Baxter further reduced the number of animals used in quality testing of certain biotherapeutic drugs and vaccines. The company also increased the amount of information collected per animal that reduced the number of animals necessary to fulfil specific regulatory requirements.

Baxter Priority Sustainability and 2015 Goals – World

8. Baxter will Strengthen Access to Healthcare through Product Development and Strategic Product Donations	
2015 Goal	**2011 Progress**
Create a new business model to improve access to healthcare for the "base of the pyramid" (developing economies).	Representatives from the organization Enterprise for a Sustainable World interviewed Baxter business leaders from around the world to understand where and how the company is currently selling products in regions with high "base of the pyramid"1 (BoP) representation or has technology well suited for use in the BoP. The company also began a review of its emerging technology portfolio.
Work with donor partners to develop and implement a strategic product donation plan beginning in 2010 that includes: being the first on the scene following disasters and tragedies, contributing most needed products to stabilize supply, and contributing most needed products in least developed and developing economies.	Baxter continued working with AmeriCares and Direct Relief International to pre-position products so they are available for emergencies as well as to meet ongoing needs in underserved communities. The company shipped products with long shelf lives to aid partners in the first and fourth quarters of 2011. These proactive strategic donations helped facilitate timely support to 75 countries.

9. Baxter will Strengthen the Company's Commitment to Education, Especially Math and Science	
2015 Goal	**2011 Progress**
Facilitate learning of math and science through biotechnology education for Chicago Public Schools teachers and students, and partner with other educational organizations to provide similar opportunities in other locations.	In the 2010-2011 school year, the Science@Work: Expanding Minds with Real-World Science program, a multi-year commitment to Chicago Public Schools, reached nearly 14,000 students and almost 150 teachers in 55 schools through the provision of in-depth biotechnology teacher training and module lesson plans (and a total of more than 45,000 students and 530 teachers in more than 150 schools since 2008). Baxter also contributed to several other educational initiatives during the year, in Chicago and in other locations.

Sustainability Awards and Recognition for Baxter Inc.

2012 – 250 Best Companies to Work for In Mexico - Great Places to Work Institute -Mexico

2012–2005 – Global 100 Most Sustainable Corporations in the World

2012–2007, 2005–2004, 2002–2000 – 100 Best Corporate Citizens - *Corporate Responsibility Magazine* (formerly Business Ethics Magazine)

2012–2011 – Maplecroft Climate Innovation Index US 100

2011–1999 – Dow Jones Sustainability Index (DJSI)

2011–2009 – First in the Healthcare Category of the Newsweek Green Rankings

2011 – Socially Responsible Company-Mexican Center for Philanthropy

2011 – AmCham Corporate Social Responsibility Award-Cartago, Costa Rica

2011 – Bloomberg-Vestas Global Corporate Renewable Energy

2010 – Chair's Award of Merit – United Way of Peel Region – Canada

2010 – Governor's Sustainability Award for Continuous Improvement - Illinois, United States

2010 – Recognition of Best Practices in Corporate Social Responsibility - Mexican Center for Philanthropy

2010 – Yangtze River Delta Pharmaceutical Corporate Social Responsibility Award - Shanghai, China

2009, 2007 – World's Most Ethical Companies – Ethisphere Council

2008 – Highly Commended (large business category) – Western Sydney Industry Awards Excellence in Business Practice -Toongabbie, New South Wales, Australia

2008 – Platinum Award for Innovative Approaches to Environmental Stewardship and Sustainability in Healthcare – Building Common Ground Conference – Burlington, Ontario, Canada

2007 – First Annual Corporate Citizen Award for Environmental Sustainability –
League of Women Voters of Illinois
(http://www.baxter.com/about_baxter/company_profile/awards_and_honors.
html)

Coca-Cola: Quenching More Than Thirst Around the World[53]

"When the well's dry, we know the worth of water." Benjamin Franklin
"By means of water, we give life to everything." The Koran

The Coca-Cola Company is the largest beverage manufacturer in the world, selling
1.7 billion servings a day of its beverages in 200 countries. The 126 year-old company
had 2012 revenues of $48 billion and operating income of $10.8 billion.[54] The only
places that Coke is not sold are North Korea, Cuba, and Myanmar.[55] For 13 years in
a row, Interbrand has named Coca-Cola the most valuable brand in the world.[56]

On average each liter of product produced by the company requires 2.26 l of
water, representing a 16 % decrease in its incremental water usage since 2004[57];
however, the story is much more complicated than this. What is clear is that without
water, Coca-Cola is out of business. Not only is water needed to produce every one
of its 3,500 products, but Coke's bottling plants also need a social license to use
local water to produce their products.

Despite its global reach, in 2002 Coca-Cola's use of water began to be questioned,
a challenge that was initiated in India. Coca-Cola's problems in India involved accusations regarding pesticides, the drainage of aquifers, pollution, and distribution of
toxic waste thought to be fertilizer,[58] but historical context is important. Coke originally went to India in 1958, but several major global companies, including IBM and
Coke, left during the 1970s during a pushback on multinationals in which India
required major ownership by native Indian investors, and asked companies to divulge
their patented secrets. In the case of IBM, it was unwilling to divulge its software
source codes and Coke was unwilling to share its secret formula. So the companies
left until the 1990s when a new government, as well as the World Trade Organization

---

[53] This case was prepared by Pauline J. Albert, St. Edward's University.

[54] The Coca-Cola Company, "2012 Year in Review," (Atlanta, GA2013).

[55] Neville Isdell and David Beasley. 2011. *Inside Coca-Cola: A CEO's life story of building the world's most popular brand*. New York: St. Martin's Griffin.

[56] Interbrand, "Best Global Brands 2012: Interbrand Releases 13th Annual Global Brands Report," Interbrand, http://www.interbrand.com/en/news-room/press-releases/2012-10-02-7543da7.aspx.

[57] The Coca-Cola Company, "The Water Stewardship and Replenish Report," (Atlanta, GA2012).

[58] Hills, Jonathan and Richard Welford. 2005. Case study: Coca-Cola and water in India. *Social Responsibility and Environmental Management* 12.

and International Monetary Funds were encouraging globalization.[59] Coke returned somewhat later than Pepsi and as Exhibit 1 illustrates, colas in general are not big sellers in India. People drink tea, coconut water, and yoghurt-based lassi. In his memoir, former CEO and chairman, Neville Isdell, who was in charge of re-opening India in the 1990s, claims that Coke did not turn a profit in the country until 2009. He reported that Coke bought the largest local soft drink company, Thums Up in 1993 and it also used local franchise bottlers. By 2005 the company had invested around $1 billion, making it one of India's largest foreign investors, with 7,000 employees, 27 wholly owned bottling plants, 17 franchise plants, supplying approximately 700,000 retail outlets across India. Coke claimed that another 125,000 jobs had been created through its supplier and distribution networks.[60]

But between 2002 and 2007, Coca-Cola encountered major problems, first in Mehdiganj, a village in the state of Uttar Pradesh near the city of Varanasi in southeast India. Varanasi is considered one of India's holiest cities. The bottling plant, Hindustan Coca-Cola Beverages, was granted the right to operate in 1999. By 2002, farmers were complaining that the water table was seriously depleted, and the local Lok Samiti, which is the "people's committee," began to complain to local magistrates. These local committees are typical in Indian villages and are formed based on the Gandhian philosophy of village democracy. The initial complaints were tied to sludge from the factory that was impacting the quality of a stream, with animals getting sick. That problem arose due to road construction in which a sewage pipe had been damaged, but problems with cows dying and drought continued.[61] The pesticide accusations involved both Pepsi and Coke, and after battling reports between multiple global organizations, the issues appeared tied to an endemic issue of pesticides in many Indian products, as the country has been one of the largest consumers of chemical products.[62] Ray Rogers, a social activist, joined forces with Amit Srivastava, an American born of Indian parents who has become a professional activist against large multinationals, and they together spearheaded a series of U.S. university student boycotts. For almost 5 years, there were numerous allegations, protests, and hunger strikes at Indian bottling plants, as well as boycotts on college campuses from Michigan to Manchester, UK. During certain periods between 2002 and 2007 many Indian plants were closed, and the company lost its social license to operate in certain states of India.[63]

[59] Blanding, Michael. 2010. *The Coke machine: The dirty truth behind the world's favorite soft drink*. New York: Avery; Isdell and Beasley. *Inside Coca-Cola: A CEO's life story of building the world's most popular brand*.

[60] Hills and Welford. *Case study: Coca-Cola and water in India*.

[61] Ibid.

[62] Burnett, Margaret and Richard Welford. 2007. Case study: Coca-Cola and water in India: Episode 2. *Corporate Social Responsibility and Environmental Management* 14.

[63] Harish, R. and Bharathi S. Gopal. 2008. Coca-Cola in India: A responsible corporate citizen? *ICFAI Journal of Corporate Governance* 7(4).

In some respects, Coke was targeted because of its size, as illustrated by the fact that local beer brewers who use more water than Coca-Cola were not attacked.[64] In early 2004, Coke lost its license to operate in Plachimada, Kerala, one of India's most prosperous states on the country's southwest coastline. The plant was re-opened and then closed as the complaints moved through the Indian court system. By the end of 2012 indications were that the plant remained closed, and there was a bill demanding that Coke pay damages to local villages that had been awaiting the signature of India's president since 2011.[65]

125 Years of Selling Fizzy Water

In 1886, John Pemberton, a patent medicine doctor wanted to create a good tasting, effective "nerve tonic" for a troubled time, America's Gilded Age. Though Coca-Cola's official history denies it, the product initially had a nice kick of coca, also known as cocaine, which contributed to its positive effect of making people feel better; less nervous, or neurotic.[66] People began to add fizzy (soda) water to the syrup creating fountain drinks that became quite popular. Pemberton was convinced that the coca was an excellent antidote to morphine to which he and many other ordinary people were addicted. Even putting this jaded past aside, a Coca-Cola historian describes the Coca-Cola Company as "emblematic of the best and worst of America and Western Civilization."[67] The company has come a long way since its patent medicine years and while emblematic of all that is American, today only 44 % of its revenues are generated in North America, and the remaining 56 % are international[68] making Coca-Cola a global corporation. The company's Turkish-born CEO and chairman, Muhtar Kent, predicts that in the not too distant future, China will be its largest market.[69] Kent's Vision 2020 includes a goal to double the company's revenues between 2010 and 2020.[70]

---

[64]Burnett and Welford. *Case study: Coca-Cola and water in India: Episode 2.*

[65]Shalya, Chinmayi. 2012. Plachimada villagers still await President's nod. *The Times of India*, September 8 2012.

[66]Pendergrast, Mark. 1993. *For God, Country and Coca-Cola: The unauthorized history of the great American soft drink and the company that makes it.* New York: Charles Scribners.

[67]Ibid., 11.

[68]Examining the historical trends, 44 % is a little deceiving, as the prior year of 2010, North American sales were only 32 % of global sales, making Coke's international business about 70 % of total sales. The 2010 increase in revenues from the Americas was tied to the company's acquisition of Coca-Cola Enterprises' North American bottling and distribution operations The Coca-Cola Company, "2011 Form 10-K Annual Report," (Atlanta, GA2012).

[69]Sellers, Patricia. 2012. Muhtar Kent's new coke, *Fortune* 165, no. 7 May 21. http://postcards.blogs.fortune.cnn.com/2012/05/10/500-coca-cola-muhtar-kent/?iid.

[70]Kent, Muhtar. 2011. Shaking things up at Coca-Cola: The HBR interview with Coca-Cola CEO Muhtar Kent. *Harvard Business Review*, October 2011; The Coca-Cola Company. 2012. *Passionately refreshing a thirsty world: 2011 annual review.* Atlanta, GA: The Coca-Cola Company.

The Coca-Cola Company's product beverage portfolio is dramatically different than it was only 10 years ago, and it is changing annually. Through the twentieth century, Coca-Cola's focus was primarily carbonated beverages. It had a few other products, such as Minute Maid, acquired in 1960[71] and it began selling Dasani water in 1999, which was largely a response to Pepsi doing so.[72] Throughout the years, there were other products than classic Coca-Cola, but most were soft drinks under the Coke label (e.g., Sprite and Fanta). Through the entire twentieth century, the company's focus was getting people to drink more Coke, and the cola wars of the 1980s and 1990s between Coke and Pepsi are infamous in corporate American history.[73] The work of increasing annual "per caps" (the number of Cokes consumed per-capita, or by every man, woman and child) was almost maniacal. Robert W. Woodruff who for 64 years (1923–1987) guided the company stated that he wanted Coke "within an arm's reach of desire," and a later president and chairman, Doug Ivester supported concepts like "a 360° landscape of Coke."[74] The goal was to have people drink Coke at breakfast, lunch, and dinner and also in between meals; after all, revenue growth depended upon it.

In the early 1980s, shortly before his death, Robert Woodruff had handpicked an unusual successor, as Coke's chairmen had long been white, American males. Robert Goizueta was a Cuban-born American with tremendous flair and charisma. His family had fled Cuba during the rise of Castro, and he was intelligent, highly driven, and charming. Goizueta brought tremendous energy and the drive of an immigrant to the job. Coke prospered during his reign from 1980 to his untimely death from lung cancer in 1997 (he was an infamous chain smoker). During the 18 years that he ran the company, its stock market value increased by 3,500 %, from $4.3 billion in 1981 to $180 billion in 1997, and sales climbed from $4 to $18 billion.[75] Goizueta was beloved by Coke enthusiasts because of the company's growth and overall success during his tenure. Other events under his leadership include the decision to move to less expensive high-fructose corn syrup instead of sugar in 1980/1981, the introduction of Diet Coke with artificial sweeteners in 1982, and he was the father of the less-than-successful introduction of New Coke in 1985. Overall, Goizueta was considered highly successful and he was admired as one of America's most successful executives of the 1990s. Like Robert Woodruff, Goizueta was personally philanthropic, though he always tried to make even his personal donations about building the Coke brand.[76] His heritage, charismatic personality,

---

[71] Pendergrast, *For God, Country and Coca-Cola: The unauthorized history of the Great American soft drink and the company that makes it.*

[72] Hays, Constance L. 2004. *The real thing: Truth and power at the Coca-Cola company.* New York: Random House.

[73] Enrico, Roger and Jesse Kornbluth. 1986. *The other guy blinked: How Pepsi won the Cola wars.* New York: Bantam ; Hays, *The real thing: Truth and power at the Coca-Cola company.*

[74] *The real thing: Truth and power at the Coca-Cola company 7.*

[75] Greising, David. 1998. *I'd like the world to buy a coke: The life and leadership of Roberto Goizueta.* New York: John Wiley, xvii.

[76] Ibid.

people orientation, philosophical worldview, and most likely his mistake with New Coke made him sensitive to the importance of listening to customers.

The 10 years following Goizueta's death were not easy ones for Coca-Cola. Muhtar Kent became president and COO in 2007 and chairman in 2009. He is the fourth person in that role since Goizueta's death in late 1997 (See Exhibit 2), and over that ten-year period a lot happened on the global front. Marketing head Minnick, and chairmen Daft, Isdell, and now Kent have done a lot to begin an expansion of the company's product portfolio buying other drink brands both in the U.S. and internationally. In the early part of the twenty-first century, then marketing vice-president, Mary Minnick received a lot of pushback from her colleagues for trying to expand the company's product portfolio, as many of the company's executives considered any other drink as competing with the company's flagship product. She felt strongly that selling a broader variety of drink products was key to long-term growth, especially in international markets. Minnick had grown up at Coke, joining the company after completing her MBA at Duke in 1983. In the 1980s, when she pushed for Coke to add other products such as sports drinks, she received nothing but accusations of being too pushy, so she got shipped abroad where she learned with even greater certainty that alternative drinks were key to long-term growth. She expanded the company's product lines first as head of the South Pacific Group, and then in Japan. Coke Chairman E. Neville Isdell, brought her back to headquarters in 2005 to implement her product expansion strategy more broadly across the world, and she was initially given a lot of freedom. She added product lines such as coffee and tea drinks to expand the company's market to a broader consumer base.[77] She was not in her position long however, and left Coke 2 years later after being passed over for the chief operating officer position.[78] Isdell confirms in his memoire that Minnick was in competition with Muhtar Kent for the top job, and that he selected Kent due to his superior experience as a general manager.[79]

Between Goizueta's and Kent's reins as company chairmen, there were several major corporate crises including the largest ever racial discrimination suit settlement payment in American history totaling over $156 million,[80] and reduction of about 20 % of the company's global workforce in layoffs that occurred in 2000 and 2003.[81] In 1999, a major Coke and Fanta product recall in France,

---

[77] Foust, Dean. "Queen of Pop," *Business Week*, August 7 2006.

[78] Rayasam, Renuka. "The Pause That Refreshes," *USNews & World Report*, no. May 20 (2007), http://www.usnews.com/usnews/biztech/articles/070520/28eespotlight.htm.

[79] Isdell and Beasley, *Inside Coca-Cola: A Ceo's life story of building the World's most popular brand*.

[80] Winter, Greg. 2000. Coca-Cola settles racial bias case. *The New York Times*. http://www.nytimes.com/2000/11/17/business/coca-cola-settles-racial-bias-case.html?pagewanted=all&src=pm.

[81] Day, Sherry. 2003. *Coca-Cola to lay off 1,000 employees in North America*, ibid.(2003), http://www.nytimes.com/2003/01/31/business/company-news-coca-cola-to-lay-off-1000-employees-in-north-america.html; Constance L. Hays. 2006. *Learning to think smaller at Coke*. ibid., no. February 6 (2000), http://www.nytimes.com/2000/02/06/business/learning-to-think-smaller-at-coke.html?pagewanted=print&src=pm.

Belgium, and Luxembourg,[82] and then another recall of 500,000 cases in 2003 when Dasani water was launched in Britain[83] cost the company both money and reputation.

Water: The Miracle Elixir

- Can you imagine being a young mother and having to walk 11 miles each day to fetch your family's daily water supply.
- Can you imagine living in Delhi and turning on the water tap, but nothing comes out. There is no water, and you are not sure when there will be.

While the United Nations has met its Millennium Goal of halving the number of people who live without sustainable water, there remain 783 million people without adequate access to clean drinking water, and about 2.5 billion without sanitation facilities. The result is that 3,000 children die each day from diarrheal diseases.[84] Clean water and sanitation were not explicitly called out by the United Nations as a "human right" until 2002[85] though the 1948 United Nations Universal Declaration of Human Rights could be interpreted as including them. Might the availability of water and sanitation be critical enabling factors for improving the lives of the 40% of the world's population (2.7 billion people) who live on less than $2.50 per day?[86]

Scientists often refer to the earth as the *water planet*, because like humans our planet is 70 % water. Water is the elixir that makes life possible. It is a finite resource and only 2.5 % of the available water is fresh and almost 70 % of that fresh water is frozen. While finite, it is re-useable over and over again and most scientists agree that with proper management, we can meet everyone's needs.[87] However, based on

[82] "Recall to Cost Coke Bottler $103 Million," *The New York Times*, no. July 13 (1999), http://www.nytimes.com/1999/07/13/business/recall-to-cost-coke-bottler-103-million.html.

[83] Cowell, Alan. 2004. *Coke recalls bottled water newly introduced in Britain*. ibid., no. March 20 (2004), http://www.nytimes.com/2004/03/20/business/20water.html.

[84] World Health Organization and UNICEF. 2012. *Millennium development goal drinking water target met; Sanitation target still lagging far behind*. Press release, no. March 6 (2012), http://www.wssinfo.org/fileadmin/user_upload/resources/Press-Release-English.pdf.

[85] In November 2002, General Comment No. 15 was adopted by the United Nation's Committee on Economic, Social and Cultural Rights and it states that water is an "indispensable prerequisite" for the achievement of other human rights and that this right "entitles everyone to sufficient, safe, acceptable, physically accessible and affordable water for personal and domestic uses." Then, on July 28, 2010, Resolution 64/292 by the United Nations General Assembly states that water and sanitation are acknowledged as required for the realization of all human rights United Nations, "The Human Right to Water and Sanitation," United Nations, http://www.un.org/waterforlifede-cade/human_right_to_water.shtml.

[86] Kristof, Nicholas D. and Sheryl WuDunn. *Half the Sky*, Kindle ed. (New York: Alfred Knopf, 2009).

[87] Black, Maggie and Jannet King. 2009. *The Atlas of water: Mapping the World's most critical resource*, 2nd edn. Berkeley, CA: University of California Press. Reference; Steven Solomon. 2010. *Water: The epic struggle for wealth, power, and civilization*, Kindle ed. New York: HarperCollins, e-Book.

current population growth projections (from 7 to 9 billion people by 2045[88]) and food requirements to sustain that population, scientists predict a 40 % gap between supply and demand by 2030. This shortfall holds the potential of creating a worsening water security crisis that could trigger a crisis in food supplies worldwide.[89] The curious thing is that the shortage is not about a reduction of total supply, but rather the amount of fresh water that lands as rain where people live and need it.[90]

Water has influenced the rise and fall of civilizations, and beginning 5000 years ago, the agricultural revolution in ancient societies such as Egypt and China emerged due to new hydraulic systems for controlling large rivers and creating irrigation systems. Ancient Rome's building of aqueducts supported the development of a new urban civilization. Medieval China's 1,100-mile-long Grand Canal created a major highway between its southern and northern rivers to support crops and the movement of goods. The invention of the steam engine using water as its fuel is largely responsible for the nineteenth century emergence of the Industrial Revolution that began in England and moved to America. Just 100 years ago, American cities began separating sewage from clean water and by 1936, filtration and chlorination systems had resulted in reducing infant mortality rates by half, and U.S. life expectancy rose from 47 to 63 years. The last 100 years has also seen America enjoying abundant water supplies resulting in its citizens becoming somewhat water illiterate. Increasing populations and climate change are creating water scarcity in certain parts of America and globally that will force a change in attitudes.[91]

In poor and dryer countries the number of children dying daily due to lack of water is equal to all the elementary school children in the state of Florida.[92] Major aspects of the conflict in the Middle East's Gaza Strip revolve around access to water,[93] and the largest number of people without clean water can be found in Sub-Saharan Africa.[94] Over the last five years, India has enjoyed GDP growth of between 5 %and 9 % per year, yet not one major city provides 24-h-per-day access to water. The tens of millions of residents living in new high-tech cities such as Bangalore and Mumbai, and the capital Delhi, have water available to them for only 1 or 2 hours per day.[95]

There are 23 United Nations agencies working water and sanitation issues, as it is endemic to all eight of the 2015 Millennium Goals (see Exhibit 3). While progress

---

[88]Worldometers, "Current World Population," http://www.worldometers.info/world-population/.

[89]The Water Resources Group. 2012. *The water resources group: Background, impact and the way forward*. Davos-Klosters, Switzerland: The World Economic Forum 2012.

[90]Black and King, *The Atlas of water: Mapping the World's most critical resource*.

[91]Fishman, Charles. 2011. *The big thirst: The secret life and turbulent future of water*, Kindle ed. New York: Free Press.

[92]Ibid.

[93]Asser, Martin. "Obstacles to Arab-Israeli Peace: Water," *BBC News*(2010), http://www.bbc.co.uk/news/world-middle-east-11101797.

[94]Watkins, Kevin. 2006. *Human development report 2006: Beyond scarcity: Power, poverty and the global water crisis*. New York: United Nations Human Development Programme (UNDP).

[95]Fishman, *The big thirst: The secret life and turbulent future of water*.

has been made toward all of the goals, they are far from completed. Similar goals were set during the 1970s and 1980s, and they were never met. Thus, some might ask why even try? Yet, in addition to there being social justice reasons for alleviating poverty through supporting people's access to basic human needs, such as water and sanitation, there are a plethora of good business reasons for participating in the achievement of the Millennium Goals. The United Nation's takes a strong stance that the root of the water crisis in poor countries is not that there is not enough water available to meet everyone's basic needs. The underlying causes are poverty, unequal power, and poor water management.[96] People need clean water to maintain their health, wellbeing, and basic dignity. Water is equally important for supporting healthy livelihoods. The UN states that problems are heavily political and institutional noting that in the high-income districts of cities in Asia, Latin-America, and Sub-Saharan Africa, the wealthy have access to hundreds of liters of water per day, while people in the slums and low-income areas in these same cities are barely surviving on 20 l or less per day. While difficult to estimate the costs and benefits, the UN notes that the water and sanitation Millennium Development Goals could be met with a $10 billion investment, which is substantially less than even these poor countries spend on their military. About a million children's lives would be saved over the next decade, and 272 million days would be gained in school attendance, while the economic benefits would be about $38 billion in increased gross domestic product (GDP). Thus, there are good economic reasons for solving these problems.[97] However, there are deep political and cultural barriers at play as well.

> In short, scarcity is manufactured through political processes and institutions that disadvantage the poor. When it comes to clean water, the pattern in many countries is that the poor get less, pay more and bear the brunt of the human development costs associated with scarcity.[98]

"Connected Capitalism" and the "Golden Triangle"

When Goizueta passed away in 1997, Coke's market value was twice as large as Pepsi, by 2005 it was just about equal.[99] Neville Isdell is perhaps the person who should receive the primary credit for initially turning the company around. Recalled from retirement, Isdell was born in Northern Ireland, but spent a significant amount of his childhood in Zambia. He began working for Coke in Johannesburg in 1972, and had retired in 2001 from Coke's European bottler. Isdell had successfully opened new markets in Africa, the Philippines, Australia, and Eastern Europe during his career with the company. His memoir[100] describes why he returned to Coke

---

[96] Watkins, "UNDP 2006 Report."

[97] Ibid.

[98] Ibid., 3.

[99] Foust, "Queen of Pop."

[100] Isdell and Beasley, *Inside Coca-Cola: A CEO's life story of building the World's most popular brand.*

in 2004, his efforts to bring on new leadership, and the development of a new corporate strategy. Morale was low when he came onboard. He brought together 150 of the company's most senior leaders for a meeting in London, out of which came a new Manifesto for Growth along with a new set of five operating principles or values (see Exhibit 4). Isdell also writes about a concept he calls "Connected Capitalism"[101] describing the linkages between a company and its stakeholders.

> My vision for Connected Capitalism advocates going much further [than Corporate Responsibility] to create a melding, a true marriage between government, nonprofit, and global corporations to fight disease and poverty, heal the planet, improve education, and ultimately, boost private sector profit. ... [Connected Capitalism] is the creation of the Socially Responsible Corporation, which examines the company's actual footprint on society and focuses on how; as part of a core business strategy, it can reduce the negative impact.[102]

Coke's former chairman wrote explicitly about the importance of corporations as good caretakers of natural resources. "A clear example is that neither Coca-Cola nor its communities where it operates can survive for long without adequate water. Their destinies are directly linked." He espoused the value of capitalism and the "triangle of sustainability – business, nonprofits, and government" and a "system that involves profit for everyone in the chain."[103]

These concepts are aligned with the "triple bottom line" acronym first espoused in the late 1990s.[104] Over the last 15 years, Elkington's ideas have become known as the sustainability revolution encompassing the three Ps (People, Profit and Planet).[105] Elkington's original premise was that sustainability involved focusing on economic priorities, environmental quality, and social justice. He was not shy about stating, "To refuse the challenge implied by the triple bottom line is to risk extinction,"[106] and in Coke's case it is true that without water it is out of business.

Isdell claimed that the most important decision he made during his 5-year tenure as Coke's chairman was his re-hiring of Muhtar Kent.[107] Today, Kent has embraced and expanded the 2004 Manifesto for Growth, and in 2010 he launched Vision 2020 (see Exhibit 4). He is building a different kind of Coca-Cola Company, and while he is promising investor growth, he is planning to achieve it differently than merely getting people in developed countries to drink more soda. The company will grow

---

[101] Ibid., 213–41.

[102] Ibid., 219.

[103] Ibid., 219, 20, 21.

[104] Elkington, John. 1997/1999. *Cannibals with forks: The triple bottom line of 21st century business.* Oxford, UK: Capstone.

[105] Edwards, Andres R.. 2005. *The sustainability revolution: Portrait of a paradigm shift.* Gabriola, Canada: New Society.

[106] Elkington, *Cannibals with Forks: The triple bottom line of 21st century business,* 2.

[107] Isdell and Beasley, *Inside Coca-Cola: A CEO's life story of building the World's most popular brand,* 170.

by both adding to its portfolio of drink products through brand extensions and acquisitions, and unlike the old path of simply fighting for market share, it is engaged with growing the market for its products in developing and emerging countries. Kent has adopted Idsell's notion of "Connected Capitalism" and refers to it now as the "Golden Triangle" that includes business, government and society working together to solve some of the world's biggest problems.[108] The Coca-Cola Vision 2020 goals reflect a focus on serving all stakeholders. Kent is credited with having "redefined Coke's culture and replaced 70 % of its senior managers"[109] between his ascension as CEO in July 2008 and mid 2010. He has been aggressively outspoken about the company's success being intertwined with the health and success of the communities in which it does business. With respect to its environmental sustainability goals, the company is involved in a broad spectrum of partnerships in which it is committed to sharing its best-known methods and learning from others.

> At the Coca-Cola Company, we are transforming the way we think and act about water stewardship. It is in the long-term interest of both our business and the communities where we operate to be good stewards of our most critical shared resource, water.[110]

The nexus between climate change, water, and food supplies has spawned the creation of a public-private-civil society partnership whose aim is to identify sustainable, best practices for corporations to conduct business, and work together to support governments in addressing their water management needs. The Water Resources Group emerged out of the 2010 World Economic Forum and the chairpersons of Nestlé, Pepsi, and Coca-Cola were instrumental in its formation. It is a partnership between the World Bank Group (orchestrated by its International Finance Corporation (IFC)) and the World Economic Forum, an organization whose mission is to support government, business, and civil society working together on global issues. Solving the water and sanitation issues of the emerging development world is simply good business. Experts at McKinsey & Company[111] describe the business quest in emerging markets as a "$30 trillion decathlon," (from report title) based on half of the world's population joining the ranks of consumers by 2025. Thus for most global corporations, and Coke especially, future growth is dependent on supporting these new customers. Some may call these efforts exploitation, others will call it good business. Coca-Cola calls its efforts in water conservation both good business and part of its goal of doubling sales by 2020, while providing "moments of happiness" around the world.[112]

---

[108] Kent, Muhtar. "The Golden Triangle: Spearheading Change the Smart Way," Coca-Cola Company, http://www.coca-colacompany.com/opinions/muhtar-kent-on-the-golden-triangle.

[109] Sellers, "Muhtar Kent's New Coke". para. 2.

[110] The Coca-Cola Company, "The Water Stewardship and Replenish Report," 1.

[111] Yuval Atsmon et al. 2012. *Winning the $30 trillion decathlon*. New York: McKinsey Quarterly.

[112] The Coca-Cola Company, "Passionately refreshing a thirsty World: 2011 annual review" 13.

Coca-Cola's Water Stewardship Programs

In an interview with Charlie Rose, Muhtar Kent speaks with enthusiasm about how he and inventor Dean Kamen are working together to provide clean drinking water for people who currently lack it.[113] Ten long years ago, Kamen, inventor of the Segway, the insulin pump, and other innovations, invented a device that uses a "vapor compression distillation system"[114] to clean any kind of water. About the size of a dorm room refrigerator the Slingshot's name is based on the Biblical story of David and Goliath, in which the small shepherd defeats the giant. As Kamen describes his metaphor, he enthusiastically quips, "The Goliath of the twenty-first century for millions of people is bad water, and those little villages need a slingshot to deal with that goliath. The twenty-first century slingshot is right here."[115] Kamen once drank his own urine while demonstrating the product at a conference.[116] His 200-employee company, DEKA Research and Development, spent 3 years developing the product and touted prototypes to foundations, companies, and non-government organizations, including the United Nations, in an attempt to get them to fund the broader mass production of the Slingshot.

The small pre-production model could generate 10 gal of clean water an hour while using less than a single kilowatt of electricity. It could use any source of power, from solar to cow dung to run its engine that used less power than a handheld blow dryer. While invented over 10 years ago, featured on "60 Minutes II" in 2003, and supported further in 2006 by Bono of U2 fame along with Angelina Jolie, the product had little hope of going into large production until recently.[117] Kamen suspected that the world's biggest beverage manufacture might be able to help him, but he was deliberate and strategic about getting in the door. In 2003, he convinced Coke to become a sponsor for FIRST, a program that gets kids involved in science and technology. Then, in 2005, the head of Coke's research lab, Nilang Patel, invited Kamen to work with him on developing a new soda fountain. Adapting technology invented to support chemotherapy, Kamen's company came up with a product that Coke branded its Freestyle fountain dispenser. The new machine could combine small amounts of syrup and soda offering consumers up to a 100 different permutations for their soft drink. Coke claims that the Freestyle has been a big success, but perhaps more importantly, it opened the door for the Slingshot. Kamen explains his quest for a partner, "We realized the NGOs aren't the ones who can help us get the

---

[113] Rose, Charlie. 2012. *Muhtar Kent, Ceo of the Coca Cola company on the global water crisis.*

[114] Geller, Martinne. 2012. Coke, Segway inventor team up on clean water project, *Reuters*, September 25 http://www.reuters.com/article/2012/09/25/us-cocacola-water-idUSBRE88O0W 120120925, para 8.

[115] Solomon, Dave. 2012. Dean Kamen's Slingshot heard 'Round the World," *New Hampshire Union Leader*, October 6 (2012), http://www.unionleader.com/article/20121007/NEWS02/71007 9913&source=RSS, para 8.

[116] Pearson, Ryan. 2005. "Segway inventor drinks his own pee (Really)," *The Orange County Register*, December 15, http://www.ocregister.com/articles/water-4371-really-people.html.

[117] Solomon, "Dean Kamen's Slingshot heard Round the World."

machine into production, scale it up, bring down the cost curve[118]. Coke is "committing millions to the development, production and deployment of the Slingshot machines in what it calls a long-term global clean water partnership."[119] The Inter-American Development Bank (IDB) and Africare, which support development projects in Latin America, the Caribbean, and Africa, are also signed up as partners. Coke's expertise will include funding and logistics. In 2011, Coke and DEKA conducted field trials of the product in five schools in Ghana providing 1,500 schoolchildren with over 140,000 l of water in a six-month period.[120] In 2012, about 30 machines were deployed to rural schools, clinics, and community centers in South Africa, Mexico, and Paraguay. Further commercializing the Slingshot will cost Coke millions of dollars, and Kent states that he will support "whatever funds are necessary" to make the project a success.[121]

Coke began measuring its water use in 2002, but in 2010 it made a significant commitment to "safely return to nature and to communities an amount of water equivalent to what we use in all our beverages and their production by 2020."[122] Coke's program involves reducing its own water use, recycling the water it uses in its bottling plants, and replenishing the water used in its finished products through supporting local water projects.

Our strategic intent is to link water stewardship to business growth by:

- Balancing global production volume with locally relevant water projects that deliver benefits equal to production volume
- Protecting reputation, brand, manufacturing capacity, and product quality and safety
- Advancing the awareness and practice of water conservation and science.[123]

Reduction programs aim to improve water efficiency of all bottling plants by 20 % by 2012, based on a 2004 base year. In 2004 the company used 2.7 l of water for every liter of product produced and it projected that by the end of 2012, it would be using only 2.16 l. Its most recent publication on the topic states that at the end of 2010 its water usage was down to 2.26 l per liter of product produced.[124] The *recycling* goal is that 100 % of its plants will treat and return water to the local environment, feeding watersheds and other downstream uses. The company's *replenish* efforts include the support of a wide variety of conservation projects, such as watershed protection, providing community's with drinking water (such as those that will

---

[118]Scanlon, Jessie. 2009. Dean Kamen reinvents Coke's soda fountain. *Bloomberg Businessweek*, no. October 9. http://www.businessweek.com/innovate/content/oct2009/id2009107_810817. htm, para. 14.

[119]Solomon, "Dean Kamen's Slingshot Heard 'Round the World". para. 13.

[120]Ibid.

[121]Geller, "Coke, Segway Inventor Team up on Clean Water Project," para. 9.

[122]The Coca-Cola Company, "The Water Stewardship and Replenish Report," 9.

[123]Ibid., 5.

[124]Ibid.

be made possible by the Slingshot), and supporting sanitation projects. Coke states that it is committed to assessing the vulnerability of both the quality and quantity of water sources for each of its bottling plants. Local bottling plants are its biggest sources of vulnerability, as demonstrated by issues in India. The company states that 100% of its bottlers have committed to its water usage sustainability standards; 95 % of their volume is currently included in the company's water risk assessment reporting; 70 % of the plants are in full compliance with its water resource sustainability standard; and 40 % are currently implementing source water protection programs.[125]

Coke is cognizant that there is still work to be done, giving itself only a grade of "B" in its 2010/2011 GRI Report. A "+" is added to the grade based on GRI's audit and endorsement of the company's self-assessment. Based in the Netherlands, GRI stands for Global Reporting Initiative, and the organization provides a framework for companies to examine their economic, environmental, and social sustainability.[126] Ceres, a Boston-based sustainability initiative, was founded shortly after the 1989, Exxon-Valdez spill, and its vision is for business and the capital markets to work with society to promote protection of the environment.[127] It also publishes standards that are more focused on corporate environmental impact. In early 2013, it unveiled an extensive report in which 600 large U.S.-based companies were assessed against Ceres' 2020 roadmap for sustainability. The report outlined that many companies have barely gotten started, but Coke in particular was commended for its on-the-ground efforts in developing nations.[128]

Working Through Partnerships

Coke's programs involve partnerships with local and national governments, non-government organizations (NGOs), and experts in water conservation. Coke outlines 386 different community water partnership (CWP) projects aimed at water replenishment. They fall into four major categories that include providing water access and sanitation, watershed protection, environmental projects that promote or improve water sustainability, and education and awareness programs. The programs involve global NGOs such as CARE, the Nature Conservancy, the World Wildlife Fund (WWF), numerous local NGOs, local governments, and schools throughout the 200 countries in which it does business.[129] Organizations that previously might

---

[125] Ibid.

[126] Global Reporting Initiative (GRI), "About GRI," https://www.globalreporting.org/Information/about-gri/Pages/default.aspx.

[127] Ceres, "Ceres in Brief," (Boston: Ceres, n.d.).

[128] "The Road to 2020: Corporate Progress on the Ceres Roadmap for Sustainability," Ceres and Sustainalytics, http://www.ceres.org/roadmap-assessment.

[129] The Coca-Cola Company. 2012. The water stewardship and replenish report," (2011); "The Water Stewardship and Replenish Report," (2012).

have been involved in criticizing Coke are now in partnership with the company, and praising its efforts. The President and CEO of World Wildlife Fund, Carter Roberts, states, "Our partnership with Coca-Cola has set the gold standard for sustainability commitments, with a specific focus on water.[130] The numerous programs with the WWF focus on five major goals that relate to water conservation in the world's seven most important water basins; improvement of water efficiency throughout the Coca-Cola system; reduction of the company's water emissions; promotion of sustainable agriculture; and promotion of water conservation around the globe.[131]

Coke has taken the additional step of trying to determine how much water is needed to produce the ingredients supplied by others for its products, for example the oranges used to make its juice products. The science of "water foot printing, also known as the measurement of "virtual water" is in its infancy (see Exhibit 5 for the nuanced definitions used in water footprinting). Agriculture uses 70 % of the world's useable water. Water foot printing involves measuring how much water is used to produce agricultural products such as oranges or beef. For example, estimates are that producing one kilogram of beef requires 15,000 l of water, and the equivalent amount of cheese requires 5,000.[132] The science is new and controversial. Some experts state that it is inaccurate or at best misleading because the water used to grow rice is not lost altogether as it "is completely recovered back into the ground, or the atmosphere, or back into the river into which the farm runoff flows."[133] In 2010, Coke and the Nature Conservancy engaged in an extensive water footprint assessment whose results were made available to the public and to the industry. The project assessed the water consumption for three products: a half liter plastic PET bottle produced by Coca-Cola Enterprises in the Netherlands; beet sugar supplied to Coke bottlers in Europe; and Minute Maid and Simply Orange juice produced for the North American market. The study noted that the agricultural products require far more water than manufacturing; acknowledging that local water constraints must be evaluated when agricultural decisions are made. In other words, no matter how much Coca-Cola does to sustain and replenish water, bottling plants must work with local governments and ensure that they are all using water responsibly. It also means that Coke needs to engage more extensively with suppliers, governments, and other stakeholders in its supply chain. The study revealed many interesting findings. For example, sugar beets from Greece require almost three times as much water from those produced in France due to irrigation requirements in the hotter country. When studying orange groves, those in Brazil and California use far less water than Florida's groves for the same reason; it is hotter in Florida. While

---

[130]"The Water Stewardship and Replenish Report," (2012), 19.

[131]The Coca-Cola Company and World Wildlife Fund, "Annual Review 2011: A Transformative Partnership to Conserve Water " (2011), 1.

[132]Black and King, *The Atlas of water: Mapping The World's most critical resource*, 57. based on 2004 data

[133]Fishman, *The big thirst: The secret life and turbulent future of water*, 18.

agricultural subsidies are extremely political in both the European Union and the U.S. Congress, company studies such as the one conducted by Coca-Cola, could impact future purchasing decisions by corporations, if they begin to take water footprints into account.

Addressing Water Shortages

Experts disagree on the timeframe, some point to 2025 while others point to 2030, but based on current population growth estimates most agree that more than two-thirds of the world will be water stressed within the next 15–20 years if usage continues at its current rate.[134] However, with focus and attention, there are emergent solutions. Not only do many major corporations (e.g. in addition to Coke, IBM, Intel, MGM Resorts and GE) now track their water use, returning purified, recycled water to the environment after its use in their manufacturing processes, but the U.S. Department of Agriculture Economic Research Service reports that U.S. farmers actually use 15 % less water today than they did in 1980, and they produce a harvest that is 70 % larger.[135] Thus, the situation is deemed manageable if appropriate actions are taken. The impact of climate change makes predicting where water shortages will be most serious difficult, if not impossible. Conservation and improving agricultural processes, as well as decisions regarding where and how crops are grown are critical. In developing countries, supporting one-acre farmers to irrigate, fertilize, and select the right crops is critical to both providing them with a livelihood, and using water in a responsible fashion.[136]

The following examples are among the almost 300 projects highlighted in Coke's annual *Replenish Reports*.[137] They illustrate both the impact that the projects are having, and highlight how Coke is engaged through NGO and government partnerships. Some involve funding through the Coca-Cola Foundation, while others are about Coca-Cola corporate learning and sharing knowledge about water use and conservation. These projects demonstrate how water and sanitation are local issues. Each project benefits a few hundred or a few thousand individuals. These are a small sampling of the projects underway.

---

[134]The Coca-Cola Company and World Wildlife Fund, "Annual Review 2011: A Transformative Partnership to Conserve Water "; The Water Resources Group, "The Water Resources Group: Background, Impact and the Way Forward."

[135]Fishman, *The big thirst: The secret life and turbulent future of water.*

[136]Polak, Paul. 2008. *Out of poverty: What works when traditional approaches fail.* San Francisco: Berrett-Koehler; Paul Polak and Stephanie Fry. 2009. Water and the Twin Challenge of Feeding 3 Billion New People and Ending Rural Poverty. In *Water Ethics: Marcelino Botin Water Forum 2007,* ed. M. Ramon Llamas, Luis Martinez-Cortina, and Mukherji. The Netherlands: CRC Press.

[137]The Coca-Cola Company, "The Water Stewardship and Replenish Report (2011)"; "The Water Stewardship and Replenish Report," (2012).

- **Water for Schools:** Coke has supported water and sanitation programs to nearly 400 schools that have benefitted more than 206,000 students in over 25 countries. One of the projects, called RAIN (Replenish Africa Initiative) supports hygiene education for both adults and children. RAIN's goal is to provide over two million Africans with clean water by 2015. Coke has made a 6-year $30 million commitment to the program. Working with South Africa's Department of Basic Education, the Mvula Trust, and H2O for Life the program provides both clean drinking water and gender-segregated latrines to 100 schools and over 60,000 students in Africa.[138] CARE and Coke have done RAIN projects to provide water for 7,500 people in some of the poorest Egyptian villages.[139] Coke has also participated in a program called SWASH+ (School Water Sanitation and Hygiene) in Central America. SWASH+ is a Netherlands-based organization and CARE's Web site features a video illustrating how African children impeccably dressed in uniforms are cleaning their own latrines, and then taking their new knowledge and skills about good hygiene back to their families.[140] Lack of separate bathrooms and the need to stay home to fetch water for their families, are among the major reasons for girls dropping out of school in many countries in Africa and in India.[141]
- **Protecting Watersheds to Ensure Clean Water to Poor Families:** Coke has funded numerous projects with the USAID Missions in a program called WADA (Water and Development Alliance). With a combined $30 million investment, WADA has supported the health of ecosystems in 23 countries in Africa, Asia, Latin America and the Middle East, providing clean water and sanitation to 55,000 people and protecting 400,000 ha of watersheds.[142]
- **Water Policy Management:** Integrated water policy management is a critical tool for municipalities and states to engage in making water policy decisions that meet needs both today and into the future. This perspective is foundational for a community's sustainability.[143] While it has had issues in India, today working through the World Economic Forum, Coke is engaged with the Karnataka, India government on transformational policies that will enhance water irrigation and agricultural productivity. Coke is supporting similar projects in Jordan, Mexico, and South Africa. In Viet Nam, Coke is working with the World Wildlife Fund on a project to preserve the natural wetlands of the Plain of Reeds ecosystem. The innovative policy statute that Coke and WWF are proposing could change the way the entire country manages its wetlands. Coke is engaged in 34 different

---

[138]"The Water Stewardship and Replenish Report,"(2012).

[139]"Coca-Cola, Care Announce Plans to Refresh Egyptian Communities with Access to Safe Water," http://216.64.210.4/dynamic/press_center/2010/08/coca-cola-care-announce-plans-to-refresh-egyptian-communities-with-access-to-safe-water-1.html.

[140]CARE, "Maintaining School Water, Sanitation, and Hygiene Services," (CARE, 2012).

[141]Watkins, "Undp 2006 Report."

[142]The Coca-Cola Company. 2012. The water stewardship and replenish report.

[143]Schmidt, Jeremy J. 2010. Water ethics and management. In *Water ethics: Foundational readings for students and professionals*, ed. Peter G. Brown and Jeremy J. Schmidt. Washington, DC: Island Press.

projects with the United Nations Development Programme to support solutions
for water supply, sanitation, resource management, and climate-change issues.
The programs are about building long-term capacity. In China an ecological
rehabilitation program will help 10 million people living in the Tarim River basin
in a sustainable agricultural program to improve the water efficiency in sugarcane cultivation.[144]

- **Supporting Women and Girls:** Each year, African women and girls spend over
  40 billion hours collecting water, which is time that could be spent learning,
  working, or earning money for their families. In 2011, through the Coca-Cola
  Africa Foundation, the company invested $6 million to support the lives of
  250,000 women and girls on the continent.[145] But, these projects are only a small
  part of Coke's efforts to support women in emerging countries.

The Coca-Cola 5 by 20 Project in Support of Women Entrepreneurship

In early 2012, Coca-Cola took its support of women to a new level with a new goal
"to enable the economic empowerment of five million women entrepreneurs across
our global value chain by 2020."[146] The program is a partnership with the Bill &
Melinda Gates Foundation, TechnoServe, which is engaged in supporting business
solutions to the poor, and the United Nations Entity for Gender Equality and the
Empowerment of Women. There is increasing evidence that empowering women is
the foundational ingredient critical to alleviating poverty in developing countries.
Based on a book[147] by the same name, the effort to empower women has come to be
known as the Half the Sky Movement. Ironically, it was China's Chairman Mao
who proclaimed, "Women hold up half the sky." While many unfortunate events
occurred during Mao's reign, he used his power to abolish child marriage, prostitution, and concubinage in China.[148]

The aim of Coca-Cola's "5 by 20 Project" is to empower women by helping them
to start new businesses or improve those they already run. One example was illustrated in the Charlie Rose TV interview with Kent and inventor Dean Kamen.[149]
Coke is considering setting up kiosks that incorporate the Slingshot water purifier as
part of a larger mobile cooler product, so a women entrepreneur can sell clean water,
as well as other Coke beverages. A solar or dung-powered cooler can also produce
enough electricity to charge cell phones, giving the business another product to sell,
or it can be used to produce electricity so the women's children can have light to

---

[144] The Coca-Cola Company, "The Water Stewardship and Replenish Report," (2012).

[145] Ibid.

[146] "5by20," The Coca-Cola Company, http://www.coca-colacompany.com/stories/5by20.

[147] Kristof and WuDunn, *Half the Sky*.

[148] "Mao Campaign Fuels Women Power," no. April 20 (2012), http://www.rfa.org/english/news/
china/women-04202012182126.html.

[149] Rose, "Muhtar Kent, CEO of the Coca Cola Company on the Global Water Crisis."

study by in the evening. Coke provides workshops in which the women learn book-keeping and merchandising techniques. Malehlohonolo Moleko started with a bakery business in which she sold cakes to construction site workers. Coke provided her with a mobile cooler and education. She learned business skills regarding purchasing of supplies and other techniques that resulted in a tripling of her profits. She talks about having peace in her family and someday buying a house. Zilda Barreto says that she feels like a "queen in a castle" in her new house made possible through Coke providing a motorcycle garbage transporter for her recycling business in one of Brazil's slums. The recyclables can be transported and sold so she can now feed her son and move into a better house.[150]

Lingering Problems

Coke's sustainable water projects appear to be producing positive results, and they are designed to support the company's business interests and reputation, such that the India problems might never happen again. For example, Coca-Cola's 2012 *Replenish Report* lists 22 projects in Mexico since 2005, and there is a 2011 project entitled "Access to Water in Rural Indigenous Communities in Huasteca Potosina" (p. B8).

However, a recent French investigative report and documentary[151] would leave one to believe that Coke's challenges are ongoing. The central premise of the documentary is the reporter's alleged search for the actual "secret" ingredients in Coca-Cola. But a segment of the hour-long documentary takes place in Chiapas, Mexico, and the French investigative reporter shows how prolific Coke is in this rural area. She and other reporters[152] critical of the company claim Chiapas is a place that at one time had plenty of water, but today the indigenous mountain people are drinking rainwater and nothing is coming out of their kitchen faucets. The French documentary, filmed in 2012, claims that the local Coca-Cola bottler is draining the aquifer near Chiapas, demonstrating that Coke may continue to encounter challenges in poor countries where poor water management and business corruption are endemic. Mexico is Coke's largest consumer, so the issues are not insignificant. In 2011 per capita consumption of Coke's beverages were higher in Mexico than anywhere else in the world by a significant percentage (see Exhibit 1). Journalists[153] report that Coke is less expensive than water, and that in both Mexico and Guatemala mothers have been known to add Coke to baby formula. In the French documentary Coke was used in religious rituals and rubbed on a child's arm to dispel evil spirits. Coke is not promoting these uses for its products, but the long-term implications of these practices are increasingly issues for the Company.

---

[150]The Coca-Cola Company, "5by20".

[151]Mokiejewski, Olivia. "Coca-Cola La Formule Secrète," (France 2 Television, 2013).

[152]Blanding, *The Coke Machine: The Dirty Truth Behind the World's Favorite Soft Drink.*

[153]Ibid; Mokiejewski, "Coca-Cola La Formule Secrète".

Exhibit 1: 2011 Per Capita Consumption of Coke's Beverage Products

Source: The Coca-Cola Company (2012), 2011 Annual Review, p. 12

Exhibit 2: Heads of Coca-Cola over Twentieth Century to Present

Robert W. Woodruff American	President 1923–1954	His father purchased the company in 1919. Remained on the board through 1984 and served as an advisor until his death in 1985
Robert Goizueta Cuban American	Named President 1979 Became Chairman in 1981 Chairman and CEO until death in 1997	Dies unexpectedly after a short illness
M. Douglas Ivester American	Chairman and CEO from 1997 to 2000	Board members Warren Buffett and Herbert Allen announce they have lost confidence in his leadership
Douglas N. Daft Australian	Chairman and CEO 2000–2004	Has stated plans to retire within 5 years when he took the position
E. Neville Isdell Irish	Chairman 2004–2009 CEO 2005-2007	Called "the man who stopped the bleeding and sutured the wounds" (Martin, 2007).
Muhtar Kent Turkish	President and COO – Dec. 2006; CEO July 2008; Chairman	Called "a veteran with the 'style of an outsider'" (Martin, 2007)

Sources: The Coca-Cola Company Heritage Timeline, Company 10Ks, and *The New York Times*[154]
(Abelson, 2006; Day, 2004; Deutsch, 2004; Martin, 2007)

---

[154] Abelson, Reed. "Head of International Unit Gets No. 2 Job at Coca-Cola," *The New York Times*, no. December 8 (2006), http://www.nytimes.com/2006/12/08/business/worldbusiness/08coke.html? ref=muhtarkent; Sherry Day, "Coke's Chief Set to Retire at End of 2004," ibid., no. February 20 (2004), http://www.nytimes.com/2004/02/20/business/coke-s-chief-set-to-retire-at-end-of-2004. html?ref=douglasndaft; Claudia H. Deutsch, "Coca-Cola Reaches into Past for New Chief," ibid., no. May 5, http://www.nytimes.com/2004/05/05/business/coca-cola-reaches-into-past-for-new-chief.html?ref=douglasndaft; Andrew Martin, "Chief of Coke to Step Down after Steering Its Recovery," ibid., no. December 7 (2007), http://www.nytimes.com/2007/12/07/business/07coke. html?ref=muhtarkent.

Exhibit 3: Links Between the United Nations Millennium Development Goals (MDGs) and Water

UN Development Goal	Role of Water Services and Management
Goal 1: Eradicate extreme poverty and hunger	People need water and sanitation to stay healthy, and be able to earn a living. Subsistent farmers need adequate access; agricultural activity needs to be improved in order to meet the demand for food at affordable prices; make water accessible, reliable, affordable and safer
Goal 2: Achieve universal primary education	Provide adequate clean water and separate toilet facilities for boys and girls; reduce time spent collecting water, and allow children to use their energy for learning, income generation, and family support. Inadequate sanitation is one of the major reasons for girls dropping out of school.
Goal 3: Promote gender equality and empower women	Make water universally accessible to women, reduce time spent collecting water, and use this time for generating income and supporting families. Inadequate sanitation correlates to a loss of dignity and creates insecurity.
Goal 4: Reduce child mortality	Homes need hygiene, nutritious food, safe drinking water, and proper feces disposal. Households without proper sanitation risk death at three to four times the level as children in rich households. Access to clean water reduces the probability of death by as much as 50 %.
Goal 5: Improve maternal health	Reduce risks of illness through access to safe water and improve the diets of both mothers and infants, especially when childbirth occurs at home
Goal 6: Combat HIV/AIDS, malaria, and other diseases	Reduce water-related diseases through better access to safe, clean water, and knowledge of proper hygiene and sanitation. With adequate water and sanitation the $1.7 billion spent on water-related disease could be diverted to resources for fighting HIV/AIDS. Poor sanitation and drainage contribute to the 1.3 million lives a year lost to malaria, with most being children.
Goal 7: Ensure environmental sustainability	Implement sustainable practices that reduce the loss of environmental resources, and further reduce the number of people who do not have access to safe drinking water and sanitation
Goal 8: Develop global partnership for development	Environmentalists, industry, researchers, and policy decision makers must engage and work cooperatively toward integrated water management solutions. Conferences have created few results. Countries with poor sanitation are spending considerably more on their military than on providing basic water and sanitation to their citizens.

Sources: *The Atlas of Water*, p. 86 (Black and King 2009); The Millennium Development Goals (United Nations, 2010, p. 134; Watkins, UNHDP, 2006, pp. 22–23)

Exhibit 4: Coke's 2004 Manifesto and 2020 Vision Goals (Established at the End of 2010)

Original Five Principles from the August 2004 Manifesto for Growth under Isdell's Direction

People	Be a great place to work where people are inspired to be the best they can be.
Portfolio	Bring to the world a portfolio of quality beverage brands that anticipate and satisfy people's desires and needs.
Partners	Nurture a winning network of customers and suppliers, creating mutual, enduring value.
Planet	Be a responsible citizen that makes a difference by helping build and support sustainable communities
Profit	Maximize long-term return to shareowners while being mindful of our overall responsibilities

Source: *Inside Coca-Cola: A CEO's Life Story of Building the World's Most Popular Brand* (Isdell and Beasley 2011, p. 183)

2020 Vision (Established at the end of 2010) under Kent's Direction

People	Be a great place to work
Partners	Be the most preferred and trusted beverage partner
Profit	More than double system revenues while increasing system margins
Portfolio	More than double our servings to over three billion a day and be No. 1 in the NARTD* beverage business in every market and every category that is of value to us.
Planet	Be a global leader in sustainable water use, packaging, energy and climate protection.
Productivity	Manage people, time and money for greatest effectiveness

NARTD = Non-alcoholic Ready To Drink
Source: 2011 Annual Report (The Coca-Cola Company, 2012, p. 35)

Exhibit 5: Definitions Used in Water Footprinting

The science of water footprinting involves understanding not only the total amount of water used to make a product, but also what kind of water is used and what can be re-used. Here is a breakdown of a few of the major definitions used in water footprinting work.

- Green water footprint refers to the use of green water resources, such as water stored in soil as moisture

- Blue water footprint: refers to the use of surface and ground water
- Grey water footprint refers to pollution or the amount of water required to assimilate the pollutants used to make a product, based on current water quality standards

For example: "Grey water results from green or blue water that is not consumed. For instance, when rain (green water) falls on agricultural land and then runs off the field, it may carry eroded soil or chemicals, such as fertilizers into an adjacent water body, thereby creating grey water" (The Coca-Cola Company and The Nature Conservancy 2010, p. 8)

Chapter 6
Finance

Introduction

An ongoing challenge for the poor is not merely that they have no money, but also that they have no means of obtaining credit. Without assets or property as collateral, banks and governments are hesitant to loan money. Thus, if you are poor and without assets, it is difficult to borrow money for new businesses, housing or even medicine. In Chap. 7 we will present three cases of organizations that attack this problem of empowering the poorest of the poor.

In this chapter, we present two cases of unusual financing vehicles. The first, "Enabling the Poor to Build Housing: Pursuing Profit and Social Development Together," describes the efforts by the large and very profitable Mexican company, Cemex, to address housing issues for underserved Mexicans by organizing communities into cooperatives that can borrow money for discounted housing materials.

The second case is even more unusual. For those of us in the economically stable world with the availability of credit, we tend to think about banking and finance as an adult phenomenon. Few of us would imagine that teen-aged children could manage their own finances or the finances of others. The Bal Vikas Bank (Children's Development Bank) belies that conclusion. These banks are created to guard the savings of homeless children, and are managed by those children with almost no theft or corruption!

There is much to be learned from these two cases, most particularly, the realization that poverty does not equate to the inability to handle financial matters, nor does just being without assets equate to defaulting on loans.

P.J. Albert et al. (eds.), *Global Poverty Alleviation: A Case Book*, The International Society   263
of Business, Economics, and Ethics Book Series 3, DOI 10.1007/978-94-007-7479-7_6,
© Springer Science+Business Media Dordrecht 2014

Enabling the Poor to Build Housing: Pursuing Profit and Social Development Together[1]

The Cemex Corporation of Mexico has launched an innovative experiment that enables very poor people to purchase building materials and upgrade their homes. It blends the pursuit of profit with significant social gain.

GUADALAJARA, Mexico – The poorest people here live in small houses constructed from raw cinder blocks or more flimsy materials like cardboard and corrugated sheet metal.

"Most of the houses aren't finished and have only one or two rooms per family," says Consuelo Silva, a resident of the Mesa Colorada settlement on the northern outskirts of Guadalajara. "Most families have at least six to ten members, and these rooms are occupied by the bedrooms and a kitchen."

Such crowding aggravates tensions that accompany life amidst poverty. "The quality of the relations between family members will determine a family's future," says Israel Moreno, director and founder of Patrimonio Hoy, an initiative of Cemex that enables poor families to finance expansion of their homes.

"Imagine one room with ten persons living together, yelling and fighting all day long. So the children are propelled out into the streets at a young age. What do they learn in the streets? Vicious delinquency, theft and prostitution. If the first thing in your life is contact with the street, your future will be the street, with its related risks."

Families in these neighborhoods tend to be resigned to making little progress on their home expansion efforts and thus to suffering the ill effects of crowding. But since it was founded 4 years ago, Patrimonio Hoy has given 20,000 families in Mexico a way to finance and build better housing in a timely manner.

Patrimonio Hoy is one of Guadalajara's most dynamic and successful programs that addresses the problems of housing in these settlements – indeed it is one of the only such programs. But what truly sets it apart is that it is neither operated nor subsidized by the government or a non-governmental organization.

Rather it is a for-profit initiative of Cemex, Mexico's largest multinational corporation. Within 5 years, one million Mexican families will benefit from this new way of doing business if the program continues to grow as planned.

Cemex manufactures cement, the principal ingredient for construction in developing countries. Cemex, along with some of the world's most savvy multinational corporations, is discovering that the poorest of the poor represent the next major frontier for companies struggling to maintain rapid growth.

---

[1] This case was prepared by Kris Herbst and is reprinted by permission of Ashoka and *Changemakers*. All rights reserved.

Pursuing Innovation and Global Expansion

Mexico is not the obvious place to find an innovative multinational corporation, much less one that is conducting a groundbreaking experiment in combining corporate social responsibility with the pursuit of profits in low-income communities. Cemex was founded in 1906 in the northern state of Nuevo Leon as Mexico's first cement company.

For nearly 90 years Cemex operated like a typical Mexican corporation in Mexico's highly-protected markets. Until the mid-1990s, it could afford to be relatively passive and slow-moving because competition between the handful of domestic cement companies was rather slack, and they competed primarily on price rather than service.

The desires of individual consumers received scant attention from the cement companies. Instead, the companies catered to a small number of large-scale customers: the government, construction companies, value-added resellers that convert raw cement to building blocks and other structural elements, and distributors that operate warehouses and stores.

During the late 1980s, Cemex consolidated its position as Mexico's largest cement company by purchasing the nation's second- and third-largest cement companies. It controlled 65 % of the market for cement within Mexico by the early 1990s, but had no operations outside Mexico's borders.

But Cemex was headed for a shake up when Lorenzo Zambrano, a 58-year-old Stanford MBA whose grandfather (also named Lorenzo) founded Cemex, rose through the ranks to assume the leadership in 1985. As chairman and CEO, Zambrano proved to be a visionary who was determined to modernize Cemex and push it into the global economy.

In a bold stroke that showed brilliant foresight – and set Cemex apart from other Mexican corporations – Zambrano shifted Cemex's attention to the world outside Mexico by acquiring Spain's two leading cement companies in 1992. Two years later, this move saved Cemex from the financial devastation that hit other Mexican companies after the 1994 peso devaluation triggered an economic crash. At the time, sales of goods and services, including cement, plunged by 50 % in Mexico.

Simultaneously, legal barriers protecting Mexico's markets began to crumble, opening the way for international competitors that promptly began eating into Mexican cement companies' market share. These Mexican companies became ripe targets for acquisition by multinational competitors as the world cement industry began consolidating.

Cemex avoided this fate by expanding and becoming a global player itself. Its newly acquired Spanish subsidiaries provided a lifeline to European capital markets that kept it afloat during the peso crisis.

The economic crisis and opening of Mexican markets in the mid-1990s was a social, political and economic upheaval that changed the rules for businesses in Mexico. Suddenly, Cemex was operating in an open, globalized market.

The very concept of marketing to consumers was new. "Prior to this time it had just been promotional products: key chains, cups, etc.," Moreno said.

"It was a breakthrough. For me, it was an explosion – a moment to create a new business model based on how employees can develop solutions that make more satisfied customers. Before, our focus was on operations – and Cemex has the highest production standards in the world – but there is another side to the business: the customer".

"When you are the customer's only option, you are making good sales – but oftentimes you forget the customer or the market. On the other hand, when you are just one of the options, customers have a choice, and they have memories. If we are not able to maintain or develop a long-term relationship with our customers, we are lost – we are out of business. That is why companies now emphasize their social responsibilities – to build long-term relations with the customer."

Zambrano led the charge to modernize Cemex by surrounding himself with executives who pursued the latest management and technology innovations in order to empower employees and streamline operations. Since the mid-1990s, "we have been acting with a new attitude of listening, awareness, innovation, and continuous improvement," Moreno said. "We need to keep very alert and awake, thinking about how to do things better, reading the markets, and listening to the customers."

Recognizing this, *Wired Magazine* added Cemex to its Wired Index mutual fund in July. For the first time, it included a manufacturer of a heavy, old-fashioned commodity like cement in its list of 40 companies that power the global economy by mastering innovation, intelligent use of new tools, strategic vision, global reach and networked communication.

Since 1995, Cemex has spent nearly $5 billion acquiring cement companies that now operate as subsidiaries in 25 countries. They have provided further access to capital markets in Europe and America, helping fuel Cemex's expansion.

Cemex has vaulted from the world's 28th-largest cement company to the third largest in the world. It produces 80 million metric tons of cement annually – enough cement to fill 1,000 football stadiums to the brim – and recorded sales of $6.9 billion in 2001.

Cemex operates 524 cement plants worldwide, and is the world's largest producer of white cement. It is also the world's leading exporter of cement and related services, using a fleet of freight ships and 54 strategically located marine terminals to sell and ship 13.2 million metric tons of cement to more than 60 countries.

Cemex acquired the U.S.-based Southdown Inc. cement company in 2000 for $2.8 billion, the largest-ever acquisition of a U.S. company by a Mexican firm. This has made Cemex the largest seller of cement in the United States, a dominant position it also enjoys in Spain, Venezuela, Panama, and the Dominican Republic.

As it has expanded, Cemex has gained a reputation for acquiring and then converting troubled cement plants to profitable operations – most of them located in developing countries – by imposing uniform strict standards of modernization and efficiency. In the process, it has become by far the world's most profitable cement company, achieving the highest cash flow, pretax margins of 37 %, and a market capitalization that reached $9.3 billion in April. Earnings before interest, taxes, depreciation and amortization have been growing at an average annual compounded rate of 20 % for the past 10 years.

By focusing on international markets, Cemex has become Mexico's top multinational corporation: nearly two-thirds of its revenues come from outside Mexico. Only two Mexican companies are larger: Pemex, the national oil and gas monopoly, and Telmex, a telecommunications monopoly that was privatized in 1990. It is the only Mexican corporation generating more profits than Cemex. These accomplishments have made Cemex's CEO Lorenzo Zambrano worth an estimated $2.8 billion, making him Mexico's third-wealthiest individual after the owners of Telmex and a booming joint Wal-Mart venture, according to *Forbes* magazine.

Discovering Opportunity in Low-Income Markets

Cemex has achieved extraordinary profitability through a shrewd strategy of targeting developing countries (Bangladesh, Egypt, Indonesia, Thailand, Philippines and countries in the Caribbean and Central and South America). Its forecasts show the world demand for cement through 2010 will grow by 4 % annually in developing countries, compared to only 1 % annually in developed countries.

The poorest residents of these developing countries represent a special opportunity for businesses. During Mexico's economic crisis in 1994, when the value of the peso crashed, Cemex noticed that the revenues from its big-ticket sales to traditional large-scale customers, and to middle- and upper-income individuals, dropped by 50 %, but sales to its low-income, do-it-yourself homebuilder customers dropped only 10–20 %.

Although the average value of a sale to a low-income customer is miniscule, their numbers are enormous compared to Cemex's better-heeled customers. This makes low-income communities a more stable market that is less affected by the cyclical fluctuations of the economy.

Cemex saw opportunities here: sales to the low-income market could offset its losses during economic downturns. And the low-income market offers the possibility of sustained growth that could offset erosion of Cemex's overall market share by international competitors.

Cemex embarked on a strategy of learning how to tap the enormous markets of low-income customers in developing countries by studying how to do business with the poor in Mexico, where 60 % of the population survives on less than $5 per day.

To help cope with the 1994 economic meltdown, a Cemex management team headed by Francisco Garza Zambrano, president of Cemex's North America Region and Trading, turned to Business Design Associates (BDA), a consulting firm founded by Fernando Flores – the philosopher, business consultant and former finance minister to Chilean President Salvador Allende. BDA led the first stage of social research in the low-income communities. Later, the Cemex team began developing the idea for Patrimonio Hoy by identifying the low-income do-it-yourself homebuilders as a neglected "last consumer segment."

Above this segment on the ladder of individual consumers are wealthy homeowners at the top, middle-class homeowners, and then low-income consumers who are part of the formal economy by virtue of having a regular job. These low-income consumers have the option of allocating deductions from their paychecks, matched by government subsidies, to help pay for their housing.

But do-it-yourself homebuilders who are outside the formal economy, living in burgeoning informal settlements, are left to fend for themselves. Significantly, they account for about 40 % of cement consumption in Mexico and have potential to be a market worth $500–600 million annually – a conservative estimate according to Cemex.

But before it could successfully enter this market, Cemex needed to figure how to help do-it-yourself homebuilders overcome their resignation about not being able to improve their housing in a timely manner. Patrimony Hoy managers began by carefully studying the methods of the Grameen Bank, the organization that invented the concept of microlending – providing tiny loans to the very poor so they can launch their own businesses and become micro-entrepreneurs.

Grameen started in Bangladesh in 1979 and has disbursed roughly $3 billion to 2.4 million borrowers. Although they lack collateral, Grameen's borrowers have an excellent repayment record – at least 90 % according to Grameen Bank figures.

Grameen discovered that women, who comprise 94 % of its customers, are highly reliable borrowers. Cemex has adopted strategies it learned from Grameen, such doing most of its business with women and shaping business procedures to fit traditional values such as a reliance on community solidarity.

Obstacles to Progress

The average low-income homebuilder takes 4 years to complete just one room, and 13 years to finish a small four-room house that typically consists of a kitchen, bathroom, bedroom and a second bedroom that doubles as a family's common space. This discouraging rate of progress reflects the many obstacles that low-income homebuilders face. Banks and other businesses will not engage with poor residents of informal settlements where the legal status of their property ownership is murky, and residents cannot document assets, collateral, references or regular sources of income.

So poor people here, as elsewhere in the world, use a traditional method for saving money: they form a savings club or tanda. Typically women form groups of ten persons who each make a small, weekly contribution of about 100 pesos (US$10) to a pool for a period of 10 weeks. Each week, one member of the tanda is selected by lottery to receive the entire pool until every member has taken the pool once.

While studying low-income communities in Mexico, Moreno found that 70 % of women who participate in tandas are saving money to construct improvements on their homes. But just 10 % actually spend the money on building materials.

Often the money is spent before a family even receives it. What little can be saved in poor communities typically gets claimed for unanticipated emergencies, loans to friends and family, school fees, and clothes, etc.

Further, a person's social status in low-income Mexican communities is measured not so much by wealth or assets, but by "social capital" – a person's reputation and participation in the life of the community.

"Much of their money goes to these festivities: weddings, music and parties," Moreno said. "There is a party for everything: my favorite soccer team won, my political party won, my neighbor's daughter just turned 15, I just put a new floor in my house. That is a very important reason why people don't have a better house, education or clothing – their money goes to non-primary necessities."

The challenges of putting aside enough money to buy a bag of cement – up to two times the average daily earnings – are great. In the past, homeowners attempted to hoard materials as a hedge against runaway price inflation, but because they lacked adequate storage they lost materials to theft and spoilage. A bag of cement left lying on the ground in front of a house will soon be rendered useless by rain, hardening before it can be put to use.

It is a common practice in the low-income communities, that the quality of building materials purchased in small lots often is poor – dealers give customers leftovers from their larger orders, prices charged by middlemen are high, and deliveries are delayed. Because most do-it-yourself homebuilders lack construction skills, they often waste materials by failing to specify the exact quantities they require. Home design and construction tends to be haphazard and suffers from substandard circulation patterns, structural integrity, ventilation and lighting.

Cemex discovered that successfully entering the low-income market will require "cultural innovation" on both sides – the values and culture of low-income communities must be shifted, but Cemex also must change the way it treats its customers. To succeed in low-income communities, companies must build bridges between a community's familiar traditional practices and a new set of more modern values. This will provide the seeds for a new way of life.

As the Patrimonio Hoy program began taking shape in October, 1999, its structure reflected this bridging approach.

Replacing Resignation with Ambition

Translated to English, Patrimonio Hoy means "Patrimony Today." Patrimony refers to the tradition of creating something of value that can be passed down to future generations.

In this sense, patrimony is seen as a statement of solidarity with the traditional community. It may be something intangible like education, personal values or a sense of personal empowerment, or it may be something material, the most substantial instance of which is a family's house.

At the same time, low-income communities are pervaded by a sense of resignation that extends to the station of life to which a person is born, fate, and an inability to reconcile traditional values – such as making expenditures for communal celebrations – with modern aspirations such as financial planning and asset accumulation. "Their mental model is 'We cannot do it, we cannot have a better life. This is my life, this has been my parents' life, and this will be my children's life'," Moreno said.

"They are resigned. We are convinced that this is a very big lie. But we are certain this will not be the model for the future because otherwise the world will be lost."

As a slogan on posters and publications, "Patrimony Today" replaces this resignation with an assertion it provides an opportunity to achieve a better way of living, more quickly, beginning today. "Our philosophy is that if we make a promise, we will make it reality," Moreno said. "This is the Patrimonio Hoy way of relating, of making transactions and doing business – no more false promises."

Banking on Social Capital

No paperwork is required to join Patrimonio Hoy: prospective members need not provide identification, proof of address, co-signers, documentation of assets, collateral or paycheck stubs. Instead, like traditional organizations such as tandas, applicants are asked to provide the one thing they do possess: social capital – their word, honor and reputation. All they need to enroll is to promise to be consistent about making weekly savings payments.

"The less economic capital you have, the more you depend on your social capital," Moreno said. "The only thing they have is social capital. Their most precious treasure is their identity, because if you don't have money you depend on your name. You must honor your commitments."

Members are invited to form savings clubs, like tandas, in which each member contributes a minimum of 120 pesos per week. Each Patrimonio Hoy savings group consists of three persons. After members join a savings group, Patrimonio Hoy calls its members "partners" rather than customers.

"We learned that the solidarity is stronger for a group with three partners than with ten because of the relationships between the partners," Moreno said. "A group of three is tightly bonded – people pick their closest relations, while a group of ten has weaker links. This system is based on trust. My leverage is that the group of three consists of the most trusted persons in each other's lives."

The structure of the saving club expands the idea of the tanda to a 70–86-week commitment to a well-defined plan. The rules of the group, such as the penalties for missing payments, are formalized and specified in advance to help prevent fraud and abuse. The lack of hidden consequences helps members trust the system.

A group's members take turns collecting payments and playing the role of contract enforcer for 1 month at time. By separating this function from Patrimonio Hoy staff, members gain a better understanding and commitment to the process.

This structure, and the use of simple, transparent rules, avoids a more familiar arrangement in low-income communities: the hierarchical relationship between patron and supplicant where care is exchanged for loyalty and the patron may be expected to forgive transgressions of the rules. Instead, Patrimonio Hoy works to develop reciprocal responsibility: it delivers quality materials and services; the customer gets the possibility of getting a better house by paying on time and doing the building.

A New and Rewarding Experience

The savings group differs from the tandas model in one all-important respect. To ensure that their savings actually get spent for housing, group members receive raw materials for building – cement, iron, etc. – rather than cash. After 2 weeks, Cemex makes a first delivery of building materials to each member of the group. Because this occurs before sufficient savings have accumulated to fully pay the bill, Cemex is, in effect, advancing credit.

Additional deliveries of materials are made to each member every 10 weeks. The structure is more fair than the tanda's system of awarding pool pay-offs by lottery because tandas give an advantage to those who receive the pool first.

Participation in the savings clubs is a breakthrough for community members because, for the first time, they are being offered a chance to do business with a legitimate corporation and to join a secure savings and credit plan. For most, it's a new and rewarding experience to be transactional equals, free to bind themselves in serious commitments to each other and to a company.

They have become accustomed to living in a culture permeated with distrust due to generations of dealings with people who have cheated and swindled them. This unhappy situation is the product of their marginal political and legal status as poor, uneducated residents of informal settlements.

This has created a risky political environment that helps explain the paucity of NGOs and other community development programs that would otherwise address the problems of these communities, such as inadequate housing. "There aren't many social entrepreneurs in the area of home construction because of difficulties over 'gray property titles'," Spinosa said.

"They also must compete with government agencies that, for many years, have been focused on ending the disorder of these communities rather than simply giving people wealth. The government's ambition and funding, although noble, gets in the way of the simple, more pragmatic wealth-building ambitions of social entrepreneurs."

High-Touch Outreach Builds Community and Trust

Patrimonio Hoy tackles these problems by employing a "high touch" method of community outreach to build community in a variety of ways. It is especially important to manage the spread of information because low-income communities are highly networked by word-of-mouth, and rumors, paranoia and jealousies spread rapidly.

Patrimonio Hoy begins operating in a city by opening an office staffed by four employees in one of the outlying areas with the greatest concentration of low-income people. Patrimonio Hoy calls these areas "cells." Typically a cell has a population of 100,000, or 20,000 families. Patrimonio Hoy is operating eight cells in Guadalajara.

The program has just come through an explosive period of expansion. It grew by 250 % last year, ballooning from 9 cells in 3 cities to 30 cells in 19 cities that are located in 15 states throughout southern and central Mexico. This rate of growth is being allowed to level off temporarily so that the program's systems and software can be upgraded and consolidated to support a large number of customers, Moreno said.

Since it was founded 4 years ago, Patrimonio Hoy has enrolled more than 20,000 families, directly affecting some 100,000 people. Even with the current pause in growth, it is adding new families at the rate of 2,000 per month, and sales are growing by 15 % monthly. "Our goal is to reach one million families in Mexico in 5 years," Moreno said.

Patrimonio Hoy targets about one-fourth of the population of a cell (5,000 families) for its services because they can afford to save 120 pesos per week and will need assistance with their housing. Rather than using advertising to reach them, Patrimonio Hoy's staff identifies and recruits informal leaders in the community, 98 % of who are women, to serve as "promoters" who will engage in a highly-personalized form of selling.

Promoters tend to be housewives who love to meet and spend time with people, and to contribute to their community. They often already are earning money by selling multilevel marketing products for companies like Avon, Tupperware and Amway.

Promoters first form a savings group with neighbors, family or friends, and then begin enrolling others to form their own savings groups. When they sign up new members, they get points, which they can exchange for cash or building materials.

Promoters are given ID badges and bright blue t-shirts emblazoned with Patrimonio Hoy logos to distinguish them from the parade of scam artists who pass through the community claiming to solicit for charities. "It's very important that people trust us," Moreno said. "We are dealing with some of the most distrustful people in the world because for many years people have been robbing them."

Women Are the Key

Patrimonio Hoy's managers have been surprised to discover how much they rely on women as their primary clients in low-income communities. They have found that women assume the responsibility for maintaining household unity and a family's progress.

"In the low-income market, the man is the provider and his only worry is what to bring to the house the next day," Moreno said. "But women see daily that the children are growing up in the streets. We discovered that women ensure the future – they are worried about what kind of life they can expect for their children, and about their education.

"When you deal with a woman, you can be more secure that she will respect agreements – on average – than if you sign with a man. It's very difficult to gain her confidence, but when we do, it's a guarantee of her loyalty."

Consuelo Silva lives with her husband and four children in the Mesa Colorada district on the northern outskirts of Guadalajara. She has been a Patrimonio Hoy promoter for 3 years.

"We are accustomed to having men be the ones who lead in Mexico," she said. "Now I know that the women also have an important role in the society, and I feel useful. I can do many more things than just being in the house.

"On average, there are 200 active partners that I have enrolled. That means a lot to me – it's a big achievement. I feel a lot more confident – like I can conquer the world."

Safety in Numbers

Community members are introduced to Patrimonio Hoy in a group session at the local Patrimonio Hoy office rather than as individuals. This helps make their first encounter a sanctioned, communal activity.

It also helps prevent new members from being socially isolated when they begin pursuing new habits that aren't a part of the traditional culture. Otherwise, envy, suspicion and misunderstanding can spread as others notice that Patrimony Hoy members are beginning to accumulate savings and improve their homes. And this can cause Patrimonio Hoy members to try to avoid notice by taking a low profile rather than proudly promoting the program to their friends and neighbors.

Introducing Patrimonio Hoy in a group setting encourages participants to talk about the problems and obstacles they face and to identify and acknowledge their resulting feelings of resignation. At this point, they are offered Cemex's guarantee of a firm and relatively quick timetable, along with technical support. In this way members are able to build the much-desired family patrimony, room-by-room.

The average do-it-yourself homebuilder in Mexico spends US$1,527 and takes 4 years to build an average size room of 100-square-feet. But participants in Patrimonio Hoy can build the same size room, with better quality, in less time – 1.5 years – and at two-thirds the cost (US$1,038, which includes the cost of materials, technical assistance from an engineer or an architect, and Patrimonio Hoy club fees).

Hearing this offer in a group increases the general level of trust in Cemex's commitment. Community members are reassured that the program is backed by Cemex, a large, credible, and well-managed company (familiar to them, if for no other reason, by its sponsorship of Mexico's most popular soccer team, Guadalajara's Chivas) that will not evaporate and leave them holding the bag.

Partner #1

"I didn't believe this plan would help me build my house in this faster and easier way – I thought maybe they will cheat me," said Rosa Magaña, the first person to join Patrimonio Hoy in 1998. Prior to joining, she and her husband had spent 8 years building a 270-square-foot, one-room house for their family of four in the Mirador Escondido settlement on the northeast edge of Guadalajara.

They had attached a kitchen area to their single-room dwelling. It was covered by a sheet of corrugated metal and would flood when it rained so that Magaña had to move her gas stove to keep it from getting wet. Family members went to a neighbor's house to use the bathroom.

"Everybody ate and slept everybody together in the same room," Magaña said. "It was very uncomfortable."

After joining Patrimonio Hoy, Magaña became the program's first promoter and she and her husband spent 2 years expanding their house into a neat, 475-square-foot, two-bedroom house complete with a kitchen and bathroom. "Now I have a house in which my family lives a much better and more dignified life," Magaña said.

"My children sleep in the other room. It was a big opportunity to be able to give 100 pesos a week to Patrimonio Hoy. I realize I have something that I couldn't have done if I hadn't known Patrimonio Hoy. My dream is to finish building my house because this is the only asset we have to pass on to our children. My plan is to start building a second floor this year."

Integrating Old and New Values

Patrimonio Hoy integrates the tradition of communal celebrations by publishing its customers' achievements in local newspapers, sponsoring block parties and open houses, and holding a twice-annual event to honor its top savers, builders, and program promoters. "We organize parties – festivals – with every delivery of materials we make," said Teresa Martinez, Patrimonio Hoy Operations Manager. "This attracts the attention of neighbors so they see that the partners are actually meeting their commitment – that they are for real."

When a family finishes a room, they become a living testimonial to the program and are issued a diploma. They also are delivered "a box with family-size soft drinks and a bowl with tacos for the party they will throw for their neighbors," Moreno said. "We call it the celebration kit."

These activities help bridge the gap between the traditional value of maintaining social status by contributing to communal celebrations, and the desire to get ahead in life. Traditionally, the latter attitude has been viewed with suspicion and envy, and seen as weakening the community fabric.

Savings group members are invited to participate in biweekly support groups to help reinforce their new values and behavior, celebrate their accomplishments and acknowledge their setbacks. "Everything is focused on these solidarity groups," Martinez said.

"I have seen cases where one of the partners broke his leg and couldn't work. The other partners helped him make his payments while he recovered. In another case, a partner was going through a divorce and he received psychological, emotional and economic support from the group."

Services Are Crucial to Low-Income Customers

Not all of a partner's 120-peso weekly payment buys building materials. Patrimony Hoy collects 15 pesos out of each payment as a "club membership" fee.

Their payments cover the cost of cement and other materials. The fee pays for services given to Patrimonio Hoy members in addition to their building supplies. Their payment for services helps reinforce the commercial nature of the transaction, as opposed to the more traditional patron-client relationship.

Patrimonio Hoy quickly discovered these extra services are crucial because simply supplying "cement by itself doesn't solve anything," Moreno said. Low-income homebuilders need a new way of doing things that includes help with financing, technical assistance and social development. "We had to retire our brain chips as a Cemex sales force and think about how to resolve these problems," Moreno said.

Patrimonio Hoy services include:

- Technical assistance from architects and engineers.
- Support for education by financing upgrades to school buildings.
- A school for beginning do-it-yourself homebuilders for those who want to cut costs by doing their own construction, freeing up more money for materials. Here they learn basic skills such as how to dig foundations, mix cement and make level walls with square corners. Some 450 homebuilders are attending the school and 1,000 have graduated.
- A more advanced school that provides professional certification for masons.
- Guaranteed quality of building materials and timely delivery. Cemex collects feedback forms from customers who evaluate the quality of the materials and delivery service they receive from Cemex's authorized dealers.
- A guaranteed freeze on the price of construction materials for 70 weeks, beginning the day a customer enrolls in the program, regardless of price fluctuations in the economy. Locking-in prices protects customers from inflation.
- Free storage of all building materials for up to 2 years to protect against spoilage and theft. A family may want to wait to claim its materials if it lacks its own storage space, or if it needs to save money to pay for the help of mason, or if a husband has gone to work in the United States for 6 months.
- An interest charge of about 12 % for the loan of building materials is incorporated into the membership fee.

See below for additional information about Sidebars on technical assistance from architects and engineers, support for education, a professional school for masons, and guaranteeing quality materials and delivery.

Doing Well While Doing Good

Cemex is determined to make a profit in low-income markets. It will not compete on price – its 110-lb bag of cement costs slightly more (about 3.5 pesos) than competing brands.

Instead, it offers a competitive package of services that it hopes will allow low-income customers to purchase a premium-quality "first world" product, and to work toward attaining a higher quality of life. "I prefer to invest in helping our partners discover ways to live a better life," Moreno said. "I think that is a more responsible and intelligent way of doing business."

So far, Patrimonio Hoy has helped the Cemex bottom line by tripling the rate of cement consumed by its low-income, do-it-yourself homebuilders. This amount has increased from 2,300 lb consumed once every 4 years, on average, to the same amount being consumed in 15 months.

Already, Cemex brands are growing stronger in low-income communities, Moreno said. "Some people say, 'Thanks to Tolteca (Cemex's premium cement brand) I have my house'," Moreno said. "'For 20 years I couldn't build my home, but now we have two more rooms, thanks to Tolteca.' When I hear testimonies like that, I know we are doing well and that our brand is well positioned."

The Patrimonio Hoy program itself is not required to generate a profit. Cemex wants the program to break even so that it covers its costs. "This program has cost the company a lot of money – millions of dollars since we started 4 years ago," Moreno said. He predicts Patrimonio Hoy will reach the break-even point by October or November 2002.

"This is not a charity organization," Moreno said. "We have to meet two objectives: we have to collaborate in providing a better life for these people and the next generations of their families, and we have to do business. If we achieve both these two objectives we will be OK. But you cannot manage this as only a business or a charity organization.

"This is my main concern: that we take both parallel courses. If you do only one of these, you will be out of business in less than 6 months. This is what wakes me up in the middle of the night."

Calle Digna: *Financing City Infrastructure*

After Patrimonio Hoy partners complete a home improvement project, they begin looking for ways to upgrade their neighborhood, Moreno said. "They say, 'Please extend the program to the streets. Let me pave my sidewalk and street with the same system'."

But residents of Mexico's informal settlements often wait years or even decades for street and utility improvements because they lack the legitimate legal status and political clout to demand such services. Nevertheless, city governments have been taking notice when Patrimonio Hoy members home improvements cause the level of investment in their neighborhood to rise, and this makes the city more likely to upgrade the public infrastructure.

"The municipal governments came to us and said we have seen what you are doing for the people and their houses, " Moreno said. "Most important, we have seen the change in attitude – you have a way of getting these people to be self-sufficient and we need that. But we don't have enough money to pave streets and create drainage."

So Patrimonio Hoy developed a program called *Calle Digna* ("Worthy Street") that allows partners to make weekly payments for public improvements to their neighborhood streets. Their payments cover the cost of cement and other materials.

The city government pays a matching amount that includes the cost of labor and engineering. The overall cost of the improvements is split 50:50 between the city and neighborhood residents.

The city installs street paving, drainage improvements and water mains. Cemex loans the building materials so that construction can begin 18 weeks after members begin making weekly payments. Patrimonio Hoy has launched the program with the paving of ten streets in the Tonala municipality in a suburban area of Guadalajara.

"Before Patrimonio Hoy was here, the people were very isolated from each other," said Gloria Noemí Cárdenas, a Patrimonio Hoy project supervisor. "But when they started working together they learned they could get more from the government."

Magaña said the government is now installing water lines in her neighborhood. "When Patrimonio Hoy got started, we started seeing construction sites everywhere and the government paid more attention," she said. "When people get organized, they start looking for other things for their own neighborhood like schools, water pipes, police officers, and buses for public transportation. So there have been some changes here."

Patrimonio Hoy Services

Technical Assistance from Architects and Engineers

Patrimonio Hoy has discovered that 50 % of homebuilders in low-income communities do their own construction rather than hire a mason to help them. This has elevated the importance of providing technical assistance to do-it-yourself homebuilders.

When a person joins Patrimonio Hoy, two things happen immediately: they make their first weekly payment and they schedule an appointment with an engineer or architect to get help with the design of their construction project. "This is one of the most – if not *the* most – appreciated service," Moreno said.

"Never before could these people have accessed a professional to design the construction of their house. They think they don't deserve these kinds of solutions because they are living in the poorest neighborhoods, and in any case they think they can't afford to pay an architect or engineer. Now, with the money they are saving each week, they can access such benefits."

Patrimonio Hoy's architects and engineers employ a software program they call "the calculator" to provide various scenarios for the exact quantity of materials required, the costs involved, and delivery and construction schedules given available laborers. This tool helps them produce high-quality designs that optimize the use of land, interior space and materials, and to account for possible future growth. They also help homeowners set priorities regarding which improvements to make first.

Rosa Magaña's first house, a single room that now serves as her kitchen, was built before she was involved in Patrimonio Hoy by bricklayers who did not guarantee their work. "My husband spent a lot of money, but it is not well built," she said. "I haven't been able to put a window there because of the way it was constructed, and the room is really dark."

She expanded the house with the assistance of a Patrimonio Hoy architect. "He really helped us," she said. "He drew a sketch and advised us how to design it. He told us the measurement of the iron beams and the exact quantity of materials we'd need, so we didn't waste any material."

Magaña, who now has three children, plans to add a second-floor that includes three bedrooms. But adding a second floor above the original one-room structure will require adding columns to support the weight "because the room has no structural support – it has a concrete beam and could collapse," she said. "Without the advice from the architect, we'd have same structural problems with our new addition."

Support for Education: *Patrimonio Hoy Escolar*

Recognizing that housing and education are the two key components of patrimony, Patrimonio Hoy links support for education to its services through a program called *Patrimonio Hoy Escolar*. It donates building materials worth about 4 % of a member's weekly club fees to the elementary school of the member's choice.

"If you ask partners about their main worries for the future, two topics will emerge: housing and education," Moreno said. "The conditions in school are very poor. When a school is not attractive and a family needs money for food, they will say, 'Sorry son, quit the school and get a job to get some money to feed this household.' So there are a lot of school drop outs. Giving parents a way to contribute to better conditions in the schools means that their sons and daughters will get a better education."

School principals meet with their local parents' representative to decide how to use the funds that accumulate in a school's Patrimonio Hoy account. Typically, Patrimonio Hoy donates about US$1,500 worth of building materials to a school each year, which is equivalent to the amount of support a school receives from the government for improvements each year.

Some 400 public preschools, kindergartens and elementary schools are receiving this support from Patrimonio Hoy. It is another way to help build community, and it motivates school principals to promote Patrimonio Hoy to students' parents.

Professional School for Masons

Those who have some building experience can professionalize their skills, or learn more advanced techniques like roof construction, by attending Patrimonio Hoy's school for mansonry (*Escuela Para Albaniles*) and get certified to work as a mason. "In many cases their knowledge comes from traditions handed down from their father and grandfathers," Moreno said.

"Many of them are still using non-functional materials like dirt or mixtures that are not well proportioned. This is the cause of much poor construction, failures, and high costs for the client."

Some 500 members have completed the school. "Now we have a database of masons, so that when the people come to us to register as partners and they say 'I don't have a mason,' we can offer them referrals to partners who have graduated from the school," Moreno said." This generates work for our partners, another benefit of being in Patrimonio Hoy. Now they have a new competency – a new way to make more money.

The school opens up new possibilities for women. "There are cases where a women is doing the construction and her husband is the helper during weekends and holidays," Moreno said. "It's surprising when you see a woman buying bricks, and impressive when you see that she is a mason's assistant."

Guaranteeing Quality Materials and Delivery

Patrimonio Hoy pays dealers of building materials from the savings it has collected from its members. "If a customer isn't satisfied, Patrimonio Hoy can penalize the dealer with a discount, or reduce or stop orders to that dealer," Moreno said.

In the past, low-income consumers who wanted to buy half truckload of sand or 55 bricks from a dealer were told they must buy the minimum full truckload, or 500 bricks – making for an expensive waste of the excess materials. "Now, if you need 55 bricks, you will get 55 bricks," Moreno said.

"Patrimonio Hoy has the information and the money, and that's changing the rules of the game in favor of the customer. We are concentrating consumer power. Now the customers have the power, not the suppliers.

"Before, the entire industry was involved in price-based competition. Now, some competitors don't know how to react to this because it has nothing to do with prices. It is value offered to the customer."

Alicia Guerrero is a dealer who began selling Cemex cement products 8 years ago. She owns the Perez hardware store in Guadalajara's Mesa Colorada settlement, a business she founded with her husband 11 years ago.

Each week Patrimonio Hoy gives Guerrero delivery orders for its members. This gives her a more consistent, reliable stream of sales and has increased her business, she said. Cemex cement products comprise about 50 % of her sales, and this percentage is growing.

"If I deliver on time to these Patrimonio Hoy customers, then I'll gain a good reputation with them and they will become my clients," she said. "I think the way Patrimonio Hoy is working is fine. I think that they should work more on their sales department – promote more – so they can keep growing."

Lessons and Innovations from Low-Income Markets

While working to create cultural innovation in low-income communities, Cemex has been forced to adjust its own business culture to meet the requirements of low-income customers. Past attempts by Cemex and other Mexican cement companies to serve this market failed when the fundamental relationship between companies and their customers did not change.

Some of the lessons learned: introduction of easy-to-carry small bags of cement designed to reduce spoilage failed because customers wanted to have large bags of cement sitting in front of their house as a status symbol. Early educational programs took on the aura of the patron-client relationship, and this weakened customers' incentive to honor payment commitments.

Opening retail outlets near low-income communities stimulated bargain-hunting behavior in customers, which suppressed the potential for profit, or discouraged customers who felt the products must be for more wealthy customers. These stores, and the technical advice they offered, sometimes made customers feel pressured to undertake home improvement projects that were too daunting for them. And stores would not extend credit to poor people who lacked formal documents.

Cemex is learning that developing a market in low-income communities is a slow process. Extra time is required to earn the trust of residents and to enable low-income customers to see themselves as producers who can afford aspirations of owning quality, mainstream products.

When introducing the program, time must be allowed for intense exploratory conversations and testimonials from community members who have already joined the program. Patrimonio Hoy encourages members to consider expanding their homes one room at a time to avoid overwhelming them with the expense and effort required for a more comprehensive expansion. Loan sizes are kept small so they are not fearful sums that paralyze borrowers.

To be viable, Patrimonio Hoy must find ways to compensate for the added cost of recruiting low-income customers. It can do so by maintaining high levels of customer retention, encouraging repeat business, and getting customers to move up to more valuable and profitable products.

It helps that its customers tend to stay engaged after completing their first 70-weeks of payments because usually they have saved enough to build walls for a 100-square-foot room, but not for the roof. By continuing to save with Patrimonio Hoy they can complete the room and are likely to want to continue adding more rooms later. As they do this, they begin to identify themselves as successful producers who can afford higher aspirations.

Members who achieve a good payment record during their first 70-week savings period get the opportunity to "ladder up" to preferred customer status, for which they get added benefits. This includes free delivery, including to relatives or friends in other states, the opportunity to belong to a smaller savings group, receive more credit, receive all building materials in 3 weeks, and to accelerate payments by paying more frequently than weekly or by making larger payments. Earning these privileges helps to make establishing a good credit record an attainable and meaningful achievement for customers without a credit record.

Through its experience with Patrimonio Hoy, Cemex is learning to develop new kinds of services that go beyond simply manufacturing and selling cement. Cemex's Construmex service is an example of such an innovation. Through a toll-free 800 number in Houston, Cemex relays calls from customers in the United States to an account center in Guadalajara.

Construmex targets Mexicans who work in the United States and want to send money back to relatives in Mexico to help them construct a house. "Statistics show that at least 40 % of the money coming to Mexico from the U.S. goes to building materials," Moreno said. "For Mexicans who go to the U.S. to make a better life, it's a very strong dream to build a house for their wife or parents."

Construmex charges a flat fee of $1 to transfer funds regardless of the amount. It's a much better deal than funds transfer services that charge commissions of 8–12 %.

Money repatriated to Mexico for home construction often gets spent for other purposes as unanticipated emergencies and other various pressing needs arise. Construmex guarantees its customers that 100 % of funds will be spent for building materials because it delivers the materials – not cash – to the recipients.

Construmex offers Cemex's guarantees of quality for materials and delivery. Over the phone, it can offer the same type of technical assistance that Patrimonio Hoy members enjoy and it can facilitate the same type of expedited, reliable construction timetable.

The Patrimonio Hoy program is an important source of lessons for how operate in more affluent markets. Through it, Cemex is learning to listen to its customers, who are becoming more intelligent and demanding at all income levels, Moreno said

"In selling to poor people, you have to treat them like producers and not consumers," said Market Expansion Partners' Spinoza. "I believe that's a shift that's coming in our culture in general. Twenty years from now, this is a cultural innovation that we will say is true for all consumers.

"More and more, the kinds of products that sell will be things that help you make changes in your life. One of the models for doing this is working with poor people. It's a cutting edge way to work with how we are going to innovate in the future."

"Second, companies are going to penetrate these markets by developing new communities. Customers are evaluating products more and more in groups instead of at home, or experiencing them individually. That is a critical change that is happening in all markets, not just in poor markets. Companies that learn how to sell to communities are going to have an enormous advantage in the new economic conditions that are emerging."

Conclusion

"Our focus is not just on material things," Moreno said. "Doing business and finding solutions for these people are of equal importance".

"Yes, it's important to have your car and bank account, but if you're not able to empower your children with an ambition, vision and mission for the future, these material things will be lost for the next generation. Our philosophy is to give them the means – a bridge to possibilities – not just the things".

"We are making promises to them about having a better future, education, housing, public infrastructure, schools, quality of life and status. But people are tired of decades of so many false promises. That's why people in this low-income market are very distrustful".

"We are trying to change that situation and mentality with these people. Cemex is committed to social responsibility and to collaborate in the making of a different Mexico".

Bal Vikas Bank: Children as Bankers[2]

In early 2001, Rita Panicker, founder and director of an Indian NGO called Butterflies, was determined to find additional ways to help the many homeless children who worked and slept on the streets of India. Butterflies had put in place a variety of programs, including education, nighttime shelter, health care, and a "Resilience Center," but there was one area that Panicker, Butterflies, and other NGOs had not addressed: the children's finances.

Many of India's homeless children begged for a living, but many did not, instead earning pittances through a range of thankless and often demeaning jobs, from "rag picking" – looking for recyclables in piles of trash – to sweeping floors and running errands for street vendors. For a variety of reasons, the children had difficulty holding on to any cash they earned, so Panicker hoped to improve the children's lives by addressing this issue. She knew that others might scoff at the idea, but helping these children gain control of their personal finances could help them gain independence, some sort of stability, and perhaps even personal pride.

---

[2]This case was prepared by Jenny Mead and Patricia H. Werhane. Copyright ©2013 University of Virginia Darden School Foundation. All rights reserved.

Rita Panicker

Prior to founding Butterflies in 1989, Panicker, who received her master's degree in Development Studies from the Institute of Social Studies in The Hague, had taught at the Women's Studies Unit at the Tata Institute of Social Sciences in Bombay (which became Mumbai in 1995). Additionally, in the early 1980s, she had helped abused women in Kerala with their legal rights; served as a consultant on children's rights to UNICEF; founded the National NGO Forum for Street and Working Children, India; founded the Delhi NGO Forum; and served as the facilitator of the Delhi Child Rights Club. She also wrote and published many articles on the rights of children, the juvenile justice system, child labor, and street children, among others. She moved to Delhi with her husband, who worked for UNICEF, in 1987.

Butterflies

With the goal of creating "a world where every child is free to be a child and has hope for the future," Butterflies[3] focused on empowering all street and working children, first in Delhi – and then, as the NGO expanded, across India. Its mission statement read:

> BUTTERFLIES addresses the challenge of making the Convention on the Rights of the Child a reality, particularly of those children who are most vulnerable, neglected, abused and exploited. BUTTERFLIES is committed within its mandate, to work towards solidarity among NGOs, Government and all Civil Society organizations for addressing the concerns of all children.[4]

Butterflies took a noninstitutional, democratic approach in dealing with the children and encouraged the children's participation in decision making in all activities, whether it was program planning, monitoring, or evaluation. Because of this participatory approach, Butterflies preferred to call itself a "program with street and working children." The organization used "the Constitution of India, Laws related to Children and UN Convention on the Rights of the Child as a major tool for ensuring government and public accountability for all."[5]

---

[3] So named because, as Rita Panicker wrote, "A butterfly is one of nature's most beautiful creatures and so is a child. The butterfly flits from flower to flower for its sustenance. Our children move constantly for their livelihood. Butterflies have very short lives; street children have very brief childhoods." From the Butterflies e-newsletter, *Learning to Fly 19*. Jan–March 2008, http://www.butterflieschildrights.org/newsletter/but_14.pdf (accessed January 9, 2013).

[4] Butterflies child rights website, http://www.butterflieschildrights.org/ (accessed December 10, 2012).

[5] "Profile," Butterflies child rights website, http://www.butterflieschildrights.org/profile.php (Accessed December 10, 2012).

Street Children in India[6]

Because of the transitory nature of street children, most of whom are homeless, it was hard for organizations to give reliable estimates of their population, but in 1994, UNICEF had estimated that there were approximately 11 million street children in India (a number that many believed was too conservative). The Indian embassy had estimated that there were approximately 315,000 street children per city in Bombay, Calcutta, Bangalore, and others, and 100,000 in Delhi. According to UNICEF and other organizations, the street children were primarily boys; 40 % were between 11 and 15 years of age and 33 % were 6–10. Among other places, the children slept in night shelters, footpaths, flyovers, bridges, parks, market places, and bus stops. While some were living with their (homeless) families, the majority had run away from home because of physical or sexual abuse, family troubles, or because they wanted to go to a larger city.

The majority of Indian street kids worked on their own, as ragpickers, firewood collectors, street vendors, cloth dyers, shoe shiners, and animal tenders. Girls often worked as prostitutes. Many of the children stole to make a living. Those children who worked for others – in shops and factories, for example – were often taken advantage of by their bosses, sometimes even enslaved without pay. Government officials, particularly the police, were known to extort from many of the children, sometimes demanding all the money they had as "bribes." The children generally had 10–13-h workdays and earned, on average, between (Indian rupee) INR200 to INR830 per month – approximately (U.S. dollars) USD4 to USD15.[7] Because they feared their money would be stolen or taken away by corrupt officials, the street children tended to spend the money as quickly as they got it, thus ensuring a continued hand-to-mouth existence.

Life on the street was difficult for these children. Malnourishment was common, with many of the children underweight, and health conditions were abysmal. Because of the constant and often brutal abuse from municipal authorities and other adults, the street children in general did not trust adults. Getting them to so much as talk to an adult, Panicker had learned, could be difficult. They generally stayed in packs for protection and avoided adults whenever possible.

Bal Vikas Bank

In thinking about the children's situation, Panicker came up with the idea of creating a type of credit union in which the youth would play an integral part. Since the children had no permanent addresses and no official identities, no mainstream financial

---

[6]Information in this section taken from "Street Children," Childline India Foundation, http://www. childlineindia.org.in/street-children-india.htm; Consortium for Street Children, Street Children Statistics, http://www.streetchildren.org.uk/; and "The Problems of Street Children," i-India, http:// www.i-indiaonline.com/sc_crisis_theproblem.htm (all accessed December 15, 2012).

[7]Kombarakaran, Francis A. 2004. Street children of Bombay. *Children and Youth Services Review* 26(9):856.

institutions would lend them money. She involved the Butterflies children in creating the idea and coming up with the program. The result was Bal Vikas Bank, or the Children's Development Bank (CDB).[8]

The basics of the CDB were: The children themselves made the rules and all the decisions. Volunteers from HSBC Bank and other financial institutions would teach the children financial and banking skills. To open an account, a child had to fill out an application form in exchange for an account number and passbook. INR20 was required as an initial minimum deposit, and the interest was 3.5 % per month – unless the child kept the money for 11 months or longer, in which case they received a bonus of 50 % interest. A committee made up primarily of children determined who could become a member of the bank.

At first, the children were extremely conservative about who could join, turning down "smokers, drinkers, drug-takers, drug-peddlers, bullies, pickpockets, or gamblers [until] they soon realized none of them would qualify for a loan"[9] and consequently relaxed the rules. If one of the children wanted to start a business (opening their own food or toy carts, for example), as quite a few did, the volunteers would help them draw up a business plan and prepare an application. A loan com-mittee, again comprising mostly children, would consider the application, question the applicant about the business and a repayment plan, and decide whether or not to approve the loan. Panicker and others at Butterflies were pleased to see that, as the CDB caught on and took in more members, many of the street children had a very strong entrepreneurial spirit.

One former ragpicker, for example, took out a loan of USD104 from the CDB to buy a pushcart from which he sold wallets, T-shirts, and other items. Another boy took out a loan to start what eventually became a tea shop. With small steps, these enterprises had the chance to grow and thrive. And while some children used their money to eat and clothe themselves, others would send their savings back to their needy families in other cities.

Lessons Learned

As Panicker suspected, the CDB experience taught the children important lessons and helped give them a sense of self-confidence and security. Not only did they learn basic principles of banking, business plans, and earning interest, but they were introduced to the "issues of democratic functioning…to negotiate, draw rules and regulations,"[10] and the responsibility of taking care of other children's money. They learned life skills, how to make decisions, and management and entrepreneurial

---

[8] Later renamed Children's Development Khazana (CDK).

[9] Baldauf, Scott. (2002). Delhi street kids bank on each other. *Christian Science Monitor* 1.

[10] "Children's Collectives – Children's Development Khazana (CDK), Butterflies child rights website, http://www.butterflieschildrights.org/developmentBank.php (accessed December 20, 2012).

practices. As Panicker said, "the bank helps children to prioritize their needs and think about how they use their money…[but] more importantly they learn that it is important to have goals and to work towards them."[11]

Further Expansion

So successful was the Delhi CDB that Panicker and Butterflies, over the years, expanded the chapters. By 2008, there were more than 3,200 Indian children who were members of the bank, which now was in eight cities in India. Chapters existed in Afghanistan, Kyrgyzstan, Nepal, Bangladesh, and Sri Lanka, with various NGOs in each new location managing the program. By early 2011, there were 199 branches in Asia, with almost 10,000 participating children. Since the program's inception, almost 30,000 children had become active members.

[11] Blakely, Rhys. 2008. Bank tips balance in favour of street children. *London Times* 67.

Chapter 7
Working at the Base of the Pyramid

Introduction

Chapter 5 illustrated creative ways in which one can help finance those without assets who are in need. In this chapter we will explore three methodologies for improving the plight of those who live "at the base of the pyramid." Some time ago C. K. Prahalad and Stuart Hart created a graphic that explicitly described the global distribution of populations and wealth (See Fig. 1, Introduction). For this book we have updated the numbers, but the distribution of wealth and poverty, although changing (see Fig. 2, Introduction) is still unacceptable.

While there is a temptation to increase philanthropic efforts in developing countries, as William Easterly explains, since the Second World War the industrial nations have contributed more than 13 trillion dollars to development, and, as he concludes, with little success, particularly in Sub-Saharan Africa and parts of Asia.[1] So the task of poverty alleviation requires us to come up with different models. This chapter illustrates three of them.

Hindustan Lever (HHL), a division of the giant global company, Unilever, located in India, saw itself as losing market share, particularly among the poorest of the poor who, despite their meager incomes, needed and bought soap products. Creating competing products and marketing to poor villagers seemed an approach that most companies would adopt. However, as you will read, HHL went much further and created jobs for local people to sell their products, and is now embarked on environmentally sustainable initiatives to make better biodegradable products.

The Grameen Bank, headed by the Nobel Prize Bangladeshi, Muhammad Yunus, was one of the first to introduce microlending, limiting clients to only those who had no assets. This approach turns upside down traditional economic approaches. Still it has been enormously successful in reducing poverty first in Bangladesh and in other countries where the model has been replicated.

---

[1] Easterly, William. 2006. *The white man's burden*. New York: Penguin Press.

P.J. Albert et al. (eds.), *Global Poverty Alleviation: A Case Book*, The International Society of Business, Economics, and Ethics Book Series 3, DOI 10.1007/978-94-007-7479-7_7,
© Springer Science+Business Media Dordrecht 2014

e-Choupal is an Indian initiative aimed and creating communication facilities between farmers in remote villages, allowing them to sell their products where they are needed rather than creating surpluses or shortages in various areas. These thee approaches demonstrate that finance, self-development, technology, and job creation, rather than philanthropy work most effectively to create economic value-added in every community, no matter how dire the economic circumstances appear to be.

Hindustan Lever Limited (HLL) and Project Sting (A)[2]

At 9:30 a.m. on a Monday morning in June 1987, the top managers of Hindustan Lever Limited (HLL), the Indian subsidiary of the giant multinational Unilever PLC, were gathered at HLL headquarters in Bombay to discuss the launch of Project STING – "Strategy to Inhibit Nirma Growth." In its more than 40 years in the Indian market, HLL had maintained a largely unbeatable reputation and performance history, so it was fairly strange that top management would spend time discussing strategies to inhibit the growth of a small company such as Nirma. Over the past decade, however, Nirma had seemingly emerged from nowhere to overtake HLL in the detergent sector. So far, HLL had ignored rural India as a potential market, but Nirma's recent success in this area had sent HLL straight to the drawing board.

At this particular meeting, HLL's top executives planned to discuss how best to regain the country's dominance in India's detergent market. The first goal of Project STING was to understand the Nirma business model and determine how this upstart company had become so successful. Following this, HLL would have to evaluate its performance and rethink the HLL strategy in order to compete effectively with Nirma and overtake them. HLL also had to decide whether it should enter the rural Indian market and, if it did, what products, strategies, and tactics would be the most effective.

Hindustan Lever Limited

Hindustan Lever Limited (HLL) was the Indian subsidiary of Unilever PLC, one of the world's largest multinational corporations. Founded in 1930 and based jointly in the Netherlands and the United Kingdom, Unilever sold its products in approximately 150 countries. Before the founding of Unilever, Lever Products arrived in India at the

---

[2] These cases were prepared by Pia S. Ahmad and Jenny Mead under the supervision of Patricia H. Werhane and Michaael Gorman. Copyright ©2004 University of Virginia Darden School Foundation. All rights reserved. The Addendum was prepared by Tim Rolph.

end of nineteenth century when India was part of the British Empire. The first Lever product introduced in India was Sunlight soap in 1888, followed by Lifebuoy in 1895, and Pears, Lux, and Vim over the next several years. Only the British citizens in India and a small section of the Indian population could afford these soaps, thus establishing early on an upscale profile typical of HLL's Indian customers.

In 1931, Unilever had established the Hindustan Vanaspati Manufacturing Company, its first Indian subsidiary, which produced *vanaspati*, granular edible oil. Two years later, Unilever created Lever Brothers India Limited specifically to manufacture soaps, and in 1935, founded United Traders Limited to market personal products. These three companies merged as Hindustan Lever Limited in 1956. Along with Lipton, Brooke Bond, Pond's, Quest, and the Assam and South India tea estates, HLL was one of Unilever's seven India-based companies. Unilever was a popular and respected company in India, in no small part because the company's "think globally, act locally" principle led it to train and appoint Indian managers instead of Europeans. Unilever realized the importance of employing managers who understood both the "Indian way" and the "Unilever way." After a series of exclusively non-Indian managers, Prakash Tandon became the first Indian director of the company in 1951. By 1955, 65 % of all managers were Indian. As in all other countries where it had a presence, Unilever brought the local managers to train at the Unilever head offices in London.

HLL was among the first foreign subsidiaries to offer Indian equity and maintained 10 % Indian participation. By the late 1970s, HLL had gained the reputation of being a role model for companies looking to succeed in India and was one of the most sought after places to work in the country. With products ranging from food and beverage to home and personal care, HLL was considered India's largest household-product packaged mass-consumption goods company. Unilever gradually divested its stake in HLL, and by 1982, held only 52 % equity in the company.

HLL was also the undisputed leader in the Indian detergent market. Traditionally, Indians had used bars or tablets of soap to wash their clothes, a process involving the scrubbing of wet garments with soap and then beating them with a club (similar to a baseball bat) or against a stone. When HLL introduced the revolutionary Surf washing powder (bright blue and packaged in a large, colorful carton) in 1959, HLL effected an enormous change as people switched from the club to the bucket. HLL's marketing strategy involved giving demonstrations of washing clothes in buckets with washing powder. Surf was an immediate success and occupied the top spot in the national detergent market.

While switching from a bar of soap to washing powder promised to revolutionize how Indian people washed clothes, only a fraction of them could afford Surf. Most of the rural poor continued to use soap bars and clubs. Expensive at the onset, Surf doubled in price in the early 1970s because of a rise in the price of crude oil and a massive increase in the cost of raw materials, placing the detergent even more out of reach of the rural people. Nonetheless, even though more new medium-sized competitors appeared in the Indian market, HLL maintained dominance until Karsanbhai Khodidas Patel, a chemist in the western state of Gujarat, and his product Nirma arrived on the clothes-washing scene.

The Rise of Nirma

In 1969, Karsanbhai Patel's life typified that of millions of other Indians. A chemist with the Gujarat Minerals Development Corporation in a dingy Ahmadabad factory in Gujarat, Patel struggled to make ends meet on a meager salary. "The work was dull," Patel would say later, "and my salary of 400 [Indian rupees] was grossly insufficient to take care of all my expenses."[3] Patel recognized, however, that there was a vacuum in the rural Indian market for affordable detergent. There were two choices: low-quality soap bars that did not wash well and were very time-intensive and upscale detergent brands that were effective but too expensive. Recognizing the need for an affordable detergent and concluding that a good product would create its own market, Patel used his background as a chemist to conduct detergent-making experiments in his kitchen. His efforts finally yielded a pale yellow powder he named "Nirma" after his then 1-year-old daughter Niranjana.

Soon Patel was producing small quantities of this washing powder and selling it to his neighbors in small, stapled, nondescript pouches. Even though Nirma's quality was inferior to Surf's, Patel's powder was far more effective for washing clothes than the traditional slab of soap had been. Every morning Patel rode his bicycle door-to-door marketing his washing powder – and sold an average of 200 kg a day. His efforts were so successful that Nirma began appearing in neighborhoods, towns, and cities all over the state of Gujarat. Wholesalers and distributors from farther away began arriving at Patel's doorstep asking to buy and distribute Nirma. In 1972, Patel registered his company as Nirma Chemical Works and opened two more production facilities over the next few years. Soon afterward, his product was available all over India, and the rural poor finally had an easier option for washing their clothes.

A New Business Model: The Nirma Way[4]

Although he hired additional employees as Nirma expanded, Patel stuck to his simple means of production for the next 10 years. He kept his company lean by outsourcing all the administrative functions and contracting out the sales, accounting, and technical production capabilities and distribution. By keeping his internal costs minimal, Patel had the flexibility to negotiate price during slow periods. Until 1985, the Nirma ingredients were simply mixed by hand, requiring no machinery or capital investment. Due to the scale of the product and the simple,

---

[3] "Karsanbhai Patel – A Clean Sweep," http://www.indiaprofile.com/people/karsanbhaipatel.htm. Accessed March 29, 2010.

[4] Butler, Charlotte, and Sumantra Ghosal 2002. *Hindustan Lever Limited: Levers for change* (302-199-1). Fontainebleau, France: INSEAD Euro-Asia Center. Much of the information in this section derives from the Butler and Ghosal case.

nonmechanized production process, Nirma was granted a number of tax exemptions and benefits for not using electricity; it did not have to pay the excise duties levied on multinationals.

As a cottage industry, Nirma was not compelled to abide by minimum-wage rules, so it saved millions in labor costs. Patel used contract workers who were paid (Indian rupees) INR85 per ton (in 1985, INR12.368 = 1 U.S. dollar) for mixing raw materials and then placing them in bags weighing 1 kg each. Because payment was by the bag and no worker was permanent, Patel did not have to pay any worker benefits. By the mid-1980s, when Nirma started to mechanize the production process, the company was well established.

Patel also kept an eye on costs when setting up a distribution system. Once the demand for Nirma had outgrown Patel's ability to make deliveries by bicycle, he moved on to using vans and then later to trucks. Nirma employed neither a field sales force nor owned a distribution network. Patel negotiated prices with truck and van suppliers on a daily basis. As sales grew, Patel eventually hired stockists, who stocked additional quantities of the goods, as commission agents, a move that helped him avoid a central sales tax. He made the stockists responsible for all transportation, octroi,[5] handling, and delivery costs. Initially, these stockists were friends or family members; but as the operation grew, others were brought into the fold. To minimize risk for Nirma, Patel established strict protocols, and distribution depended on prepayment for stocks. Despite small trade margins, these stockists remained intensely loyal to Patel because of the high volume, quick turnover, and business opportunity (and increased income) that he and Nirma had provided.

At first, Patel did not advertise, but as television slowly spread throughout rural India in the late 1970s, he placed Nirma ads – with simple messages and catchy jingles – on television. By the early 1980s, Nirma became synonymous with good quality and low price. The stockists were also responsible for promotions, and they funded 50 % of the promotional expenditure for their goods. Nirma's sales reached a growth rate two to three times that of the industry in general. As a result of all these measures, Nirma survived and flourished on what looked like a miniscule margin per unit. Patel even created a new word "nirmagenic," in the late 1990s, to describe a product's successful production and ongoing strength in the marketplace.[6]

Nirma's extremely simple distribution system stood in sharp contrast with HLL's multilayered system. Put into place in the late 1940s, HLL's system had four tiers: factories, carrying and forwarding agents, redistribution stockists, and retailers. While this system provided an extensive network for the sale of HLL products, it also contributed to their higher cost.

---

[5] Octroi is essentially a regional import tax applicable to goods to be locally sold, used, or consumed.

[6] "We Don't Feel the Need to Adopt Any Hardsell." *Economic Times* (India), (July 23, 1999).

Marketing, Packaging, and Other Innovative Nirma Ploys

At first, packets of Nirma featured a generic picture of a woman washing clothes. In 1973, Patel put a picture of his daughter, for whom the soap was named, on the package, giving it a distinctive and personal aspect that helped Nirma stand out from the other detergents. Patel then embarked on some innovative marketing strategies. To gain trade acceptance, he hired women to go into retail shops and ask for the product. The company then began holding contest drawings, giving large sums of money as reward. The Nirma calendar along with plastic shop boards were introduced in 1982, and Nirma was the only Indian company to advertise at the 1980 Moscow Olympics. To spread its name recognition even farther, the company plastered Nirma advertisements in stores, village shops, newspapers, and vans. Television and radio ads featured a constant stream of Nirma ads accompanied by the catchy jingle, "Nirma washes clothes white as milk." By 1986, Nirma had the highest "top-of-mind" recall and an overall aware-ness level of 90 %.

Nirma first caught HLL's eye and piqued its curiosity in 1977, during an offi-cial tour of North India, when S. Sen, a former HLL marketing director, noticed that Nirma was ubiquitous, whether in shops, on posters, or in advertisements plastered throughout remote villages and in newspapers. Sen's mental calculator had been at work, and he soon began to realize that this small upstart detergent was taking away business that could have belonged to HLL. Curious to meet the reclusive Karsanbhai Patel, Sen went to Patel's office but was turned away before he could gain an audience with him. Thinking quickly, Sen asked for a cup of water, a request that could not be refused in this polite society and a tactic that brought him into the Nirma offices. Once there and face to face with his eventual competitor, Patel told Sen:

> You are selling detergents. I am selling detergents. We are competing. I don't want to talk. Soon, you see, I will be bigger than Surf. I will be number one in India. After that, I will be number one in the world.[7]

Despite Patel's strong words and Sen's genuine concern that this competitor was probably right, it still took many years for HLL to take Nirma seriously.

Product Differences

The key difference between Surf and Nirma was the price, but the ingredients also set the two products apart. Aware that soda ash, the main raw material for his product, was abundant in Gujarat, Patel set up shop in the vicinity. In designing his product, Patel kept things simple and essentially violated all of HLL's detergent-design rules.

---

[7] Butler and Ghosal, 11.

Nirma contained no "active detergent," whitener, perfume, or softener. Indeed, tests performed on Nirma confirmed that it was hard on the skin and could cause blisters. Despite these differences, Nirma soap was a success.

Understanding the Rural Market

HLL's dismissal of the huge market segment of India's rural poor was based in part on traditional business theories. C. K. Prahalad and Allen Hammond, however, have likened the worldwide market to a four-tiered pyramid.[8] (See Fig. 1 in the Introduction for the World Pyramid.) The top tier consisted of the 75 million to 100 million people earning more than $20,000 a year. These people were considered to belong to the elite and middle- and upper-income segments of society, with most of them living in the developed world. The second and third tiers (estimated at approximately 1.75 billion people) consisted of the rising middle classes that lived mostly in developing countries and earned between $2,000 and $20,000 a year. At the bottom of the pyramid, in tier 4, approximately four billion people lived mostly in developing countries, earning less than $2,000 a year.

Typically, multinational companies (MNCs) focused on the first tier since it provided for the highest margin of returns. In many cases, people in the second and third tiers of the pyramid received attention, but the people at the bottom of the pyramid were usually ignored. It is interesting to note, however, that the top three tiers represented only 34 % of the world's population. MNCs have made the assumption that people in tier 4 do not have any disposable income and so cannot afford most products. Nirma's success in rural India, however, dispelled this myth. Additionally, MNCs ignored tier 4 markets because they were considered a "disorganized sector" in which a lack of infrastructure and development made effective marketing and distribution of products almost impossible. MNCs' high overhead costs also made it hard to be price competitive with local companies and thus serve as an additional barrier to entering this market.

The Case of Rural India

With an estimated annual growth rate of 1.7 % in the early 1980s, India was the second most-populous country in the world. The country's total population was around 750 million, with 70 % living in rural areas. (See Exhibit 1 for a map of

---

[8] Prahalad, C. K., and Stuart L. Hart. The fortune at the bottom of the pyramid, *strategy + business* 26, First Quarter 2002, 48–57. Booz Allen Hamilton.

India). This 70 % – or 525 million people – was almost twice the population of the United States and constituted 12 % of the world's population. By the year 2010, its population was expected to reach 1.15 billion.

Despite the sheer size and potential volume of business in India's rural areas, HLL avoided this potential market for the simple reason that it was physically very difficult to penetrate. Rural Indians lived in approximately 570,000 villages spread across the Indian countryside. Approximately 90 % of these villages were small (populations of fewer than 2,000) and extremely remote. Most villages lacked electricity and running water as well as telephones and Internet access. Because of a lack of infrastructure, only 45 % of the villages were accessible by road, and many of these roads were impassable in bad weather.

HLL had been deterred from entering this market not only because of the physical challenges, but also because of these villages' "social and cultural" climates and the ineffectiveness of conventional marketing and advertising tactics. MNCs had never approached this rural "client group." Creating product awareness through banners and leaflets was ineffective because only 43 % of the rural population could read; television and radio were almost equally ineffective given that only 57 % of the population was reachable by mass media. A media campaign was complicated by the country's 15 recognized languages and several hundred dialects. If HLL was going to make any dent in this market, it would have to be extremely innovative in its approach.

HLL Slumbers While Nirma Overtakes Surf: The War of the Bubbles

Even though Nirma was the second-largest volume seller in the country by 1977, other companies did not take the product seriously, believing that it was a regional product that would have only temporary success. HLL marketing executives predicted that at such a low price, the Patel was making margins per unit that would not sustain his business for long. HLL believed itself a superior company with a superior brand and that the only clients worth pursuing were the Indian middle class and the elite. HLL continued to avoid the rural and low-income market, believing that the rural market was too disorganized and too poor and that HLL's high overhead costs would restrict it from producing a low-cost detergent. Besides, HLL did not consider Nirma a true threat and decided to wait and watch.

Despite its somewhat inferior quality, Nirma was in high demand by rural housewives because it sold at a third of the typical soap price. By 1977, with a 12 % market share, Nirma was the second-largest volume seller of detergent in India; Surf was the leader with 33 %. Still, HLL did not consider Nirma a threat; it laughed at the minuscule per-unit margins Nirma was making and simply waited for its bubble to burst. But by 1984, Nirma was the number-one brand in Asia.[9] Patel explained the phenomenal growth:

> I found a massive market segment that was hungry for a good-quality product at an affordable price, so I decided to keep my margins very low and was happy if I could net between 3 % and 5 %...profits really came from the huge volumes we generated.[10]

With its leap from no market share in 1976 to 61.6 % of the market share in 1987, Nirma had pushed HLL from the top spot. Despite being ousted from the top by the little detergent upstart, HLL still did not reduce the price of Surf, which remained 2.5–3.6 times as expensive as Nirma. According to HLL – and proven by laboratory tests – Nirma did not contain any whitening ingredient, had insufficient active detergent, had no perfume, and was rough on the skin. In short, "Nirma was inferior to Surf and other premium powders on every single characteristic normally measured."[11] Yet despite all these factors, Nirma had outperformed Surf in the market.

HLL Reacts

By 1985, Nirma was outselling Surf three to one. While Nirma had a market share of 58 %, Surf's had dropped to 8.4 %. From nowhere, Nirma had risen to become one of the largest-selling detergent brands in the world, not only increasing its share of the pie but increasing the size of the pie itself. Moving into a thus far untapped market, Patel was responsible for expanding the detergent market tenfold.

HLL researchers continued to examine Nirma for safety and effectiveness. They reported that persistent use of Nirma caused blisters on the skin and damaged clothes by weakening fabric in the long run. According to HLL's R&D team, these side effects were due to Nirma's high soda ash content. Despite these criticisms, Nirma was being perceived as a much cheaper and fairly comparable alternative to Surf.

Consumer preference and HLL's massive decrease in sales forced the company to finally "get it," recognizing that Nirma was here to stay and that it was successfully toppling the giant from the bottom of the pyramid. Finally, in 1986, Nirma started testing a new detergent bar that would be directly marketed as a challenge to Rin, HLL's leading and most profitable detergent bar at the time. At this point, HLL was aware that Nirma was systematically undermining its dominance in the industry and, for the first time, HLL got a glimpse of what could be the "beginning of the end" of their detergent business. It was time for HLL to react. The company had taken the first step with the creation of Project STING; now it had to put its plan into action.

---

[9] "One Man Show Rivals Multi Nationals". *Responsive Database Services, Inc., Business and Industry* 37(2):26.

[10] "A Clean Sweep."

[11] Butler and Ghosal, 8.

Exhibit 1: Hindustan Lever Limited (HLL) and Project Sting (A)

Map of India

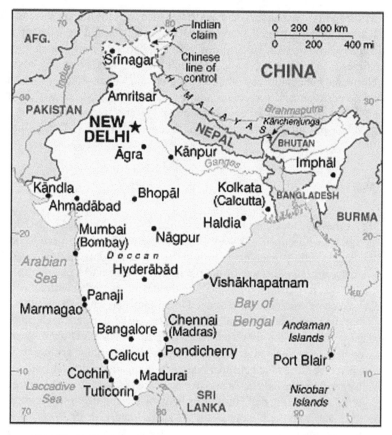

(Source: CIA World Factbook, https://www.cia.gov/library/publications/the-world-factbook/geos/in.html (Accessed March 29, 2010))

Hindustan Lever Limited (HLL) and Project Sting (B)

Hindustan Lever Limited's New Strategy

The success story of Karsanbhai Patel's Nirma detergent had shown that many people in rural India did in fact have the money to buy packaged goods – if only the products could be delivered to them cheaply enough. Because Nirma threatened the very existence of Hindustan Lever Limited's (HLL) detergent business, HLL had formed Project STING in 1987 to develop a strategy to inhibit its growth. Project STING's participants had decided that HLL should enter the rural market, and now HLL needed to decide how best to compete with Nirma and its efficient and lean low-cost business model. This was a big step for HLL, and everyone was watching: Unilever, the parent company, Nirma, the competition, and all the critics. Under tremendous pressure to succeed, HLL faced some daunting questions.

Could the company even produce a product that was competitive to Nirma in price? There were several options to consider. Should they repackage Surf for rural consumption? Should they give the uneducated rural consumer a cheaper version of the urban counterpart or should they design a new product for the rural market? What would be the research and development costs involved in developing a new product? Additionally, HLL had to strategize distribution; unless the company could ensure the availability of its products at all centers and to all vendors on a continuous basis, entering rural India was not a worthwhile endeavor.

As had been evident from Nirma's success, the bottom of the pyramid could be very profitable as long as a company understood that low costs combined with high unit sales were essential. In rural India, the game was about volume and capital efficiency. HLL had to ensure that every aspect of the process, be it product design, marketing, or distribution, was as innovative as possible. As C. K. Prahalad and Stuart Hart state in their analysis of the world's market, which they divided into a four-tiered pyramid, "The bottom of the pyramid poses a fundamentally new question: How do we marry low cost, good quality, sustainability, and profitability at the same time?"[12] HLL needed to think of all these issues during the product design stage.

If HLL could understand the everyday needs of this new client group, the company could develop a product for the poor. Unlike Patel's kitchen, HLL had its own R&D facilities, as well as those of Unilever's subsidiaries in other countries. In addition, if their product became a success, they would not only profit in India but also would have the choice of exporting it and related technologies to other Unilever markets.

Entering rural India would be a costly experiment for HLL if the new product failed; however, if it were a success, Unilever would be the MNC that led the way into the tier 4-market. This would give the company an additional advantage in the other developing markets where it did business. At the same time, the Indian government was opening its doors to more companies, and, with liberalization around the corner, HLL was well aware that they would soon be faced with even more competition. The positive side of these deregulation policies was that HLL would now face far fewer constraints on output volume and taxes and could be more competitive in terms of price.

---

[12] Prahalad, C. K., and Stuart L. Hart. The fortune at the bottom of the pyramid, *strategy + business* 26, First Quarter 2002, 48–57. Booz Allen Hamilton.

Analyzing the Market

Fraught with difficulties, rural India, with its 525 million people spread across a country the size of continental Western Europe, was both a challenging and attractive market. As part of their background work, HLL conducted research on rural income levels. Contrary to the popular belief that rural people were poor, the company's research showed that a typical rural family earned approximately 4,800 rupees ($103) a year from crops and odd jobs in the city.[13] In most cases, unlike city dwellers, rural Indians did not pay for either food or housing. While they had less total income, rural Indians had a higher percentage of disposable income than their urban counterparts who paid for both food and rent. India's rural market was comprised of 525 million people, approximately 12 % of the world's population. Once HLL had established the fact that rural Indians had the ability to buy goods, the company decided to go the extra distance to bring their goods to this new, unusual but sizeable, client group.

HLL did not define this market in the traditional fashion of calculating the number of times rural Indians used detergent, but instead looked at the number of times these potential customers washed their clothes. Rural clients did not use detergent every time they washed their clothes; unlike their urban counterparts, detergent was a luxury for rural Indians, so they would only use a detergent "x percent" of the time. HLL's goal was not to get 50 % of the existing detergent market, but to get customers to increase the number of times they washed in a year and then to ensure that 50 % of all these "washes" were done with the HLL product. An increased percentage of washes done with washing powder meant an increase in demand for that detergent.

While HLL seemed to be on the right track, the problem was how to increase the number of washes per year in rural areas where most villagers did not even have running water. If people often washed their clothes and bathed in the same river water, would multiplying the number of times they washed their clothes result in a more polluted river? Higher pollution levels would not help HLL in the long run because people would stop buying the company's products, and the number of washes would decrease. In addition, how would HLL convince rural consumers to buy more detergent when they had a limited amount of disposable income? Stimulating demand by launching a convincing and appealing ad campaign would have to be part of the process.

Designing a Product to Fit the Needs of a Market

Many questions and issues confronted HLL in its design of an appropriate product for the rural Indian market. The company could just reprice and repackage a

---

[13] Balu, Rekha. 2001. Strategic innovation: Hindustan Level Ltd. *Fast Company* 47:120.

mediocre version of the urban variant of the product and sell it in rural India. This would not build brand loyalty but it would keep costs down for HLL, and the poor might not even know the difference. While there were different opinions within the company about whether the rural consumer were savvy enough to tell the difference between a low-end and high-end detergent, HLL decided to go with the latter. To create brand loyalty and win customers away from Nirma, HLL reasoned that its product would have to be both high-quality and a good value for the money. Peddling low-quality products at cheap prices would not motivate clients to buy their products in the future. HLL decided that building brand loyalty was essential because the hope was that someday the residents of each rural village would join India's ever-growing middle class and trade up to more expensive HLL products. In a market where people gravitated toward the cheapest product, building brand loyalty was a challenge, and product quality was the essential first step.

Understanding the consumer was important in product design. Rural Indian consumers were very different from any of HLL's previous clients. Because rural consumers bathed and washed their clothes in the same river water, low toxicity and pollution levels were a vital element in the product design. Additionally, consumers lived in remote places, difficult to access by traditional means of transport, so the product had to be durable. Poor storage facilities in rural areas necessitated a product able to withstand heat and dust exposure. Unlike their urban counterparts, who bought in bulk at the Sam's Clubs and Coscos of India, the rural consumer would never have the spare income to follow suit. Consequently, HLL would have to package the product in small packets so that per-unit costs could be kept low. HLL was hoping to make a profit not on margin per unit but on total volume.

For the top managers at HLL, effective project design meant coming up with a product that would fulfill the following criteria[14]:

- High quality (superior to Nirma)
- Lack of toxicity with minimal pollution
- Sufficient durability for rough transportation conditions
- Tolerant of heat and dust, with a long shelf life
- High value for the money
- Low unit price and high functionality
- Self-visibility and display
- Packaging and contents that were disposable and dispensable
- Availability in small packages
- A strong but cost efficient marketing campaign
- Wide distribution throughout rural India

---

[14] Hart, Stuart L., C. K. Prahalad, and S. Ramachander. 1998. The concept of marketing insight: linking innovation to business goals. Presentation, International Conference on Corporate Marketing Communications, University of Strathclyde.

A New Definition of Product Design

In its attempt to create brand equity and develop long-term relationships with rural consumers, HLL had to keep in mind how the product would be used (in rivers) and focus on defining the benefits of its product to rural consumers. In determining the pricing strategy, HLL had to understand that the rural Indian had little money to spare. Finally, because HLL thought its product was superior to Nirma, part of its marketing strategy had to be convincing the consumer of that superiority; as it stood, consumers had started to perceive Nirma as a cheaper substitute for Surf. The perception of a new product would not be based solely on product performance and quality but on a combination of factors, and HLL had defined and articulated these factors. The list of demands for product design and marketing was long and unusual, and the top managers on the Project STING team needed to determine how HLL could fulfill these demands and then move forward.

Hindustan Lever 2013 Case Addendum

Since the writing of this case, Hindustan Lever's (HLL) Wheel soap has continued its strong market presence, but in late 2011 Ghari, a product of RSPL (Rohit Surfactancts Pvt. Ltd.), edged out Wheel for largest market share. At that time, Ghari held a market share of 17.4 %, Wheel 16.9 %, and Nirma less than 6 %,[15] with the latter having lost significant ground when multinational brands began cutting prices in 2004.[16]

Ghari, launched in 1987, spends under 2 % of sales on advertising and promotion, but uses it to aggressively target rural customers and convert them from low-quality unbranded local products. Ghari is built on Nirma's low-cost, high-volume model[17] and also uses roadshow-style promotions. Perhaps its most recognizable campaign is the Ghari Detergent Express, a train with the exterior covered in Ghari advertisements that ran for several months, traveling to and from various rural locations. Ghari's slogan loosely translates to "Use it and then Believe it."[18]

Ghari also shuns the use of celebrity advertisements, as opposed to Wheel, as it feels that it is inconsistent with the spirit of the brand. Ghari has a network of over

---

[15] http://articles.economictimes.indiatimes.com/2012-01-10/news/30611850_1_bimal-kumar-gyanchandani-ghari-laundry-market

[16] http://articles.economictimes.indiatimes.com/2011-04-22/news/29463111_1_ghari-detergents-indian-detergent-market-detergent-brands

[17] http://articles.economictimes.indiatimes.com/2011-05-06/news/29517095_1_ghari-detergent-brand-nirma

[18] http://www.business-standard.com/article/management/watch-out-for-ghari-express-110110100048_1.html

3,500 dealers across 19 Indian states and offers the dealers a profit margin of 9 % compared to the 6 % or 7 % of its competitors.[19] Ghari has also recently implemented mobile phone technology to streamline booking and tracking sales.[20]

Part of Wheel's continued success is due to its innovative marketing strategies, which include a 'mobile campaign' in which, during early 2012, Wheel promoted a toll-free number to consumers on radio stations throughout the country. Consumers were encouraged to give a 'missed call' to the number, after which they would receive a call back that would play humorous conversation snippets between a husband and wife. There were eight possible jokes, and each set was tailored to specific regions. The campaign generated over five million missed calls, and was considered a major success, especially owing to the program's low cost for HLL and it being completely free for consumers.[21]

Two other HLL initiatives are important to mention. First, Hindustan Lever has worked tirelessly to reduce its environmental footprint. According to its website, "We have set ourselves three big goals to achieve by 2020: Halve the environmental footprint of our products, Help more than 1 billion people take action to improve their health and well-being, Source 100 % of our agricultural raw materials sustainably." At the end of 2012, the company reported the following results against its 2020 "Sustainable Living" goals:

- Lifebuoy soap has reached 47 million people with handwashing programmes since 2010.
- 45 million people globally gained access to safe drinking water from Pureit in-home water purifier, till 2012.
- By the end of 2012, 66 % of our food portfolio (by volume) is compliant with the 5 g salt target
- We have more than 30,000 freezers with Hydrocarbon (HC) technology deployed in India.
- Over 60 % of tomatoes used in Kissan Ketchup in India are from sustainable sources.
- A total of 77 Tea estates in Assam, West Bengal and Tamil Nadu have been certified 'Sustainable Estates' by the Rainforest Alliance™ till the end of 2012.
- Number of Shakti entrepreneurs scaled up to 48,000; No. of Shaktimaans scaled up to more than 30,000.
- Kwality Wall's mobile vending operations provide entrepreneurship opportunities to over 6,500 migrant labourers across India.
- By 2015, we expect 70 billion litres of water to be harvested, one million people to benefit and 15 % rise in crop production expected in villages across India.

---

[19] http://www.business-standard.com/article/management/watch-out-for-ghari-express-110110100048_1.html

[20] http://www.business-standard.com/article/technology/using-mobiles-to-book-sales-track-distributors-111092100021_1.html

[21] http://www.hul.co.in/brands-in-action/detail/Active-Wheel-s-Mobile-Campaign-a-huge-success-in-U-P--and-Bihar/301896/

- CO emissions per tonne of production in India reduced by 22 %, water use by 29 % and waste by 77 % compared to 2008*. (*per tonne of production in 2012 over 2008 baseline)
- 30 sites became Zero-discharge site out of 38 sites; Rainwater harvesting implemented in 22 sites
- Launched Magic water saver & Comfort 1 Rinse in laundry – Comfort 1 Rinse saves 2 buckets of water per wash; Magic water saver saves 3 buckets of water per wash. [22]

By 2012, Project Shakti had 48,000 entrepreneurs (Shakti *ammas*) in 15 states. The Shakti *ammas* now cover over 135,000 villages and serve 3.3 million households. The door-to-door selling operation effectively serves poor rural communities.

HLL aims to increase the number of Shakti entrepreneurs to 75,000 by 2015. (It operates similar schemes in Bangladesh, Sri Lanka and Vietnam, and HLL is committed to expanding these programs, as well.)[23]

The Grameen Bank and Muhammad Yunus[24]

> The world has always visualized capitalism by saying that the driving force is greed. But Grameen is a capitalist institution. We are gung-ho about maximizing profits. Now you cannot say that greed is moving this bank, so your theory will have a shock coming.[25]
>
> – Muhammad Yunus

The year was 1971 and Bangladesh had finally become independent from Pakistan. Bangladesh's population had almost passed 68 million, with 92 % living in rural areas. With a total land area slightly less than the state of Iowa, many areas of Bangladesh were facing overcrowding, with an average of 514 people per square kilometer. The country's new government did little to combat the poverty, and even in 2012, with a population of 165 million, 76 % of the population lives on under $2.00 a day.[26]

Muhammad Yunus, a professor of economics at Chittagong University in Bangladesh, had returned to his native country in 1972 after receiving a Ph. D. in Economics from Vanderbilt University. That year Bangladesh was experiencing widespread famine, and Yunus spent a considerable amount of time speaking to people in the village of Jobra near his university. He began experimenting with

---

[22] http://www.hul.co.in/. Accessed June 7, 2013.

[23] http://www.hul.co.in/Images/USLP%E2%80%93India-2012-Progress-Report_tcm114-241468. pdf. Accessed June 7, 2013.

[24] This case was prepared by Tim Rolph under the direction of Patricia Werhane, DePaul University.

[25] Bornstein, David. 1996. *The price of a dream*, 342. New York: Simon and Schuster.

[26] http://databank.worldbank.org. Accessed June 1, 2013.

several programs and innovations to increase and better manage the yield of the villagers' crops. But these programs did not benefit those most in need – the rural landless poor.[27] How could these people be best supported?

A New Model

Most of the population of Jobra was poor and these people had the fewest assets of all, though not because they lacked skills or ambition. They were at the mercy of those who rented them rickshaws, bought and sold them bamboo, and especially those who loaned them money. Once a worker's operating costs were covered, he or she was often left with an income of several pennies per day. Yunus realized the landless poor lacked access to what they needed to overcome chronic poverty.

Yunus and his university students surveyed the villagers in Jobra to determine how much money would be required for them to purchase materials and work freely, without having to return most of their profit to suppliers and lenders. They surveyed 42 people, and learned that they needed a total of 856 taka – just less than $27.[28]

Yunus offered them his own money as a loan without interest, but realized that this was not a long-term solution. He approached the Janata Bank about lending small sums to impoverished populations, but they balked at the idea of lending to those without collateral or financial history. After extended negotiations, the bank finally authorized a loan with Yunus as the guarantor. As a middleman, he lent over 100,000 taka to the villagers with near-perfect repayment rates, and made several key discoveries: that the lending opportunities needed to be extended to women, who were traditionally excluded from commercial activity; that the formation of self-supervising groups within the village would harness the culture's effective social pressure and ensure high rates of repayment; that each borrower needed to save one taka per week.[29]

While successful, facilitating the growing number of requests proved too much for both Yunus and his staff, as well as the Janata Bank, who did not anticipate the quantity of demand. So in 1977, Yunus spoke with A. M. Anisuzzaman, the managing director of the large Bangladesh Krishi Bank. Anisuzzaman allowed Yunus to open a pseudo-branch in Jobra. Yunus named it the Experimental Grameen Branch.[30] As the loans were distributed and the groups formed, Yunus created savings funds within each group, for both small short-term loans and emergencies, that the members would pay into and then control the disbursement, giving them further financial independence.

---

[27] Bornstein, pp. 31–34.

[28] Ibid., p. 39.

[29] Ibid., pp. 44–47.

[30] Muhammad Yunus, with Alan Jolis. 2007. *Banker to the poor*, 89. New York: Public Affairs.

Though Yunus wanted to expand his lending project to include an entire district, everyone he approached was convinced that his success in Jobra was unique, dependent on his personal involvement and reputation, and not reproducible on a larger scale. He took up their challenge and, taking a leave of absence from his professorship, relocated to Tangail, a district closer to Dhaka. Here, each of the seven national banks made several branches available to his project, though each lending decision had to be reviewed by the local branch, and larger project adjustments were subject to the input of all.

In 1981, anxious to continue expansion, Yunus traded on his success to secure $800,000 from the Ford Foundation as a guarantee fund, and a $3.4 million loan from the International Fund for Agricultural Development, as well as a matching loan from the Bangladesh Central Bank. Grameen would expand to five districts – by the end of 1981, its cumulative loan disbursement was $13.4 million, and during 1982, it increased by an additional $10.5 million. By the end of 1982, the Grameen bank had 30,000 members.[31] By 1998 it had repaid all its development loans. Since that time it has accepted no additional financial assistance and has been and remains fiscally independent.

A Private Bank

In order to gain flexibility and control, the next step was for Grameen to become a private institution. Many supporters believed, however, that Grameen would fail without the support of the cooperating national banks. But Yunus was in luck. A long-time friend of his became Minister of Finance following a government coup, and Yunus was allowed to privatize the Bank.

The Grameen bank officially became an independent entity on October 2, 1983. The bank could now hire permanent staff, and recruit young and enthusiastic workers. Grameen continued to push for an increase in women borrowers, and without the skepticism of the national banks, by 1984, the number of women borrowers exceeded the number of male borrowers, 68,000 to 53,000.[32] Grameen opened approximately one hundred new branches every year[33] during the 1980s, and expanded to offer $300 housing loans. By 2007, 650,000 homes had been financed.[34]

---

[31] Bornstein

[32] Ibid.

[33] Yunus, *Banker to the Poor*, p. 127.

[34] Muhammad Yunus, with Karl Weber. 2007. *Creating a world without poverty*, 57. New York, Public Affairs.

The Sixteen Decisions

In 1984 at its annual workshop, the bank center leaders developed the Sixteen Decisions that became pledges that every member would take. This list of commitments, promises, and principles was, and continues to be, a cornerstone of Grameen culture and operation. The list is as follows:

1. We shall follow and advance the four principles of Grameen Bank – Discipline, Unity, Courage and Hard work – in all walks of out lives.
2. Prosperity we shall bring to our families.
3. We shall not live in dilapidated houses. We shall repair our houses and work towards constructing new houses at the earliest.
4. We shall grow vegetables all the year round. We shall eat plenty of them and sell the surplus.
5. During the plantation seasons, we shall plant as many seedlings as possible.
6. We shall plan to keep our families small. We shall minimize our expenditures. We shall look after our health.
7. We shall educate our children and ensure that they can earn to pay for their education.
8. We shall always keep our children and the environment clean.
9. We shall build and use pit-latrines.
10. We shall drink water from tube wells. If it is not available, we shall boil water or use alum.
11. We shall not take any dowry at our sons' weddings, neither shall we give any dowry at our daughters wedding. We shall keep our centre free from the curse of dowry. We shall not practice child marriage.
12. We shall not inflict any injustice on anyone, neither shall we allow anyone to do so.
13. We shall collectively undertake bigger investments for higher incomes.
14. We shall always be ready to help each other. If anyone is in difficulty, we shall all help him or her.
15. If we come to know of any breach of discipline in any centre, we shall all go there and help restore discipline.
16. We shall take part in all social activities collectively.[35]

Yunus placed much emphasis on the sense of self and empowerment that borrowing and repaying from Grameen provides. Though any year in Bangladesh may be rife with natural disasters, Grameen does not forgive loans made to those affected. Instead, it encourages borrowers to take a new loan to restart their activities at a reduced repayment rate. Yunus argued that, "This discipline is meant to boost the borrower's sense of self-reliance, price and confidence. To forgive a loan can undo

---

[35] http://www.grameen-info.org/index.php?option=com_content&task=view&id=22&Ite mid=109. Accessed May 28, 2013.

years of difficult work in getting that borrower to believe in his or her own ability."[36] When women gain equality, the birth rate also declines, as being brought into industry and education curbs younger marriage and large families.

In April of 1996, Grameen gave its one-billionth dollar in loans, and 2 years later, its two-billionth dollar.[37] In the 1990s, Grameen again expanded its loan offerings to include cellular telephones, seasonal loans for sharecroppers, tube well loans for those without safe drinking water, and lease-to-own agreements for live-stock and equipment. It has since begun offering higher education loans at no interest during the education period and a 5 % interest rate after completion, and gives around 3,700 scholarships to children, especially girls, every year. Grameen's loan repayment rates, from its inception to present day, have hovered between 95 % and 98 %.[38]

Assessment

In an effort to assess whether borrower branches were "poverty-free," Yunus and Grameen had to determine what "poverty-free" meant. After a series of interviews with borrowers, they developed ten indicators to evaluate whether a member has moved out of poverty. They are:

1. The family lives in a house worth at least Tk. 25,000 or a house with a tin roof, and each member of the family is able to sleep on a bed instead of on the floor.
2. Family members drink pure water of tube-wells, boiled water or water purified by using alum, arsenic-free, purifying tablets or pitcher filters.
3. All children in the family over 6 years of age are all going to school or finished primary school.
4. Minimum weekly loan installment of the borrower is Tk. 200 or more.
5. Family uses sanitary latrine.
6. Family members have adequate clothing for everyday use, warm clothing for winter, such as shawls, sweaters, blankets, etc, and mosquito-nets to protect themselves from mosquitoes.
7. Family has sources of additional income, such as vegetable garden, fruit-bearing trees, etc, so that they are able to fall back on these sources of income when they need additional money.
8. The borrower maintains an average annual balance of Tk. 5,000 in her savings accounts.

---

[36] Yunus, *Banker to the Poor*, p. 137.

[37] Ibid., p. 199.

[38] http://www.grameenfoundation.org/what-we-do/microfinance-basics

9. Family experiences no difficulty in having three square meals a day throughout the year, i.e. no member of the family goes hungry any time of the year.
10. Family can take care of its health. If any member of the family falls ill, family can afford to take all necessary steps to seek adequate healthcare.[39]

Grameen II

In 2000, Grameen began to retool its existing structure and methods in response to a wave of loan defaults following the extreme flooding of 1998. Striving for greater flexibility in both the bank's savings and the borrowers' repayments, the organization collaborated to develop improvements and solutions to problems in operations. On August 7, 2002, every Grameen branch had transitioned to Grameen II. The new system featured improvements such as: a flexible loan option for struggling borrowers who cannot meet their repayment schedule; a pension savings requirement for larger borrowers, wherein after 10 years, they receive almost double what they have saved; an insurance provision under which, following the death of a borrower, the family is not held accountable for the loan.[40]

A program designed specifically for beggars was introduced in 2004. The loans are for around $15, with no interest and no timetable for repayment. They use this money to purchase small items to sell when they beg door to door. In the first 3 years of the program, it had acquired 100,000 members, 10,000 of which were selling products full-time, and almost 63 of the 95 million taka borrowed had been repaid.[41]

In 2006 Muhammad Yunus and the Grameen Bank were awarded the prestigious Nobel Peace Prize for, "Their efforts to create economic and social development from below."[42]

As of 2011, Grameen had 2,565 branches and almost 8.5 million members across 80,000 villages, 96 % of which are women. 2011 was a landmark year in that Yunus left Grameen as it transitioned to new management, focusing his efforts since on social business – a concept he had experimented with and honed in the implementation of a series of Grameen-based companies that offer opportunities and services such as cellular phones, internet, fisheries, health services, and technology training. Yunus defines a social business as, "A non-loss, non-dividend enterprise, created with the intention to do good to people, to bring positive changes to the world, without any short-term expectation of making money out of it."[43]

---

[39] http://www.grameen-info.org/index.php?option=com_content&task=view&id=23&Itemid=126

[40] Yunus, *Banker to the Poor*, pp. 235–243.

[41] Yunus, *Creating a World Without Poverty*, p. 65.

[42] http://www.nobelprize.org/nobel_prizes/peace/laureates/2006/

[43] Yunus, *Banker to the Poor*, p. 266.

As Yunus' and Grameen's achievements were recognized, microlending projects have spread throughout the world. The first pilot projects were in Malaysia and the Philippines. While both, like Grameen in Bangladesh, had early struggles adapting to the culture and implementing a framework, they have been successful since. Though more potential microlending institutions were devised for other countries, many encountered difficulties finding funding. In response, Yunus started a specific fund within the Grameen Trust to fund replicator projects, which, as of 2013, total 150 organizations across 40 countries.[44]

Bangladesh has come a long way since 1971, and while it remains extremely poor, the garment industry, Grameen's programs, and other trade and agricultural-related programs have improved conditions. See World Bank for current statistics on poverty in Bangladesh at: http://data.worldbank.org/country/bangladesh

The e-Choupal Initiative[45]

What is needed is a better approach to help the poor, an approach that involves partnering with them to innovate and achieve sustainable win-win scenarios where the poor are actively engaged and, at the same time, the companies providing products and services to them are profitable.

–C. K. Prahalad, The Fortune at the Bottom of the Pyramid[46]

In 2007, S. Sivakumar could look back on 18 years as chief executive of ITC International's Agriculture Business Division with satisfaction and one major point of pride: the e-Choupal initiative that he helped launch in 2000. This initiative had strengthened ITC's international competitiveness by streamlining its supply chain management and, perhaps most gratifying to Sivakumar, had improved the lives of many Indian farmers and made their operations more efficient. Sivakumar sat in his office in Secunderabad, in the Hyderabad province of India, pondering the successes of the initiative. He also thought about the bigger and more difficult challenge that lay ahead: expanding the e-Choupal initiative throughout the country.

When Sivakumar joined ITC's International Business Division (IBD) in 1989, he had several concerns. IBD, the agricultural commodities export division of ITC, had lagged in performance behind the other divisions. This inefficient performance was hurting ITC's international competitiveness. In addition, Sivakumar was well aware of the plight of the Indian farmer, who was generally poor, beleaguered,

---

[44] Grameen Trust Partner Organizations, Monthly Statement, April 2013. http://www.grameentrust.org/MonthlyStatement.pdf

[45] This case was prepared by Anne Laure Thiemele, Jenny Mead, S. Venkataraman, and Alexander Horniman. Copyright © 2009 University of Virginia Darden School Foundation. All rights reserved.

[46] Prahalad, C. K. 2005. *The fortune at the bottom of the pyramid: Eradicating poverty through profits*, 3–4. Upper Saddle River: Wharton School Publishing.

and – because of a number of factors – inefficient and nonproductive. As Sivakumar would explain several years later in an interview:

> [There was concern about] the international part of our agriculture business [and also] over social responsibility. It was the time when the international market was becoming more competitive and looking at higher-cost markets and higher quality of produce. This created the immediate need to reorganize the supply chain to serve our customers in the higher market. At a broader context, we are not only looking for commercial interests but also at the place where we gave weightage to the social environmental angle.[47]

In 2000, with the support of ITC Chair Y. C. Deveshwar, Sivakumar had launched e-Choupal, an information technology initiative designed to connect farmers for the procurement of agricultural products, as a pilot project in Madhya Pradesh with soybean farmers. e-Choupal's main goals were to improve ITC's international competitiveness and to transform and develop rural India. Over the years, the program had been enormously successful, evolving through several phases beyond the original concept. Now, Sivakumar was determined to find innovative ways to introduce the concept to the rest of the country and make it sustainable. Given India's size and the various challenges involved, expansion would not be an easy task; Sivakumar was encouraged and inspired, however, by the successes of the past 7 years (see Exhibit 1 for e-Choupal 2007 milestones and 2012 goals).

ITC Limited

Indian Tobacco Company Limited (ITC) was one of India's largest private-sector companies, with a market capitalization of more than $15 billion. ITC had a diversified presence in various industries: tobacco, hotels, paperboards and specialty papers, packaging, agribusiness, packaged foods, confectionary products, and greeting cards.[48] The company's divisions each contributed significantly to the company's financial performance and, in the twenty-first century, to its increasing role in social and ecological capital The company was founded in August 1910 in Kolkata, India; by 2007, it had more than 21,000 employees at more than 60 locations across the country. Indians were proud of ITC, considering it a true Indian company. Y. C. ("Yogi") Deveshwar, who had become ITC chair in 1996, had devised a "three V" strategy – "Vision, Values, and Vitality" – that had powered the company's transformation during his first decade as CEO and had helped ITC sustain superior wealth creation in an increasingly competitive environment.

---

[47] "MBAUniverse.com Exclusive Interview: 'India Needs Specialized MBA Programmes for Emerging Industries,' says Dr Bakul Dholakia," http://www.mbauniverse.com/innerPage.php?id=oi&pageId=40 (accessed October 22, 2008).

[48] "The ITC Profile". http://www.itcportal.com/sets/itc_frameset.htm (accessed October 20, 2008).

In a 2006 speech at ITC's 95th annual general meeting, Deveshwar defined the three Vs:

- A compelling *vision* creates and forges corporate identity. It imparts a larger purpose and meaning to individual endeavor. It is aspirational, unifying, and motivational.
- *Values* refers to the institutional standards of behavior that strengthen commitment to the *vision* and guide strategy formulation and purpose[ful] action. The core values of your company are shaped around the belief that enterprises exist to serve society.
- *Vitality* enables robust strategy formulation and world-class strategy execution. Vitality in ITC is manifest in many ways, including the strengthening competitive capability, the deepening consumer insight, the breakthrough innovations in products and processes, the ability to rapidly absorb knowledge and harness technology, the widening bandwidth of distributed leadership, [and] a growing nimbleness to proactively manage change and adaptiveness to continuously leverage market opportunities.[49]

International Business Division

ITC's International Business Division, the agriculture business arm of ITC Limited, specialized in the exports of agriculture products to international customers. Founded in 1990, the division contributed more than 60 % of the company's total foreign exchange earnings; its main commodities were feed ingredients, food grains, coffee, edible nuts, and processed fruits. Sivakumar led the division, supervising a team of qualified and experienced professionals. The Indian government had recognized IBD as one of the top exporters of commodities in the country; the division had also received several awards for its e-Choupal initiative. In a special address, the former president of India, Dr. A. P. J. Abdul Kalam, said, "ITC has taken the role of a network orchestrator in this market by bringing together an end-to-end solution by synergizing and unleashing the power of partnerships in public, private, and not-for-profit sectors through the e-Choupal."[50] Through both the e-Choupal and its Social and Farm Forestry initiative,[51] ITC had demonstrated the financial benefits of being a good corporate citizen.

---

[49] Shri Y. C. Deveshwar, Vision, Values, and Vitality, speech at the 95th Annual General Meeting, July 21, 2006. http://www.itcportal.com/chairman_speaks/chairman_2006.html (accessed November 3, 2008).

[50] Dr. A. P. J. Abdul Kalam, Special Address, "Agriculture Cannot Wait: New Horizons," the National Symposium to Commemorate 60th Year of Independence: New Delhi, June 5, 2007. http://www.itcportal.com/newsroom/press06june07-a.htm (accessed November 3, 2008).

[51] The objective of ITC's Social and Farm Forestry initiative was to plant trees or seeds to transform and regenerate wasteland and forest and also to enhance farm incomes and generate sustainable employment.

Agriculture in India and the Plight of the Farmer

Agriculture was, according to C. K. Prahalad, "economically, nutritionally, and socially vital to India."[52] As of 2003, it represented 23 % of India's GDP, employed 66 % of the country's work force, and fed one billion people.[53] After India gained independence in 1947, the agricultural sector had underperformed for a number of years for a variety of reasons, including heavy legislation and an archaic, corrupt system. From the mid-1940s through the mid-1960s, India tried, with mixed success, to achieve food self-sufficiency, primarily by expanding the country's agricultural areas. In the 1960s, however, India participated in the "green revolution,"[54] which focused on three areas: expanding the farmland, double-cropping (planting two crops) each season, and using high-yield, genetically superior seeds. During this time, there was increased use of fertilizer and heavy irrigation.

While the green revolution had several positive results, including making India a net exporter of most food grains, it created several social and economic problems. First, the profitability of agriculture increased and land values rose, leading land-owners to eject their tenants; consequently, small and marginal farmers were squeezed off the land. Second, the new agricultural technology was expensive, and the poorer farmers did not have the cash to buy inputs and lay out capital expenditures. As a result, small farmers were at a disadvantage because of lower profits. Finally, "[b]ecause of labor constraints, the need to maximize family survival possibilities, and the low profit margins of small-scale grain farming, the smaller farmers may have found the monoculture revolution centered on hybrid wheat or rice unattractive and unprofitable."[55]

Even as agriculture's share of the GDP declined slightly in the 1990s, employment in this sector was still high, which meant that farmers earned less. Few farmers left agriculture for another job sector, and as the rural population grew to 72 %,[56] even less land was available. Consequently, there was an increasing number of small and midsize holdings and a larger marginalization of the farmers.[57] By the mid-1990s, despite countrywide agricultural advances, the Indian farmer was in bad shape. He had limited land and "a very small-scale operation measured in fractions of acres."[58] As the twenty-first century dawned, India's nonagricultural economy experienced a boom because of increasing industry and services' influence on the

---

[52] Prahalad, 320.

[53] Annamalai, Kuttayan, and Sachin Rao. 2003. *What works: ITC's e-Choupal and profitable rural transformation.* World Resources Institute.

[54] The "green revolution" was not specific to India, although it was considered most successful there.

[55] Nicholson.

[56] "Census of India". http://www.censusindia.gov.in/Census_Data_2001/India_at_glance/rural. aspx (accessed October 21, 2008).

[57] "Agricultural Census," Indian Ministry of Agriculture. http://agcensus.nic.in/ (accessed January 16, 2009).

[58] Prahalad, 321.

GDP, but agriculture declined. Whereas agriculture represented 32 % of the GDP in 1990–91, it represented only 17.8 % in 2007–08.[59] The underlying causes of this recession were lack of infrastructure, increasing production risks, lack of livelihood opportunities, and institutional neglect.

In short, India's agricultural market and its rural farmers suffered from a series of "lows;" they were "trapped by low investment, low productivity, weak market orientation, low value addition, low margin, and low risk-taking ability."[60] The situation took its toll on the farmers who, in addition, were excluded from the country's mainstream development. Suicides increased; in 2003, a record 17,107 farmers committed suicide.[61]

Specific problems assailed farmers. Agriculture, of course, was dependent on adequate rainfall. The monsoon season in India was essential to helping farmers grow their crops. But the weather was capricious and if there were not enough rain, drought conditions led to fluctuating production and sometimes crop failure.[62] Although irrigation techniques and best practices had been introduced during the green revolution, not all farmers had access to them. The unequal distribution of water resources and limited availability of irrigation across the country contributed to the declining productivity level and to unpredictable yield. Many farmers, through lack of knowledge, overused fertilizers and pesticides; the result was soil depletion. Additionally, few farmers had access to institutional credit; according to World Bank estimates, "87 % of marginal farmers who own less than two hectares of land and 70 % of small farmers have no access to credit from a formal financial institution in India."[63] Farmers often borrowed from unscrupulous moneylenders who charged extremely high interest rates (sometimes as high as 150 %).

There was an urgent need for reform in rural India to integrate and incorporate the small and marginal farmers into the agricultural system, and to create an adequate support system that could provide them with tools and techniques that would make them more productive and increase their wealth. Further challenges for Indian agriculture included increasingly smaller farms, lack of infrastructure, and the existence of various intermediaries that led to structural deficiencies and results in the exploitation of the farmers. Potential solutions included access to fair and timely institutional credit; insurance policies for farmers to protect them against various endemic risks (crop, weather, and price risk); finally, rejuvenating the agricultural sector would require improvement in infrastructure, technological support, and investment in general in order to rejuvenate the agricultural sector.

---

[59] "The Global Capitalist Crisis and India: Time to Start the Discussion," *Analytical Monthly Review* (West Bengal, India), December 22, 2008. http://www.monthlyreview.org/mrzine/amr221208.html (accessed January 15, 2009).

[60] Kim, Do Kyun, Ketan Chitnis, P. N. Vasanti, and Arvind Singhai. 2007. Opinion leadership in Indian villages and diffusion of E-Choupal. *Journal of Creative Communications* 2(3):346.

[61] Sengupta, Somini. On India's farms, a plague of suicide. *New York Times*, September 19, 2006.

[62] Bailay,Rasual. 2003. Monsoon driven. *Far Eastern Economic Review*, 166(27): 45.

[63] Mohindru, Sameer, and Prasenjit Bhattacharya. In India's boom, its farmers suffer. *Wall Street Journal*, October 30, 2007:A8.

The e-Choupal Initiative

In 2000, Sivakumar initiated the e-Choupal model, designed to fill the rural community's information gap, increase farmers' productivity by giving them access to current commodity prices, and provide direct sourcing of crops at lower cost for ITC. Sivakumar's graduate diploma from the Institute of Rural Management and his 6 years' experience working for a farmers' cooperative gave him the knowledge and understanding of the dire situation Indian farmers faced. With this initiative, IBD would be able to provide an innovative solution that would empower farmers through transparent information and improve the efficiency of the farming community. Initially, however, the villages' remote locations presented many obstacles for Sivakumar and his team in getting the system ready and finding solutions that would make the e-Choupal system work.

The Hindi word *choupal* meant "the village meeting place," and Sivakumar wanted to preserve its traditional system of information- and knowledge-sharing in the e-Choupal model. The e-Choupal would therefore be an Internet-based market-place where local farmers would gather to exchange and get information about crops, prices, and volumes traded, and to communicate with ITC about its products. The model started with an Internet kiosk installed at a farmer's house; from this kiosk, all the villagers had access to weather forecasts, seed and chemical information, and best farming practices. Each e-Choupal typically served approximately 600 farmers spread throughout eight to ten villages located within a 5 km area. Each village's e-Choupal maintained a base of operations at the home of a *sanchalak* (a designated liaison between the farmers and ITC), with a computer and printer, a dial-up modem or VSAT modem to make up for the weak telecommunication infrastructure, and a solar battery charger to ensure that the computer would be available consistently.

The e-Choupal offered farmers an alternative to the traditional *mandi* system, which was an institutionalized market yard where they had to sell their products through an auction. To reach the *mandi*, a farmer had to travel for a long time at his own expense; once there, the commission agents, who were either purchasing agents or brokers who made all *mandi* transactions, assessed the quality of the seeds very casually and then proceeded to the auction. Only at the auction did farmers learn what price their seeds would bring. Farmers had no alternative but to sell at a very low margin. After the auction, the farmers had to bag and weigh their goods, but the *mandi* employees handled the bags of seeds carelessly, often spilling them (sometimes up to 2–3 kg/t). The commission agents never paid the farmers in full and inevitably extracted a large transaction fee, forcing the farmer to return later at his own cost to collect the remaining payment. The high transaction costs and the commission agents' exploitation left the farmers with the lowest price in the entire chain. The farmer lost both on the sale side and the purchasing side; there was a lack of transparency in supply sales and little honest advice about which crops might grow best in a farmer's soil.

The Sanchalak

The human hub of the e-Choupal model was the *sanchalak*. Chosen for his respectability in the village and his ability to read and write (most farmers were illiterate), the sanchalak had an Internet-access kiosk in his house and received training from ITC on many fronts. He learned basic computer skills for operating the kiosks; business skills for running the e-Choupal profitably; and seed quality assessment techniques to be able to test the farmers' products and advise them on improving the quality of their produce and selling them the adequate ITC inputs. As motivation, ITC paid the sanchalaks a commission based on the number of transactions that took place in the kiosk. The sanchalak also had to take an oath during a ceremony in front of the entire village and pledge that he would act in the best interests of both the community and ITC. The company's requirements and responsibilities increased the sanchalak's social stature and motivated him to act with integrity. In short, sanchalaks were the unique communication tool by which ITC reached out and connected with local farmers. They were crucial to the entire e-Choupal model. Trust was very important in rural India, and the sanchalak was an approachable human "interface" and someone from the community instead of a stranger whom the farmers could not trust.

The Samyojak

Another key player in the business model was the *samyojak*, a former commission agent who worked in the mandi. He acted as an intermediary, helping the company in the selection of the sanchalaks, in ITC's warehousing hub where the farmers sold their grains, and in other logistical activities such as bagging and weighing at the hub and handling cash for payment. The samyojaks' motivation for working with ITC was the higher commission they got from working in the e-Choupal than in the mandi and the fact that ITC continued to employ them for certain transactions at the mandi. This collaboration among ITC, the sanchalaks, and the samyojaks was the basis of the e-Choupal success. The company did not destroy the traditional roles but leveraged the system. In addition, by bringing the company directly to the farmers and reducing the middleman, ITC used the farmers' resourcefulness and collaborated with them in finding a win-win solution for each party.

The e-Choupal Process

The e-Choupal process was simple. The sanchalak would go online and connect to the e-Choupal Web site (http://www.echoupal.com [accessed April 29, 2009]) whenever the farmers needed information or to make a decision about the sale of

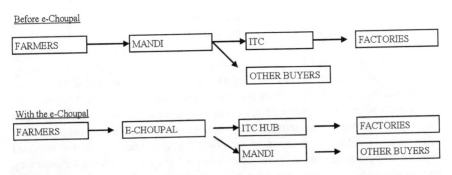

Fig. 7.1 The supply chain before and with the e-Choupal

crops. The e-Choupal Web site featured weather information, best practices, crop information, market information, a Q&A forum, and news. Once connected to the Web site, the farmers could access different prices, such as the mandi price and the ITC price (which was the "fair average quality price" based on the previous day's mandi closing price). Sanchalaks, who knew more about the commodities market and wanted to follow the world price, could access the Chicago Board of Trades (CBOT) prices. Once aware of prices, farmers could pursue various options: They could go to the ITC hub and sell their crops immediately; go to the mandi; or simply wait for a better price. For example, if the CBOT indicated a potential increase in future prices, the sanchalak would usually advise farmers to hold off selling and thus benefit from the predicted price increase. The Internet kiosk was always walking distance from the local farmers so they could visit it regularly, and the ITC hubs were within driving distance from the villages. The e-Choupal was a way for the company to obtain supplies but also to sell its own input products such as fertilizers, herbicides, and seeds. The sanchalak had an inventory of ITC products and was responsible for aggregating village demand and placing orders with the company. Farmers could also get inputs by visiting the ITC hub, where they could use part of their compensation to pay for such items. Farmers also used the Internet for other types of information: market prices, entertainment, sports, education, and e-mail.

Leading Transformation in Rural India

Reorganizing the Supply Chain

One of Sivakumar's goals was to make the IBD more competitive internationally by improving ITC's supply chain efficiency and integrating more price transparency and lower transaction costs. The mandi system, with its various intermediaries, was rife with information blockage and increasing costs on both sides of the transaction (Fig. 7.1).

Although the mandi process produced lower margins for the entire chain, Sivakumar's idea was to use the existing rural system and complement it without destroying the basis of the traditional model so that every level of the supply chain could benefit from the e-Choupal. The IBD's initiative had re-engineered the supply chain and had offered farmers an alternative to the farmers; they could continue to use the mandi system, but now they had the information ahead of time to make their decisions. The company even reimbursed the farmers for transportation costs when they sold their crops at the hubs, paying them in full so that there was no need for them to return at their own expenses to collect the remainder, which was standard practice in the mandi system. With fewer intermediaries in the chain, the company had greater control over its purchase of produce and lowered its expenses; at the same time, local farmers were able to increase their profits and focus on improving their productivity. ITC benefited from the e-Choupal model by having access to critical information about its customers; a database crafted from kiosk patterns gave ITC information the company could use to better track the farmers' needs and customize its Web site.

The e-Choupal Advantage

With its e-Choupal model, IBD had been able to enhance the lives of the farmers and benefit the company and its shareholders. The farmers' increased empowerment was a direct consequence of the e-Choupal, which gave them the decision-making ability they did not have before. There was also greater transparency and increased access to information, which created trust between the farmers and ITC. The farmers felt like they were treated fairly, something that was nonexistent in the traditional system. With this trust and fairness as well as ITC's policy of paying a premium for higher-quality products, the farmers were now motivated to try new techniques; they could decide the time, location, and price for selling their produce. And they could align their production with customer demand inside and outside of India. The farmers' wealth increased because their margins were higher than in the traditional system. Fewer intermediaries and faster transaction times led to decreasing costs, and farmers could focus on higher quality and increased productivity.

Naturally, the e-Choupal also led to the evolution of the Internet in rural India. Not only could farmers check for important information regarding their sales, but also they could communicate with family and friends worldwide. In addition, the farmers' children used the Internet for schoolwork and games. Additionally, the Internet offered rural India the potential for development: During gatherings at the sanchalak's house, farmers could discover best practices and raise their awareness of how things were done in other parts of the world; they could also communicate with the company and give their feedback on how to make things better.

As for IBD, the e-Choupal offered control over the quality of the crops and lower procurement costs but also a great marketing channel: when farmers received their payment at the hub, they could buy appropriate inputs and goods for their products. Moreover, the hub also included laboratories that offered soil-testing capabilities and customized help and advice to the farmers. Not only did e-Choupal increase farmers' productivity and efficiency, but it also had boosted soy production from 50 % to 90 % since the beginning of the initiative.[64] The e-Choupal had been a platform for the reorganization of supply and demand through a collaborative and unique business model, giving ITC an opportunity to compete more effectively internationally.[65]

By 2007, the statistics on the e-Choupal were extremely encouraging. Farmers' incomes had increased by 20 %, with productivity rising from 14 % to 29 %. Approximately 87 % of the farmers in the e-Choupal areas knew about e-Choupal services, and 78 % were using them. More than four million farmers in about 40,000 villages were involved with one of the 6,500 e-Choupals across eight Indian states. Finally, ITC estimated "a payback period of 7 years on its total investments in the e-Choupal initiative with full bouquet of services to the farmers and rural customers."[66]

Extending the Concept

From its launch in 2000 as a pilot project with soybean farmers, e-Choupal had grown and expanded to other crops, including wheat, rice, pulse, and coffee, as well as marine products such as shrimp and prawns. Sivakumar had pioneered a strong model and built a solid network that he was now leveraging in other parts of the agricultural business. The initiative's geographical reach included nine states: Madhya Pradesh, Haryana, Uttaranchal, Karnataka, Andhra Pradesh, Uttar Pradesh, Maharashtra, Rajasthan, and Kerala. In 2005, after many successes, Sivakumar wanted to leverage the e-Choupal infrastructure to sell products and provide rural market services. As a result, IBD decided to start a second phase of expansion: the *Choupal Sagar*. The Sagar was a retail-shopping complex or hypermarket, which was at the time the company's first rural hypermarket. The hypermarket bought and sold agricultural commodities, offered training for farmers, and provided lectures from agricultural scientists. By 2007, the company had more than 10 Choupal Sagars across the country.

The next phase of the e-Choupal initiative was the horticultural phase, started in three states: Maharashtra, Andhra Pradesh, and Chandigarh. In this phase, farmers sold fresh vegetables and fruits daily to the "Choupal Fresh," a retail initiative of IBD. The company set up a supply chain that ensured retail stores would procure fresh produce. The difference between this phase and the first phase was the type of investment that the IBD would have to make: cold chain storage and technologies instead of IT investments. There were many advantages in the horticultural phase: a

---

[64] Annamalai and Rao.

[65] Annamalai and Rao.

[66] A. P. J. Abdul Kalam, President of India, "Agriculture Cannot Wait: New Horizons," speech to the National Symposium to Commemorate 60th Year of Independence, New Delhi, May 6, 2007.

higher output per hectare in horticulture than in grain, for example, which would give the company a higher return on investment. Additionally, this wave of products was expected to benefit ITC's other food businesses, increasing the project's benefits for the entire company.

At the same time, Sivakumar was developing credit and insurance services that would help the rural communities. Farmers had a very limited access to institutional credits; banks were reluctant to offer any type of products and services to rural populations because of the potentially high nonrepayment risks and lack of information. Sivakumar saw access to credit as one of the best ways to reduce poverty. He decided to partner with financial institutions in order to help them access more information on farmers and offer more services to rural communities. With the help and knowledge of the sanchalaks, banks would be able to assess farmers' credit worthiness. As a result, banks would offer noncash loans or loans to sanchalaks who would then lend to farmers. In addition, Sivakumar and his team tried to structure payments with insurance companies so that farmers could pay their premiums more easily.

IBD also began offering health care and education services for rural communities. The company was partnering with health care providers to offer their services to remote villages using telemedicine through the e-Choupal. IBD also proposed to offer education services and various distant learning programs to rural communities to battle illiteracy.

The Road Ahead

The e-Choupal had created a small revolution in the villages where it was installed. Farmers who were once accustomed to traditional farming methods had, at the click of a mouse, access to information that could change their lives. The e-Choupal was a model that could mitigate rural isolation, connect the remotest villages in India with the world, and offer services and advantages that transformed the farmer from a passive, exploited worker to a proactive, empowered entrepreneur who could make his own decisions and influence the fate of his community. IBD's e-Choupal had started a transformation of rural India that brought increasing wealth and opportunities to farmers, and fostered their innovation and risk-taking abilities.[67] Sivakumar and his team wanted to show the world that Indian farmers were incredibly resourceful and that, indeed, a fortune could be made at the bottom of the pyramid.

In 2005, Sivakumar and his team received several awards, including a $100,000 development prize by the Development Gateway Organization. Their various prizes recognized their successful use of information technology to enhance and transform

---

[67] Sivakumar, S. *Role of ITC and collaboration and development*, http://unpan1.un.org/intradoc/groups/public/documents/APCITY/UNPAN022803.pdf. Accessed January 15, 2009.

the quality of life for India's rural communities. The e-Choupal platform had triggered continuous innovation and dynamic leadership. The initiative had succeeded where many organizations had failed. The challenges Sivakumar had faced at the beginning of the initiative were not to be taken lightly; however, his vision, his commitment to contributing to sustainable wealth creation for ITC's stakeholders' needs, and his belief in rural communities made the e-Choupal a revolution and a success across the country that was recognized around the world.

Gazing through his office window at Hyderabad, Sivakumar thought of how far the e-Choupal had come since its beginning in 2000. He knew that ITC wanted to scale up the initiative to reach 10 million farmers in 100,000 villages by 2012. Sivakumar wondered how the initiative would evolve and remain sustainable given the challenges that lay ahead – the changing trends in the food sector and the fluctuations in commodities markets around the world.

Exhibit 1: The e-Choupal Initiative

e-Choupal at a Glance

Milestones, July 2007

- States covered: 9
- Village covered: 38,500
- e-Choupal installation: 6,400
- Choupal Saagars established: 10
- Empowered farmers: 3.5 million

Agenda for 2012

- States to be covered: 15
- Villages to be covered: 100,000
- e-Choupals to be installed: 20,000
- Choupal Saagars to establish: 700
- Farmers to be empowered: 10 million

Source: "e-Choupal: E-empowering Indian Farmers," www.itcportal.com/ruraldevp_philosophy/echoupal.htm (accessed January 15, 2009).

Chapter 8
Global Corporations and Supply Chain Management

Introduction

We end this book with two important cases on supply chain management. In the 1990s Nike faced a great deal of criticism that some of its manufacturing units, all franchises not owned by Nike, were basically sweatshops, mistreating workers, paying low wages, and not providing decent working environments even by local standards. Nike listened to those criticisms, and ever since has been engaged in the process of changing these conditions. The case in this collection illustrates these efforts in its Vietnamese franchises.

Walmart, the world's largest retailer, is working on its Chinese suppliers, trying to encourage environmentally sustainable processes and products while at the same time squeezing the lowest price from its supply chain. Whether and how these efforts will be successful is its challenge.

Both cases illustrate the struggles of large companies in their work to be profitable, global, and sensitive to poverty and environmental issues in the communities in which they operate.

P.J. Albert et al. (eds.), *Global Poverty Alleviation: A Case Book*, The International Society   321
of Business, Economics, and Ethics Book Series 3, DOI 10.1007/978-94-007-7479-7_8,
© Springer Science+Business Media Dordrecht 2014

Nike, Inc.: Corporate Social Responsibility and Workplace Standard Initiatives in Vietnam[1]

Corporate Overview

Nike was founded in 1964 by Philip H. Knight as "BRS (Blue Ribbon Sports)"; in 1972 the name was changed to "Nike." Phil Knight remains Nike's owner, chairman, and CEO today. Nike, based in Beaverton, Oregon, has more than 22,000 and over 300 contracted suppliers in about 52 countries throughout the world, employing more than 550,000 workers on any given day creating sports and fitness footwear, apparel, equipment, and accessories for worldwide distribution (over 400 of these suppliers are located in Asia). Approximately 175 million pairs of shoes are manufactured each year for Nike, contributing in part to Nike's annual revenue for 2001, which totaled almost $10 billion.[2] Nike's Code of Conduct, first sent out to manufacturers in 1992 and the second code to be developed in the entire industry binds all Nike contract manufacturers and requires that all "manufacturing partners must post this Code in all major workspaces, translated into the language of the worker, and must endeavor to train workers on their rights and obligations as defined by this Code and applicable labor laws."[3] In its code, Nike sets a standard for its partnerships by seeking contractors who are committed to best practices and continuous improvement in the following areas:

– Employing management practices that respect the rights of all employees, including the right to free association and collective bargaining
– Minimizing the impact on the Environment
– Providing a safe and healthy workplace
– Promoting the health and well-being of all employees

Specifically, Nike's code binds its partners to core standards of conduct concerning the following issues:

1. Forced labor.
2. Child labor.
3. Compensation.
4. Benefits.
5. Hours of work/overtime.

---

[1] This case was originally published in *Rising Above Sweatshops,* edited by Laura P. Hartman, Denis G. Arnold, and Richard E. Wokutch. Westport CT: Praeger Publishers. 2003. Reprinted by permission of the publisher. The 2013 case Addendum was prepared by Tim Rolph.

[2] Nike Inc. "Corporate Responsibility Report 2001," p. See also Amanda Tucker, Nike Director of Compliance for Americas, transcribed by Richard Wokutch, "Nike and its Critics," *Organization and Environment* 14, (June 2001), 207–34; 212.

[3] Nike. "Code of conduct." www.nike.com/nikebiz/nikebiz/jhtml?page=25&cat=compliance&subc at=code (accessed July 15, 2002)

6. Environment, safety, and health: The Nike Corporate Responsibility Compliance Production SHAPE (Safety, Health, Attitude of Management, People Investment & Environment).
7. Documentation and inspection.[4]

When Nike chooses to establish a relationship with a new production factory, it requires that the factory agree to, pay for, and undergo a presourcing audit conducted by a third party, as well as a Nike internal SHAPE inspection.[5] The goal is that SHAPE inspections will take place at least four times a year for footwear factories and twice a year for each apparel or equipment factory. For the relationship to continue or for an order to be placed, both of the inspections described above must conclude that the factory is in "substantial compliance" with the Nike code of conduct. If not, the factory may choose to resubmit at a later date, striving toward compliance at that time. The entire monitoring process strives to achieve the following schedule of events:

– Factory identified by Nike production/sourcing staff
– SHAPE inspection carried out by production and/or LP manager
– Presourcing monitoring visit conducted by Global Social Compliance/ PricewaterhouseCoopers (PwC)
– Factory approved by vice president of compliance
– Production begins in the factory
– SHAPE inspections carried out quarterly for footwear manufacturers and biannually for apparel and equipment manufacturers
– When noncompliance issues identified, recommended action plan compiled for factory by Nike labor practice department working in conjunction with Nike production staff
– Follow-up monitoring visit done to measure corrective action taken by factory

Nike has developed a new management audit designed to quantitatively measure a contract factory's compliance with Nike management standards concerning pay, wage, benefits, forced labor, nondiscrimination, age, freedom of association, and the treatment of workers. This new instrument is in-depth, and Nike is focusing on global consistency, striving to find ways to link performance on this audit with sourcing decisions and incentive schemes. The audit evaluates contract factories on the basis of four areas of risk assessment: country location, size of factory, type of operation, and factory-specific historical compliance performance record. In conjunction with the development of the audit, Nike's president Mark Parker approved the of 21 new internal labor compliance auditors for the compliance department. On the basis of Nike's assessment of its contract factories, these auditors will

---

[4] Ibid, n. 4.
[5] See Nike, Inc. An online look: inside Nike's contract factories. www.nike.com/nikebiz/nikebiz/ jh=html?page=25&cat=overview&subcat=facftorytour. Accessed July 15, 2002.

categorize them as high, medium, and low risk. Each year, using this tool, Nike plans to audit 100 % of high-risk factories, 50 % of medium-risk factories, and 10 % of low-risk factories.[6]

Evolution of Nike's Approach to Global Labor Issues

Attention to the labor practices of Nike's suppliers began about 1988 when journalists focused several news stories on the situation in Nike's Jakarta, Indonesia, suppliers. USAID then funded a large-scale survey to document wage law violations that was later supported by a study of the Indonesian shoe industry. Between 1988 and 1996 the minimum wage rate in Indonesia rose more than 300 % (from $.86 to $2.46 per day), in large part due to this attention and efforts by large MNEs such as Nike.[7] The rate of inflation in Indonesia for the same time period was 205 %.[8] On May 12. 1998, Nike CEO Phil Knight delivered a speech at the National Press Club that became a turning point in Nike's approach to the issues facing its suppliers.[9] In that speech, Knight accepted responsibility at the corporate level for the labor activities of Nike's suppliers by establishing six initiatives for the firm. Knight explained that, as of that day, Nike committed to the following:

– Increasing the minimum age of new footwear factory workers to 18, and the minimum age for all other new light-manufacturing workers (apparel, accessories, equipment) to 16.
– Adopting the personal exposure limits (PEL) of the U.S. Occupational Safety and Health Administration (OSHA) as the standard for indoor air quality for all footwear factories.
– Funding university research and open forums to explore issues related to global manufacturing and responsible business practices such as independent monitoring and air quality standards.
– Expanding worker education programs, including middle and high school equivalency courses, for workers in all Nike footwear factories.
– Increasing support of its current microenterprise loan program to 1,000 families each in Vietnam, Indonesia, Pakistan, and Thailand; expanding its current independent monitoring programs to include nongovernmental organizations

---

[6]Discussion with Amanda Tucker, Director of Compliance, Nike, Inc, and Fukumi Hauser, Director of Global Compliance, Monitoring, and Training (4 November 2002) and e-mail from Amanda Tucker (26 July 2002).

[7]Balinger, Jeff. Once again, Nike's voice looms larger than that of its workers. www. BehindTheLabel.org/oped.php?etor_id=22. Accessed July 15, 2002.

[8]World Bank International Economics Department. Development Data Group, World Development Indicators. (1999).

[9]http://www.nike.com/nikebiz/news/pressrelease.jhtml?year=2001&month=05&letter=g (accessed July 15, 2002). See also, http://cbae.nmsu.edu/~dboje/NIKphilspeech.html (accessed July 15, 2002).

(NGOs), foundations, and educational institutions; and making summaries of the findings public.
- Involving NGOs in the process of factory monitoring, with summaries released to the public.[10]

The *New York Times* applauded Knight's commitments, claiming that they "set a standard that other companies should match."[11] To the contrary, however, some critics chastised Knight for not including several other commitments, including the protection of whistle-blowers in the factories, Nike-directed worker rights education programs, guarantee of living wages and reasonable working hours, and protection of workers' right to freedom of association.[12]

Since the time of Knight's pronouncement, Nike has developed a system of comprehensive monitoring and remediation.[13] This includes a health management and safety audit program and a significant global labor practice team that visits factories on an everyday basis[14] and conducts training and awareness initiatives. In connection with auditing programs, not only has Nike coordinated these activities from inside, but it has also engaged external auditors, as well as NGOs, to monitor, audit, and report on ongoing activities from an external perspective. Nike is also a founding member of the Fair Labor Association and has committed to external independent monitoring throughout its factory base. Though many have praised these efforts,[15] not all of Nike's critics have been pacified by them, as is specifically evidenced by scholar Dara O'Rourke's critique of the PwC labor-monitoring program, in which he claims not only that PwC failed to catch and assess several violations, but also that it allowed for management bias in the audits and failed to effectively gather information.[16]

In 2001 Nike invited Global Alliance For Workers and Communities (GA) to evaluate challenges existing in its suppliers' factories in Indonesia, Thailand, and

---

[10] http://cbae.nmsu.edu/~dboje/NIKphilspeech.html (accessed July 15, 2002); *see also* http://www.nikebiz.com/labor/time.shtml

[11] Connor, Tim. 2001. *Still waiting for Nike to do it.* San Francisco, CA: Global Exchange; http://www.globalexchange.org/economy/corporations/nike/stillwaiting.html (accessed July 15, 2002), p. 1.

[12] Connor, op. cirt. N. 12, p. 5.

[13] For Nike's overview of the challenges and successes of these initiatives to date, see http://www.nike.com/nikebiz/news/pr/2001/p_challenges.jhtml (accessed July 28, 2002).

[14] Currently, there are over 100 individuals in Nike's Compliance Department, including more than 20 people permanently housed overseas.

[15] Daniel Akst, "Nike in Indonesia, through a different lens," *New York Times* (March 4, 2001), sec. 3 p. 4; Editorial, "Smelly sneakers," *The Asian Wall Street Journal* (March 2, 2001), p. 6; "Knight speaks out on improving globalization," *Financial Times* (August 1, 2000), p 15; Holger Jensen, "A Tale of Two Swooshes in Indonesia," Rockymountainnews.com, 7/2/2000 [related article in the *San Jose Mercury News* (July 5, 2000), p B6]; David Lamb, "Economic Program Revitalizing Thailand's Countryside," *Los Angeles Times* (February 27, 2000), p. A34; Business Brief, "Indonesian Workers to Get Boost in Entry-Level Wages," *Wall Street Journal* (March 24, 1999), p. B2; Editorial, "For Citizens of Vietnam, Nike is the Place to Work," *Oregonian* (March 6, 1999), p. C7.

[16] O'Rourke, Dara. Monitoring the monitors: a critique of pricewaterhousecoopers labor monitoring. http://web.mit.edu.dorourke/www/pdf/wc.pdf. Accessed July 15, 2002.

Vietnam. Though some have questioned the validity and credibility of GA's work as a result of its relationship with Nike (along with The Gap, St. John's University, Kent State University, the World Bank, and the John D. and Catherine T. MacArthur Foundation, Nike has contributed funds to GA),[17] GA maintains strict standards relating to conflicts of interest and autonomy of its research. As a result of Nike's invitation, GA produced a report titled "Workers' Voices: An Interim Report on Workers' Needs and Aspirations in Nine Nike Contract Factories in Indonesia." The report was based on interviews with more than 4,450 workers at nine Nike supplier factories.[18] Currently, GA is engaged with Nike in a tailored training program focused on supervisory skills in Thailand, Indonesia, Vietnam, India, and China.

Most recently, in September 2001, Knight and Nike's board of directors created a Corporate Responsibility Committee of the Board. The committee's responsibility is to review, report, and make recommendations to the full board regarding Nike's alignment with corporate responsibility commitments. Issues to be addressed include labor compliance initiatives, environmental practices, community affairs programs, human resources, diversity issues, and philanthropic efforts.

Vietnam Operations

Nike has been manufacturing in Vietnam through factory partners since 1995, currently employing more than 43,000 workers making 22 million shoes annually and exporting apparel totaling over $450 million. Nike production accounts for 8 % of Vietnam's manufactured exports and 32 % of its footwear exports.[19]

Based in Ho Chi Minh City, Vietnam, American Chris Helzer served as Nike's director of government affairs for Southeast Asia and Australia for two and a half years. Lalit Monteiro is the general manager of Nike Vietnam and works on ethics-related issues with Steve Hewitt, the corporate responsibility and compliance manager. As a modification to Nike's earlier compliance structure, the vice president for apparel sourcing now has the oversight for corporate responsibility and may veto any given source as a result of its failure to comply with corporate responsibility standards.

Leverage toward compliance is much greater in the Vietnam footwear industry than in apparel or other industries since most footwear factories serve Nike 100 % and since there is little, if any, slow season. Of Nike's more than 850 supplier factories worldwide, 68 are footwear factories (5 footwear and 7 apparel factories are located in Vietnam). Nike has 46,000 workers in Vietnam with a current turnover of only 1 %, which is usually due to lack of desire on the part of female workers to return after pregnancy or marriage. As the largest employer in Vietnam, Nike has a

---

[17]Balinger, ibid. n.8.

[18]Results of the report can be found at www.theglobalalliance.org/section/cfm/6/3/. Accessed July 15, 2002.

[19]"Envor Defends Nike's Practices in Vietnam." *Financial Times*, April 12, 1999, p. 4.

significant impact on the Vietnamese economy. While the discussion above evidences prior challenges, even one of Nike's harshest critics, Medea Benjamin of Global Exchange, notes that "things are changing for the better" [20] and that the firm has made an "astounding turnaround."[21]

Nike, Inc.: Program Analyses

Program 1: After-Hours Education Program

Inspiration and Vision Setting: Idea Generation/Inception

The inspiration or vision-setting process for the Nike after-hours education program began during one of the ongoing meetings with suppliers coordinated by Nike when Dae Shin, the Korean owner of a supplier located in Vietnam, noted that the workers have requested and would benefit from an education program that could be attended after working hours. It was determined by this supplier and others interested that the best program would be one that balanced worker interest, slots available, and the nature of the educational need. In his May 1998 initiatives speech, Knight made the education program a Nike standard, promising that by the end of 2001 Nike would order footwear only from manufacturers that offer a "Jobs + Education" program to workers.

Integration: The Approval Process

The approval process for this project was informal. A group of individuals involved in supply chain compliance and integrity at Nike, including CEO Phil Knight and President Dave Taylor, sat down to explore how Nike might be able to best support this project. During this stage of the project's establishment, group members discussed the parameters of their corporate responsibility as well as the investment they hoped to make, not only in these suppliers, but also in the workers and the countries in which they lived, highlighting the importance of top management commitment to the responsibility vision Nike was establishing. It was determined that the most effective program would he one that was coordinated in partnership with the Ministry of Education to ensure GED compliance where desired by the students. (GED-equivalent is the norm for Vietnam. However, in other counties, workers were more interested in obtaining life and other skills. Thus, education programs in same countries do not necessarily result in granting of GED equivalency.)

---

[20] Interview with Steve Hewitt, Nike-Vietnam. *Corporate Responsibility Manager.* 7/6/01.
[21] "Nike Critic Praises Gain in Air Quality at Vietnam Factory". *New York Times*, March 12, 1999.

Integration, Establishment, and Implementation

The supplier, in partnership with Nike and the Ministry of Education, worked together in the integration process and established GED programs by hiring teachers and renting classrooms in local educational facilities near the factories. The program covers the expenses of each student including books and other supplies and a meal allowance. Nike currently participates in the after-hours education program by funding 50 % of the cost of the program to each supplier. All Nike footwear suppliers in Vietnam currently have active education programs in accordance with this model. One of the factory owners involved identifies the program as a foundation for personal development, "We would like to be able to promote from within and can only do that once these workers have additional educations." In fact, this owner has already promoted several Vietnamese workers to line management positions on completion of the education program. He explains that he and his firm "want to go beyond compliance, both for the business relationship with Nike as well as for its own impact on the workers and our organization. To achieve our profits, we have to address the employees from an emotional perspective, as well."

As these practices are integrated into Nike's training programs, they serve as a Foundation for long-term relationships,[22] Dusty Kidd, Nike's Vice President for Compliance, explains that these programs are valuable not just as a gesture of Nike's commitment to the workforce and the supplier's future, they are valuable because they also result in long-term efficiencies that can be realized by investing in education. By investing matching funds ranging on average from $15,000 to $20,000 per supplier, Nike "can touch 300 people for a lifetime."[23] To date, over 10,000 contract workers have participated in these programs. The education program at one factory, Chang Shin, is currently the largest program, with 400 students having originally enrolled and an 85 % completion rate, which are important indicators of success that provide a basis for improvement and innovation. In addition, the Chang Shin Vietnam factory suggested a literacy program for the workers, jointly funded with Nike, Chang Shin Vietnam, and the local government, to which Nike agreed. Chang Shin Vietnam also offers "livelihood training" for interested workers, coordinating sessions on hand-knitting, embroidery, and other skills that the workers can then also teach their relatives. It is hoped that this program might offer the workers' families skills that they could use for additional income.

Though the subjects vary depending on worker demand and interest, the programs themselves range from high school equivalency, to vocational, to short-term education programs on specific subjects such as personal health or financial management. After-hours education programs now exist in Korea, Vietnam, Taiwan, China, Thailand, and Indonesia. Educators are generally hired from the local region to best meet the needs of the workers and to comply with education regulations of the education ministries in various countries.

---

[22] Nike has done business with many of the same Vietnamese suppliers for over 25 years.
[23] Conversation with Dusty Kidd, April 27, 2001.

Indicators: Continued Program Assessment

For program assessment, Nike considers the following factors as important indicators that help measure performance during its biannual audit visit:

- Are students remaining in the classes? If not, is it because of lack of interest, lack of time from work, the level or quality of the instruction, or other variables? (In one situation, Nike learned that the students did not feel that the quality of instruction was good, so the company worked with local programs to find more high-quality instructors an a better curriculum.)
- Are the students able to learn from and complete the coursework?
- What is the absentee rate? Why?
- Are the programs offered at appropriate times? Appropriate, accessible locations?
- What does our monitoring program report in connection with these programs? What do we learn from pretests and posttests or GED completion rates?

Since the workers have expressed a great deal of satisfaction with this program and encourage its continuation, Nike has encouraged its suppliers and suppliers of other companies from Vietnam and throughout Southeast Asia to visit the factory and learn about the program. To date, factory owners and others from adidas, Fuiitsu, and Nike itself have visited the program. Nike has institutionalized these types of visits to allow its suppliers to share best practices, providing a basis for ongoing improvement initiatives. Once a month, general managers from each factory come together in a different factory and discuss accomplishments and challenges. Every 6 months this same group travels to factories in other countries to learn about their processes (with Nike financial support).

As of June, 1999, there were 20 separate education programs in the factories of 37 Asian Nike footwear contractors, including five footwear factories in Vietnam, six footwear factories in Indonesia, six in China, and three in Thailand. In Vietnam, this program has been extended to include two contract apparel factories, and a third will begin participating soon.

Exit Strategy

In terms of an exit strategy, Nike expects that it will remain as long as necessary or as long as it has a relationship with that supplier. However, by participating in this program, Nike also hopes that it might affect the general standard of education in that country such that the supplemental programs are no longer necessary, as regional education programs are enhanced.

Program 2: The Nike Labs and Microenterprise Program

Inspiration and Vision Setting: Idea Generation/Inception

Conceived in 1997 and beginning in 1998, Nike established a microenterprise loan program to provide some support for women in the communities surrounding its suppliers. The inspiration or vision for the program originated in Vietnam and was later expanded to include Thailand and Indonesia. The purpose of the program is to allow women a chance to build small businesses that will ultimately boost their family's economic well-being, as well as contribute to the community's overall development. Though there is no direct financial gain for Nike, "the microloan program helps to create a more healthy community, which then provides other sources of income in the community, better workers, and additional sources of support for the families of current workers, raising the whole village's standard of living,' says Helzer.

Microloans respond to another difficult challenge in the Southeast Asian region. Nike has a global prohibition against any at-home work. However, this might have the impact of discriminating against women who, for social and cultural reasons, have either chosen not to work or are not allowed to work outside of the home. Therefore, because of the prohibition against any at-home outsourcing, these women may not have any financial means to protect their rights in other areas. The microloan program can provide this financial stability without outsourcing Nike manufacturing.

Integration, Establishment, and Implementation

In each country in which the program is located, Nike has teamed with local NGOs in an effort to ensure that ongoing support is available for borrowers and that the programs are well integrated. The Vietnam programs were established as a joint effort between Nike, Colorado-based Friendship Bridge (an NGO devoted to creating loan programs for developing economies that was involved in the first 3 years of the program), and the local Vietnamese Women's Unions (who notify and solicit the borrowers). Currently, there have been approximately 3,200 loans in place, with the average loan standing at approximately $65 [maximum loan = 1 million Vietnamese Dong (VND) (~U.S.$75) and the minimum loan = 500,000 VND (~U.S. $37)]. Total Nike investment to date has been approximately 3.5 billion VND (U.S.$244,755), which includes an administrative fee paid to Friendship Bridge. Usually women will borrow the minimum amount for their first loan and increase the amounts for subsequent loans.

The Vietnam program includes potential borrowers within a 30-mile radius of Nike suppliers. The loan program currently operates in 6 villages in the Dong Nai province and 12 villages in the Cu Chi province. The borrowers must submit a business plan and go through basic business training and health seminars before the plans and loans are approved. The business plan must include a provision for saving a part of the money earned, and mini-classes are available to borrowers regarding good saving habits. An additional component of the program requires children of borrowers to remain in school.

Those receiving the loans included groups of women who team together to borrow funding to raise small livestock, to produce incense sticks and other basic manufactured items (garments), or to tend to rice fields in the production of rice paper for spring rolls. More than 2,300 rural women and former workers have received funds to help them in creating small businesses and, in Vietnam specifically, there have been no defaults and the loans.[24]

The loans are granted in a "trust bank" format to teams of individuals to build in a support structure to the program. The 5–20 team members of each trust bank guarantee each other's loans. The borrowers meet weekly or monthly to make loan repayments, share business tips, address community concerns, and receive training in business topics such as financial management as well as personal subjects such as nutrition, hygiene, child care, and so on. After repaying loans, trust bank members can qualify for larger loans, and their payments are recycled to others in the form of new loans. Trust Bank clients have maintained an average repayment rate of 97 % or better.

In Indonesia the microenterprise loan program is offered in conjunction with Opportunity International, an NGO whose primary goal is fighting global poverty. The basis of the program is the belief that a very small loan (such as less than U.S. $100) may allow individuals to expand their inventory or to buy their raw materials in bulk, so that they can increase their profit margin, improve their business, and perhaps begin to accumulate savings.

Through a partnership with an NGO called the Population and Community Development Association and Union Footwear, Nike also supports a micro-enterprise program in northeastern Thailand, where it helped to establish a rural village stitching center and surrounding infrastructure, such as a vegetable bank, a tree bank, a school, and a women's empowerment center. Nike invested to build cash crop projects, to provide jobs, and to support the rural development of the region, which reversed migration to the city. By providing this kind of small business loan assistance, Nike can potentially put thousands of individuals to work. Significant local community improvement and innovation efforts are associated with the program.

Case Example: In conducting research for this report, one author visited the home of one of the Vietnamese microloan borrowers in the Cu Chi province. This young woman had borrowed money from the program each year for the past 4 years and had used the funds to purchase equipment to create rice paper. Before her involvement in the program, this woman engaged in a variety of domestic services in neighboring communities but never held a stable job until she began this work for herself. Currently, she produces between 10 and 20 kg a day of rice paper (depending on the weather) and is the sole support for her family of four. Although her youngest child is still in school, her husband and daughter assist in the production. With proceeds from the sale of her rice paper, this woman was able to rebuild her house using a

---

[24]Phil Knight, "New Labor Initiatives," (May 12, 1998), text at http://cbae.nmsu.edu/~dboje/ NIKphilspeech.html (accessed July 15, 2002), also reported in "PBS Newshour," http://www.pbs. org/newshour/forum/may98/nike.html (accessed July 15, 2002) (confirmed in discussion with Dusty Kidd). For additional information on the loan program, see http://www.nike.com/nikebiz/ nikebiz.jhtml?page=26&item=asia (accessed July 15, 2002) and http://www.nike.com/nikebiz/ nikebiz.jhtml?page=25&cat=communityprograms&subcat=smbixloans (accessed July 15, 2002).

brick structure and has been able to repay each of the four loans on time. Admittedly, although she earns significantly more money than she would earn in a factory working the same hours, she has no benefits available to her and is joined in her work by other family members.

Indicators: Continued Program Assessment

Until the program reaches self-sufficiency, Nike receives quarterly or biannual reports from the program coordinators as indicators of progress.

Exit Strategy

The program was developed and structured with the intent of self-sufficiency within several years. On the basis of interest charged and reinvestment of capital, the program will soon be able to afford its loans with no additional infusion of capital from Nike.

Program 3: Nike Cultural Sensitivity Training Program

Inspiration and Vision Setting: Idea Generation/Inception

Nike's Office of Labor Practices (now called Corporate Responsibility Compliance) was established in 1996. Al that time one of the more pressing issues revolved around a culture gap apparent in Vietnamese, Korean, and Taiwanese-owned factories between the Vietnam nationals and the foreign supervisors. The Korean- and Taiwanese-owned suppliers used local labor in Vietnam and found that they were faced with significant management challenges in connection with cultural issues.

In early 1997 Nike asked Andrew Young to visit the factories in China, Indonesia, and Vietnam for purposes of assessing how well Nike's code of conduct was being implemented. Young also reported on the cultural gap between the workers and the managers in these particular factories and identified specific areas of challenge in connection with cultural differences. He suggested that special human relations and cultural sensitivity programs should be designed and organized and that participation should be mandatory for all expatriate management.[25] His report, combined with the earlier identification of the problem, served as the inspiration for the vision-setting process that was to occur at Nike.

It should be noted that Young's report was not received without criticism. Critics contended that Young avoided the main issues and used a flawed research method

---

[25]Good Works International, LLC. "Report: The Nike Code of Conduct." (1997) pp. 33, 47–48.

that did not uncover the facts about conditions facing workers who produce Nike products. He was criticized for relying in part on previous, purportedly imprecise Ernst & Young audit reports; for failing to meet with certain NGO's; for spending insufficient time in various factories; and for issuing vague recommendations.[26] However, other investigators reported agreement with Young' 5 findings.[27]

In response to Young's report on cultural challenges, Nike determined that it should assist the factories in bridging the cultural divide by assigning human resource expert Fukumi Hauser as its global training manager. (Hauser is currently Nike director of global compliance, monitoring, and training.) These findings were also later supported by the work of the Center for Economic and Social Applications (CESAIS, now Troung Doan), which visited seven Vietnamese footwear factories in 1999. They found that one of the primary issues facing these Vietnamese workers was better relations between workers and managers.[28] Hauser visited the factories herself and identified several specific hurdles she might be able to help the suppliers overcome.

First, on the most basic level, there were language differences. These differences in language served to exacerbate other differences because of a general inability to communicate. Second, the Taiwanese and Korean supervisors managed the Vietnamese workers according to their home standards, rather than those in place in Vietnam. However, when the Vietnamese workers were displeased, they did not come forward for fear of losing their jobs or because sharing concerns was not encouraged. Other cultural management differences abounded. A specific example related to Taiwanese culture is the Taiwanese response to illness. If Taiwanese people are sick, they will often look to their ancestors, their graves, their ancestral homes, to determine whether something is amiss, perceiving the illness to be a sign that the ancestors are disturbed. The Vietnamese culture does not share that perception and therefore would consider medicinal remedies instead to mend the illness if a worker were sick Understanding these distinctions was vital to working together.

Third, the Vietnamese workers were accustomed to a rural, self-paced agricultural work routine and found it hard to adjust to a regimented factory routine with thousands of co-workers. Fourth, the Vietnamese workers did not have a great deal of education and therefore were not aware of their basic worker rights. This naiveté discouraged them from coming forward to assert their rights, as they did not know the parameters of those rights.

---

[26] Tim Connor, "A Response to Andrew Young's Report into Nike's Code of Conduct," The Nike-watch campaign at Oxfam community aid abroad, http://www.caa.org.au/campaigns/nike/young.html (accessed July 15, 2002); Campaign for Labor Rights, "The Andrew Young/Good Works Report on Nike," *Labor Alerts* (June 28, 1997), http://www.hartford-hwp.com/archives/26/004.html (accessed July 15, 2002); Eric Lourmand, "Nike drops the Ball: The Andrew Young Report," http://www-personal.umich.edu/~lormand/poli/nike/nike101-5.htm (accessed July 15, 2002).

[27] Kahle, Lynn et al. 2000. Good morning, Vietnam: an ethical analysis of Nike activities in southeast Asia. *Sport Marketing Quarterly* 9(1):43–52.

[28] Nike, Inc. "Corporate responsibility report, 2001." p. 35.

When an expectation gap resulting from different management styles is merged with a language barrier that prevents free-flowing communication, a power differential, and a lack of awareness regarding rights, the result is lower productivity, higher attrition, a possible abridgement of rights, and a consequent low sense of morale in the workplace. These conditions, obviously, make stakeholder engagement difficult.

Integration, Establishment, and Implementation: Cultural Sensitivity Training

Confronted with these significant barriers to healthy working relationships, Hauser considered her options. In lieu of asking the Vietnamese workers to modify their perceptions and to learn new communication skills, Hauser concluded that those in power had the responsibility to learn about those with whom they worked. Hauser developed an awareness campaign and, after training the top management staff from Nike footwear supplier sites in Vietnam, Indonesia, and China (and simultaneously creating top management commitment), she was asked to go to the home offices of the suppliers in Korea and Taiwan. Currently, the cultural training program has been integrated into Nike's monitoring program, which is called SHAPE (Safety, Health, Attitude of Management, People Investment, Environment).

The cultural sensitivity campaign encompassed three segments. The training began by exploring the nature of a "culture." What is culture? We all are part of some culture, but how do we define those cultures beyond simply food and language distinctions to differences in respect, relationships, communication styles, and so on? For example, cultures differ based on whether they are future-oriented or past-oriented. This is critical to understand since a past-oriented culture will place great weight on how a person has acted, while a future-oriented culture will place great weight on how a person modifies her or his actions. The second segment of the training asked the participants to identify for themselves their own particular culture and its specific components. Finally, Hauser explores with the participants the nature of Vietnamese culture to allow them to better understand their subordinates.

She explains the impact of this type of awareness by referring to American culture and its impact on American workers. For instance, in the United States, we often hear about "The American Dream," insinuating that anything is possible; if a person just reaches for a goal, it can be attained. However, consider the implications of these messages for American workers. Where a supervisor manages workers on the basis of this cultural belief system, workers' failure must only be their own. If a person can do anything, the failure to do something is also the person's responsibility.

Moreover, if someone has a problem, that person is expected to speak up and voice the problem in an attempt to solve it. In other cultures, speaking up causes conflicts in two areas. First, it may be viewed as dull-witted since silence connotes wisdom and understanding. Second, in certain cultures, individuals with a problem expect the manager to know their problem, even if they have not voiced it. By voicing a problem, a person may be implying that the manager did not know enough to be aware of that issue. Therefore, it may be insulting to the manager if a person raises a problem – not a good result. Also specifically "American" are the concepts of individualism and freedom of choice. As with those discussed above, these values are not necessarily considered to be "positive" values in some other cultures. In a culture that focuses its attention on the past and is slow to forgive, mistakes such as these are not easily forgotten.

Hauser relates this to the Vietnamese situation by sharing the following example. One issue of cultural conflict has to do with the basic sounds of the different languages. Vietnamese is a language that is spoken in a soft, somewhat singsong, tone that has been compared to "birds chirping." Korean, on the other hand, is spoken quite boisterously. There were bound to be instances in which, as a result at the language barrier, the Vietnamese workers misinterpreted a Korean manager's statement to be full of anger when it was simply basic speech.

Issues of age and respect also play a role in fleeting possible workplace conflicts. In Vietnam, no matter one's position, the younger worker owes strong respect to an older worker. Consequently, in instances in which a younger foreign supervisor manages an older Vietnamese line worker, the elder worker may respond indignantly if the manager does not respect the cultural mores connected with age.

Another example of distinction refers to communication styles, as opposed to the words or sounds that are used. Hauser explains that the Korean and Taiwanese managers expressed concern that the Vietnamese workers were making mistakes but refused to accept responsibility for them. "They would deny it and I would ask them to admit it." They then found that the workers would giggle and laugh at them as they continued to try to get the worker to own up to his or her mistake. The managers explain that all they wanted was for the worker to accept responsibility and things would be all right.

Hauser was able to diffuse this type of conflict by explaining to the managers that, in Vietnamese culture, (1) reproach should be handled in private, (2) public reproach is the source of shame and embarrassment, (3) workers smile or giggle when they are embarrassed or ashamed, and (4) Vietnamese expect to have to pay harshly for their mistakes. Therefore, the managers learned that the more they reproached the individual for not accepting responsibility, the more likely it was that the worker would smile or laugh. As the manager would get more and more angry, the worker would continue to be ashamed and, therefore, smile. It was also very difficult for the Vietnamese workers to trust that they would not be fired when a manager expresses anger at a mistake.

As a resolution of this issue, Hauser did not suggest that the managers refrain from pointing out mistakes; instead she suggested through her training program that the reproach take place in a private area and that the trust would grow as workers were able to see that every mistake did not result in a termination. The response: "Aha! We had no idea!" Thus by explaining differences, Hauser was able to allow for greater understanding and compassion, and these improvements could be integrated into daily management practice.

Finally, cultural differences exist in connection with reporting violations. Predictably, when people feel that they are not protected by promises of due process, reporting a supervisor's violation is an extremely risky venture. Moreover, when that retribution may be inordinately more severe than the violation, people are discouraged from bearing that responsibility. In one instance, a journalist reported a violation by a Vietnamese line supervisor but refused to offer the person's name for fear of inappropriate punishment. In that situation, Nike resorted to retraining all management in this particular area.

Integration, Establishment, and Implementation: Management Training

It is critical that these suppliers be able to promote from within to management positions because not only do expatriate managers often choose to return home after a stint overseas, but also because fewer and fewer managers choose to go into this industry and accept foreign postings. Consider today's young Taiwanese and Koreans. As education standards in their own countries have increased, these individuals are less likely to go into footwear manufacturing but instead will gravitate toward other, more attractive and lucrative industries such as these in the hi-tech arena. Therefore, there is a shortage of possible managers, and these Korean- and Taiwanese-owned firms must be able to recruit management and supervisors from within their Vietnamese ranks.

As a result, while there was improved communication between expatriate managers and the Vietnamese workers, there was one additional challenge in connection with training that had been left unsolved. During newly implemented exit interviews, the suppliers were finding that Vietnamese workers who were promoted to first-level supervisory roles found themselves in those roles with no management training. Therefore, they simply replicated some of the original management styles of the Korean and Taiwanese managers who first supervised them. They were often under the impression that this was what was expected of a manager and, if their style failed to resemble the foreign management style, they might be fired.

To create a management training program appropriate for the Vietnamese workers, Hauser enlisted the assistance of a Vietnamese-American trainer named Tuan Nguyen, who was experienced in management training through Levi Straus and other firms in the United States. Together, Hauser and Nguyen created and coordinated a 5-day supervisor training program for Vietnamese workers. The training program was designed to improve management abilities by enhancing self-awareness, improving communication skills, and working with cultural differences. Nike paid fully for a pilot of the weeklong program, first with five workers from each factory. After responding to feedback from the pilot effort, Nguyen returned for 22 weeks, training 100 supervisors from each of the five participating factories. For this segment of the training, Nike covered two-thirds of the cost, with the supplier covering one-third.

The aim of the program was to create a self-sustaining system in which trainers were available in each factory, and training materials were tailored for each factory's needs, so that later training could be initiated and be fully paid for by the supplier. This integration into factory-specific systems allows individual factories to develop the improvement process needed for their specific situation.

Currently, managers in many of Nike's suppliers receive support materials regarding some of these issues on joining the factory. For instance, expatriate managers in one factory received a booklet titled "Vietnamese Language for Daily Communication." In this way, though all foreign managers or supervisors are required to learn the local language, they also have additional support tools to help in day-to-day operations. In one factory, Vietnamese line managers and above are chosen to participate in the factory's "Innovation School," in which additional business skills are developed.

Indicators: Continued Program Assessment

Currently, each footwear factory in Vietnam conducts its own ongoing supervisor training using the modified material. Continued regular dialogues with workers, departmental representatives, and the trade unions; surveys; suggestion boxes; and self-reviews provide indicators that allow Nike both to ascertain the efficacy of the programs and to identify areas that continue to need to be addressed. (In fact, one firm receives thousands of suggestions each month.) For instance, during one review, a problem was identified about gift giving. It seems that Vietnamese culture dictates small gifts on certain occasions, holidays, accomplishments, and so on. The factory owner, a Korean, was unfamiliar with this practice, so the workers simply believed that he chose not to do so. Once notified of this error, he instituted certain awards or benefits such as calendars, raincoats, or token amounts of money on appropriate occasions. The same challenge proved surmountable when one Korean factory president, C. T. Park, realized that female workers no longer spoke to him and some even sneered at him from time to time. Later he learned that this "snub" treatment was the result of his failure to attend or even respond to their wedding invitations – a major cultural faux pas and one that could be easily be ameliorated.[29]

One unexpected consequence of the training, however, is that workers are confused by the modified behavior. Hauser reports that workers have asked their supervisors, "Why are you like this now? Why are you treating me differently?" When asked to create additional training materials to help them to "integrate" into the workplace, Hauser responded that what was needed was not more training, but more problem-solving sessions that would empower the workers and the supervisors to jointly explore challenges and resolve issues on their own.

Nike Addendum 2013

Though not without challenges, Nike has continued its commitments to improving the quality of working life in its Vietnam contract factories. Between 2002 and 2004, Nike conducted over 600 audits across its contract factories, with a focus on

---

[29] Samantha Marchall, "Executive action: cultural sensitivity on the assembly line."

problematic sites that did not meet performance standards. In 2005, Nike published a complete list of the factories it contracts with, as well as a thorough report on conditions and pay in those factories including problems, and it became the first company in its industry to make such information public.[30]

In 2008, over 20,000 workers at a Vietnamese footwear contract factory went on strike, demanding better pay and arguing that the current salary (approximately $59 per month, 14 % more than minimum wage) was not enough to cope with Vietnam's rising inflation, nor were the cafeteria lunches adequate to maintain energy during the work day.[31] After 2 days, a 10 % raise and new lunch program were agreed upon.[32]

As of end of fiscal year 2011, in 79 % of its focus factories, Nike had: implemented the Human Resources Management training program; implemented the Freedom of Association education program; and formally surveyed workers on conditions and satisfaction.[33]

Nike aims to source only from those factories that meet at least a Bronze rating on the Sourcing & Manufacturing Sustainability Index by the end of its 2020 fiscal year. Nike has prioritized the reduction of excessive overtime (defined as more than 60 h worked in 1 week, or less than 1 day off in 7), and declared its focus on lean manufacturing and its benefits for the workforce, which Nike has pledged to study by the end of fiscal year 2015. Nike also has committed to investing a minimum of 1.5 % of pre-tax profit in the communities of its workers towards, "Combining capital, engaging in innovative partnerships, and developing marketing, business acumen, and public policy advocacy in new ways to drive change at scale."[34]

Can Walmart Rise to a Transformational Challenge in China?[35]

Introduction

On October 24, 2005, CEO, Lee Scott broadcast his "Twenty First Century Leadership" speech to over 2 million Walmart associates in nearly 10,000 stores in 28 countries around the world. Scott's message went out as well to a network of

---

[30]Nisen, Max. How Nike solved its sweatshop problem. *Business Insider.* http://www.businessinsider.com/how-nike-solved-its-sweatshop-problem-2013-5#ixzz2W0cbrPpT. Accessed June 12, 2013.

[31]http://news.bbc.co.uk/2/hi/business/7324242.stm

[32]http://www.teamsweat.org/2008/04/02/nike-ends-strike-in-vietnam/

[33]http://www.nikeresponsibility.com/report/content/chapter/targets-and-performance#topic-performance-against-past-targets

[34]http://www.nikeresponsibility.com/report/content/chapter/targets-and-performance#Community

[35]This case was prepared by Jerry M. Calton, University of Hawaii, Hilo.

over 100,000 suppliers in 60 countries. Around 70 % of Walmart's vast global supply chain is located in China. Scott's speech signaled a remarkably ambitious transformational change effort in the retail giant's relationships with its stakeholders, which had traditionally been defined by its corporate slogan: *Always low prices, always*. October 24, 2005, is celebrated within the company as a "defining day in the history of Walmart."[36] The transformational challenge for Walmart executives, associates, and suppliers is how their single-minded focus on lowering prices by squeezing costs throughout its global supply chain could be reconciled with new initiatives to improve social and environmental performance via ethical supply chain management.

In his talk, Scott staked out Walmart's claim to environmental responsibility, and less directly to social responsibility: "Environmental loss threatens our health and the health of the natural systems we depend on." He affirmed that as "one of the largest companies in the world, with an expanding global presence, environmental problems are *our* problems."[37] He acknowledged that some would "think that if a company addresses the environment, it will lose its shirt." He countered that they are wrong: "I believe, in fact, that being a good steward of the environment and in our communities, and being an efficient and profitable business, are not mutually exclusive. In fact, they are one and the same."[38] In effect, Scott argued that Walmart's relentless focus on low cost leadership potentially could be reconciled with social and environmental goals so seamlessly that they would be subsumed into a more complex, *but still unitary*, framework for corporate performance outcomes.

Scott laid out Walmart's three long-term transformational goals for *doing well by doing good*:

1. To be supplied 100 % by renewable energy.
2. To create zero waste.
3. To sell products that sustain our resources and environment.

Scott characterized these goals as "both ambitious and aspirational." Notably, he went on to confess that he was "not sure how to achieve them, at least not yet."[39] He recognized that Walmart's emergent, more complex framework of performance aspirations would be a work in progress, as Walmart executives learned how to rethink relationships with stakeholders, particularly Chinese suppliers. The reputational impact of Scott's sustainability leadership was more immediate, since he was ranked near the top of the 100 Most Influential People in Business Ethics in 2008.

---

[36] Schell, O. 2011. How Wall-Mart is changing China and vice versa. *Atlantic* (December) :86.
[37] Schell 2011, p. 84.
[38] Ibid.
[39] Ibid.

How Did Lee Scott Arrive at His "Now Think" Moment?

Dennis Gioia, in reflecting on why he failed as Ford's recall coordinator to recall the subcompact Pinto car in the 1970s after evidence mounted that it was prone to lighting up after a rear end collision, called attention to the role of *cognitive scripts* in limiting the discretion available to decision-makers, such as himself. He argued that Ford's cultural cues, such as elevating "rational" over "emotional" criteria for triggering a recall, and the restrictive "rule of 2000" dollars and pounds in building the subcompact car comprised mental knots that effectively tied his hands. Gioia, who went on to become a professor of business ethics after leaving Ford before the deluge of product liability suits began, encouraged decision-makers to remain open to "Now think" moments.[40] These reflective interludes can prompt questioning of the limits of cognitive scripts, followed hopefully by rewriting scripts to reframe the shared problem domain in a more meaningful way. Such epiphanies can take into account new information, new ways of thinking, and a wider range of stakeholder perspectives, values, and interests. This would enable inclusion of ethical as well as operational considerations in the decision frame. Patricia Werhane has characterized this emergent process of cognitive reframing as *moral imagination*. She offers it as a remedy for the syndrome of *moral amnesia* brought on by the tendency to cast business decisions narrowly in terms of economic or technical parameters, prompting a "setting aside of moral considerations in the pace of business activities."[41]

When CEO Lee Scott made his twenty first century leadership speech in 2005, he was responding to a history of troubled and deteriorating stakeholder relationships as Walmart expanded exponentially from its home base in Bentonville, Arkansas. The unconventional, folksy persona of Walmart's founder and cultural icon, Sam Walton, masked these stakeholder problems, which arose, ultimately from Walmart's narrow, near obsessive focus on cost-cutting as a way to build competitive advantage via aggressive and innovative supply chain management. Sam's pithy sayings and his remarkable ability to remember the names, faces, and stories of associates provided cultural cohesion as Walmart expanded from its rural, southern, small town roots into a regional, national, and ultimately global retailing juggernaut. Sam's stories, such as his *ten foot rule* that associates who came within ten feet of a customer must ask how they can help, were cultivated by his successors to nurture a paternalistic, extended family culture in which associates pulled together to serve customers and, ultimately, the company and its shareholders.

Walmart's relations with stakeholders outside its primary focus on creating value for customers and shareholders began to deteriorate, particularly after the death of Sam Walton to cancer in 1992. These tensions were generated primarily by Walmart's relentless cost-driven growth strategy, which accelerated after it started to develop

---

[40] Gioia, Dennis. 1992. "Pinto fires and personal ethics" a script analysis of missed opportunities. *Journal of Business Ethics* 11:388.

[41] Werhane, Patricia H. 1999. *Moral imagination and management decision-making*, 11. New York: Oxford University Press.

and extend its global supply chain later in the 1990s. Ironically, Sam Walton's *Buy American* initiative served to mask this shift toward global sourcing – particularly toward China. Walmart's large and small US suppliers were forced to abandon wholesale middlemen and shift to direct buying relationships in Vendorville, an office complex that grew up near the Bentonville corporate headquarters in Arkansas. As a condition for maintaining a relationship with Walmart, suppliers were required to disclose their cost and profit data and to agree to an annual 5 % reduction in unit costs. In short order, suppliers were faced with the choice of bankruptcy or outsourcing production, preferably to China.[42]

To avoid the appearance of working directly with the Chinese Communist government, particularly after the Chinese democracy movement was brutally suppressed in Tiananmen Square in 1989, Walton set up a buying agency in Hong Kong, Pacific Resources Export Limited (PREL). Headed by Sam Walton's tennis buddy, George Billingsley, PREL became Walmart's exclusive buying agent, with 29 offices throughout Asia but focusing primarily on China. Shortly after China joined the World Trade Organization (WTO) in 2001, Walmart shifted toward direct buying arrangements with 5,000 Chinese suppliers at a new Vendorville East base in the rising industrial city of Shenzhen, in southern China. Very much like Walmart's remaining US suppliers, these Chinese suppliers became dependent price-takers, drawn by the promise of high-volume orders from the retail giant, but held captive by the shrinking profit margins dictated by Walmart's relentless cost-cutting pressure. This dependent relationship is an extension of the new "pull" system of manufacturing pioneered by Walmart and other big box retailers. Rather than make consumer goods and then try to push them out the door via wholesale distributors, even large manufacturers such as Procter and Gamble and Rubbermaid, were subordinated to taking orders from massive computerized inventory control systems that monitor big box consumer purchases.[43]

Walmart was drawn to China by the seemingly inexhaustible source of low cost, young, energetic (mostly female) workers streaming into newly created Special Economic Zones from China's poor rural hinterland. Also attractive was the Chinese government's recent embrace of globalization to attract foreign investment in their new "export platform" special economic zones, such as the zone along the Pearl River that encompasses Shenzhen. American, as well as Taiwanese, Korean, Japanese, and European companies were offered low taxes and minimal regulation so long as they were prepared to take on a Chinese (often a government) joint venture partner, transfer product and process technology to the local partner, and export the output back to international markets. Also attractive was the Chinese government's 40 % devaluation of the yuan against the US dollar, dramatically lowering the cost of Chinese exports, increasing the US trade deficit, and triggering massive Chinese foreign exchange earnings. This inflow of export income would have driven up the value of the yuan

---

[42]Lichtenstein, N. 2011. Wal-Mart's long march to China: How a Mid-American retailer came to stake its future on the Chinese economy. In *Wal-Mart in China*, ed. Anita Chan, 13–14. Ithaca: ILR Press.

[43]Lichtenstein 2011, pp. 13–14.

against the dollar if the Chinese government had not purchased over $1 trillion in US treasury bonds, engineering a Chinese capital account deficit to counter the trade surplus. While some cite these trends as evidence of a Chinese threat to US national security and economic well-being, others argue that the Chinese are *playing our game* (e.g., Steinfeld 2010) and that the primary beneficiaries of China's central role as workshop of the world in emerging global supply chain networks are the big box retailers, such as Walmart, that control them. In 2006, Walmart exported US$27 billion from China, up from US$9.5 billion in 2001. This makes Walmart China's 12th largest trading partner.[44] Some have observed that Walmart and the Chinese government are bound together virtually in a joint venture partnership and that Walmart's *culture of Sam* bears a striking resemblance to the Chinese reverence for Chairman Mao.[45]

Supplier Dependence Within Walmart's Ethical Supply Chain Management System

The dependent position of Chinese suppliers in this relationship is captured in the plaint of Mr. Liu, a purveyor of craft goods:

> A Walmart order gives a very low profit, even when compared with other large American retailers; for example, it is usually 10 % lower than Target, but the size of a Walmart order is at least five times that of a Target order. It is the large volume that makes it worth dealing with Walmart. Walmart really exploits our company, though. Usually, the price of our products in Walmart stores in the U.S. is at least six times what Walmart pays us.[46]

Walmart's insistence on maintaining a low cost advantage within its global supply chain has raised serious doubts as to whether corporate executives are sincere in their determination to improve social and environmental performance. To the extent that financial, social, and environmental goals are compatible (such as saving energy and recycling packaging), real progress has been made toward improving Walmart's triple bottom line. However, when improvement in employee conditions in Chinese supplier firms impacts Walmart's bottom line, rather than just supplier firm profit margins, a less salutary picture emerges.

Walmart embarked on its Ethical Standards program in 1992, after a scathing NBC expose on child labor and other deplorable sweatshop conditions one of Walmart's Bangladesh supplier factories. A broad-based anti-sweat movement in the U.S. during the 1990s targeted other apparel firms as well, such as Liz Claiborne and Nike. These branded firms were more vulnerable to consumer backlash than Walmart, which pushed lower cost private brands and appealed to a more price-sensitive clientele.

---

[44]Lichtenstein 2011, p. 29.

[45]Schell 2011; Davis, D. J. 2011. Corporate Cadres: Management and corporate culture in Wal-Mart China." In ed. Chan, 97–129.

[46]Hong, Xue. 2011. Outsourcing in China: Wal-Mart and Chinese Manufacturers. In ed. Chan, 41.

Nevertheless, Walmart's factory certification system looks impressive. The Ethical Standards program covers a supplier's compliance with local and national laws and regulations, compensation, hours of work, no forced/prison labor, no underage labor, no discrimination, freedom of association and collective bargaining, health and safety, environment, and the right to audit by Walmart. Over 200 inspectors were hired, and 100 were assigned to monitor Chinese suppliers. At least once a year, 5,300 factories from which Walmart *buys directly* are inspected. A green-yellow-red reporting system was established to flag violators. Annually, 1 % of its Chinese suppliers are dropped from Walmart's supply chain for non-compliance.[47]

While this code enforcement framework sounds effective, a comment from a Chinese supplier, Mr. Hua, raises a question as to whether, in the context of supplier dependence, compliance or evasion is the operative response to Walmart's ethical compliance system:

> Doing business with Walmart is like a battle. If you want to win, you have to know the enemy very well. Sometimes you have to obey Walmart's rules, but sometimes you don't have to comply with all of them. Walmart's number-one rule is low price; that one you have to satisfy. I don't think its requirements on labor rights are very important. Of course, you have to trick Walmart to make higher profits.[48]

This rather cynical observation suggests that Walmart is primarily concerned with preserving its low cost advantage and that its ethical code procedures, particularly with respect to labor conditions in its supplier factories, are designed to preserve the appearance of compliance. A study of ethical compliance among Walmart's Chinese toy suppliers, concluded that CSR consultants, rather than factory employees, were the primary beneficiaries of Walmart's enforcement efforts. Walmart's self-policing system forces suppliers to demonstrate compliance as a condition for contract renewal. This places the burden for compliance upon supplier firms and invites a search for *creative* ways to simulate compliance. Thus, CSR consultants provide aid to supplier firms in preparing a separate set of books to show that limits on involuntary overtime have been enforced and that domestic minimum wage and child labor laws have been obeyed. Walmart's insistence that suppliers respond quickly to a surge in orders that are triggered by its pull inventory controls virtually forces suppliers to violate limits on involuntary overtime. Suppliers typically know in advance when ethics inspectors are coming and they coach employees on how to respond to questions, while giving under age workers the day off. Factory managers warn that if employees complain, Walmart might cancel the supply contract, throwing everyone out of work. In some cases, a model factory is built for inspection purposes, while a nearby non-complying parallel factory runs full bore.[49]

Since a substantial, but loosely monitored, amount of the work of Walmart suppliers is sub-contracted out to factories not subject to Walmart inspections, a significant gap in supplier oversight exists. The devastating fire in a Bangladesh

---

[47]Lichtenstein 2011, pp. 30–31.

[48]Xue 2001, p. 42.

[49]Xue 2001, pp. 46–48.

apparel factory in December 2012, which killed 112 workers, highlights the reputational risk of such partial oversight of Walmart's global supply chain. Initially, Walmart spokespersons denied any involvement with the factory, which had failed a recent fire inspection. Walmart subsequently learned that its local supplier had sub-contracted production to this factory after Walmart tagged clothing was discovered in the burned debris. Walmart's response was to hold its suppliers accountable for inspecting the factories of their sub-contractors.[50]

Can Walmart Forge a More Collaborative Relationship with Its Chinese Suppliers?

Walmart's push to create new supplier partnerships in China after Lee Scott's twenty first century leadership speech provides the best test of whether Walmart and its supplier network can rise to the transformational challenge. The focus is on improving product quality and food safety by forging closer, more collaborative relationships with Chinese suppliers. The question remains – has Walmart turned over a new leaf based on efforts to build trust and collaborative partnerships? The jury is still out on this question.

Toward the end of his term as CEO, Lee Scott convened a China Sustainability Summit in the Grand Ballroom of Beijing's Shangri-La Hotel. On October 22, 2008, he told representatives of the 1,000 Chinese suppliers in attendance that a year from now "each and every one of you who chooses to make a commitment will be a more socially and environmentally responsible company." He went on to warn:

> Meeting social and environmental standards is not optional. I firmly believe that a company that cheats on overtime and on the age of its labor, that dumps its scraps and its chemicals in our rivers, that does not pay its taxes or honor its contracts, will ultimately cheat on the quality of its products.[51]

Scott assured the suppliers in attendance that Walmart would "work with" them in assuring compliance to the new sustainability standards. However, he went on to reveal the hammer within the velvet glove:

> If a factory does not meet these requirements, they will be expected to put forth a plan to fix any problems. If they still do not improve, they will be banned from making products for Walmart.[52]

The timing of Walmart's embrace of the green mantle in China was fortuitous, since the Chinese government had just shifted its Five Year Plan from rampant economic development to *scientific* or *sustainable* growth toward more *harmonious*

---

[50] J. Wohl, 2012 "After Bangladesh fire, Wal-Mart vows to address supply chain risks." http://www.insurancejournal.com/news/national/2012/12/14/274050.htm

[51] Schell 2011, p. 88.

[52] Schell 2011, pp. 88–89.

social relationships. The emerging middle class in China's bustling cities was becoming increasingly concerned about rampant air pollution, cancer villages poisoned by the effluent from unregulated chemical plants along China's waterways, and by adulteration of the food supply for financial gain, often with the complicity of local or regional government officials. One infamous case was the 2008 *milk scandal* in which milk distributors in Inner Mongolia laced baby food and powdered milk with melamine, a coal-based by-product. This chemical, which induced a false positive reading for higher protein to boost sales, had the unfortunate side-effect of causing kidney stones, renal failure, and even death, particularly among infants. In another case, a "lean meat powder" containing toxic chemicals was used to produce less fatty pork for the burgeoning middle class palate. A new Food Safety Law went into effect in 2009, but enforcement, given local government indifference and corruption, was problematic. Thus Walmart was well positioned to partner with China's national government in cleaning and greening its Chinese supply chain, though enforcement of supplier compliance remains challenging.[53]

Walmart's strategic and cultural shift toward sustainability in China aligned well, not only with the new shift in government priorities, but also with middle class consumer preferences. Thus, in its 352 stores in 130 Chinese cities, Walmart emphasized the quality and safety of its product offerings as much as their low price. Gravitating toward *organic, green,* and *hazard-free* labels in the produce section, one Chinese customer chose organic "because there are so many fake products on the market, and I am worried about my health." A woman confessed: "In my local supermarket, who knows? But I trust Walmart to buy the best."[54] To deliver on these promises, Walmart managers have had to forge a new, closer, virtually *evangelical* relationship with key Chinese stakeholders. The big box giant expanded a Direct Farm Program begun in 2007, sponsoring the organization of regional farm cooperatives. This gave farmers expanded market access for their produce beyond local farmers markets, while Walmart could eliminate middlemen and assure adherence to food quality standards. Continuing food controversies, such as Walmart's mislabeling of pork as organic in Chongqing suggest that Walmart's quality controls are less than seamless.[55] (Lee 2011)

A related push by Walmart for energy savings among its suppliers is instructive. Loftex, a Walmart supplier of high-end bath towels, joined the Energy Efficiency Program, which sought a 20 % savings in energy use by 2012. Particularly encouraging is Walmart's close relationship with NGOs, such as the Environmental Defense Fund, the National Resources Defense Council, and Business for Social Responsibility as allies in working with suppliers to increase energy efficiency. Driving through Loftex's plant gates in the regional city of Binzhou, the visitor is

---

[53]Schell 2011, p. 89; L. Burkitt. 2012. "Wal-Mart faces new food-safety complaints in China." http://online.wsj.com/article/SB10001424052702303410404577466.

[54]Schell 2011, p. 90.

[55]M. Lee. 2011. "Wall-Mart's pork scandal highlights struggles in China." http://www.reuters.com/assets/print?aid=USTRE79D1SO20111014

greeted by hortatory banners such as "Boldly Revolutionize the Towel" followed by the admonition that "Enterprises Must Develop, But First They Must Protect the Environment." At Walmart's prompting, Loftex has invested $660,000 in energy efficiency, cutting electricity use by 25 % and water use by 35 %.[56]

The question remains, is Loftex a leading indicator of a new, more collaborative relationship with an emerging network of sustainable, socially responsible Chinese suppliers? Or are seemingly eager recruits to the green cause mere *Potemkin villages* held out for show, but with little substance to back up the facade – akin to the *parallel plants* set aside for Walmart's complicit or clueless ethics inspectors? Xue Hong, one of the contributors to the book, *Walmart in China* edited by Anita Chan argues that ethical supply chain management has become little more than "a cat and mouse game between suppliers and their buyers"[57] The point is not that most Chinese suppliers are inherently unethical; only that Walmart's persistent pressure upon suppliers to lower costs has forced them to assume most if not all of the additional costs to improve social and environmental performance.

Walmart's Authoritarian Management Model of Cultural Solidarity

Walmart managers have worked to counter this pluralist tendency for suppliers to look after their own interests by drawing upon the rhetoric of revolutionary solidarity – curiously reminiscent of the Chinese Communist doctrine of *democratic centralism*. Walmart's *Cult of Sam* is taking on the absolutist aura of Chairman Mao. Paralleling evangelical exhortations for suppliers to revolutionize the towel, David Davies, another contributor to *Walmart in China*, has found Maoist undertones in the training of mid-management *cadres* in Walmart's Chinese stores:

> References to egalitarianism, loyalty, service, shared sacrifice, and delayed gratification for a utopian future of corporate success – combined with images of a great leader – evoke uncanny associations with recent Maoist ideologies of the ideal workplace…. [The] logic of this culture lies in the correct management of internal thoughts and attitudes. In such a community, compliance to the culture is not measured according to an abstract standard, but modeled for employees through social relationships – attempting to forge a sense of shared obligation and mutual responsibility for corporate success.[58]

A large portrait of Sam smiling benignly and waving somewhat diffidently is displayed prominently near the entrance of all Walmart stores in China. Walmart associates in China are called *tongren*, which translates as "hearts united," to suggest the centrality of cultural solidarity as a management tool for manufacturing employee loyalty and commitment to the company cause. Sam's sayings, such as the *ten foot*

---

[56] Schell 2011, p. 94.

[57] Chan 2001, p. 46.

[58] Davis 2011, p. 99.

rule (converted into the *three meter rule*) for helping any customer who falls within the perimeter are converted into transformational moral principles for interacting with Walmart's stakeholders. Walmart China's employee manual stipulates:

> These [principles] are not simply rules for a style of work, but are "a kind of way of life": we must take these convictions and dissolve them into every hour and every minute of our lives, furthermore embody them as colleagues work together in the process of serving our customers. [59]

This moral commitment to customer service is reinforced by such symbolic devices as clipping a one yuan note to each employee's uniform. A customer is free to take the money if she feels the employee has failed a service obligation. Store managers are not exempt from this practice. They must append a five *yuan* note on their uniform! Loss of a monetary token is widely noted and taken as a justification for serious moral introspection and rededication to the cause of restoring the solidarity of employee-customer relationships. [60]

Conclusion

Lee Scott's call for a new transformational relationship with Walmart stakeholders, and particularly with the Chinese *partners* in its global supply chain, has garnered a definite reputational bump for the company. Michael Duke, Scott's successor as CEO, has affirmed that the new focus on social and environmental performance is the "new normal" for the company. [61] And yet, Walmart's Chinese experiments in relational transformation pose troubling questions. Can a single-minded insistence on cost cutting within its global value chain be reconciled with new aspirational goals to do *good* in the context of improved social and environmental performance while also doing *well* financially? Walmart's attempt to answer this question in the affirmative drew upon the Chinese authoritarian tradition of inculcating personal transformation to achieve cultural solidarity within a putative harmonious social, political, or corporate order. This authoritarian approach to transforming stakeholder relationships seems at odds with the more open and democratic movement toward multi-sector collaboration within stakeholder networks. [62] Such *community conversations* bring to the table different interests and voices to engage in multi-stakeholder dialogue to craft mutually agreeable standards of global practice relating to labor or human rights or environmental sustainability. Rules of engagement

---

[59] Davis 2011, p. 115.

[60] Ibid., p. 125.

[61] Schell 2011, p. 98.

[62] Waddell, S. 2011. *Global action networks: Creating our future together.* New York: Palgrave Macmillan; Waddock, S. 2006. *Leading corporate citizens: vision, values, value-added.* New York: McGraw Hill/Irwin.

for such open-ended, problem-driven conversations require inclusion of different perspectives, respect for all parties at the table, and a willingness to engage in a process of co-creative discovery to find common ground within the pluralist problem domain. The key ingredient for finding common ground among the contending voices is the capacity to build and maintain trust among all of the parties at the table.[63]

Given the above considerations, it is not at all clear that Walmart China can forge a harmonious community of practice where cost-driven profitability goals and social and environmental performance can be subsumed in Lee Scott's transformational vision that all goals could be "one and the same." At the time of his twenty first century leadership speech in 2005, Lee confessed that he was not sure how to achieve this aspirational vision "at least not yet." [64]

While Walmart has managed to forge cooperative relationships with NGOs in China to improve social and environmental performance within its value chain, it is worth noting that the Communist Chinese government regards civil society associations with great trepidation, since they seem to represent potentially subversive private and plural rather than common public/private interests. It is not at all clear that Walmart will be successful in extending its authoritarian *cultural solidarity* model for reconciling financial, social, and environmental performance once the low hanging fruit of energy efficiency and recycling gains have been reaped. An ever-expanding consumers suspended precariously over a massive carbon footprint seems a fragile platform upon which to build a sustainable and prosperous world order. More "Now think" moments[65] to encourage rewriting of cognitive scripts in Walmart's further transformational efforts would seem to be in order.

---

[63]Calton, J. M., and S. Payne. 2003. Coping with paradox: Multi-stakeholder learning dialogue as a pluralist sense making process. *Business & Society* 42:7–42.

[64]Schell 2011, p. 86.

[65]Gioia 1992, p. 182.

About the Editors

Pauline J. Albert is an independent researcher and writer. Over the last decade she taught a wide variety of courses in the U.S. and Europe as a faculty member at St. Edward's University. Before joining the academy, she had a lengthy career in the high-tech, consulting, and banking industries working both in the U.S. and abroad.

Patricia H. Werhane is Wicklander Chair of Business Ethics, DePaul University and Professor Emeritus, University of Virginia. Her latest book is *Obstacles to Ethical Decision-Making*, with Hartman, Archer, Englehardt and Pritchard, Cambridge University Press, 2013.

P.J. Albert et al. (eds.), *Global Poverty Alleviation: A Case Book*, The International Society   349
of Business, Economics, and Ethics Book Series 3, DOI 10.1007/978-94-007-7479-7,
© Springer Science+Business Media Dordrecht 2014

Index

A

Abbott Laboratories, 226
ACER Africa, 189
Acres International Ltd., 49
Africare, 251
Agriculture, 39, 41–43, 73, 118, 154, 190, 253, 309–312, 317. *See also* Farmers, farming
Ahmad, P.S., 288
Akosombo Dam, 30, 31, 34, 35, 37–39, 42, 44, 46, 55, 56
Albert, J., 142
Albert, P.J., 32, 56–88, 240–257
Allende, S., 267
Allgood, G., 140–142
Amway, 272
Anisuzzaman, A.M., 303
Apple, 100, 111
Aquaya Institute, 139–142
Archer, C., 56–88
Aristide, J.-B., 69, 70, 96
Armani, 111
Arnold, D.G., 322
Arthur D. Little Inc., 221, 222, 225
Ashoka, 215, 264
Austin, A., 54, 150, 152, 211
Australia, 35, 120, 239, 247, 326
Austria, 196, 235
Avina, 216
Avon, 272

B

Bal Vikas Bank, 263, 282–286
Bangladesh, 8, 86, 131, 267, 268, 286, 287, 302–305, 308, 342–344

Banking, 6, 170, 263, 270–271, 285
Bardel, N., 81
Barreto, Z., 257
Barrett, C.R., 57, 61, 62
Barrymore, D., 152
Base of the pyramid, 236, 287–319
Battery Ventures, 170
Baxter International, 5, 6, 213, 216–240
Belgium, 81, 196, 197, 200, 201, 208, 211, 217, 245
Beluluane, 187–189, 191, 193
Benjamin, M., 327
Berry, S., 5, 36
BHP Billiton, 4, 167, 182–195
Billingsley, G., 341
Biodegradable product(s), 287
Blackburn, W., 218, 237
Body Shop, 211
Bogaerts, F., 196
Bogaerts, H., 200
Borneo, 141–143
Botswana, 139
Bottom of the pyramid. *See* Base of the pyramid
BP, 231
BrainPOP, 81, 82
Brazil, 4, 7, 60, 119, 131, 164, 191, 215, 225, 253, 257
Brazil, Russia, India, China (BRIC), 7
Bremans, Mike, 212
BRIC. *See* Brazil, Russia, India, China (BRIC)
Bristol-Myers Squibb, 126
British Council, 81
Brooke Bond, 289
Bugaboo Strollers, 111
Business Design Associates (BDA), 267
Business for Social Responsibility, 345

C

Calton, J.M., 338–348
Canada, 33, 49, 72, 78, 134, 222, 239
Cárdenas, G.N., 277
CARE, 65, 86, 140, 252, 255
Cargill, 231
Carson, R., 218
Cartwright, J., 56, 57, 64, 66, 78–83
Cawood, W., 177–181
Cemex, 6, 263–269, 271, 273, 275–277,
    279–282
Center for Economic and Social Applications
    (CESAIS), 333
Centers for Disease Control (CDC), 138, 141,
    144, 164, 165
Ceres, 4, 5, 225, 252
Chan, A., 341, 342, 345
Chartex International, 145
Chatterjee, J., 66
Children, 3, 6, 11, 26, 43, 57, 65, 67, 68,
    70–78, 81, 83, 86, 94, 97, 98, 106,
    114–116, 119–127, 129, 133–141,
    144, 154, 155, 175, 180, 190, 197,
    213, 245–247, 255, 256, 259, 263,
    264, 270, 273, 274, 278, 282–286,
    305, 306, 316, 330
Children's banking, 285
Chile, Chilean, 267
China, 7, 34, 60, 62, 63, 170, 178, 217, 239,
    242, 246, 256, 326, 328, 329, 332,
    334, 338–348
Cholera, 141, 214
Christmas, D., 88–90
Ciba-Geigy, 116–118
Climate change, 1, 33, 226, 246, 249, 254, 256
Climate Change Capital, 171
Clinton, B. (President), 47, 52
Clorox, 136, 212
Clugage, J., 57, 64–67, 78, 81, 84, 85
CMS Energy Corporation (CMS), 49
Coca-Cola Company (The), 5, 6, 240, 242,
    243, 248–258, 260, 261
Collins and Aikman Floorcoverings, 230
Columbia, 171
Communication, 56, 61, 62, 77, 117, 132, 150,
    152, 153, 155, 178, 197, 223, 224,
    226, 227, 266, 267, 288, 299, 314,
    334–336
Computers, computing, 3, 84, 97, 106, 190,
    194, 313, 314
    education, 57–61, 63, 64, 66, 80, 82, 84
Connected Capitalism, 247–249
Converse, 111
Cook, B., 177

Corporate social responsibility (CSR), 2, 64,
    132, 265, 322–338, 343
Corporate sustainability initiatives, 218
Cosco, 299
Creole, 67, 73, 74, 77, 80, 98, 107
Critical Links, 78, 80–82
Cuba, 240, 243, 258
Cunningham, B.D., 14–24

D

da Costa, D., 78
Daft, D.N., 258
Dams, 2, 30–32, 34–38, 41, 42, 44, 46, 51, 52,
    55, 56, 194
Danish Consumer Organization, 198
DEKA Research and Development, 250
Dell, 59, 100
de Loayza, H., 89
Denmark, 31
Dessalines, J.-J., 68
Detergent, 4, 134, 137, 196–206, 208–212,
    288–290, 292–299
Developing country, countries, 2, 60, 61, 94,
    113, 115, 118, 119, 127, 129, 130,
    133, 135–137, 139–141, 152, 176,
    183, 254, 256, 264, 266, 267, 287,
    293
Deveshwar, Y.C., 309, 310
DFJ, 170
Dhanda, K.K., 216–240
Dian Desa Foundation, 142
Disease, 13, 40, 41, 67, 92, 113, 115,
    117, 131, 133–135, 138, 140,
    143–146, 163, 182, 188, 214,
    232, 245, 248, 259
Dominican Republic (Saint Domingue),
    67, 96
Dow Chemical Company, 231
Driessen, A.M., 81
Duguid, S., 211
Duke, M., 347
DuPont, 231
Duvalier, F. (aka Papa Doc), 69, 96
Duvalier, J.-C. (aka Baby Doc), 69, 96

E

Earthquake, 56, 57, 67, 69–76, 79, 96,
    100, 135
Easterly, W., 287
eBeam, 82
E-Choupal, 9, 288, 308–319
Ecover, 167, 195–212

Education, 2–4, 9, 13, 43, 56–88, 94, 97, 98, 106–109, 115, 118, 130, 131, 135, 136, 141, 142, 147, 154, 163, 175, 190, 191, 194, 209, 211, 215, 219, 248, 252, 255, 257, 259, 269, 273, 275, 278, 282, 305, 306, 315, 318, 324, 325, 327–333, 336, 338
Egypt, 86, 246, 267
Electricity
  husk powered, 168, 169, 171–174
  hydroelectric, 33, 35
  solar, 30, 177, 178, 180
Elizabeth II (Queen), 37
Elkington, J., 248
Emerging markets, 2, 3, 57, 60–65, 67, 83, 168, 170, 171, 249
Energy, 4, 13, 15, 20, 21, 24, 29–31, 35–37, 41, 43, 44, 47, 49–52, 56, 133, 154, 167–173, 176–182, 199, 200, 202, 212, 224–227, 229, 231, 234, 235, 243, 259, 260, 338, 342, 345, 346, 348
Entrepreneur, entrepreneurship, 2, 4–6, 8, 10, 103, 136, 143, 197, 205, 210, 214–216, 256–257, 271, 302, 318
Environment, 2, 10, 23, 40–42, 49, 64, 87–89, 97, 107–109, 122, 125, 153, 168, 178, 188, 190, 197–201, 203–208, 213, 216, 220, 224, 251, 252, 254, 271, 305, 309, 321–323, 334, 339, 343
Environmental Defense Fund, 345
Environmental Detergent Manufacturers Association, 209
Environmental sustainability, 4, 131, 213, 219, 235, 237, 240, 249, 259, 347
Erie, J.-M., 78, 79
Ernst & Young, 126, 333
Escover, 4
Eskom, 2, 13–30
Esprit, 211
Exxon, 252

F
Fafo, 72, 73
Farmers, farming, 9, 40, 42, 51, 69, 173, 189, 193, 194, 241, 254, 288, 308–319, 345
FATEM. See Foundation for the Technological and Economic Advancement of Mirebalais (FATEM)
Female condom, 3, 113, 143–153, 163–165
Female Health Company (FHC), 3, 6, 13, 143–151, 153, 155–165

Filose, Luke, 78, 79, 81, 83–85
Finance, 16, 17, 23, 32, 126, 127, 164, 168, 201, 226, 263–288
Fisher House, 92, 99
Fishing, 39, 42, 51
Flores, F., 267
Fonkoze, 93, 95–99, 110
Ford (Motor Company), 340
  Foundation, 304
Foundation for the Technological and Economic Advancement of Mirebalais (FATEM), 76, 77, 93, 95–98, 106, 107, 109
France, 69, 78, 211, 244, 253
Franchises, 92–95, 241, 321
Friendship Bridge, 330

G
Games, gaming, 3, 6, 9, 13, 58, 77, 88–111, 279, 297, 316, 346
Gap, Inc. (The Gap), 100, 111, 326
Garbage, 213, 214, 216, 257
Gasifier, 173
Gates, Bill and Melinda Foundation, 256
Geigy, R., 117
General Electric (GE), 49
Germann, S., 119, 123
Germany, 81, 134, 196, 211
Ghana, 30–39, 41–56, 81, 251
Gibson, A., 227
Gioia, D., 340
Glaxo Wellcome, 116, 117, 126
Global Alliance for Workers and Communities (GA), 64, 325
Global Exchange, 327
Global Reporting Initiative (GRI), 225, 226, 234, 252
Goizueta, R., 243, 244, 247, 258
Gold Coast, 31–34, 47, 55
Golden Triangle, 10, 247–249
Good Energies, 171
Gorman, M.E., 14–22, 180, 288
Graham, W., 219
Grameen Bank, 6, 231, 268, 287, 302–308
Greece, 253
Greenpeace, 9
GreenPoint Partners, 168, 170–171
GRI. See Global Reporting Initiative (GRI)
Grove, A., 3
Guatemala, 64, 138, 139, 257
Guerrero, A., 279
Guinea, 36, 42, 51

H

Haiti, 3, 13, 56–88, 92, 93, 95–100, 104, 105,
    107, 109, 138, 141
Half the Sky, 6, 256
Hallmark, 10, 111
Hammond, A., 172, 293
Hartman, L.P., 56–89, 91–94, 96, 97, 99, 102,
    103, 106, 109, 133–141, 184, 322–338
Hart, S.L., 7, 53, 287, 297, 299
Hastings, A., 98
Hauser, F., 324, 333–337
Hayford, E.K.K., 48, 53
Health, 13, 24, 39, 41, 68, 69, 98, 99, 106, 107,
    110, 113–165, 182–188, 196–199,
    203, 205, 206, 211, 214, 217, 219,
    221, 222, 225, 247, 249, 255, 259,
    282, 284, 301, 305, 307, 318,
    322–325, 328, 330, 334, 339,
    343, 345
Heini, 142, 143
Helzer, C., 326, 330
Herbst, K., 264–282
Hessel, L., 145
Hewitt, S., 326
Hindustan Coca-Cola Beverages, 241
Hindustan Lever/Hindustus Unilver, 6, 8, 287,
    300–302
HIV/AIDS, 113–132, 143–145, 149, 152–155,
    163, 164, 188, 259
  RED, 99, 100
Hochmouth, F., 177
Hoechst Marion Roussel, 126
H2O for Life, 255
Holland, 31, 211
Holtgrave, D., 165
Homeless, homelessness, 6, 114, 263, 282, 284
Honda, 231
Honeywell, 231
Hong Kong, 341
Horniman, A., 308–319
Housing, 15, 18, 21, 22, 182, 191, 263–282,
    298, 304, 314
Human rights(s), 4, 70, 96, 118, 124, 138, 144,
    245, 347
Huntington's Disease Society of America
    (HDSA), 92
Husk Power Systems, 167–177

I

IBM, 59, 240, 254
IDB. *See* Inter-American Development
    Bank (IDB)

IFC. *See* International Finance Corporation (IFC)
India, 4, 6–9, 14, 17, 60, 63, 66, 86, 119, 164,
    168–172, 174, 176, 178, 215, 217,
    231, 235, 240–242, 246, 252, 255,
    257, 282–284, 286–299, 301, 302,
    308–312, 314–318, 326
Indian Tobacco Company (ITC) Limited,
    9, 308–310, 313–318
Indonesia, 140, 142, 267, 324–326,
    328–332, 334
Industrial Development Corporation (IDC), 187
Infrastructure (capacity building), 13, 20, 25,
    29, 31, 32, 36, 37, 45, 49, 52, 57,
    60, 66, 68, 72, 73, 75, 76, 83, 97
Innova Pure Water, 136
Intel
  Classmate PC, 63, 65
  Foundation, 61
  Intel Education Service Corp (IESC),
    57, 64–67, 77–86
Inter-American Development Bank (IDB),
    64, 74, 75, 251
International Council of Nurses (ICN), 138
International Finance Corporation (IFC), 186,
    188, 189, 192–195, 249
International Fund for Agricultural
    Development, 304
International Rescue Committee, 139
Ionics, 136
Ireland, 59, 78, 224, 247
Isdell, E.N., 241, 244, 247, 248, 258
ITC. *See* Indian Tobacco Company Limited
    (ITC)
Ivester, M.D., 243, 258
Ivory Coast (Cote d'Ivoire), 38, 50, 51, 81

J

Jamaica, 36, 45
Janata Bank, 303
Japan, 24, 60, 63, 187, 211, 224, 244, 341
Job creation, 28, 288
Job training, 3, 190–191
John Bird, C., 32, 33, 42, 55
Johnson & Johnson, 126, 231

K

Kaiser, E., 35–38, 53, 55
Kaiser Aluminum, 36, 55
Kalam, A.P.J.A., 310, 317
Kamen, D., 250, 251, 256
Kennedy, J.F. (President), 36–38

Kent, M., 10, 242, 244, 248–250, 256, 258
Kenya, 83, 86, 139, 140
Khan Academy, 82
Khosla, V., 171
Khrushchev, N., 37
Kidd, D., 328
Kimberly-Clark, 215
Kitson, A., 32, 55
Kleiner Perkins Caufield and Byers, 170
Knight, P.H. (Phil), 9, 322, 326, 327
Kouyate, L., 50
Kraemer, H., 225, 226
Kramer, M.R., 62
Krishi Bank, 303

L
Larson, A., 195
Latham, V., 205, 207, 210
Leeper, M.A., 143–147, 149–155, 162, 163, 165
L'Ecole de Choix (School of Choice),
        13, 56–88, 99, 100, 107–109
LEGO, 63, 81, 82, 84
Leisinger, K., 114, 118, 121
Lenovo, 59, 63
Leprosy, 3, 113, 117, 119, 124, 129, 131
Levi Straus, 336
Liberia, 139
Lipton, 289
Liz Claiborne, 342
Loftex, 345, 346
London, T., 7
Loucks, V., 223
Loutskina, E., 168–177
Lunde, H., 71–73

M
MacArthur Foundation (John D.
        and Catherine T.), 326
Madagascar, 119
Madöri, K., 114, 119, 121
Magaña, R., 274, 277, 278
Majekodunmi, B., 95
Malaria, 41, 113, 117, 119, 124, 131,
        182–185, 259
Malawi, 139
Malaysia, 163, 308
Mandela, N., 190
Manufacturing, 58, 134, 145, 150, 187, 199, 203,
        208, 210, 212, 217, 220, 221, 224–227,
        251, 253, 254, 281, 321, 322, 324,
        326, 330, 336, 338, 341, 346

Mao, Tse-Tung/Chairman Mao/Maoist,
        37, 253, 342, 346
Marchand, P., 205, 210
Maree, J., 23–24
Maree, P., 26
Marketing, marketing to the poor, 4, 56,
        134, 137, 139–141, 145, 146,
        149, 150, 152, 163, 195, 197,
        199, 201–204, 206–212, 214,
        244, 266, 272, 287, 289, 290,
        292–294, 297, 300, 301,
        316, 338
Martelly, M., 70, 75
Martens, L., 210
Martinez, T., 274
McArthur, V., 93, 94, 99, 102
McCloskey, P., 218
McDonald's, 100
McKinsey and Company, 2, 249
Mead, J., 56–88, 114–136, 182–184,
        213–216, 282–286, 288–302,
        308–319
Meissen, R., 218, 227, 237
Merck, 126
Method Products, 212
Mexico, 4, 78, 81, 215, 239, 251, 255, 257,
        264, 265, 267, 268, 272, 273, 276,
        281, 282
MGM Resorts, 254
Microfinance, 6, 93, 99
Microloans, 330
Microsoft, 59
Millipore, 136
Milojkovic, M., 237
Mining, 18, 19, 29, 32, 45, 167
Minnick, M., 244
Mioxx Corporation, 136
Mirebalais, H., 56, 76–77, 97, 107–109
Mitsubishi Corporation, 187
Moleko, M., 257
Monteiro, L., 326
Moore, G., 57–59, 116
Moral imagination, 1, 2, 4, 10, 340
Moreno, I., 264, 266, 268–270, 272–279,
        281, 282
Motorola, 59, 100
Moxon, J., 32, 37
Mozal, 167, 182–195
Mozambique, 167, 182–189, 191–195
Murphy, R., 219, 220
Mvula Trust, 255
Myanmar, 240
Mythware, 82

N

Namibia, 85, 86
National Audubon Society, 99
National Resources Defense Council, 345
National Women's Health Network
    (NWHN), 145
Nature Conservancy World Wildlife Fund
    (WWF), 252, 253, 255
Nelson, G., 218
Netherlands, 81, 196, 252–254, 288
New Enterprise Associates, 170
Nguyen, T., 336
Nigeria, 50, 51
Nike, 5, 9, 111, 230, 321–338, 342
Nirma, 288–297, 299, 300
Nixon, R. (President), 218
Nkrumah, K., 30, 33–38, 55
North Korea, 240
Novartis, 3
    Foundation, 114–133
Ntem, Y., 81
Nyamukapa, D., 149, 152

O

Ohene-Kena, F., 51
Opportunity International, 331
Organization for Economic Cooperation
    and Development (OECD), 198
O'Rourke, D., 325
Otellini, P., 60

P

Pacific Resources Export Limited (PREL), 341
Pakistan, 142, 302, 324
Pall, 136
Panama, 266
Pandey, G., 169, 173
Panicker, R., 6, 282–286
Paraguay, 251
Park, C.T., 337
Parker, M., 323
Parkinson, R.L. (Bob), 226, 227, 233
Partnerships, partners, 1, 3, 10, 33, 49, 57, 60,
    63, 64, 66, 67, 75, 77, 80, 83–85,
    89, 92–97, 99, 100, 107, 108, 113,
    124, 127–128, 132, 138–139, 141,
    146, 147, 150–152, 155, 162, 164,
    170, 174–176, 185–187, 189, 194,
    215, 227, 249–254, 256, 260, 270,
    274–279, 310, 318, 322, 326–328,
    331, 338, 341, 342, 344, 345

PASCO, 81, 82
Pasternik, S., 168, 170
Patel, K.K., 289–293, 295
Patel, N., 250
Pauli, G., 196, 197, 200, 201, 203, 209
Pearson, G., 85
Pemberton, J., 242
Pemex, 267
Pepsi, 241, 243, 247, 249
Peru, 4, 213–216
Pfizer, 126
Philanthropy, 2, 14, 128, 288
Philip (Prince), 37
Philippe, J., 98
Philippines, 247, 267, 308
Pincus, M., 77, 88–96, 101–103
Planned Parenthood, 143, 151, 164
PlusPetrol, 215
Pond's, 289
Population and Community Development
    Association, 331
Population Services International (PSI),
    139–140
Porter, M., 59, 62
Portugal/Portuguese, 31, 55, 78
Poverty, systemic poverty, 14
Powell, L., 143–149
Prahalad, C.K., 7, 60, 63, 287, 293, 297, 298,
    308, 311
Préval, E., 74
Préval, R., 69, 70, 96
Proctor & Gamble, 3, 113, 212, 231
Prussia, 31
PUR, 3, 113, 136–143

Q

Quest, 289

R

Ransler, C., 168–177
Reichart, J., 195
Reynolds Metal Company, Reynolds
    Aluminum, 36
Rhodes, C., 153
Rhodesia, 153
Rice husks, 4, 169, 172–176
Riverton, J., 30–56
Roberts, C., 253
Roche Pharmaceuticals, 126
Rogers, R., 241
Rohit Surfactancts Pvt. Ltd. (RSPL), 300

Rolph, T., 29–30, 56–88, 177, 195, 211–212,
        300–308, 337–338
Rose, C., 32, 250, 256
Rose, D., 32, 55
Ruiz, A., 4, 213–216

S
SAIL Venture Partners, 170
Sainsbury, 211, 240
Sam's Club, 299
Samsung, 63
Sandoz, 116–118
San Francisco Society for the Prevention
        of Cruelty to Animals (SF SPCA), 92
Save the Children, 65, 67, 77, 86
Schmitt, K., 114, 118, 119, 121, 126–132
Schools, 13, 14, 20, 22, 23, 39, 43, 57, 63–66,
        71–80, 82, 83, 85, 88, 97, 100,
        106–109, 122, 125, 135, 169, 1
        90, 246, 247, 251, 252, 255, 259,
        269, 275, 277–279, 282, 306,
        324, 330, 331
School Water Sanitation and Hygiene
        (SWASH+), 255
Schwab Foundation for Social
        Entrepreneurship, 214–216
Scott, L., 338–342, 344, 347, 348
SELF. *See* Solar Electric Light Fund (SELF)
Sen, S., 292
Sequoia Capital, 170
Sexually transmitted diseases (STDs), 145,
        146, 163, 188
Seychelles, 85, 86
Shakti, 8, 301, 302
Shared Value, 62
Shaye, G., 67
Sheehan, J., 133–136
Shell, 231
Silva, C., 264, 273
Sinha, M., 168–177
Sivakumar, S., 308–310, 313, 315–319
SKOOOL, 81
Soap products, 167, 287
Solar Electric Light Fund (SELF), 4, 6, 167,
        177–179
Solar power, 52, 167
Sonenshein, S., 177–182
Sourcing & Manufacturing Sustainability
        Index, 338
South Africa, 13, 14, 17–26, 28–30, 32, 33,
        114–132, 177–182, 187, 191, 193,
        251, 255

Soviet Union, 34, 37
Spain, 67, 235, 265, 266
Spiro, L., 195
Sri Lanka, 119, 129, 131, 142, 286, 302
Srivastava, A., 241
Starbucks, 100, 111
STDs. *See* Sexually transmitted
        diseases (STDs)
Stewardship, 225, 249, 251
Sub-Saharan Africa, 3, 113–115, 120, 125,
        131, 153, 246, 247, 287
Sullivan, B., 136, 137
Supply chain, 5, 9, 10, 149, 237, 253, 309,
        315–317
    management, 308, 321–348
Sustainability (sustainable development),
        4, 113–132, 182, 186, 190, 197,
        216, 225
Sustainable Value Framework, 229, 230, 232
SWASH+. *See* School Water Sanitation and
        Hygiene (SWASH+)
Swaziland, 187
Sweatshops, 9, 321, 342
Sweden, 31, 197, 205, 218
Swedish-American Company (SKANSA), 51
Switzerland, 114, 116, 132, 196, 235
Systems thinking, 1

T
Tandon, P., 289
Tanzania, 86, 113, 114, 117, 119–123, 129, 131
Taylor, D., 327
Technology, 2–4, 9, 13–111, 136–138, 140,
        169–174, 178, 179, 181, 217, 226,
        229–231, 250, 266, 288, 297, 301,
        307, 309–312, 317, 318, 341
TechnoServe, 256
Telmex, 267
Thiemele, A.L., 308–319
Toyota, 231
Trash, 214, 215, 282
    collection, 213
Triple bottom line, 1, 248, 342
Tucker, A., 322, 324
Tupperware, 272
Turkey/Turkish, 242, 258

U
U.K. Board of Trade, 37
Unilever, 8, 32, 204, 287, 288, 297
Union Footwear, 331

United Kingdom (UK) England, 33, 81, 204, 206, 235, 288
United Nations
 Millennium Goals, 245–247
 Stockholm Conference, 218
 United Nations Children's Fund (UNCEF), 75, 123, 140, 283, 284
 United Nations Educational Scientific and Cultural Organization (UNESCO), 72
United States (U.S.), 3, 8, 15, 31, 34, 35, 37, 39, 45, 49, 52, 56, 60, 68–70, 72, 78, 80, 85, 96, 113, 136, 144–146, 150, 153, 163–165, 169–171, 198, 202, 204, 211, 212, 216–218, 220, 224, 226, 235, 236, 244, 246, 254, 281, 284, 291, 294, 324, 334, 336, 342
United Technologies, 231
U.S. Agency for Economic Development (USAID), 37, 73, 115, 255, 324
U.S. Department of Agriculture Economic Research Service, 254
U.S. Environmental Protection Agency (EPA), 218, 220
U.S. Export-Import Bank (EXIM), 37
U.S. Food and Drug Administration (FDA), 143
U.S. Occupational Safety and Health Administration (OSHA), 324

V
van Rooyen, C., 25, 26
Vatican, 68
Venezuela, 266
Venkataraman, S., 308–319
Vietnam, 65, 86, 142, 178, 302, 322–338
Volta Aluminum Corporation (VALCO), 31, 35–37, 44–46, 52, 53, 55
Volta River, Volta River Project, Volta River Authority (VRA), 2, 13, 30–56

W
Wages, living wage, 9, 77, 315, 321, 323–325, 338, 343
Walmart, 9, 10, 321, 338–348
Walton, S., 10, 340, 341
Water
 clean, 3–5, 15, 113, 133, 135, 138, 213, 245–247, 250, 251, 256, 259
 footprinting, 253, 260–261
 PUR, 113, 136–143
 purification, 113, 136, 140
 shortages, 2, 135, 140, 141, 254–256
Waterford Institute, 64, 80
Werhane, P.H., 7, 14–24, 30–56, 60, 88–111, 114, 133–136, 177, 182–184, 195, 213–216, 282–286, 288, 340
Whole Foods, 167
Wiggins, M., 78
Wisconsin Pharmacal, 145, 146, 150
Wokutch, R.E., 322–338
Woodruff, R.W., 243, 258
World Bank, 30, 37, 49, 50, 53, 64, 70, 76, 308, 312, 326
World Economic Forum, 75, 249, 255
World Health Organization (WHO), 119, 140, 152, 155, 163
World Trade Organization (WTO), 341

Y
Yadav, R., 169, 173, 174
Yemen, G., 143–149
Young, A., 126, 332, 333
Yunus, M., 6, 8, 287, 302–308

Z
Zambrano, F.G., 267
Zambrano, L., 265–267
Zimbabwe, 119, 124, 139, 153–155
Zynga, 13, 77, 81, 89–95, 97, 99–102, 104

tion can be obtained
ing.com
A
819
0002B/6/P

9 789400 774780

CPSIA inform
at www.ICGtest
Printed in the US
LVHW08032227
628964LV0